DONNE AT SERMONS

Donne at Sermons

A CHRISTIAN EXISTENTIAL WORLD

GALE H. CARRITHERS, JR.

State University of New York Press Albany 1972

Donne at Sermons

First Edition

Published by State University of New York Press,

99 Washington Avenue, Albany, New York 12201

Printed in the United States of America
Designed by Richard Hendel

Library of Congress Cataloging in Publication Data

Carrithers, Gale H 1932–
Donne at sermons.

Includes the complete texts of four sermons by Donne: The sermon of valediction, The third sermon on John 1.8, The sermon on Pslam 63.7, The two-part sermon on fishers of men.
Includes bibliographical references.
1. Donne, John, 1572–1631. 2. Preaching—History—England. 3. Church of England—Sermons. 4. Sermons, English. I. Donne, John, 1572–1631. Selected works. 1972.
PR2248.C35 252'.03 74-171183
ISBN 0-87395-122-0
ISBN 0-87395-161-1 (microfiche)

Gale H. Carrithers Jr. is Professor of English at the State University of New York, Buffalo.

To J.L.C.

CONTENTS

Part I. The Sermonic World

Part II. Single Sermons

PREFACE

This study makes a three-fold attempt: to distinguish the genius of "the sermon" among generic ways of relating to the world (chapter 1), to explicate some Donnean existential convictions in action (chapter 2), and to document John Donne's achievement in putting his own world together (chapters 3–6). Hence this joins other studies which have attempted—mainly in terms of differing paradigms—to transmit to our age the work of Donne, who was one of the chief wonders of his own.

Insofar as this helps anyone, it will testify to years of help for me from a long train of people to whom I am joyously grateful. Louis Martz supervised my Yale dissertation on Donne's sermons at Lincoln's Inn. Very little indeed of that remains in this, thanks in part to Louis's continuing friendly encouragement. At an early stage the unforgettable Charles A. Fenton encouraged a rethinking of the subject, and the Duke University Research Council underwrote some research time and travel to that end. Early and late my friend the Rev. Layton Zimmer has encouraged reconceptions of the work as his own thoughts and mine have changed. Similarly, my friend Calvin Cabell Tennis, now Dean of the Episcopal Cathedral in Seattle, helped me toward some crucial recognitions. Albert Cook, Edgar Dryden, and Joseph Riddel—friends who are colleagues—have aided variously in conversation about writing problems, organizational problems, and critical ideas. The SUNY Research Council has provided summer research fellowships, and SUNY Buffalo Research Council has provided travel funds for work at Yale's Beinecke Library, that super-elegant well of conscious cerebration. Initially the manuscript owed much to Linda Wachob, who proved herself more than a match for my handwriting, and Hilda Ludwig, more than a match for the memory-bank typewriter. For the Press, Margaret Mirabelli, as copy-editor, lobbied tirelessly for clarity. I hope that all the generous people, the readers and members of the State University of New York Press, will cheerily accept my failure to take more of their good advice and write a more conclusive book. I can but try to affiliate myself with Donne when he prefers Plato to Aristotle and Calvin to "Melanchton" because "the best men are but Problematicall, Onely the Holy Ghost is Dogmaticall." I will try to restrict my own dogmatism to assertion of the very special steadfastness acknowledged by the dedication.

Part I
The Sermonic World

1
DONNE AND THE SERMONIC MUSE

i. Sermon Genre, Literary Interest, and Human Direction

What is generic, imaginative, or even literary about sermons? Granted sermons can have literary bits *in* them, but like raisins in a muffin? T. S. Eliot long ago accused Donne of writing that kind of sermon. He offered for praiseworthy contrast the relative homogeneity of Lancelot Andrewes. Recently Joan Webber ably expanded the case for Andrewes,[1] though he seems no preacher for every taste even yet. But our question really is larger. Should not a sermon differ in some *essential* way from what we oddly call "straight exposition"? Donne certainly thought so, once even remarking firmly to his congregation "We are not upon a lecture but a sermon." He seems to have meant by *lecture* what we mean by straight exposition: practical discourse which can conform to the shape of its container as water or sand does, or be repeatingly modular like bricks, discourse to which the humanity of the speaker and the rise and fall of human action are not integral. A confused jumbling of sermon and lecture these past three centuries may have a great deal to do with the sermon's present low estate among most readers, many listeners, and not a few practitioners.

Christian preachers since patristic times have traditionally preached "on" biblical texts, though there has also been a rival tradition of preaching on a general topic like sin or obedience to authority. The text for a sermon might be a verse, incident, parable, or occasionally even whole psalm or book from the Bible. Chaucer's Pardoner, who preached always on the verse "Radix malorum est cupiditas," delivered the Canterbury Pilgrims a narrative "exemplum" illustrating his text. By Donne's time, the norm was more expository than narrative. A preacher would usually *place* his text in a biblical or congregational context. He would then *divide* his text into the *parts* which would become the sections of his sermon. The parts might be words or phrases of the text or features of the life to which the text referred, such as biblical history, the moral life of the congregation, or connection with transcendent divine power, offer of eternal redemption, and judgment. Often preachers would at transition points refer to the parts announced in the division of the text. Like classical orators, Renaissance preachers might use rhetorical figures and formal argument, citations of authority (especially related biblical and patristic passages), refutations of opposing arguments (by pagans or rascals of adversive sects), illustrative anecdote and emotive conclusion. The Renaissance preachers attempted to remobilize classical oratory in biblical terms.

On the levels of generality and literary achievement we are considering just now, it is practical to make the assumption that identifications of genre do not of themselves evaluate. A tragedy may be good or bad. "A bad tragedy" is neither an oxymoronic label nor a euphemism for some nameless monster. Certainly there are bad sermons, as we shall see illustrated by Donne's contemporaries.

Donne may serve to epitomize the art of the sermon for us for three reasons. First, we can more fruitfully scrutinize the *essentia* of the sermon, that which makes it hold together and communicate, than that which disables it. Second, Donne has been called, and for his sermons, "a king . . . of wit," preëminent among "that race of giants," and by such disparate students as Thomas Carew and Samuel Taylor Coleridge; their astonishing remarks seem, on investigation, quite warranted. Third, the powerful operation of Donne's genius among all the prescriptions and practices of the Anglican sermon elegantly presents the synergistic relation of convention and innovation, or—an alternative appraisal of the same activity—freedom operating amid necessities, or tradition and the individual talent, as Eliot put it.

Our exploratory investigations will be phenomenological in temper and existential in assumptions in ways analogous to Donne's own assumptions. Such inquiry can profit from the flexibly particular concreteness of a limiting term like *Anglican* and flexibly particular concreteness of a body of data like *Donne's* sermons, 160 of which survive. There will be a risk of course, in this attempt to order phenomena—risk of either violating the phenomena with ordering mechanisms alien to them, or leaving them a humanly unassimilable welter. More particularly, there is a risk of circular argument: "this is what a sermon should be because this is what Donne did; Donne is good because he did this." That we have been told how many observations (perhaps all worthwhile ones) interfere with the thing observed does not comfort us. But Samuel Johnson's reminder that there is always an appeal to general nature applies. If, in defining the generic sermon and the Donnean sermon in terms of one another, we can avoid Procrustean lopping and stretching, then the views of sermonizing and of Donnean practice need not be interdependent in any damaging way.

Since literary works unfold line by line and action to reaction, genre theory ought to take as good account of dynamic facts as of static facts. That is, it should treat action and temporality and temporal relationship as no less *real* than matters of syntax, length, number of speakers, subject, projected audience, formality, and the like. Moreover, since literary works involve human nature by representation or at least by implication, and human life-in-time continuously entails evaluative activity of some order, genre theory ought to take serious account of literary tone and other tactics of evaluation (tone here meaning whatever *attitude* is revealed by a speaker's *language*).

The notions of genre on which my sense of the sermon rests may be briefly put as follows. Structurally simple literary forms present the sense of experience of some certain kind of person (any kind, but particularized because people are particular) in some certain situation (any situation, but particularized because history never quite repeats itself). Structurally simple literary forms, such as most lyric poems, present the protagonist's situation as oriented toward *one* of the three sectors of time (or else they are not simple). It may be the future:

Western wind, when wilt thou blow . . .
Time will not be ours forever . . .
When by they scorne, O murdresse, I am dead . . .

It may be the present:

This bed thy center is, these walls thy spheare . . .
The proper study of mankind is man . . .
Kind pity chokes my spleen, brave scorn forbids . . .

It may be the past:

I have done one braver thing,/Then all the *Worthies* did . . .
A gentle knight was pricking on the plaine . . .
Whilst yet to prove,/I thought there was some Deitie in love . . .

The examples are arranged to illustrate the further truth that all orientations are evaluative in ways that can be roughly characterized: appreciative (the first example in each group), analytic (the second, relatively detached or reportorial example), and antipathetic (the third, rather uncommon in simple literary works oriented toward the past except as debunking biography).[2]

Complex literary forms obviously encompass more than one of these nine divisions. But it seems useful to regard each complex form as having a kind of center-of-gravity in one or two. Tragedy is clearly a case in point. In the tragic play or novel or whatever, we watch the action begin pregnant with future possibilities, and—in a play at least—the action continues as a present-tense thing. But its conclusion and thematic and emotional weight accumulate on what is irrecoverably lost to the past. Great Antony or Hamlet or Brutus or Samson is dead. And in retrospect we can see easily what we may well have glimpsed all along—the ominous weight of the past, whether antecedent action or irrevocable decision executed after the curtain's rise. Care and sorrow and suffering predominate in the tones of such works, jaunty gravediggers notwithstanding. Occasionally we hear indictment: "Murder most foul!" or "Why was sight to such a tender ball as the eye confined?" Past action—of a murderer or a god or the protagonist—weighs heavily even when a speaker ostensibly looks to the future, as in the unhopeful formula "we shall not see such another." Comedy traditionally has complemented tragedy: it is future oriented and affirmative in tone because the past is not irrevocable in any crushing way. The future means survival, of a person or way of life or a society. This is often signalized by a marriage, and the individual's inevitable end is not in focus.[3]

Some latter-day black comedy, by gravitating about as far as possible toward tragedy, has ended up in a posture closely akin to epic and to sermon. Samuel Becket's *Happy Days,* for example, presents the animated conversation of an aging wife with her mostly out-of-sight and almost monosyllabic husband; she is up to her waist in a literal and allegorical sand dune in Act One, up to her chin in Act Two, the last act; he is less concretely but almost equally immobilized behind her. The tragic life-world might be delineated as one wherein "you die of living, of being what you are, and if you live remarkably then you merely die more remarkably." Clearly that world stands as close to *Happy Days* as does the comic, wherein "you die to live" (like Kate the Shrew or Benedick and Beatrice or Hero and Claudio or Vincentio's Vienna), "you put off the old life to put on the new." The audience at *Happy Days* may wonder if they are being "put on" when the wife recurrently talks of "many blessings" and "this will be a happy day." The wife and husband are dying of living, dying by being what they are, but reluctantly and not quite yet. That is their comic triumph of life.

Epic may usefully be considered as the philosophical poem gone more conspicuously existential, *De Rerum Natura* or *Essay on Man* made more obviously matters of personal, temporal, action and relationship. Hence there can be works of variously intermediate station not really so unclassifiable as they may initially seem: *Works and Days,* the *Georgics, Paradise Regain'd,* Byron's *Don Juan,* Pound's *Cantos.* First, all are essentially oriented toward the present. An epic bard often winnows a mythic past, yes, but he conveys his treasures to his present audience not because they are quaintly unrelated to his and his audience's present, or have a cause and effect relationship to it; rather, the bard's tale is an epitome or a thematic foundation (in the Renaissance sense a "mirror") for the present. The philosophical poet's preoccupation with ostensibly timeless truth comes to the same thing. Second, all these works adopt a relatively detached and unemotional posture toward their material. Their discourse tends to move analytically or reportorially. Passionate cries of evaluation tend to be distanced by metrics, syntax, or diction: a refrain in epic's miniature cousin the ballad or Byron's wit. Milton's exclamations in *Paradise Lost* are the more remarkable because atypical ("Oh shame to men! Devil with devil damn'd firm concord holds").[4]

Milton's song soars often with no middle flight. Donne's muse normally treads on the ground. Yet our own circle through matters of simple lyric to bards and epics has brought us closer to the sermon. Almost any sermon, to be sure, has legitimate entries to the highest celebration or profoundest condemnation or lament: the creativity or the grace of God, for example, or betrayals (both mythic and historic) of god, or such a betrayal by ourselves. Donne exploits more of that spectrum of tone in dealing with such occasions, and does so more regularly, than Andrewes or other contemporaries or subsequent Anglican preachers. Yet like theirs, his ordinary tone is deliberative. The honorable rationale for his deliberative tone and the virtue of his divergences will be examined in a moment.

The sermon characteristically exhibits in its temporal concerns versatility similar to its tonal versatility. Like philosophical poetry, epic, and elements of all drama, it looks to the present. Like epic, it will look to the past, but precisely because of that past's present vitality. Unlike much tragedy, the sermon does not treat the past as crushing. Like comedy, the sermon has in the present some sort of heading toward a bright future. Like a kind of white tragedy reverse to black comedy, the sermon may present generalized protagonists who through mysterious *choices* die effortfully and painfully into life whereas their antagonists glide on easy paths to eternal deprivation. In sum: a Christian sermon is the activity of a certain figure—a *preacher*—dealing concretely (because the preacher's God was Incarnate), and conventionally in prose, with what by definition is a *free* challenge of the highest import. That he is a preacher implies he addresses himself not so much to himself or to his God as to a group of *neighbors,* and that he addresses them with some faith in their hearing. Protestant Christianity in particular has emphasized the priesthood of all believers. The challenge, some Godly claim of highest importance, is free in the sense that, unlike a knife at the throat, it permits *deliberative actions* and affords more than one *alternative* not instantly fatal. The Anglican preachers of Donne's half-century who were emancipated from the Book of Homilies took the challenge not in terms of an abstract point of doctrine or ethics or civic order so much as in the terms of a passage of Scripture. The terms might be dealt with analytically as they often were by Andrewes, each word yielding description and doctrine, or casually in the course of a dominating argument as by many lesser preachers, or synthetically, as often by Donne, each word indicating a landmark in the life-world of the Old and New Adam or crossroads in his pilgrimage.

ii. Church, Liturgy, and Preaching Situation

The assertion of all this in somewhat abstract generalities must be quickly complemented by concrete generalities of groundwork. The Anglican church-interior anyone enters, virtually anywhere, proclaims itself architecturally and aesthetically a symbolic space and presents itself as communal lived space. Certainly this was so in Donne's generation, and he knew it. He knew, too, that the invitation to share and participate could be rejected, as by a parishioner or communicant present in body only, or by half-hearted conformists.

Some details may be added about that symbolic space, as to the exploitable significance of the pulpit and preacher's bearing there and as to the auditor's possible relation to him within the practices of Prayer-Book worship. Typically, images and shrines had been cleared away by order of the reformers. But stained-glass windows, the royal arms, and the tables of the decalogue were permitted and seem to have been fairly regular features of décor.[5]

The body of the church thus tended to become somewhat simpler, in aim at least more distraction free and better unified, just as the service was simplified and cast in the vernacular language. In large churches where a permanent rood screen divided the nave and chancel into markedly distinct rooms, the congregation usually would join the celebrant in the chancel for holy communion, just as the preacher for centuries had, and still does, come out into the nave to be with his congregation for the sermon. Often, a small church would have no screen or other architectural obstacle to concerted work by the whole body of the faithful at every point in the service.[6] Such was probably the situation for Donne at old Lincoln's Inn Chapel, since it was replaced (in 1623) as crowded and inadequate.[7] Or the priest might bring the consecrated elements out into the nave, among the congregation, getting the body of the faithful as much together for communion as for sermon in that way. Such diversely corporate worship agreed perfectly well with an attitude that viewed altar, pulpit, and baptismal font as separate but commensurable foci of worship.

Donne's friend George Herbert refers to the priest's pulpit as "his joy and his throne" (*A Priest to the Temple,* chap. 7). As for the congregation:

> The evidence is conclusive, from a variety of early manuals, that it was considered as much a Christian man's duty to hear sermons as to hear Mass. There is a popular notion that much preaching, and consequently the multiplication of pulpits, came in with the Reformation; but this notion is completely false. . . . The stone pulpits of pre-Reformation date yet extant in our churches number upwards of sixty [the wooden ones "upwards

> of one hundred"] . . . almost invariably . . . from the 15th century. . . . The craftsmanship is always excellent.[8]

In short, revitalization of preaching and listening, as of rhetoric generally, antedates the Reformation in England.

The Book of Common Prayer has from its first version in 1549 prescribed a dual ministry of word and sacrament. Conflicting forces in balance tend to become unbalanced or rearranged with one subordinate to the other; a dual ministry threatens always to become a ministry primarily of word or primarily of sacrament. Before the late-medieval revival of preaching, many services no doubt featured a "sermon" that was no more than a casual exhortation or brief pious colloquium delivered from a flimsy—even a portable—wooden pulpit. Which came first, the function or the form? The symbolic *proportions* of even an ambitious sermon may be reduced by the elaboration of a sung Eucharist with lengthy procession and incense, all in conjunction with Counter-Reformation splendor. It is hard to imagine any preacher or sermon so dynamic as not to be subsumed by the decoration, the panoramas of angels and cherubim to be seen around some continental baroque pulpits. At the opposite extreme, the preoccupation of some Puritan groups with all that can be verbalized and with private, individual apprehension eventuated in the familiar preaching auditoriums: there the pulpit at one side is replaced by a central lectern, which stands above or in lieu of a holy table.

But what are the inevitabilities and possibilities in a normal Anglican church? Pews there are low enough to permit visual "community" of worshippers.[9] The symbolic space is small enough to be an auditory space because all can hear as the preacher in raised pulpit between them and the altar mediates and interprets and guides and questions. Erwin Straus, in his brilliant collection of essays *Phenomenological Psychology,* addressed himself to "The Forms of Spatiality." Quotation at some length from him can help us with this provocative issue.

> Space filled with sound is enough to establish a connection between viewer and picture [compare TV with the sound off]. Optical space is the space of directed, measured, and purposive movement; acoustical space is the space of dance. . . . Walking, we move *through* space . . . dancing we move *within* space. . . . Acoustical space is different from optical space, whose structure is given in terms of the analytical, geometric categories

> of distance, measure, and direction. We achieve goals, realize our life history, in optical space. In acoustical space, on the other hand, we live only in the present, forgetting past and future; we accomplish nothing concrete, and we experience only the union between ourselves and our surroundings.[10]

The time that tends to be forgotten in acoustical space, as Straus makes clear, is the time of impending needs, in which last Sunday's dinner sustains no one today. Notice that the pulpit, situated at once in optical and in acoustical space both amply furnished with symbolic referents to the auditor's life-world, has at least the possibility of leading attention to the total space in which the auditor's "life history" works itself out.

Straus's reference to dance appears by design here. A priest could deliver his sermon from behind a screen (or "by public address system to the meeting room, for those members of the congregation who are unable to be seated in the sanctuary"), or from behind a lectern or communion table, or even—it is barely conceivable—from a kneeling or prostrate position before the altar. But in fact the priest moves variously about in front of the congregation and at the appointed time walks to the pulpit. He stands there, very much a *bodily* figure, in a place that enforces somewhat upright posture, that permits a modicum of purposive movement, and that invites the affective and symbolic movements evidently so much a part of the Renaissance elocutionary vocabulary. Straus comments:

> In conversation, we talk with one another about something. Conversation, therefore, demands distance in three directions: from the acoustical signs, so that the phoneme can be perceived in its pure form [i.e. as symbolic medium, not sign]; from things, so that they can be the object of common discourse; from the other person, so that speech can mediate between the speaker and listener. Upright posture produces such distances. It lifts us from the ground, puts us opposite to things, and confronts us with one another. . . . the essential point for an understanding of human inquisitiveness is that man is able to suspend all direct action toward his environment; to reflect upon himself; to see himself within his environment; still more, to see himself together with his environment; and, finally, to relate the unit of this particular situation to the structure of the whole to which it belongs.[11]

This admirably summarizes some of the opportunities and dangers latent in the pulpit. The preacher, lifted farther from the ground than his audience, may unfortunately so "suspend all direct action" as to see only his own situation or only static counters of data. These he passes to his auditors as self-indulgence in the first case or flat lecture in the second. The pulpit aptly symbolizes the upright position mediate between earth and heaven. Donne explicates the upright posture and concurrent dialogue-relationship as a complex given by grace but vulnerable to sinful choice:

> But as when man was nothing but a body, he lay flat upon the earth, his mouth kissed the earth, his hands embraced the earth his eyes respected the earth; and then God breathed the breath of life into him, and that raised him so farre from the earth, as that onely one part of his body, (the soles of his feet) touches it, And yet man, so raised by God, by sin fell lower to the earth againe, then before, from the face of the earth, to the womb, to the bowels, to the grave;
>
> (6. S2. 264–271) in the edition of G. R. Potter and Evelyn Simpson; spot citations will be from this edition by volume, sermon number, and line) [12]

Donne's dynamic efforts to make the sermon enlist its auditors in both optical and acoustical space seem to me demonstrably better executed than those of any other Anglican. Partly, no doubt, because he felt sharply the dangers.

He charted the dangers explicitly, often by brilliant use of matters in the biography of his own or another man's Christian *essentia*. He rejected the *idiosyncratically* autobiographical because:

> . . . perchance you would rather fixe your thoughts upon my illnesse, and wonder at that, then at Gods goodnesse, and glorifie him in that; rather wonder at my sins, then at his mercies, rather consider how ill a man I was, then how good a God he is.
>
> (St. Paul's, evening prayer, 25 December 1624: 6. S8. 126–129)

He recognized the failures of communication which result from feeble or misoriented or divided attention:

> . . . betweene these two, this licencious comming, and this treacherous comming, there are many commings to Church, commings

for company, for observation, for musique. . . . He that brings any collateral respect . . . to a Sermon, looses the blessing of Gods ordinance in that Sermon; hee heares but the Logique, or the Retorique or the Ethique, or the poetry of the Sermon, but the Sermon of the Sermon he heares not.

(St. Paul's, 25 December 1626;
7. S11. 503–512)

Preaching is potentially a kind of parallel on a lower plane to divinely efficacious language, to words of Godly comfort. By implication, the preacher's great task (at the tactical level) is to mobilize positively all the random and wayward "affections" of his congregation. Hooker proposed the crucial task in 1593: "there will come a time when three words uttered with charity and meekness shall receive a far more blessed reward than three thousand volumes written with a disdainful sharpness of wit."[13] Donne endorses that distinction in 1617, in one of the earliest of his surviving sermons:

. . . here, not in the School, but in the Pulpit, not in Disputation, but in Application

(1. S4. 429–430)

"Application" suggests that he engages in a *dramatic* enterprise, about which more in a moment. Any Anglican preacher "applies" in a context of worship formulated by the Book of Common Prayer. Private prayer might be left to numberless manuals of devotion and to private initiative, but an act of Parliament institutionalized a matrix and much of the substance for group devotional activity with regard to sacraments, Bible, and priest. In the services of Morning and Evening Prayer, of Holy Communion, and occasional services like Baptism or Holy Matrimony, the Prayer Book works most fundamentally to *unite* in dramatic *actions* regarded as crucial a group of people regarded as essentially *communal* (diverse though they might be in worldly condition).

Clarifying the generic and literary relevance of all this to sermons calls, I think, for language not exclusively ecclesiastical. Hence the careful formula just above, and hence a resort again to the antiphonal voice of Erwin Straus. His argument that from the moment of awaking anyone lives and moves within reality can serve us as an arresting gloss on the Prayer Book's omnipresent *assumption* that life is rudimentarily or incipiently dramatic:

> We do not use our eyes and other sense organs like binoculars to watch events on a distant stage; we ourselves are on the stage; awake, we find ourselves within the world; we experience ourselves in the world, together with the world, in relation to the world. Self-awareness does not precede awareness of the world; the one is not before the other; the one is not without the other. . . . Awake, we experience the power of reality in our and the world's counteraction—in its resistance and our suffering. . . . Experienced reality is not the theme of a theoretical proposition. Its counterpart is not unreality but destruction and death. The question is to be or not to be.

Straus argues that similarly one is no more detached from his own body. In any but reflex movements:

> . . . in our actions, we are directed to objects which, in their visibility, lie ahead of us. The motor response can never reach a stimulus, but we, as experiencing beings, move toward a goal. Only a motile being, capable of disengaging itself from the ground, can face objects and can meet, in sensory experience, the Other; only a sentient being, to whom an environment is opened, can move spontaneously.[14]

"All the world's a stage," Straus might agree (since Jaques' claim is qualified by Hamlet's question), and Donne too (at, for example, 1. S3. 899 and 4. S10. 6). Everyman's identity is involved with the stage-setting and furniture, and Hamlet's question is Everyman's question. Prayer Book worship particularizes and insists on the *communal* quality of the *mutual* involvement in the waking world.

The Anglican liturgy is "the people's work," in the language of the people. It engages a congregation understood as a local element of the body of Christ in closely communal acts of worship in response to, or dialogue or unison with, the priest. No single point about external influences on Donne's preaching is more important.

Cranmer's Prayer Book of 1549 was revised in 1552, 1559, 1604, and 1662. Those usages of 1604 which particularly concern us here are to be found in modern Prayer Books in almost identical language.

In Morning Prayer, there was no short form for bidding confession. The officiant used the long form beginning "Dearly beloved brethren," and further spelled out the congregation's status in the family of God by the phrase "before the face of Almighty God our heavenly father;" he went on to insist that the congregation dramatize its corporate quality by making confession:

> . . . chiefly . . . when we assemble and meet together to render thanks for the great benefits that we have received at his hands, to set forth his most worthy praise, to hear his most holy word, and to ask those things which are requisite and necessary, as well for the body as the soul. Wherefore I pray and beseech you, as many as are here present, to *accompany me with* a pure *heart,* and humble *voice, unto* the throne of heavenly grace, saying after me [the "General Confession"]. (my italics)

Thus, the exhortation among other things made the congregation newly aware of the major *acts* in the service to follow. The concerted confession, Lord's Prayer (following "The Declaration of Absolution, or Remission of Sins"), and subsequent congregational statements establishing the congregation as unified Christian brothers, sinners, but confessing, penitent, and reverent, charitable toward trespassers against themselves, and thankfully no less aware of transcendent holy laws, kingdom, grace, and glory than of sin, temptation, and evil. Whatever an individual worshipper's daily doubts, or weakness, or saintliness, this was his *formal* status after the successive acts of the service prepared and presented him as auditor of the sermon.

This formal status may be compared with that of the Renaissance theatergoer. Consider the Prologue to *Henry the Fifth.* After the Prologue has spoken, the theater audience "knows" that dramatic art is apart from life, that art will present a significant selection from life, that the selection will be presented formally by a kind of representative fraction, and that they, the audience, will complete the process by the supplementary action of their imaginations.

The Jacobean Anglican preacher's congregation was analogously "prepared" for him every Sunday by Morning Prayer—right down to recitation in unison of articles of belief in the Apostles' Creed (or occasionally the Nicene Creed)—if only he knew what to do about it. Moreover, the insistence on the Holy Ghost in the Creed and the following dialogue, and in the earlier Absolution [15] made it possible for a man such as Donne, in the primitive party of the church, to conceive of the Anglican dual ministry of word and sacrament as two in one. Proper preaching and the proper reception, or "application" of it he took to be working toward a right relation to the *logos,* to be hearing "in the words of the preacher the Word of God."

> . . . we *make* the naturall body of Christ Jesus appliable to our soules, by the words of Consecration in the Sacrament, and our soules apprehensive, and capable of that body, by the word Preached.
>
> (3. S12. 137–139, my italics)

Consider Donne's sense of involvement with the crucified and resurrected Christ. This can instance how pervasively he exploited the preparation afforded by Prayer Book worship; later on we shall consider his unusually great resourcefulness in doing this. Among the 160 surviving sermons, 101 by my count make in their concluding moments historical or liturgical reference to the Crucifixion, Resurrection, or Ascension, some 71 of the 101 making the reference in specifically liturgical terms; 18 end with the formula "the inestimable price of his incorruptible Blood."

Granted the inherent dramatic circumstances of a priest's confrontation with his congregation upon his ascent to the pulpit, how in particular would he develop and shape the possibilities? Any priest of a liturgically oriented Christian denomination would appear in a distinctive costume that would tend to universalize, stylize, and objectify that priest's presence. An Anglican of Donne's generation, in accord with Canons 58 and 74 of 1604, would appear in cassock, gown (derived from the medieval scholar's gown), tippet, and hood.[16]

Any Renaisance public speaker would know the need for elocutionary and gestural art, "the whole bodie stirring altogether," as Thomas Wilson prescribed in 1560. Abraham Fraunce in 1588 cautioned that gesture should change with the voice, "yet not parasiticallie as stage plaiers use, but gravelie and decentlie as becommeth men of greater calling."[17] Evidently Donne was a master of the "powerful kinde of preaching by his gesture and Rhetoriquall expression:"

> Yet have I seene thee in the pulpit stand,
> Where we might take notes from thy looke, and hand;
> And from thy speaking action beare away
> More Sermon, then some teachers use to say.
> Such was thy carriage, and thy gesture such,
> As could divide the heart, and conscience touch.

Thy motion did confute, and wee might see
An error vanquished by delivery.[18]

Such vigor of gesture goes with the assumption that each man lives outward from his bodily self. That accords with the doctrine of the Incarnation, as we shall notice again later. Sermonizing, as a liturgical activity, begins communally with its general direction and momentum already established, but with wide latitude of goal and route.

iii. Preacher as Uniformed Orator

Any Renaissance Anglican might well have accepted—as Donne did—St. Augustine's revision of the three classical rhetorical styles. The preacher will not be using a low style for trivial matters, middle for intermediate, and high for momentous ones, because everything he deals with is a great matter (*re magna*). But he may proceed self-effacingly (*submisse*) for factual instruction, or temperately (*temperate*) in the voice of mutual involvement, or powerfully (*granditer*) to overwhelm opposition.[19] Some sense of this appears in the practice of diverse Anglicans—Hugh Latimer, Andrewes, William Laud, John Bowle, John Rawlinson, Jerome Phillips, Ephraim Udall, for instance.

Of them all Donne shows the greatest vitality and resourcefulness in styling and restyling *himself* as a variety of typical-yet-individualized characters and in characterizing his *congregation* as a variety of corporate identities. The visible preacher is unchanging in costume but metamorphic in gesture. If the audible preacher persists in his convictions—in the Creedal sense—he nevertheless moves and shifts in his relation to them. Donne states a particular case in point:

> You may remember that I proposed to *exercise* your devotions and religious meditations in these *exercises,* with words that might *present* to you first the severall persons in the Trinity, and the benefits which we *receive, in receiving* God *in* those distant notions of Father, Son, and holy Ghost; And then with

> other words which might *present* those sins, and the danger of those sins which are most particularly opposed against those severall persons.
>
> (3. S13. 1–7; my italics)

He will *exercise* and *present,* thereby making the sermon a form of drama akin to masque, wherein cast and audience may share or exchange roles. His listeners have joined him previously in Prayer Book actions of affirming belief in the Trinity and confessing sins. He will propose, oppose, and receive with his auditors in a kind of contest.

> . . . to come to a doubt, and to a debatement in any religious duty, it is the voyce of God in our conscience . . . as no man resolves of anything wisely, firmely, safely, of which he never doubted, never debated, so neither doth God withdraw a resolution from any man that doubts with an humble purpose to settle his owne faith, and not with a wrangling purpose to shake another mans.
>
> (5. S1. 105–112) [20]

He will personify, on occasion, both sides of a debate, two sides which may reflect any man's two minds on the matter.

> . . . man is that creature, who onely of all other creatures can answer the inspiration of God, when his grace comes, and exhibit acceptable service to him, and cooperate with him.
>
> (1. S7. 126–129)

Since Donne naturally regarded the Bible as inspired, these lines seem to imply that a proper sermon on a biblical text will embody that answer in some service or acts of cooperation.

His word *answer* indicates the fundamentally dialogic nature of his sermons. The foundation dialogue of action and responsive action would appear to be the restless, mysterious relationship of freedom to necessity. That relationship nourishes almost endlessly varied exchanges, exclamations, debates, colloquia, symposia. They take place among the preacher's personations, which are different much as Shakespeare's Henry the Fifth is variously the worried monarch, the triumphantly witty courtier, the detector of subversion, the captain of men, the lover. By his rhetoric the preacher's adversaries are made almost as present as the on-stage adversaries of King Henry;

and contemporary auditors felt their own numbers supplied the physical representations of his rhetorical construction.

He can be found to style himself Everyman-fallen:[21]

> Because I am drousie, I will be kept awake, with the obsenities and scurrilities of a Comedy, or the drums and ejulations of a Tragedy:
>
> (3. S12. 577–579)[22]

Or, not quite antithetically, as high priest of godlike discernment to a congregation of fallen men, he may speak with the almost incantatory parallelism of a psalmist:

> as thy high Priest . . . if he looke narrowly,
> is able to finde some spot in thy purest Lambe,
> some sin in thy holiest action,
> some deviation in thy prayer,
> some ostentation in thine alms,
> some vaine glory in thy Preaching,
> some hypocrisie in thy hearing,
> some concealing in thy confessions,
> some reservation in thy restitutions,
> some relapses in thy reconciliations:
> since thou callest him Father,
> feare him as thy high priest . . . .
>
> (3. S13. 345–352)

The high priest in the last line is God, and preaching typifies the speaker no less than hearing does his parishioners, so the initial magisterial air is ironically qualified. Preacher is both above his congregation in pulpit and judgment and among them in prayer and reconciliations.

Another, less schematic and almost lyrical passage suggests even further the range of resource Donne commanded in this situation:

> . . . Since you, to whom God sends us, doe as well make up our Crown, as we doe yours, since your being wrought upon, and our working upon you conduce to both our Crowns, call you the labour, and diligence of your Pastors, (for that's all the suffering they are called to, till our sins together call in a persecution) call you their painfulnesse your Crown, and we shall call your applyablenesse to the Gospel, which we preach, our

> Crown, for both conduce to both; but especially childrens children, are the Crown of the Elders, says *Solomon:* If when we have begot you in Christ, by our preaching, you also beget others by your holy life and conversation, you have added another generation unto us, and you have preached over our Sermons again, as fruitfully as we our selves; you shall be our Crown, and they shall be your Crowns, and Christ Jesus a Crown of everlasting glory to us all. Amen.
>
> (3. S16. 540–553)

The whole scene is a "world" of self and society freely created and sustained by on-going commitment. The preacher is by turns servant, master, and brother-in-Christ to all Sons of God. The logical positions attendant on these permutations repay scrutiny. He begins with an analysis of the situation which is, not incidentally, a kind of summary of the sermon. At the same time he creates a bridge between the simple conditional proposition ("if *a,* then *b*") and the simple eduction ("*a,* therefore *b*"). We have, in effect, rhetoric of expectation: "Since *a,* as *b* (*b* and *a* being statements drawn from knowledge and faith together), therefore *c* and *d* if directions are followed)." There follows the citation of Solomonic precedent, and the rather straightforward conditional construction, "If when . . . [then] you have. . . ." He concludes with a statement from which the "if" and "then" have evaporated. The condition has been apprehended as a foregone conclusion in witness to a regenerate and charitably inclusive faith.

Finally, it may be inferred that he sees all such available versions of the self as partial and provisional contributions toward some consummation of the self. In one of his most famous passages, from which too often the key opening clause is omitted, he says of heaven:

> I shall be all there . . . I am not all here, I am here now preaching upon this text, and I am at home in my Library considering whether *Saint Gregory,* or *Saint Hierome,* have said best of this text, before. I am here speaking to you, and yet I consider by the way, in the same instant, what it is likely you will say to one another, when I have done. You are not all here neither; you are here now, hearing me, and yet you are thinking that you have heard a better Sermon somewhere else, of this text before; you are here, and yet you think you could have heard some other doctrine of downright *Predestination* and

Reprobation roundly delivered somewhere else with more edification to you; you are here, and you remember your selves that now you think of it, this had been the fittest time, now, when every body else is at Church, to have made such and such a private visit; and because you would bee there, you are there. I cannot say, you cannot say so perfectly, so entirely now, as at the Resurrection, Ego, I am here . . . .

(3. S3. 691–707)

iv. Metaphoric Figure and Metaphor Maker

If the sermon is a communal, inclusive, dramatic "exercise," if it involves in "debatement" all the capabilities of the personality—in short if it is imaginative in nature—then it will energetically use metaphor. It may well use metaphor extended or elaborated into narration, which generally describes what the English Renaissance meant by the term allegory. Presumably, almost necessarily, chief metaphors or allegories in sermons as in epics and inclusive comic or tragic dramas will be familiar ones.

The most pervasive metaphor of Donne's sermons is *living* as *travelling*. For him, Christians not sunk in apathy or "lethargy" are constantly on the move. As preacher he guides his congregation through biblical texts which may be imaged, houselike, as the structuring and furnishing of living space with "rooms," or as having "branches," outlinelike, through which to course the understanding or, riverlike, up which to sail. Or again a text may be a region of heaven through which to sail or a torch to light the way.

We can easily recognize the propriety of journeying as a shaping sermonic metaphor and its congeniality to Donne in particular. It is a metaphor biblical, patristic, medieval, Anglican, and familiar to his hearers in literally numberless devotional and secular ways, evidently ever capable of new turns. The "journey of existence" integrates beginnings and endings and diverse events in between. This journey metaphor unifies, but not in a way that need collapse all into a reductive present, because journey always implies time, place, and condition *from which,* just as it implies time, place, and condition *to which*. Journeying involves effort and resistance within the body-self and in such external ways as foot-to-ground or wind-to-sail-to-boat-to-water. Moreover, effort and resistance implicit in such a metaphor adjust more readily to Christian charity than the hostilities of Donne's early Ovidian elegies and satires or the more cynical of his *Songs and Sonets*. Similarly, effort in travel can dramatize singlemindedness of commitment, as direction can readily dramatize the validity (or not) of the traveller's values. In any such case, humility, even penitence, may readily be reported or invited, because by Christian definition the traveller has not reached his goal.

The content and implications of Donne's journey metaphors naturally call for much more extended inspection later. The cursory identification here has to do with the generic fact that metaphor and allegory are frequently used in sermons. Other preachers might well achieve as much for the sermon with the same metaphor although I have not found any Renaissance Englishmen who seem to me to have done so. Others might achieve as much with a different metaphor, although I cannot guess what it might be. Donne himself in the nonsermonic *Devotions* used illness as allegory. I intend no frivolity in saying he did not get as far.

Allegory can be one way for an imaginative sensibility to counterattack overstatic, conceptualistic modes of thought. It slyly hypostatizes these terms and concepts into gods, demons, heroes, and monsters, thereby revealing their arbitrariness and involvement in passions, and so attesting indirectly to the freedom and dignity of man. Theology tends to lapse into a condition inviting such a counterattack. That inept allegory has now and then discredited the mode by leaving unseemly gaps and unbridgeable distances between tenor and vehicle need not concern us. The Renaissance thought allegory legitimate according to whether done well or ill. I will assume that modern criticism, with a debt in particular to Northrop Frye, has sufficiently reestablished that potential legitimacy for our purposes.

In these terms, the sermon is a tour of duty provoked by the more-or-less limited emergency of the biblical text. In the better sermons the challenge of the text is convincingly, comprehensively serious; in the poor ones it is not and the prose sags into merely cerebral exposition and ready explication. An earlier quotation spoke of any man fairly resolving any devotional point (hence almost any vital issue) only by coming to a "debatement" with his own conscience. That this agrees with tendencies in Martin Heidegger, Paul Tillich,

Gabriel Marcel and others to define man as the questioning being should not be too surprising.

The Donnean sermon then certainly, and the essential sermon quite possibly, must be understood in part as allegory. Donne's allegory tends to be unobtrusive because tenor and vehicle often stay close together (Church Fathers like orators on street corners, for example) rather than far apart, as in the occasional "seas" of Christ's blood or "seas" of iniquities. "Baroque" images like the sea of Christ's blood do not, it should be noted, violate the existential decorum and rationale of any such sermon as Donne's. Instead they attest to the personality's capacity to inhabit a life-world shaped by its own intensity of direction and wholeheartedness of commitment. Christ's blood is a sea to the men carried by it and whose homeland is moated by it.

Epic orders time by taking images from some mythic time superior to calendars and presenting them as examples significant for current reference. Somewhat similarly, Christian exegetes have since early days ordered time by connecting an event in a time under divine surveillance with an event in a time of divine presence. Such is the essence of typology.

Donne occupies a middleground of caution in exploiting typological possibilities of local metaphor and allegory. His typological constructions extend beyond strict usage, the prefiguration of New Testament events by Old Testament events, but the extension is not vague or careless. Biblical situations, whether Old Testament Egypt, Goshen, promised land, or New Testament "Land of the Gergesens," figure more or less current situations. There is some ambiguity in the relationship: obviously the biblical account, dictated by the Holy Ghost (as any Renaissance Anglican would put it) has definitive exemplary status and in that sense is the fulfillment, the antitype; yet just as obviously the "type" in this variation, the current situations or options have a kind of existential status as fulfillments for preacher and congregation. In other instances, a current situation may bear the same relation to an eschatological future as Old Testament types conventionally bore to New Testament antitypic fulfillments;

> If you will heare so, as you have contracted with God in your Baptisme, the holy Ghost shall fall upon you, whilst you heare, here . . . and the holy Ghost shall accompany you home to your own houses, and make your domestique peace there, a type of

> your union with God in heaven; and make your eating and drinking there, a type of the abundance, and fulnesse of heaven; and make every dayes rising to you there a type of your joyfull Resurrection to heaven; and every nights rest, a type of your eternall Sabbath; and your very dreames:[23] prayers, and meditations, and sacrifices to Almighty God.
>
> (5. S1. 789–798, concluding a sermon on Acts 10.44. "While Peter yet spake these words, the holy Ghost fell on them which heard the Word")

The current situation, in the context of the whole sermon, *may* duplicate the New Testament situation of Peter's audience. Donne used such variations of typology oftener than he used the basic convention.

Finally, though Donne never forgot the imponderability of the future and the unpredictability of grace (and no Anglican of that generation would be likely to), he used typology less to insist on the foreordained character of history than on the intermittent availability of free choices, open crossroads. The past itself has a certain elasticity or Protean changefulness—as the quotation above shows—since what is past *to* a man (existentially *the* past for *him*) is what he launches himself from towards a future accordingly hopeful or hopeless. Every crossroads turn, setting him in a different direction, may be taken to put him in a different line of typological kinships, a different past, a different history.

All this is so notwithstanding the repetitiousness of certain situations and choices. The liturgical year of Prayer Book worship *insists* on returning human attention to certain events and seasons unique by definition. But these unique, historical events are seen as the paradigm for new beginnings in a particular life. It may be that the sermon is the genre of all others most accessible to both the repetitious and the unique in human affairs. Hence an obvious way for a sermon to fail would be through failure to control that difficult balance. Donne's peculiar brilliance depends in part exactly on his accommodation of the unique and the recurrent. It was on the special festival of the Holy Ghost, Whitsunday, that he preached those lines about "your eating . . . a type of the abundance . . . every nights rest, a type of your eternall Sabbath." His exploitation of the journey metaphor abets such a sense of numberless encounters—with places mysteriously the same yet new, with personal relationships mysteriously the same yet new.

> Yet I am loath to depart my selfe, loath to dismisse you from this ayre of Paradise, of Gods comming, and returning to us. Therefore we consider againe, that as God came longe agoe, six thousand years agoe, in nature, when we were created in Adam, and then in nature returned to us, in the generation of our Parents: so our Saviour Christ Jesus came to us long agoe, sixteene hundred yeares agoe, in grace, and yet in grace returnes to us, as often as he assembles us, in these holy Convocations. He came to us then, as the Wisemen came to him with treasure, and gifts, and gold, and incense, and myrrhe;
>
> (5. S18. 287–295, on Ps. 6. 4–5)

The English Renaissance frequently thought in terms of the "order of nature" and "the order of grace." These notions, if conceived as a polarity, could make the increasingly lively Renaissance notion of history somewhat awkward. A sense of awkwardness or perplexity over getting the three orders of experience together can be seen in such diverse places as Shakespeare's histories, Donne's "Anniversaries," and Marvell's poems. We notice in the quotation above, though, that the three orders are conceived to accord, at least potentially. History features unique events, some of them sacred events, like God's creation of human nature in Adam and the Incarnation of Christ. The order of nature has featured recurring generation of and by parents, even recurring convocations among men. The order of grace can reconcile the two by renewing history, as a refreshed Incarnation in the hearts of a group of believers, or new Epiphany to their natural perceptions. (Presumably he distances with simile, *"as* the Wisemen," because the Wisemen were less than divine; Christians of Donne's generation, to my knowledge, took the Wisemen as literal history, not as metaphor and certainly not as mere legend.)

Each celebration of Epiphany, each repetition of the communion liturgy even—certainly each sermon referring to it—will be in some measure unique. Grace, including working through the sermon, may serve to *renew* events which have the uniqueness characteristic of history. Of course even grace cannot reverse time, which remains irreversible for animal, God, Renaissance man, and twentieth century phenomenologist.

But we notice the "six thousand years," the "sixteene hundred years," the "often": even if preacher or hearer is estranged from grace, whether the concept of grace is even meaningful to the latter or not, each stands outside the mere "order of nature" or of animal life, in a world of imagination wherein the question "When?" can be answered with reference to "objective time," that elegant communal fiction. Similarly the *wheres* of Donnean and other sermons not similarly animated by journey metaphors refer to a realm beyond the naturalistic animal cycles of path and goal, hunger-satiety, or the like. They refer to an order of experience in which questing yields experience and "debatements" answers that can be "bequeathed" so that there can possibly be an imaginative "ascent to a new level" (Straus, *Phenomenological Psychology,* p. 186).

Donne could be as insistent as any phenomenologist that human experience exceeds path-goal, stimulus-response organization. Perhaps the generic sermon inherently shows that the cycle of nature can afford no lasting satiety nor adequate security. Sermons tend to stay actively aware of transcendence and of particular needs to achieve transcendence, as for some mysterious aid like grace. One example from scores:

> In the beginning of the world we presume all things to have been produced in their best state; all was perfect, and yet how soon a decay! All was summer, and yet how soon a fall of the leaf! a fall in Paradise, not of the leaf, but of the Tree it self, Adam fell; a fall before that, in heaven it self, Angels fell: Better security than Adam, then Angels had there, we cannot have, we cannot look for here.
>
> (4. S4. 142–147;
> Ascension Day, 1622)

This dark bit exemplifies a motif familiar in Renaissance and much subsequent literature: those who live merely by Nature die by nature (often the dark side of secular comedy). The passage comes from a sermon on Deuteronomy 12.30, about following false gods, and hence shows journey-events melding with other imagery: missteps, falls in place, trees of self, typological alternatives. Finally, as a moment in a sermon commemorating a unique Ascension, it brings us back to the sermonic obligation to treat uniqueness and Donne's response.

Comic butts conventionally reform; comic heroes and heroines conventionally marry. Hence the movement is toward typical life.[24] Tragic heroes, though in some respects symbolic of general human attributes, remain obviously special. Hence we can say that uniqueness and the kind of historicity antithetical to natural cyclicism figure centrally in tragedy. Expectably in the sermon the tragic aspect of the unique or extraordinary tends to be lightened or redeemed. This because the crucial death has by definition already occurred: the Crucifixion means for the believer a perennial offer of unending redemption, a turning point toward an eternal action, not the end. Donne's excells in identifying with detailed and concrete vividness multiple subtle choices among experiences ordinarily either natural, transcendently special, or comically or tragically or Christianly unique. He schematically identifies some while speaking of posture upright "in nature, much more in grace":

> . . . and to make that which God intended for our way, and our rise to heaven, (the blessings of this world) the way to hell; this is a manifest Declination from this Uprightnesse, from this Rectitude. Nay, to goe so far towards the love of the earth, as to be in love with the grave, to be impatient of the calamities of this life, and murmur at Gods detaining in this prison, to sinke into a sordid melancholy, or irreligious dejection of spirit; this is also a Declination from this Rectitude, this Uprightnesse. So is it too, to decline towards the left hand, to Modifications, and Temporisings in matter or forme of Religion, and to thinke all indifferent, all one; or to decline towards the right hand, in an over-vehement zeale. To pardon no errors, to abate nothing of heresie, if a man beleeve not all, and just all that we beleeve; To abate nothing of Reprobation, if a man live not just as we live; this is also a Diversion, a Deviation, a Deflection, a Defection from this Rectitude, this Uprightnesse. For, the word of this Text, *Iashar,* signifies *Rectitudinem,* and *Planiciem;* It signifies a direct way, for, the Devils way was Circular, Compassing the Earth; but the Angels way to heaven upon Iacobs ladder, was a straight, a direct way. And then it signifies, as a direct and straight, so a plaine, a smooth, an even way, a way that the Fathers, and the Church have walked in before, and not a discovery made by our curiosity, or our confidence, in venturing from our selves, or embracing from others, new doctrines and opinions.
>
> (7. S9. 244–267, on Ps. 64.10
> "And all the upright in heart shall glory" 1626)

Turning aside, sinking, throwing down, leaning left or right, are all ordinarily natural activities, the stuff of comic action prior to its resolution, or of satire. Perhaps "to thinke all indifferent" characterizes absurdist comedy; certainly it opposes the tragic potentialities of "an overvehement zeale." Jacob's ladder was triumphantly unique; the Church's "way" triumphantly special. Donne's expeditions on that way often involve some Fathers controverting others on particular steps, and sometimes he follows the Fathers' spirit of appraising evidence, but to conclusions concretely different from most of them. Still, his activities would not oppose any of the theological positions taken by his listener during the course of Prayer Book worship. For him and for them Creation, Incarnation, Passion, Resurrection, and Ascension are unique and fundamental, not symbolic; other actions of God, devil, angels, or men can thanks to their repeatability be symbolic. Liturgy and sermon, at their best, partake of that uniqueness as well as of that symbolic quality.

In a passage not uncharacteristic he presents something like a conventional line-up of imagery with tragic and comic dénouements:

> His hailestones, and his thunder-bolts, and his showres of bloud (emblemes and instruments of his Judgements) fall downe in a direct line, and affect and strike some one person, or place: His Sun, and Moone, and Starres, (Emblemes and Instruments of his Blessings) move circularly, and communicate themselves to all. His Church is his chariot; in that, he moves more gloriously, then in the Sun. . . .
>
> (6. S8. 192–193)

Yet this detached and analytic view dilutes the pity and terror of single man confronting the gods as antagonist. Such detachment, with cosmic panorama and *deus ex machina,* accords better with divine and human comedy, perhaps. But it is in any case more characteristic (as we shall observe) of the early moments in his sermons than the late moments.

Typically, a path is validly straight, instead of deflected or "a vertiginous circle" (6. S11. 170) or "the Devils way . . . Compassing the Earth," only by virtue of dynamic heading toward divine transcendence. Among the nostalgic would-be "primitive churchmen" and variant warring moderns, Donne accorded a *judicious* recognition to the effect defined by Straus as complementary to natural cyclicism: questions and answers follow one another incrementally. The path they mark may deflect into error or be lost to the forgetter but for those who know, it will inevitably be on-going. Donne's references to the biblical text or antiphonal patristic interpretations often exemplify his sense of a "way" at once special, traditional, and incremental:

> For the Fathers, it may be sufficient to insist upon St. *Augustine;* not because he is alwayes to be preferred before all, but because in this point, he hath best collected all that were before him, and is best followed of all that come after.
>
> (7. S13. 635–638)

The progressive revelation of truth by man and to man (including restoration of truth) is presumably a special case of God's progressive revelation of Himself to man, one medium of the divine comedy. And the incremental nature of knowledge, the progressive feature of the journey imposes its own demands:

> They saw not whither they went, and therefore were loath to goe. . . . But . . . their excuses will not be applicable to us. We have a full cleernesse of the state of the soule after this life, not onely above those of the old Law, but above those of the Primitive Christian Church, which, in some hundreds of yeares, *came not to* a cleare understanding in that point . . . whether the soule could not die, or onely should not die. Or (because that may be without any constant cleerenesse yet) that was not cleare to them, (which concerns our case neerer) whether the soule *came to* a present fruition of the sight of God after death or no. But God . . . afforded us cleernesse in that. . . .
>
> (5. S19. 182–195; my italics)

Fruition and *cleernesse*—enjoyment and illumination—*as goals* are metaphors that suggest something about the Donnean notion of life and sermon alike.

v. Donne and the Generic Sermon, a Summary

But what in *general* is the tenor of Donne's pervasive allegorical journey, and what *summary* remarks do the preceding observations warrant about the genre of sermon that were not accessible at the beginning? Can we make our circle just, as Donne liked to do with his?

We can say: the Donnean sermon presents the action of faithfulness in moving the speaking self (1), and hopefully the listener (2), from static, atomistic nonattachment (3), to (4) a dynamically inclusive attachment (5). This action works out in contest with all kinds of adversities (6); that is, apathy or inattention, confusion or error, and willful or sinful counteraction. These points may be considered one at a time.

At Whitehall in 1618, early in his ministerial career, Donne observed:

> It is but little, that man is proportioned to the working of God; but yet man is that creature, who onely of all other creatures can answer the inspiration of God, when his grace comes, and exhibit acceptable service to him, and cooperate with him.
>
> (1. S7. 126–129)

The priest's sermon is part of *his* "answer," a dramatic interchange betokening the way any man may respond constructively to crucial challenge. Such challenges call not the righteous, but sinners, readers of St. Luke will recall.

Any preacher might, in Donne's sense, "exhibit . . . service;" he can proceed along a path; he can even, like Donne, join with alternative versions of himself or otherwise include on that journey possible selves of his auditors. But obviously no preacher not a Pelagian heretic can pretend to carry them surely to a transcendent goal:

> I will but paraphrase the words of the Text, and so leave you in that, which, I hope, is your *gallery* to heaven, your own meditations. . . .
>
> (6. S7. 549–551)

The sermon may well of all generic forms be the most fundamentally open-ended or inconclusive or contingent. The tragic protagonist dies; the comic pair marry; the bard has produced his definitive story. Donne clearly knows his sermons are not conclusive, either because all will have to be done over again, or there will be a continuing, incremental effect in "your meditations." And Heaven, by definition, cannot be taken by violence or delivered in a package. So perhaps all sermons should, like his, make heavy use of conditionals, subjunctives, and optatives, especially toward the end.

In the early parts of the Donnean sermon there is less contingency and more assurance. But it is the inconclusive or uncreative assurance of what Donne distinguishes from faith as *knowledge* and our contemporary Gabriel Marcel distinguishes from faith as "opinion."[25]

> Be pleased therefore to give me leave in this exercise, to shift the scene thrice, and to present to your religious considerations three objects, three subjects: first, a secular mariage in Paradise; secondly, a spirituall mariage in the Church; and thirdly, an eternal mariage in heaven.
>
> (3. S11. 20–25)

The preacher stage-managing, object-shuffling, furniture-moving, or diagram-drawing at the beginning of a sermon defines by radical contrast the man all-involved at the end. He had complained years earlier about the kind of preacher unable to emerge from the world of dead artifacts to the drama of human involvement:

> That the Divines of these times, are become meer Advocates, as though Religion were a temporall inheritance; they plead for it with all sophistications, and illusions, and forgeries: And herein are they likest Advocates, that though they be feed by the way, with Dignities, and other recompenses, yet that for which they plead is none of theirs. They write for Religion without it.
>
> (letter to Sir Henry Goodyer, 1609) [26]

A hearer may always be in some measure dynamically involved in the matters being communicated. He both receives and broadcasts again to his own understanding the words in his ears, in Walter J. Ong's argument.[27] Yet Donne identifies several stations of possible involvement:

> I know what dead carkasses things written are, in respect of things spoken. But in things of this kind, that soul that inanimates them, receives debts from them: The Spirit of God that dictates them in the speaker or writer, and is present in his tongue or hand, meets himself again (as we meet ourselves in a glass) in the eies and eares and hearts of the hearers and readers: and that Spirit, which is ever the same to an equall devotion, makes a writing and speaking equall means to edification.
>
> (2. S8, Dedicatory Letter)

Accordingly, he recognized that an auditor might be sharing membership with him in the changing worlds from the opening scene of mere furniture to the subsequent worlds of involvement. The sermon ought to allow for that and for lesser particpations, or at least acknowledge them:

> It is not the depth, nor the wit, nor the eloquence of the Preacher that pierces us, but his nearenesse; that hee speaks to my conscience as though he had been behinde the hangings when I sinned, and as though he had read the book of the day of Judgement already. Something *Abraham* saw in this Angel above the rest, which drew him, which *Moses* does not expresse; Something a man finds in one Preacher above another, which he cannot expresse, and he may very lawfully make his spiritual benefit of that, so that that be no ocasion of neglecting due respects to others.
>
> (3. S5. 295–304)

Note that "nearenesse" is so central that the preacher himself is a fellow auditor: "pierces *us*." God Himself "is absent when I doe not discerne his presence." (5. S18. 156–157).

For Donne, worship moves toward both nearness and inclusiveness:

> I can build a Church at my bed side; when I prostrate my self in humble prayer there, I do so. . . . yet, I finde the highest exaltations, and the noblest elevations of my devotion, when 'I give thanks in the great Congregation, and praise him among much people' (Ps. 35. 18), for, so me thinks, I come nearer and nearer to the Communion of Saints in Heaven. . . .
>
> (4. S2. 782–789, slightly repunctuated)

Properly all attention develops into social activity:

> To that we must come, to *practise*. For in this respect, an *University* is but a *wildernesse,* though we gather our learning there, our private meditation is but a wildernesse, though we contemplate God there, nay our *being here,* is but a wildernesse, though we serve God here, if our service end so, if we do not proceed to *action,* and glorifie God in the publique.
>
> (4. S5. 548–553)

The preacher's living-into-existence of his own integrity, then, properly parallels any man's journey from coldly atomistic finitude to infinitely satisfying nearness and inclusiveness, at the behest of a transcendent invitation.

The Donne who sometimes ends a sermon with a description of heaven both paradoxical and suggestive of defects and limitations in earthly life (e.g., 2. S11 and 7. S4)—who during his ministerial years was wont to "consider our ascension in this life (that which *David* speaks of, *Who shall ascend into the hill of the Lord?*)"—that Donne has changed from the poignantly troubled yet confident youth of the 1590s who wrote:

On a huge hill,
Cragged, and steep, Truth stands, and hee that will
Reach her, about must, and about must goe. . . .

In his sermons—surely with generic propriety—no reified abstraction has so commanding a place. Truth remains accessible though sometimes difficultly so, but accessible more as a way of life than as a trophy to be seized or even as a "love-object." And the journey, though often enough imaged as uphill, heads in the sermons into regions less completely known, less ponderable. Adversities are more extensively and variously dealt with because recognized as more various and formidable than "hills suddenness."

Exhortation in any sermon, like celebration there or in a lyric poem, like exhortation to oneself to be better or even to pray to be better, fights against *neglect,* the human tendency to lapse into indifference, inattention, atomistic self-absorption. No one knew it better than Donne:[28]

> . . . which of us ever, ever sayes over that short Prayer, with a deliberate understanding of every Petition as we passe, or without deviations, and extravagancies of our thoughts, in that halfe-minute of our Devotion? . . . I throw my selfe downe in my Chamber, and I call in, and invite God, and his Angels thither, and when they are there, I neglect God and his Angels, for the noise of a Flie, for the ratling of a Coach, for the whining of a doore; I talke on, in the same posture of praying; Eyes lifted up; knees bowed downe; as though I prayed to God; and, if God, or his Angels should aske me, when I thought last of God in that prayer, I cannot tell: Sometimes I finde that I had forgot what I was about, but when I began to forget it, I cannot tell. A memory of yesterdays pleasures, a feare of to morrows dangers, a straw under my knee, a noise in mine eare, a light in mine eye, an any thing, a nothing, a fancy, a Chimera in my braine, troubles me in my prayer. So certainely is there nothing, nothing in spirituall things, perfect in this world.
>
> (7. S10. 259–286)

The very confrontation of the challenge in a particular text may be seen to imply a call for penitence. The Word, after all, has been there. Why has not the priesthood of believers responded before?

The response will dramatize and imply obstacles. The struggle against faltering attention and the curse of emptiness does not bulk nearly as large in the Donnean sermon as the contention against meaninglessness. The central good thing sought in such passages is valid knowledge, understanding. The deliberative or analytic portions of the sermons, like the deliberative, relatively dispassionate literary modes in general (epic, ballad, philosophical poem, history) aim for harmoniously meaningful wholeness, the opposite of chaos. In heaven, remarks Donne soberly,

> I shall see all problematicall things come to be dogmaticall, I shall see all these rocks in Divinity, come to be smoothe alleys; I shall see Prophesies untyed, Riddles dissolved, controversies reconciled. . . .
>
> (3. S3. 743–746)

We have noted his identification of the curse of oblivion and the curse of confusion. There is a third, which appears to be second in the perspective of Donne's concerns, the curse of guilt. Humility, contrition, "holy scorn," the not-so-holy scorn (in Donne's view) of satire in sermons, as in lyric poems or whatever, battle against the *agents* of guilt; the first two see the self as agent, while the third sees others. Donne's God, like Milton's, occupies a throne altogether unshaken. But neighbors in Donne's city, like Milton's fallen angels, may fancy they inhabit a Manichaean landscape:

> *Gods House is the house of Prayer:* It is his Court of Requests; There he receives petitions, there he gives Order upon them. And you come to God in his House, as though you came to keepe him company, to sit downe, and talke with him halfe an houre; or you come as Ambassadors, covered in his presence, as though ye came from as great a Prince as he. You meet below, and there make your bargaines, for biting, for devouring Usury, and then you come up hither to prayers, and so make God your Broker. You rob, and spoile, and eat his people as bread, by Extortion, and bribery, and deceitfull waights and measures, and deluding oathes in buying and selling, and then come hither, and so make God your Receiver, and his house a den of Thieves. His house is *Sanctum Sanctorum,* The holiest of holies, and you make it

> onely *Sanctuarium;* It should be a place sanctified by your devotions, and you make it onely a Sanctuary to priviledge Malefactors, A place that may redeeme you from the ill opinion of men, who must in charity be bound to thinke well of you, because they see you here.
>
> (7. S12. 643–659)

The effects of such demonic, anti-Eucharistic activity may indeed be a temporary, local hegemony. Donne, like Augustine and Milton, does not claim to fathom the mystery of the evil will. But he speaks as buoyantly as they do (and as any sermon almost necessarily must) about divine beneficence and potency in a world at large which will no more than a whole sermon seem *entirely* relevant or favorable to any one particular observer:

> And for the refreshing of . . . one span of ground, God lets fall a whole showr of rain . . . if thou remember that which concerned thy sin, and thy soul, if thou meditate upon that, apply that, thou has brought away all the Sermon, all that was intended by the Holy Ghost to be preached to thee.
>
> (7. S13. 126–139)

Despite such particularity, can there be an inclusive, general activity in the sermon? What shall any of us hear if he is not to hear "but the Logique, or the Rhetorique, or the Ethique or the poetry of the Sermon, but the Sermon of the Sermon he heares not" (7. S11. 510–512)? To speak generally, Donne preaching is a man seeking the mystery and perfection of inclusive, integrated wholeness; but he preaches of that quest as a journey with way-stations of error and crossroads of dispute on the way to what he elsewhere spoke of as the place and activity of "the sacred choir." In short, he will be a man faithful to the place he has brought himself to, the pulpit, and healthily balanced in profound respect both for his immediacies and his ultimates, diligent in finding and furthering their closer relation.

> Beloved . . . It is not halfe our worke to be godly men, to confesse a God in generall; we must be Christians too; to confesse God so, as God hath manifested himselfe to us. I, to whom God hath manifested himselfe in the Christian Church, am as much an Atheist, if I deny Christ, as if I deny God; And I deny Christ, as much, if I deny him in the truth of his Worship, in

my religion, as if I denyed him in his Person. And therefore . . . If I doe not remember *Thee,* If I doe not professe *Thee* in thy Truth, I am falne into this *Death,* and buried in this *Grave* which *David* deprecates in this Text, *For in death there is no remembrance of thee; and in the grave, who shall give thee thanks?* [Ps. 6. 5]

(5. S19. 315–334)

❦ 2 ❦

THE EXISTENTIAL ORDER OF DISCOURSE

i. Definitions

We have considered what sermons are artistically and some leading features of these sermons. Our preoccupations were mainly aesthetic and literary, although inevitably those interact with concerns either more general or more particular. This chapter begins not with mindfulness of broad distinctions between market square and Anglican church, Anglican sermon and comic play or epic poem, but rather with ideas about the world. Argument from this direction attends hardly at all to sermons as a generic entity, but looks to the assumptions and developed implications that animate Donne's sermons. This is not to make any confusing or fruitless distinction between style and content, only to act on the common-sense observation that *structure* and content are complementary and quite different places to begin, though they share some bits of ground which we will consider later.

The first chapter emphasized these sermons as 160 objects, similar in shape (or movement) but differing somewhat in size and quality according to no particular pattern. This chapter treats them more as one homogeneous body, a sort of granitic mountain which will yield the same proportion of components wherever a core sample is taken. These practices naturally distort, although not as severely as my analogies might suggest. But any critical method and any critical thesis distorts. The biases of Chapters 1 and 2 tend to correct one another.

One assertion, repeated by Potter and Simpson, goes that Donne's adeptness at sermons underwent a marked "curve of development." They mean curve upward and their placement of all undated sermons, some quite good, as late as possible perhaps adds invalid weight to their argument. I would enlist with the late Charles Coffin in suggesting these claims are exaggerated. There are good sermons and poor ones both early and late. There are changes with the decorum of the church year: penitential tones and terms for Lent, joyous for Christimas, and the like. There are adjustments for the tone and degree of complication in the Scriptural texts Donne chose as the foundation for sermons. He adjusted the density of argument for his audience, although I think this too can easily be exaggerated. Sermons to congregations at St. Paul's or St. Dunstan's or occasional audiences at weddings and funerals tend to be a *little* less demanding, by their complexity of syntax and pace of argument and illustration, than sermons preached to the learned King James or the university audience at Lincoln's Inn. But the conclusions in Chapters 1 and 2 do not say or imply that any large number of sermons grouped by place or year of delivery or biblical source shows marked superiority to other groups. I am not convinced any such superiority exists or can be shown, though arguments can readily be made for or against particular sermons and for or against different strategies of sermonizing.[1]

For a twentieth-century reader stalking the rationale of these sermons, their epistemology will present little immediate difficulty. Donne obviously conceives that he *knows* by experience. Informative experience includes the sensory, the ratiocinative and deductive, the meditative, that which derives from personal relations, and knowledge by revelation through the Bible. He may know by personal revelation through God's grace as the Church Fathers sometimes knew; but obviously it would be hubris to claim grace as if it were his by seizure. And he expects his congregation to know likewise; as a private believer Donne repeatedly petitions for grace in "Holy Sonnets: Divine Mediations."

But this rough-and-ready epistemology can be refined if we begin closer to the heart of his sermons and consider ontology. His ontology appears more sophisticated than that of his preaching contemporaries and markedly more congenial to many twentieth-century readers than the ontology of Anglican preachers of the following century.

The obvious term to use for Donne's way of being-in-the-pulpit and being-in-the-world is *existential*. The term may have jarring associations for the literary-minded because of Sartrian existentialism, but the reader coming from theology may comfortably recall more appropriate conceptions, such as this advanced by Paul Tillich:

> An interpretation of religion is existential if it emphasizes the two-way character of every genuine religious experience: the involvement of the whole man in the religious situation, and the impossibility of having God outside this situation.[2]

Identification of these sermons' generic properties involves the problem which enlivens recent generic criticism and no doubt provokes some of the flourishing generic experimentation by current writers: how to reconfirm generic organization in this generation's lived experience, how to bring together that tradition and this world. Identifying Donne's ontology, to the contrary, involves finding lines of direction, as in grain or magnetic orientations in that granitic mountain of sermonic material. Four points seem central; each is both a Donnean assumption and a theme:

1. several kinds of thing are real;
2. human life is characterized by *limitation;*
3. (a logical consequence of 1 and 2) the *relativity* of human perception, cognition, and constancy;
4. men live not in the world as God sees it or as any measuring instrument sees it but in a life-world of past, present, and future involvements.

These points may be considered one at a time.

ii. Multiple Realities

Donne, like any theocentric existentialist opposing assorted materialists or idealists, asserts that several elements of human life and experience are *real,* not just weights or measures or deductions. Sometimes he will use traditional terminology:

> A naturall man is not made of Reason alone, but of Reason, and Sense: A Regenerate man is not mode of Faith alone, but of Faith and Reason; and Signes, externall things, assist us all. (6. S8. 262–265; 1624)

Again, speaking of Revelations 7.3 and 7.14, he speaks of *matter* and *form* as meaning *concept* and *concrete process,* and as being complementary:

> In which words, we shall consider for order and distinction, first the *matter,* and then the *form:* by the *matter* we mean the purpose and *intention* of the Holy Ghost in these words; and by the *form,* the declaring, the proving, the *illustrating,* and the heightning of that purpose of his. For that matter, we take this *imprinting of the Seal* of the living God in the forehead of the Elect, and his *washing in the blood* of the Lamb, to be intended of the *Sacrament of Baptisme:* In that which we call the *form,* which is the *illustrating* of this, we shall first look upon the great benefits and blessings which these servants of God so *sealed,* and so *washed,* are made partakers of. . . .
>
> (5. S4. 74–83; probably before 1628)

The "matter" and the "form" are equally real (and important) in men's lived experiences.

In a sermon on Philippians 3.2 ("Beware of the concision"), Donne reminds his congregation of a Psalmist's assertion familiar to them from the regular readings in Prayer Book worship: "The heavens declare the glory of God" (Ps. 19.1). He goes on to argue that any believer "may heare God in the motions of the [spheres], in the seasons of the yeare, in the vicissitudes and revolutions of Church, and State, in the voice of Thunder, and lightnings. . ." (10. S4. 247–249). Natural cycles then, or changes in institutional structure or content, or natural events all can refer equally to the God who is "the way, the truth, and the life." He then goes on to preach about St. Paul's "concision" as referring to destructive rendings, and contends that preaching records two modes of reality in a double way:

> . . . . musicall cadence and agnomination, *Circumcision,* and *Concision;* But then this delicacy, and juvenility presents matter of gravity and soundnesse. Language must waite upon matter, and *words* upon *things.* In this case, (which indeed makes it a strange case) the matter is the forme; The matter, that is, the doctrine that we preach, is the forme, that is, the Soule, the *Essence;* the language and words wee preach in, is but the Body, but the *existence.*
>
> (10. S4. 327–331)

This sermon cannot be dated except as subsequent to his appointment as Dean of St. Paul's in November 1621. More will be said later about what he calls here "but the Body," "the language and words." So let it suffice now to note that the seeming disparagement of language comes in a context which implies no more than a common-sense recognition: some doctrinal essences could be conveyed just as well in French or Greek—at least if they were addressed to a Frenchman or a Greek. His major point about the usual difference, occasional congruity and equivalent importance of matter and form—that point could well have been enunciated at any time in his ministry.

In a characteristic preacherly activity, he seeks to *define* a feature of experience, sin in this instance He defines it as real, in opposition to the Scholastic formula that sin is a privation of being, *peccatum nihil.* Of sin and the Redemption he says:

> that that needed that ransome (say the Schoole men what they will of privations) cannot be meerely, absolutely nothing, but the greatest thing that can be conceived; and yet that shall be forgiven. That, and all that; *Sin* and all *sin:* And there is not so much of any thing in the world, as of sin. Every vertue hath two extreames, two vices opposed to it; there is two to one; But *Abrahams* taske was an easie taske to tell the stars of Heaven; so it were to tell the sands, or haires, or atomes, in respect of telling but our owne sins.
>
> (5. S3. 136–146; at St. Paul's, Whitsunday, probably 1623) [3]

Somewhat analogously, because with regard to similar causes and effects, he insists *wonder* is real.

> *Nil admirari* is but the Philosophers wisdome; He thinks it a weaknesse, to wonder at any thing, That any thing should be strange to him: But Christian Philosophy that is rooted in humility, tels us, in the mouth of *Clement* of *Alexandria, Principium veritatis est res admirari,* The first step to faith, is to wonder, to stand, and consider with a holy admiration, the waies and proceedings of God with man: for, Admiration, wonder, stands as in the midst, betweene knowledge and faith, and hath an eye towards both. If I know a thing, or beleeve a thing, I do no longer wonder: but when I finde that I have reason to stop upon the consideration of a thing, so, as that I see enough to induce admiration, to make me wonder, I come by that step, and God leads me by that hand, to a knowledge, if it be of a naturall or

civill thing, or to a faith, if it be of a supernaturall, and spiritu-all thing.

(6. S13. 101–115; "at St. Paul's, in the evening, upon Easter Day," 1625)

Wonder is real much as sin, knowledge, or faith is real: as a consequence of certain combinations of attitude and experience, and as a "step" toward further consequences. Notice John Donne rather than "Christian Philosophy" puts that wayfaring metaphor of "step to" into the real enough mouth of *Clement*.

Such proceeding often suggests that abstractly definable *relationship* had reality as much as any physically experiential matter. Thus, with a bow to "the Schools" whose view of sin and evil he elsewhere repudiated for its abstraction:

King and subjects are Relatives, and cannot be considered in execution of their duties, but together. The greatest Mystery in Earth, or Heaven, which is *the Trinity,* is conveyed to our understanding, no other way, then so, as they have reference to one another *by Relation,* as we say in the Schools; for, God could not be a Father without a Son, nor the Holy Ghost *Spiritus sine spirante.* As in Divinity, so in Humanity too, *Relations* constitute one another, King and subject come at once and together into consideration. Neither is it so pertinent a consideration, which of them was made for others sake [any more than "whether the Egge, or the Hen were first in the world" he has earlier said], as they were both made for Gods sake, and equally bound to advance his glory.

(1. S3. 25–34; at Paul's Cross, 1617)

Duty, reciprocal relationship, function, pertinence are all as real as an egg, a hen, or a deduction.

It may just be that during the years of his surviving sermons, that is from age 43 to 58, he grew increasingly phenomenological and existential. Some allegations about Donne's "development" as a preacher seem exaggerated, but the difference between the last quotation, from 1617, and this from 1629 may be suggestive:

And as no lesse light then Faith it selfe, can show you what Faith is, what it is to believe; so no lesse time then Damnation shall last, can show you what Damnation is: for the very form of Damnation is the everlastingness of it. . . .

(8. S15. 652–655) [4]

Indeed, this sounds almost like a definition by example of the phenomenological method. It can stand moreover as introductory evidence for his sense of human limitations, his theocentric relativism, and his conception of the life-world, which are discussed in parts iii, iv, and v through ix.

iii. Human Limitations

Donne countenances multiple modes of reality then, which are more or less on equal footing, as illustrated in the foregoing section. That and the familiar notion of human limitation provide much of the ground for Donne's usual profusion, for what his listeners appreciated as proper copiousness. The listener insensitive to one mode of reality very likely can be approached from some different direction. Quasi reasons all in a troop are opposed by sound reason and confuted by metaphor (1. S4. 110–140). What is meant for the Holy Ghost to *fall* on Peter's auditors (as reported in Acts 10.44) gets glossed in cumulative analogy to falling waters and stooping hawk and invading army, in a metaphoric distinction from New Testament revelation, in Old Testament myth, in general social terms, and in a metaphor of natural process (5. S1. 508–534). Before concluding that "there is an infinite sweetnesse, and infinite latitude in every Metaphor . . . of the Scripture," he proposes the "consideration" of sin as *burden* (referring to Ps. 38.4) in terms of the following categories: any man's personal history, a metaphoric distinction, contrasting sceptical ratiocination, timeless bodily analogies, secular political analogy, Old Testament myth, Old Testament testimony and history, and prophetic psychology (2. S4. 186–400); and my listing temporarily ignores preacher-auditor relationships as vehicles and components of meaning.

A survey of the importance Donne accords human limitations should begin with the most general. He does not say "I think erroneously, therefore I am" nor "I die, therefore I am," but rather "I am dying, but in expectation of restoration to life." Almost any sermon would provide abundant illustration of these fundamental convictions, but an early one at Whitehall serves conveniently, a sermon on 1 Corinthians 15.26. "The last enemie that shall be destroyed, is death."

> Death is the last, and in that respect the worst enemy. . . . We have other Enemies; Satan about us, sin within us; but the power of both those, this enemie shall destroy; but when they are destroyed, he shall retain a hostile, and triumphant dominion over us. But . . . .
> How long O Lord? for ever? No, *Abolebitur:* wee see this Enemy all the way, and all the way we feele him; but we shall see him destroyed. . . .
>
> (4. S1. 379, 46–51)

The experiential richness and communal tones of this make a provocative contrast with the fine but conceptualistic, vocative bravado of "Death, be not proud."

Equally general and almost equally pervasive in the sermons are his attentions to the little deaths of strength or resolution or attention or fidelity, but with the difference of earlier and more constant Christian emphasis:

> I shall be all there, my body, and my soul, and all my body, and all my soul. I am not all here. . . You are not all here neither; you are here now, hearing me, and yet you are thinking that you have heard a better Sermon somewhere else . . . and because you would bee there, you are there. I cannot say, you cannot say so perfectly, so entirely now, as at the Resurrection, *Ego,* I am here; I, body and soul; I, soul and faculties; as Christ said to *Peter . . . Fear nothing, it is I.*
>
> (3. S3. 691–708; more fully in Chap. 1. in a different connection) [5]

> Now though Christ were farre from both, yet he came nearer to an excesse of passion, then to an Indolencie, to a senselesnesse, to a privation of naturall affections. Inordinatenesse of affections may sometimes make some men like some beasts; but indolencie, absence, emptinesse, privation of affections, makes any man at all times, like stones, like dirt.
>
> (4. S13. 208–213; 1623)

Death, emptiness, inconstancy, and guilt are for Donne not only omnipresent elements of the human condition but echoes of the original fall from grace, terrain features along a fallen way of life.

In this orthodox view, sin limits and distorts man's being, knowing, and doing.

> . . . *thy sins are forgiven thee?* Does he mean all my sins? He knowes what original sin is, and I do not; and will he forgive me sin in that roote, and sin in the branches, originall sin, and actuall sin too? He knowes my secret sins, and I doe not . . . and will he forgive my faint repentances and my rebellious relapses after them? . . . Will he forgive that dim sight which I have of sin now, when sins scarce appeare to be sins unto me, and will he forgive that over-quick sight, when I shall see my sins through Satans multiplying glasse of desperation, when I shall thinke them greater then his mercy, upon my deathbed?
> (5. S3. 146–166; perhaps 1623)

> we see [God] in the Church, but men have made it a riddle, which is the Church; we see him in the Sacrament, but men have made it a riddle, by what light, and at what window: Doe I see him at the window of bread and wine; Is he in that; or doe I see him by the window of faith; and is he only in that? . . . I shall not live till I see God; and when I have seen him I shall never dye. What have I ever seen in this world, that hath been truly the same thing that it seemed to me?
> (3. S3. 735–751; perhaps 1620)

He laments being subject even during prayer to "powers and principalities": "The spirit of slumber . . . the spirit of deviation . . . the spirit of error . . . *Hosea's spiritus fornicationis* . . . some unclean spirit" (10. S1. 553–572; probably 1623).

The disabling nature and effects of sin constitute a leading theme in Christianity from the very first, the very thing that makes the Good News needful and good, and Donne's frequent quotations from patristic and New Testament sources attest his awareness of exploring a well-worn line of attention. Here again sensitivity and richness of observation, rather than pioneering search, distinguish him. He will now and then touch hands with an Old Testament forefather of the tradition, as by the reference above to Hosea, or to Jeremiah 17.9: " 'The heart is deceitfull above all things, and desperately wicked, who can know it?' " (10. S2. 640; 1624 or 1625). The theme is familiar to many in Spenser's and Shakespeare's countless variations on discrepancies between seeming and being. There the devotional orthodoxy of the theme has escaped some readers, perhaps because of the scarcity of biblical and patristic names. Here the imaginative vigor may escape attention amid the names. In any case, Donne notes the full range of possibilities: deceiving, being deceived, self-deception, consequent ill action, attendant damaged being. "The sinner will see nothing, till he can see nothing; and when he sees any thing . . . he thinks it but a little cloud, but a melancholique fit" (2. S3. 491–493), he observes, neatly refusing to pamper that Elizabethan malady, melancholia. He continues, in this third of five sermons on Psalms 38. 2, 3, and 4:

> and in an instant, (for 7 years make but an instant to that man, that thinks of himself, but once in 7 years) . . . his sins are got above him, and his way out is stopp'd. . . . if a man come to walk in the counsel of the ungodly, he wil come to sit in the seat of the scornful; for that's the sinners progress, in the first warning that *David* gives in the beginning of his first *Psalm*. . . . The Organ that God hath given the naturall man, is the *eye;* he sees God in the creature. The Organ that God hath given the Christian, is the *ear;* he hears God in his Word. But when we are under water, both senses, both Organs are vitiated and depraved, if not defeated. The habitual and manifold sinner, sees nothing aright; Hee sees a *judgement,* and cals it an *accident*. He hears nothing aright; He hears the Ordinance of *Preaching* for salvation in the next world, and he cals it an invention of the State, for subjection in this world.
>
> (2. S3. 494–703)

Although this series of five sermons does not, I think, differ from the other 155 in convictions about sin, the series does focus on sin with an imaginative energy usually focussed some other way, with sin a matter of intermittent attention. The five form a superbly *sustained* imaginative exploration of the phenomenology of sin. They were preached at Lincoln's Inn, perhaps in 1618 or 1617, no later than 1621, and seem to me to argue for early mastery of the sermonic mode.

What becomes apparent in such moments of the sermons—and they occur constantly—is that ontology and epistemology merge in the murk after the Fall. What becomes increasingly distinct are conditions *here* and conditions *there:* "What have I ever seen in this world, that hath been truly the same thing that it seemed to me?" but there "I shall see all problematicall things come to be dogmaticall, I shall see all these rocks in Divinity, come to bee smooth alleys; I shall see Prophesies untyed, Riddles dissolved, controversies reconciled" (3. S3. 750, 743–746). It is in that sense of distinction that "our mortality and our immortality . . . are the two reall Texts, and Subjects of all our Sermons" (2. S18. 485–486; at White-hall, the first Friday in Lent, 1620).

iv. Human Relativity, Presence, and Temporality

In the substance and structure of the sermons, the largest-looming consequence of the human limitations imposed by the Fall is the *relativising* of human certainty and human involvement. My certainty and involvement tend to decrease as their object, any object, becomes more distant, relative to some existential "center" of my self. Hence the counterforce of liturgy, with singing and saying in dialogue and seeing and changing bodily position. Hence the bread and wine of communion. Hence "thou must say, as [St. Paul] did . . . that thou art a greater sinner than thou *knowest* any other man to be" (6. S10. 233, my italics). The relativism here comes from human privateness in the negative sense, not the private self told to "be still and know that I am God" but the private self in contrast to the omnipresence and omniscience of God, which hereafter we may call the *parochial* self.

The point is not that nothing is truly real or intelligible; for Donne the universe is both complex and mysterious, not absurd. Nor is it impossible for a fallen man to get at the truth of a human circumstance. The man may by the grace of God have the truth; but either he cannot properly be sure he has it, or if he can confidently conclude (as Donne frequently does in sermons) that he has grasped an element of the truth in a given situation, he cannot be sure that he has all the elements that matter. Or he cannot be certain he has applied the truth to himself, cannot be sure that he has related himself to it adequately and appropriately. Donne's relativism, then, should be seen not as ultimately nihilistic universal relativism but as a contingent mundane relativism of certainty and of *presence* (that is, interactive immediacy). That "life of the world to come," in which priest and congregation reaffirm their belief before each sermon, is by definition beyond deceit or distraction or attenuation.

The excerpts above which illustrate Donne's sense of limitations on human life, and many of the excerpts near the end of the previous chapter, concur in illustrating at the same time the relativism of certainty. He "sees nothing aright. . . . He hears nothing aright." "What have I ever seen in this world, that hath been truly the same thing that it seemed to me?" Obviously, charitable caution must often be the style of the preacher's utterance and of the believer's life.[6]

> In the matter, The difference of degrees of Glory [of angels], we will not differ; In the manner, we would not differ so, as to induce a Schisme, if they would handle such points Problematically, and no farther. But when upon matter of fact they will induce matter of faith, when they will extend Problematicall Divinity to Dogmaticall . . . then wee must necessarily call them to the Rule of all Doctrines, the Scriptures.
>
> (7. S4. 498–509; 1626)

But charity is just the question, the problem, the issue, for Donne the mystery. Any "affection of the will" partakes of reconciling "our mortality and our immortality"[7] satisfactorily, the ground action of all these sermons. More particularly and immediately charity or other affections of the will determine by their intensity and direction the relative presence of anything.

With the composition of *Songs and Sonets,* seemingly after his poetic apprenticeship, Donne began to testify to his sensitivity to presence. With the usual exception of Shakespeare, he had as much awareness as anyone in his generation of differing degrees of existential presence, that is, presence as receptivity of the self toward the other and the other toward the self, as differentiated from simple sensory or ideational acknowledgement. That mystery the will, dazzling yet plain for all to see, lies at the heart of the matter:

> *Tolle voluntatem, et non est infernus* /Bernard/: If thou couldst quench thine owne will, thou hadst quenched hell; If thou couldst be content, willing to be in hell, hell were not hell. So, if God save a man against his will, heaven is not heaven; If he be loath to come thither, sorry that he shall be there, he hath not the joy of heaven, and then heaven is not heaven.
>
> (10. S1. 810–815; probably 1623)

And the presence of what is perceived, like the validity of the perception, depends to a great measure on the orientation, the bearing, as well as the vitality of the will.

> This I gain by letting *in* the fear of the Lord [into the self's being, not just the registration of the phrase on the rational consciousness], into my naturall fear; that whereas the naturall object of my naturall fear is *malum,* something that I apprehend *sub ratione mali,* as it is *ill, ill* for *me,* (for, if I did not conceive it to be *ill,* I would not fear it) yet when I come to thaw this Ice, when I come to discusse this cloud, and attenuate this damp, by the light and heat of *Grace,* and the illustration of the Spirit of God, breathing in his word, I change my *object,* or at least, I look upon it in *another line,* in *another angle* . . . .
>
> (6. S4., 386–394; 1624; at St. Dunstan's)

He goes on to describe how he will attend now to serving the glory of God by overcoming the immediate ill by the grace of God. Hence orientation of the will toward the God of Being ("Essence, Beeing: Beeing is the name of God, and of God onely" 8.S5.523) presents an existentially different world with different angles, a cloudlessly larger world, and a warmer brighter world. In short, a present world, precisely antithetical to the egotistical world, wherein the self closes on the self and tends in consequence toward solipsism and finally oblivion.

> All knowledge that begins not, and ends not with his glory, is but a giddy, but a vertiginous circle, but an elaborate and exquisite ignorance. He would learn of him, and what? *Quid boni Faciam,* What good things shall I do? Still he refers to the future; to do as well as to have done: and still to be doing so. Blessed are they that bring their knowledge into practise; and blessed again, that crown their former practise with future perseverance.
>
> (6. S11. 169–175; 1625)

Thus having any future at all is relative to orientation Godwards.

But it should be noticed in the quotations above, even the last because of its emphasis on doing and practice, that any orientation begins with and from the body-self. The difference for Donne between egocentricity and regeneracy or grace is not that the self gets displaced from the center of its own cosmos to a remote orbit, but rather that the self with whole will opens and orients itself to the God of "Beeing" both incarnate and transcending all incarnation. No wonder that Donne, somewhat like Milton, continued to find as much existential resonance in the image of a geocentric cosmos as he found experimental validity in a heliocentric cosmos. In 1614 or 1615 he wrote to Sir Henry Goodyer of astronomical distances between the self and salvation:

> *Copernicisme* in the Mathematiques hath carried earth farther up, from the stupid Center; and yet not honoured it, because for the necessity of saving appearances, it hath carried heaven so much higher from it: so the *Roman* profession seems to exhale, and refine our wills from earthly Drugs, and Lees, more than the Reformed, and so seems to bring us nearer heaven; but then that carries heaven farther from us . . . .[7]

If the self has oriented and opened its self to the "light and heat of *Grace,* and the illustration of the Spirit" in this life, the life to come may be imaged as something like a geocentric system interfused within the all-embracing sun of a heliocentric system. The soul's *here,* relative to *there,* may be paradoxically subsumed by the miraculous there, the self paradoxically exalted in being subsumed in a mysterious other:

> But then in her Resurrection, her measure is enlarged, and filled at once; There she reads without spelling, and knowes without thinking, and concludes without arguing; she is at the end of her race, without running; In her triumph, without fighting; In her Haven, without sayling; A free-man, without any prentiship; at full yeares, without any wardship; and a Doctor, without any proceeding: She knowes truly, and easily, and immediately, and entirely, and everlastingly . . . For though this world be a sea, yet (which is most strange) our Harbour is larger then the sea; Heaven infinitely larger than this world. . . .
>
> (6. S2. 523–534; 1624)

But if the self attends elsewhere, thereby denying availability to grace or whatever messenger of larger reality is at hand, then the self's situation must be characterized in varying degrees of bleakness or emptiness. One of the most extensive and explicit treatments of this came rather early in his preaching career. He often made the impoverishment of the self-that-refuses-presence a point of familiar reference, but at Whitehall in April 1618 he gave an anatomy (in several senses) of human limitation in this regard and relative degrees of presence. The sermon is the second of two on 1 Timothy 1.15: "This is a faithfull saying, and worthy of all acceptation, that *Christ Jesus* come into the world to save sinners; of which I am the chiefest." He reflects and questions:

> At least be sure that he is so far come into the world, as that he be come into thee. Thou art but a little world, a world but of a few spanns in length; and yet Christ was sooner carried from east to west, from *Jerusalem* to these parts, then thou canst carry him over the faculties of thy Soul and Body; He hath been in a pilgrimage towards thee long, coming towards thee, perchance 50, perchance 60 years; and how far is he got into thee yet? Is he yet come to thine eyes? Have they made *Jobs* Covenant, that they will not look upon a Maid; yet is he not come into thine ear? still thou hast an itching ear, delighting in the libellous defamation of other men. Is he come to thine ear? Art thou rectified in that sense? yet voluptuousness in thy tast, or inordinateness in thy other senses keep him out in those. He is come into thy mouth, to thy tongue; but he is come thither as a diseased person is taken into a spittle to have his blood drawn, to have his flesh cauterized, to have his bones sawd; Christ Jesus is in thy mouth, but in such execrations, in such blasphemies, as would be Earthquaks to us if we were earth; but we are all stones, and rocks, obdurate in a senselesnes of those wounds which are inflicted upon our God. He may be come to the skirts, to the borders, to an outward show in thine actions, and yet not be come into the land, into thy heart. He entred into thee, at baptism; He hath crept farther and farther into thee, in catechisms and other infusions of his doctrine into thee; He hath pierced into thee deeper by the powerful threatnings of his Judgements, in the mouths of his messengers; He hath made some survey over thee, in bringing thee to call thy self to an account of some sinful actions; and yet Christ is not come into thee; either thou makest some new discoveries, and fallest into some new ways of sin; and art loth that Christ should come . . . should trouble thy conscience in that sin, till thou hadst made some convenient profit of it; thou hast studied and must gain, thou hast bought and must sell, and therefore art loth to be troubled yet; or else thou hast some land in thee,

> which thy self hast never discover'd, some waies of sin which thou hast never apprehended, nor considered to be sin; and thither Christ is not come yet: He is not come into thee with that comfort which belongs to his coming in this Text, except he have overshadowed thee all, and be in thee intirely.
>
> (1. S9. 255–290, a central paragraph)

Some readers will be struck by the imperial deftness with which Renaissance commonplaces about the macrocosm and microcosm, or Son of God as Sun of Heaven, have been manipulated; others by Donne's apparent elaboration from "I am a little world made cunningly" to "I am a world self-made all too cunningly."[8] In any case, the passage can stand as a sufficiently anatomic distinction between existential presence and physical propinquity.

In a sermon at St. Dunstan's in the West on Trinity Sunday 1624, he spoke of knowing the Trinity by "the book of creatures" or other means. The means most present is voice, always suggestive of response. But the voice can be fruitfully present or stultifyingly present or corrosively present depending on whether it is or is not that mobilizing and as it were heliocentric voice:

> And then, continue this first way of knowledge, to the last, and powerfullest proofe of all, which is the power of miracles, not this weake beginning, not this powerfull end, not this *Alpha* of Creatures, not this *Omega* of miracles, can imprint in us that knowledge, which is our saving knowledge, nor any other meanes then a voyce; for this knowing is beleeving, And, *how should they beleeve, except they heare?* sayes the Apostle. It must be *Vox, A voyce,* And *Vox de coelis, A voyce from heaven:* For, we have had *voces de terra,* voyces of men, who have indeed but diminished the dignity of the Doctrine of the Trinity, by going about to prove it by humane reason, or to illustrate it by weak and low comparisons; And we have had *voces de Inferis,* voyces from the Devill himselfe, in the mouthes of many Heretiques, blasphemously impugning this Doctrine; Wee have had *voces de profundis,* voyces fetched from the depth of the malice of the Devill, Heretiques; and *voces de medio,* voyces taken from the ordinary strength of Morall men, Philosophers; But this is *vox de Excelsis,* onely that voyce that comes from Heaven, belongs to us in this mystery: And then lastly, it is *vox dicens, a voyce saying,* speaking, which is proper to man,

> for nothing speaks but man; It is Gods voyce, but presented to us in the ministery of man; And this is our way; To behold, that is, to depart from our own blindnesse, and to behold a way, that is shewed us; but shewed us in the word, and in the word of God, and in that word of God, preached by man.
>
> (6. S6. 61–83)

Voice tends to orient the listener, for good or ill, or can reinforce his orientation. The listener who resists all external voices except those that amplify his egotistic inner voices will by Donnean terms suffer a kind of closure, vertiginous circling, and diminution.

In the fallen world, a speaker, too, may be left feeling empty by the inaccessibility and unresponsiveness of a resistant listener.

> Now if these blessed Fathers, these Angels of the Church, these Archangels of the Primitive Church, were thus affected, if they were not frequented, but neglected for other entertainments; or if they were not hearkned to, when they were heard, but heard perfunctorily, fragmentarily, here and there a rag, a piece of a sentence; Or if they were not understood, because they that heard were scattered, and distracted with other thoughts, and so withdrawne from their observation; or if they were not liked, because the Auditory had some pre-contracts with other Preachers, that they liked better; how may we think, that those holy and blessed spirits were troubled, if they were not beleeved? This destroyes and demolishes the whole body of our building; this evacuates the whole function of our Ministery, if we lose our credibility; if we may not be beleeved. . . .
>
> (8. S5. 717–729; 1627)

Demolishes, evacuates; the substantiality of the self is relative to its presence to others and constructive function in concert with them.

At least one auditor testified to Donne's preaching activity in just such terms of presence. In one of the commendatory elegies attached to the first edition of Donne's poems, Sidney Godolphin wrote:

> Pious dissector: thy one houre did treate
> The thousand mazes of the hearts deceipt;
> Thou didst pursue our lov'd and subtill sinne,
> Through all the foldings wee had wrapt it in,
> And in thine owne large minde finding the way
> By which our selves we from our selves convey,

> Didst in us, narrow models, know the same
> Angles, though darker, in our meaner frame.[9]

Godolphin was himself of "meaner frame," but evidently of sympathetic bearing and agility. Donne would seem to have been over severe in that sermon in which he denied that he himself or any auditor was "all here" for the hour.

Donne pondered how the profit of that "hour" and its presence could shift as variously for different auditors (including himself) as the sands in his glass, and less predictably. Poets like other men must always have known time is relative. Donne simply knew better than most, and better than other Anglican preachers articulated time's qualities as a function of orientation and existential presence.

In treating time as the shape of dialogue, the shape of growth, the shape of degeneration and regeneration, Donne attempts both positive and negative actions. Positively, he would keep faith with the injunction "to preach deliverance to the captives, and recovering of sight to the blind, to set at liberty them that are bruised, to preach the acceptable year of the Lord" (Luke 4. 19).

He makes countless references to time, references which give time a great variety of attention. But for all their variety, they can be characterized: normally they are poised or genial in tone, the outstanding exceptions being when he quotes such biblical phrases as "Time shall be no more" or "Fool, this night they shall fetch away thy soul;" their essential focus centers on the time-span of liberation. By the clock, such a period might be anything from a moment of recognition ("sight to the blind"), to a Christian Year in Prayer Book worship, to half a lifetime reoriented to a graceful path.

This contrasts with what we are probably accustomed to, reading twentieth-century prose. There and in some poetry we may readily find time by the span of sense-datum or experience, time by the phases of body-self's inner relationships, time by the stage of family relationships in one generation, time less often by the generations. Yet all such treatments of time threaten to be inhumane, in contrast to time by the opportunity of liberation. Or so Donne saw the matter, adverting to the downhill slide of a merely biological cosmos, to "the fall of the leaf, at the end of the year." Similarly, the scale of merely fallen human nature, although not so heavily cyclical, offers dreariness enough: "every age" of a person "a diverse sinne pursueth" he had written in 1609 ("Elegie on Mistress Boulstred," ln. 54) and "it is but living a few years, and then the prodigall becomes covetous" (2. S3. 664).

> I need not call in new Philosophy, that denies a settlednesse, an acquiescence in the very body of the Earth, but makes the Earth to move in that place, where we thought the Sunne had moved; I need not that helpe, that the Earth it selfe is in Motion to prove this, That nothing upon Earth is permanent . . . .
> A Monarchy will ruine, as a haire will grow gray, of it selfe. In the Elements themselves, of which all sub-elementary things are composed, there is no acquiescence, but a vicissitudinary transmutation into one another; Ayre condensed becomes water, a more solid body, And Ayre rarified becomes fire, a body more disputable, and inapparant. It is so in the Conditions of men, too; A Merchant condensed, kneaded and packed up in a great estate, becomes a Lord; And a Merchant rarified, blown up by a perfidious Factor, or by a riotous Sonne, evaporates into ayre, into nothing, and is not seen.
>
> (7. S10. 515–537; 1626)

Donne unquestionably recognized abstract time as another threat. He may have been ahead of his age in recognizing the potential inhumanity of time conceived as abstracted from lived experience, essentially amenable to mechanical measurement and hence annihilatingly indistinguishable. Certainly he could speak vehemently on the matter:

> The whole body and frame of the *Sermon* is opposed against one pestilent calumny . . . that wee have cast off all distinction of places, and of dayes, and all outward meanes of assisting the devotion of the Congregation.
>
> (4. S15. preface; Ascension Day 1623)

He would of course hardly need to take that line so explicitly very often, because he had constantly present the insistence of Prayer Book attention to the sequential opportunities of the Christian Year, and a great weight of biblical tradition. All concurred in affirming that days are not indistinguishable or interchangeable, but can on the contrary be constituted special by God or man or both together.

> Why doth one day excell another? When as all the light of every day in the yeere is of the Sunne. By the knowledge of the Lord they were distinguished: and he altered seasons and feasts.

> Some of them hath hee made high dayes, and hallowed *them,* and some of them hath hee made ordinary dayes.
>
> (Ecclus. 33. 7–9)
>
> See then that yee walke circumspectly, not as fooles, but as wise, Redeeming the time, because the dayes are evill.
>
> (Eph. 5. 15–16)

The days of our years are not all the same, and accordingly the ethical presence and quality of some feature of life may be relative to its point on a large curve of social time:

> Certainly the limits of adorning and beautifying the body are not so narrow, so strict, as by some sowre men they are sometimes conceived to be. Differences of Ranks, of Ages, of Nations, of Customes, make great differences in the enlarging, or contracting of these limits, in adorning the body; and that may come neare sin at some time, and in some places, which is not so alwaies, nor every where.
>
> (5. S15. 220–225)

This cultural relativism on Donne's part, cautious and guarded though it will seem to some modern readers, sufficiently fights for distinctions that are vivid in lived experience, against abolition by abstract time.

But such limited cultural relativism Donne subsumes in an orthodox Christian sense of history as an incomplete, generally ascending line oriented toward a mysterious consummation fully known only to God. This again controverts static or cyclical views of history, whether they have sprung from the idolatry of concepts or idolatry of natural cyclicism. And he rebuts with wry verve:

> The *Judiciall* law of *Moses,* was certainly the most absolute, and perfect law of government, which could have been given *to that people,* for whom it was given; but yet to thinke, that all *States* are bound to observe those lawes, because God gave them, hath no more ground, then that all Men are bound to goe clothed in *beasts skinnes,* because God apparelled *Adam,* and *Eve* in that fashion.
>
> (5. S7. 33–39; date uncertain)

But believing in a linear concept of history, and even denying other views in the name of lived experience oriented toward a divine freedom, even this does not dramatically contend with some heavy implications of other views of time. Time cannot be present as a liberating moment, event, or experience if naturalistically conceived, because then "the thing that hath been is that which shall be" and "Putrefaction is the end / Of all that Nature doth intend," as Herrick put it. To recognize that while nature always repeats itself but history never does, yet conceive history as undifferentiated and hence meaningless flux is to impose an intolerable burden on the present. Differentiating time and history mechanically makes the present just as much a cage, by tick-tocking the past remorselessly farther away.

Donne obviously participates in the Christine *doctrines* which controvert such perennial attitudes: history, far from being flux or entropy, articulates itself in terms of gracious divine acts like creation, deliverance from bondage to promised land, Incarnation of the Son of God, His Passion and Resurrection, and the orientation toward Last Judgment; the future need be no bondage because death shall die and heaven may be attained, and so on.[10] But less familiar are the tactics by which he dramatized and made present his conviction that time need be no bondage and indeed may be experienced best as the action of liberation.

The present—where his auditors are and so where he begins—need be no cage because the preacher can prompt their memories and teach them typologies.

> But the *memory* is so familiar, and so present, and so ready a faculty, as will always answer, if we will but speak to it, and aske it, *what God hath done for us, or for others.* The art of *salvation,* is but the art of *memory.*
>
> (2. S2. 49–52)

His particular tactics of fostering sacramental remembrance will claim further attention later, but this fragment suggests one of his usual strategies for enriching the present and ordering the past's multeity.

He could also set aside the presence of a burdensome, all-too-natural past by making concrete the doctrinal alternative and celebrating that new and acceptable year of the Lord. Perhaps no Anglican has excelled him at such celebration:

> In paradise, the fruits were ripe, the first minute, and in heaven it is alwaies Autumne, his mercies are ever in their maturity. We ask *panem quotidianum,* our daily bread, and God never

> sayes you should have come yesterday, he never says you must againe to morrow, but *to day if you will heare his voice,* to day he will heare you. If some King of the earth have so large an extent of Dominion, in North, and South, as that he hath Winter and Summer together in his Dominions, so large an extent East and West, as that he hath day and night together in his Dominions, much more hath God mercy and judgement together: He brought light out of darknesse, not out of a lesser light; he can bring thy Summer out of Winter, though thou have no Spring; though in the wayes of fortune, or understanding, or conscience, thou have been benighted till now, wintred and frozen, clouded and eclypsed, damped and benummed, smothered and stupified till now, now God comes to thee, not as in the dawning of the day, not as in the bud of the spring, but as the Sun at noon to illustrate all shadowes, as the sheaves in harvest, to fill all penuries, all occasions invite his mercies, and all times are his seasons.
>
> (6. S8. 135–152, Christmas, 1624)

Typology likewise argues that the past does not either remain burdensomely close, nor recede everlastingly farther away. Types and figures, cautiously assayed, can cut between the tyranny of natural cycles and the nightmare of flux to delineate moral hierarchies in time, present to the understanding and will now. Early in his series of sermons on Psalm 38, for example, he spoke of a large-scale general use of the method and suggested the Augustinian criterion of friendliness to the reign of love (*ad regnem caritatis*) as the check and balance.

> for this Psalm, some of our Expositors take to be a *historicall,* and *personall* Psalm, determin'd in *David;* some, a *Catholique,* and *universall* Psalm, extended to the whole condition of *man;* and some a *Propheticall* and *Evangelicall* Psalm, directed upon *Christ.* None of them inconveniently; for we receive help and health, from every one of these acceptations; first, *Adam* was the *Patient,* and so, his promise, the promise that he received of a *Messiah,* is our *physick;* And then *David* was the *Patient,* and there, his *Example* is our *physick;* And lastly, *Christ Jesus* was the *Patient,* and so, his *blood* is our physick.
>
> (2. S2. 123–132) [11]

He dealt judiciously—even tough-mindedly—with typological readings of Old Testament events as prefiguring New Testament antitypes. But he extends that strict construction of typology generously and imaginatively. To Donne's auditor David will be more present, nearer and more companionable, than Henry the Seventh or Eighth and that auditor will from time to time be invited to find in his London, like "marble mileposts in an alluvial land" in Auden's fine phrase, Goshens in his Egypts and warnings against smelling after Egyptian onions. He also will hear history invoked to reinforce his faith and thereby make a benign future more present:

> . . . let him beleeve; yea, for Gods sake let him take heed of not beleeving that we shall know one another, *Actions* and *Persons,* in the Resurrection, as the Apostles did know Christ at the Transfiguration, which was a Type of it.
>
> (3. S4. 221–224)

Or a vividly present immediate moment, like a newly pronounced marriage, may be extended as the visible couple's possible future time and an "earnest" of the witnesses' hoped for eternity:

> And in the mean time, bless these thy servants, with making this secular mariage a type of the spirituall, and the spirituall an earnest of that eternall, which they and we, by thy mercy, shall have in the Kingdome which thy Son our Saviour hath purchased with the inestimable price of his incorruptible blood.
>
> (3. S11. 518–523; 1621, at the marriage of Mistress Margaret Washington)

Thus the temporally present and knowable persons are used to help make existentially present a future otherwise either fearful or abstract.

v. Self, from Center Outward

Few of us would argue against the proposition that a man lives—in some sense—in his skin. Donne insisted on the self as a bodily self, as we shall have occasion to reiterate. Then, too, a man lives in his clothes. Chaucer's portraits and Donne's use of St. Paul's injunctions to "put on the armour of light . . . put ye on the Lord Jesus Christ" (Romans 13. 12, 14)—all owe some force to our common sense of our clothes: they give us protection from objectifying weather and objectifying gazes and give us "a face to meet the faces that we meet." But anyone's reluctance to be an object and his feeling of injustice if accosted as an object derives from a more fundamental truth, or so Donne would have it. *Man lives, the self becomes real, in a field of care and concern and lived expectation.*

No one would suppose Donne unique in his own century in developing a philosophical position which has been called Europe's greatest twentieth-century gift to the English-speaking world. This chapter and parts of those following argue not his uniqueness (unless in degree) but his sophistication and sensitivity in developing the position. Still, a suggestion or two is in order about the company he moved with. For example, St. Augustine. The sense of man as more the inhabitant of a life-world than of merely physical space, like the notion of man as occupant of historical, interfused, and alternative cities, concurs with that Father who was overwhelmingly Donne's most frequent patristic reference.[12] He seems to have been familiar with *De Civitate Dei* by 1608 at the latest. What that could mean may be suggested by slivers from Books One and Eleven (given here as they appeared "Englished" by John Healey in 1610):

> That most glorious society and celestiall City of Gods faithfull, which is partly seated *in the course of these declining times, wherein* "he that liveth by faith" / Habakkuk 2. [4] /, is a Pilgrim amongst the wicked; and partly *in* that solid estate of *eternitie* . . . have I undertaken to defend in this work. . . . The worke is great and difficult, but God the maister of all difficulties is our helper. For I know well what strong arguments are required to make the proud know the vertue of humilitie, by which (not being enhanced by humane glory, but endowed with divine grace) it surmounts all earthly loftinesse, which totters through the [i.e. its] owne transitory instability.
> (p. 1, my italics)

The self, it seems, lives *in* and through a community partly *in* "these declining times," partly here, partly *in* modes of being (like eternity) not locally measurable. The self can do and be by a relinquishment of aspiration—as if a subsiding into the self—which makes way for mysterious recruitment that extends the self, to surmount remote obstacles. These biblical ideas had scarcely any champion so effective as Augustine in the fifteen centuries after St. Paul.

> Thus as these contraries [in 2 Corinthians 1. 6–10, of sufferings and consolations] opposed doe give the saying an excellent grace, so is the worlds beauty composed of contrarieties, not in figure, but in nature. This is plaine in Ecclesiasticus . . . [33.13] "Against evill, is good, and against death is life, so is the Godly against the sinner: So looke for in all the workes of the highest, two and two, one against one."
>
> (p. 422)

Donne naturally read Augustine's Latin, as earlier noted. But a contemporary could have made out even through Healey's somewhat desperate English the central animating conviction: men's lives are *in* times of attitude, will, and action more profoundly than they are *in* space like peas in a pod (though that latter figure might characterize their *dead* bodies). Care and concern and lived expectation, like the two cities, imply alternatives in contention, rib to elbow. Like Augustine, Donne follows St. Paul's convictions that belief in Christ offers the believer a "new creation" and that "all things work for good to those who love the Lord." Hence, too, he worries about teaching the "vertue of humilitie" not so much to the ignorant as to the proud. All of this rests on the general assumption that history is divinely teleological, though vicissitudinal, and that a man's lively freedom requires commitment to such a view.

Perhaps more Augustinian than otherwise, Luther spoke of two life-worlds in "A Sermon of the Kingdom of God" in *Special and Chosen Sermons* . . . Englished by W. G[ace]" (London, 1581):

> For even as a wor[l]dly and temporall kingdom is ordayned to this ende, that man may live quietly and peaceably one with another: So the kingdom of God giveth these things spiritually, and destroyeth the kingdome of sinne, and is nothing else, but an abolishing and pardoning of offences, God reigneth in the hartes, inasmuch as he worketh in them by his word, peace quietnes and consolation: even as sinne worketh the contrary, namely, unquietnes, anguish, and all kinde of evills.
>
> (p. 153)[13]

But God's new creation comes through the working of a good deal more than "his word," in hearts, to Donne's way of thinking, as we shall see further. Though generally Luther and Donne do not stand far apart on the notion of radically different life-worlds, coexistent or interfused in space, Luther's splitting of the two into relationship by *analogy* here, and demotion of worldly-temporal kingdom to illustrative term, defines partly by contrast.

Finally, Donne's congregation would have reminders in that vein before every sermon from Prayer Book liturgy. They would say together in the General Confession, "We have *erred,* and *strayed* from thy ways like lost sheep. We have *followed* too much the devices and desires of our own hearts. . . . But thou, O Lord . . . *Restore* thou those who are penitent" (my italics). That adumbration of a quasi-physical relocation to be effected immediately by a change of heart gets reinforcement in the Absolution. There the priest means "starting here and now" when he speaks of God desiring "not the death of a sinner, but rather, that he may turn from his wickedness and live."

Similarly, after saying together the Apostles' Creed, they would hear the preacher pronounce what was in 1604 "The Second Collect for Peace," beginning with the familiar but remarkable formulas: "O God, who art the author of peace and lover of concord, in knowledge of whom standeth our eternal life, whose service is perfect freedom. . . ." The present tense of *standeth* and *is* designates the here and now. To "author" something like concord among men implies establishment of a relationship and condition of life that excludes other simultaneously available relationships and conditions. A prayer for the king asks that all those in authority "may always *incline to* thy will, and walk in thy *way*" (my italics) implying different life-worlds as matters of different bearings simultaneously available.

Even more emphatically than the foregoing from the service of Morning Prayer, the service of Holy Communion insists on coexisting life-worlds differentiated by will, attitude, and action. In the 1604 order (since altered) the priest, just before consecrating the bread and wine, would say, "Grant us therefore, gracious Lord, *so* to eat the flesh of thy dear Son Jesus Christ, and to drink his blood, that our sinful bodies may be made clean by his body, and our souls washed through his most precious blood, and that we may *evermore dwell in him and he in us*" (my italics). The gently ambiguous *so* of "so to eat . . . and to drink" papers over once-violent doctrinal controversies which need not concern us here. But the *evermore* means "starting (or continuing) from now on." Similarly, after the reception of the consecrated bread and wine, in the prayer of thanksgiving, the priest (and perhaps the people) would say "we most heartily thank thee, for that thou dost vouchsafe to feed us, which have duly received these holy mysteries . . . and that we be very members incorporate in thy mystical body which is the blessed company of all faithful people; and be also heirs through hope of thy everlasting kingdom." There is the ambiguity and contingency about who has *duly received,* and consequent subjunctive *be*'s (indicative *are*'s in later revisions), all of which strengthens rather than weakens the existential quality of difference between status as a fallen man, self-disinherited, and status as an "heir through hope."

When Donne in 1609 began one of his Holy Sonnets "At the round earths imagin'd corners, blow/Your trumpets, Angells," he alluded to Revelation 7.1, and presumably (as in other Divine Poems) to contemporary maps, often decorated at the corners with angelic trumpeters or wind-blowing cherubim. But more to our point is what his composition of place says about the imagination's substantiality in the meditator's world of lived experience. Angels can stand on corners provided by the imagination, whether mapmaker's, poet's, or reader's. Preaching on Revelation 7. 2–3, perhaps in 1623, he expanded on just such possibilities in that image.

> Take thy selfe at the largest, as thou art a world, there are foure Angels at thy foure corners; Let thy foure corners be thy worldly profession, thy calling, and another thy bodily refection, thy eating, and drinking, and sleeping, and a third thy honest and allowable recreations, and a fourth thy religious service of God in this place, (which two last, that is, recreation, and religion, God hath been pleased to joyn together in the Sabbath, in which he intended his own glory in our service of him, and then the rest of the Creature too) let these foure, thy calling, thy sleeping, thy recreation, thy religion be the foure corners of thy world, and thou shalt find an Angel of tentation at every corner: . . . .
>
> (10. S1. 595–605)

Very like his sonnets to focus on Last Things; very like his sermons to focus on daily things as a way to Last Things; very like both to ponder man as somehow *one* in the circle of self yet *many* in corners and bearings and turns. Certainly the preacher tended to bring macrocosmic angels in close to microcosmic action; and he tended to point out choices free in their initial "Let . . . be's" but relentless in their consequences.

The self, then, rather than being a self-contained and self-sufficient circle (as God might be imagined) extends out cornerwise into various modes of interest and care. Nevertheless, the self's diffusion outward in fields or vectors of concern never for Donne countenances schisms in the self. He can be quite explicit about this:

> That whereas God hath made the body to be the Organ of the soule, and the soule to be the breath of that Organ, and bound them to a mutuall relation to one another, Man sometimes withdrawes the soule from the body, by neglecting the duties of this life, for imaginary speculations; and oftner withdrawes the body from the soule, which should be subject to the soule, but does maintain a war; and should be a wife to the soule, and does stand out in a divorce. . . . we must love God with all our soule, yet it is not with our soule alone; Our body also must testifie and expresse our love, not onely in a reverentiall humiliation thereof, in the dispositions, and postures, and motions, and actions of the body, when we present our selves at Gods Service, in his house but the discharge of our bodily duties, and the sociable offices of our callings, towards one another: Not to run away from that Service of God, by hiding our selves in a superstitious Monastery, or in a secular Monastery, in our owne house, by an unprofitable retirednesse, and absenting our selves from the necessary businesses of this world: Not to avoid a Calling, by taking none: Not to make void a Calling, by neglecting the due offices thereof. In a word, To understand, and to performe in the best measure we can, the duties of the body and of the soule, this is the resurrection from the first fall, The fall into a divorce of body and soule.
>
> (7. S3. 354–387; 1626)

The powerful metaphors of marriage and resurrection make this profoundly antischizoid, the more easily understandable as such to its first audience, because it was preached at evening prayer on Easter, a day when the morning service would have included Holy Communion. Hence Donne himself was enacting the dual charge of *his* calling, the dual ministry of Word and sacrament.

As to characterization, ethical judgment, and selection of rhetorical resources, all this points the same way: insistence on the primacy of lived experience. Passages from two widely separated years will illustrate. Speaking of the self as nurturing parent to good actions sired by the Holy Ghost, he says:

> I will not stop mine eares to thy Word, my heart shall not doubt of thy word, my life shall expresse my having heard and harkened to thy word . . . for hearing is but the conception, meditation is but the quickning, purposing is but the birth, but practising is the growth of this blessed childe.
>
> (1. S8. 327–333; 1618)

In a sermon on Matthew 19.17, and a passage partly on churchmanship, he emphasizes the biblical context ("sell . . . give to the poor . . . and follow me") and the church as the company of faithful people in action:

> I heare them say they would have it thus [i.e. live devoutly, with constancy], this is Rhetorique to my soule; When I see their Laws enjoyne it to be thus, this is Logick to my soul; but when I see them actually, really, clearly, constantly do thus, this is a Demonstration to my soule, and Demonstration is the powerfullest proofe: The eloquence of inferiours is in words, the eloquence of superiours is in action. . . . as all example is powerfull upon us, so our own example most of all; in this case we are most immediately bound by our selves; still to be so good, as we our selves have been before.
>
> (6. S11. 136–151; 1625)

"Still" of course means "always," and "immediately" betokens yet once more his concern with existential "neerness," with life from the heart outwards.

A theological consequence of such existentialism is an anti-Pelagianism reaching far beyond insistence on the agency of grace and Christ, beyond simple exhortations to a churchmanship more than merely formal. He argues against the notion "That the merits of one man may be applied to another," in an emphatically Reformist sermon on Esther 4.16:

> When Queen *Esther* appoints others to fast for her, she knew she could no more be the better for their fasting then she could be the leaner . . . but because she was to have benefit by the subsequent act, by their prayers, she provokes them to that, by which their prayers might be the more acceptable and effectual . . . but . . . she and her own maids will fast likewise. As in spiritual things, charity begins with our selves, and I am bound to wish my own salvation, rather then any other mans; so I am bound to trust to my making sure of my salvation, by that which I

> do my self, rather then by that which I procure others to do for me . . . teach thine own eyes to weep, thine own body to fulfill the sufferings of Christ. . . . Come and participate of the devotions of the Church; but yet also in thy Chappel of ease, in thine own Bed-chamber, provide that thy self and thy servants, all thy senses, and all thy faculties, may also fast and pray; and so go on with a religious confidence as *Esther* did, about all thy other worldly businesses and undertakings.
>
> (5. S11. 159–308)

If as seems likely this was preached in 1615,[14] then this passage in the light of the two above suggests a chicken-or-egg problem. Did his convictions about lively churchmanship lead him to a conviction of the primacy of lived experience or the other way around? Either position could be argued, using biographical information about his ecclesiastical studies on the one side or the imaginative life of the *Songs and Sonets* on the other.

However that was, phrases like "charity begins with our selves" in the passage above and many others in similar vein witness that he sees any man, Everyman, as living from the center outward:

> We should be more sensible of the publique, but because private and personall things doe affect us most, the Commandment here goes to the particular.
>
> (3. S18. 143–145)

Accordingly, too, "the root of all societies is in families (2. S17. 29–30); "Cities are built of families, and so are Churches, too" (4. S9. 983). Donne always fights solipsism and hence sees living from the center outward as necessarily a dynamic thrust. He will acknowledge occasion for contraction into the self for meditation, but will see over all a "God, who ever, *for our example,* prefers the publique before the private" (2. S17. 284). He preaches a sermon on Mark 4.24: "Take heed what you heare." The whole argument, diffuse and difficult to represent by brief quotation, maintains that we must hear all that is good and none that is bad. And we must do both, it seems, the better to make such intaking and inward living worthy outward action through society to the circle of transcendence:

> What Christ tels us in the darke, he bids us speake in the light . . . every man hath Scriptures in his own heart, to hearken to . . . In declaring ill affections towards others, the Holy Ghost hath imprinted these steps. First . . . home, . . . then . . . out

> into Cities . . . the State . . . thence . . . to the highest upon earth . . . thence to the highest in heaven. . . . The ear in such cases, is as the clift in the walls, that receives the voice, and then the Echo is below, in the heart, for the most part, the heart affords a returne, and an inclination to those things that are willingly received at the ear; The Echo returnes the last syllables;
>
> (7. S16. 124, 387, 515–566; 1627) [15]

Finally, he adumbrates a boundary to the outward thrust, a boundary in this world determined externally and internally alike by good will:

> And in that sense, I may use the words of the Apostle, *As much as in me is, I am ready to preach the Gospel to them also that are at Rome:* at *Rome* in their hearts; at *Rome,* that is, of *Rome,* reconciled to *Rome.* I would preach to them, if they would have me, if they would hear me; and that were *opportune, in season.* But though we preach *importune, out of season* to their ends, and their purposes, yet we much preach, though they would not have it done: for we are debters to all, because all are our Neighbours. *Proximus tuus est antequam Christianus est:* A man is thy Neighbor, by his Humanity, not by his Divinity; by his Nature, not by his Religion: a Virginian is thy Neighbor, as well as a Londoner; and all men are in every good mans Diocess, and Parish.
>
> (4. S3. 761–773)

This issue of living vigorously outward from a center introduces the matter—difficult to characterize—adverted to by terms like *orientation* or *heading* or *bearing.* Intention is some combination of aptitude and orientation:

> *Ecce, Behold,* leave your blindnesse, look up, shake off your stupidity, look one way or another; A Christian must not goe on implicitely, inconsiderately, indifferently, he must look up, he must intend a calling. . . .
>
> (6. S6. 46–49; 1624)

Calling and intention may coalesce as lived expectation:

> . . . (for this world to the righteous is *Atrium templi,* and heaven is that Temple it selfe, the Militant Church, is the porch, the Triumphant, is the *Sanctum Sanctorum,* this Church and that Church are all under one roofe, Christ Jesus) . . .
>
> (5. S10. 421–424) [16]

The Donnean epitome of proper bearing and lived expectation may be illustrated even to definition by contrast, in the following from a Lincoln's Inn sermon of (probably) 1621.

> Carry *back* your comfort to the root, and *bring* that comfort *to* the fruit, and confesse, that God who is both, is "the God of all comfort." *Follow* God in the execution of this good purpose upon thee, *to* thy Vocation, and heare him, who hath left East, and West, and North, and South, in their dimnesse, and dumnesse, and deafnesse, and hath called thee *to* a participation of himselfe *in* his Church. *Go on* with him *to* thy justification, That when in the congregation one sits at thy right hand, and beleeves but historically (It may be as true which is said of Christ as of WILLIAM the Conquerour, and as of JULIUS CAESAR) and another at thy left hand, and beleeves Christ but civilly, (It was a Religion well invented, and keeps people well in order) and thou betweene them beleevest it *to* salvation *in* an *applying* faith; *proceed* a step farther, to feele this fire burning out, thy faith declared *in* works, thy justification growne *into* sanctification, And then thou wilt be *upon* the last staire of all, That great day of thy glorification will breake out even *in* this life, and either *in* the possessing of the good things of this world, thou shalt see the glory, and *in* possessing the comforts of this World, see the joy of Heaven, or else, (which is another of his *wayes*) *in* the want of all these, thou shalt have more comfort then others have. . . .
>
> (3. S12. 611–630; my italics)

Such a life-world, integrating all the *back to's* and *bring to's* of interiority and exteriority, of body and faculties, of history and commitment and cause—such a life-world contrasts with the flaccid historical belief "at thy right hand" and complacent civil belief "at the left" precisely as what St. Paul calls *a new creation* (2 Corinthians 5. 17–19).

The preacher's body and vestments may go near to filling the pulpit, but obviously the feature which fills the congregational space with the felt sense of his lived vocation is his voice, as suggested above by his remark on ear and heart's echo. Its presence summons to equivalent faithfulness-in-vocation on the part of his parish-congregation. He appears to them—so Donne believes—more in that than in spectacle:

> . . . for the most part, he that will speak, lies as open to me, as I to him . . . God hath made other creatures *Gregalia,* sociable . . . Man only can speak; silence makes it but a Herding: That that makes Conversation, is speech . . . To declare Gods goodness, that hath enabled us to speak, we are bound to speak: speech is the Glue, the Cyment, the soul of Conversation, and of Religion too.
>
> (8. S15. 99–112)

> the Organ of the Gospel is the Ear, for faith comes by hearing;[17] but then the Organ of faith it self, is the Hand too; A Hand that lays hold upon the Merits of Christ, for my self; and a Hand that delivers me over to the Church of God in a holy life, and exemplary actions, for the edification of others.
>
> (8. S15. 289–293; 1629)

This preacher's hands will figure in actions of dispensing Eucharistic bread and wine, of course, and in the actions of elocutionary delivery, but his voice will be the most pervasive evidence that he "intends a calling" which heads toward some divine fulfillment. His voice, we might say, is the medium and the unifying element in the life-world he constructs within the church walls, designed to help listeners maintain similar life-worlds or at least similar orientations outside the church walls, where he would have each man recognize God's good will for mankind as the only true boundaries. To this furnishing of life-worlds we turn now.

vi. Outward in Words

The preacher's voice pervades the auditory space of the church interior. His voice reaches from his interior to each auditor's, and his voice answers essentially in *words* the commission to serve the Lord and preach "the true and lively word." Donne remarks that a "whole Sermon is not the word of God. But yet all the Sermon is the Ordinance of God" (5. S1. 767–768). His voice furnishes the congregational life-world with words, participates and contributes to making biblical-ecclesiastical matters present, and furnishes in so doing some words whose referents suggest an imagistic world. Finally, his words come in syntactic units which might be different and which therefore have significance; their parade in syntax looks toward movement and action, which will thereupon claim our attention. But the fact of words, of Donne's many words, must concern us first.

Of course the cutting edges of the matter were apparent to Donne and his auditors:

> *Mens in sermonibus nostris habitat, & gubernat verba* [Ambrose]: The soul of a man is incorporate in his words; As he speaks, we think he thinks. . . .
>
> (8. S15. 220–221) [18]

> As fine words (truly) as you would desire,
> But (verily) but a bad edifer.
>
> ("doctrine men," commenting on a Donne sermon [19])

What are we to make of his language, these multitudinous words he incorporated himself in? Many of them have vivid concrete referents; accordingly a good deal can be said about his imagery, and his use of biblical material, and something of his use of patristic references. These last two categories shade from imagistic language's heavily *referential* import to the conspicuously *relational* import interpersonal communications may have. Ultimately these remarks will bear on that, inevitably so if Father Ong has it right in his assertion that "communication in human society, although it uses external media of all sorts, is basically a transaction between two or more unique and inviolable interiors." [20]

Donne's well-wrought sermons attempt to *unify* even more passionately than his major poems did, attempt to make "one little room" in some sense an everywhere. This aim calls for contributions from all kinds of *form* which would be irrelevant to such an anecdotal writer as John Aubrey gathering the "tumultuary" scrapbook of his *Brief Lives*. Some formal elements of Donne's language afford at least three kinds of insight into his mastery of the sermon. These formal elements inhere in the words somewhat apart from what they refer to and contribute to or sometimes even control the relational meanings attendant on Donne-the-familiar-preacher using those words to his congregation. We should in this regard notice his linguistic *elevation,* his *selectivity,* and his assumptions and practice with regard to *validity*.

The meaning of *linguistic elevation* comes partly from convention, partly from the user's stipulations. First, a word's elevation must be accounted part of its public meaning, not a coterie matter. The *general* public meaning of a word is the group of its significations, and its historically characteristic associations and suggestions which might be catalogued in a dictionary, but which in any case would be apprehended by contemporary readers or hearers with a maximum of agreement among themselves and with a minimum of aid from context. The public *local* meaning of the word would of course be that which it owes to context, as an extension or a restriction of its normal meaning, and which the reader could perceive *only* with the aid of context. Donne often takes imposing pains to establish a local meaning public at least to his congregation and readers.

Second, linguistic elevation appears to be expression which achieves exactitude of meaning—especially a high degree of exactitude—primarily through *choice* of words. Context, rather than choice, might make the phrase "black market research" mean either "research on illegal commodity transactions" or "research on black community market needs." Elevated diction tends to be painstaking, then, but only incidentaly is it fussy (as in the two glosses above). A given elevated word or phrase is likely to carry with it associations with one or another rigorously *authoritative* activity—law court or royal court or laboratory determination, liturgy or conference. Fussiness is a *fault* of diction, not a necessary feature of elevated diction. Precision and economy of effort might prescribe the word *schismatic,* say, over any equivalent word or phrase. Either fussiness or unachieved precision at any level will imply that the writer has not seen clearly at all, or at least has not placed first things first, or carried his message faithfully all the way to the addressee. Such consequences are moral issues, and hence not surprisingly matters of Donne's attention in sermons.

Of course we see many a writer rely on other resources than on word choice, as he tries to be understood in his single meanings and his ambiguities. He may exploit syntactic parallels or logical sequence, as Pope does in those famous couplets in "The Rape of the Lock"; or logical incongruity and dramatic disposition, as in Othello's "put up your bright swords, for the dew will rust them." He may list *things,* whose incongruity or range is most important, but whose names are less so, as when Pope says "Puffs, Powders, Patches, Bibles, Billet-doux," or Shakespeare's Antony says, "The hearts / That spaniel'd me at heels, to whom I gave / Their wishes, do discandy, melt their sweets / On blossoming Caesar: and this pine is bark'd. . . ." In these sermons, those resources, and dramatic disposition of voices, all require attention. But in Donne's and nearly anyone's case, the painstaking air and the momentous associations of elevated words work to suggest either that serious matters are afoot or that (as in Augustan mock-pieces) pretension is abroad.

Donne's manipulation of formality offers a ready entry to the rationale of his "fine words." The characteristic level of a given writer's diction can be gauged, or at least some aspects of it can be gauged, with greater succinctness than can most other elements of verbal style.

For convenience here, we can indicate relationships comparatively, using proportions based on the correlation between categories of etymological derivation and degree of elevation in diction. In practice, that category of words used since Old English times is the most colloquial group, as well as being overwhelmingly the largest; it is both a verbal instrument in its own right and a sort of matrix for the other groups. Words which passed colloquially from Vulgar Latin through Old French to English (and which often issued from market place to print shop markedly changed in pronunciation and spelling) form a second and only slightly less colloquial category.[21] Literary loan-words from Classical Latin into Old French form a third and more elevated category. And literary loan-words from Latin, Greek, and Hebrew form a small but stylistically vital fourth category.[22]

Even small samples give a momentarily useful numerical definition to what some readers have presumably sensed: OE—81.7 percent, Vulgar Latin through Old French—3.9 percent, Classical Latin through Old French—8.3 percent, literary loans—6.1 percent. For Andrewes, seemingly the other most illustrious English preacher of Donne's generation, the figures differ significantly: OE—89.6 percent, VL/OF—3.4 percent, CL/OF—5.2 percent, loans—2.3 percent.[23] The Authorized Version, the group translation of the Bible over which Andrewes presided and which by direction made heavy use of sixteenth-century translations, seems to show an even heavier preponderance of native English words, and so too the sermons of Hugh Latimer. Of course no such figures prove much; rather they offer a rough profile of probabilities and sharpen some further questions. How low, for example, is Donne's low? How high is his high? He employs words from the top three categories much more often than Andrewes does; what are we to make of this frequency?[24]

With Donne, the range is great, from an infrequent colloquial word like *tush* (2. S3. 188) and *roughcast* (2. S4. 379) and *laies about him* (9. S6. 152) to words like *concupiscence* (2. S3. 780, 781, 803) and *Chabad* (transliterated Hebrew, 2. S4. 371). The few such elevated words, *more* than half again as frequent as in Andrewes, color the whole realm of discourse.[25] Once one has heard the figure in the pulpit say *Banim* and *Elohim* (6. S4. 35, 462), or *latreia* and *Synedrion* (9. S6. 225, 279, 289), things are never quite the same. He exploits some such word or two or three in nearly every sermon. And the slangily colloquial word is rare. The rhetorical implication becomes clear. The practice comes to be a reassurance to the auditor, a reassurance stronger with each recondite word and substantial explanation, that the preacher has vast resources of vital knowledge and power of communication rigorously marshalled at hand, and therefore that *each* word he presents bears an unusual weight of philosophical commitment—it may well be the necessary and conclusive word. Thus, the practice of employing a wide range in diction, with unusual richness in the most elevated category, serves him well. It builds the auditor's and reader's confidence that the preacher speaks "the true and lively word" expertly. It remains beyond the scope of this study, but worth attention, to determine at what proportion assimilation of loan-words, giving loan-words as much utility-in-place as Old English matrix words, would start to sound like a catalogue.

Donne seems by no means unconscious of these considerations. One more-than-usually explicit statement, made after ten years of his preaching ministry, connects the elevated word additionally with that fear of the Lord which evidently he always deemed the beginning of wisdom:

> we should not make Religion too homely a thing, but come alwayes to all Acts, and Exercises of Religion, with reverence, with feare, and trembling, and make a difference, between Religious, and Civill Actions. In the frame and constitution of al Religions, these Materials, these Elements have ever entred; Some words of a remote signification, not vulgarly understood, some actions of a kinde of halfe-horror and amazement, some places of reservation and retirednesse, and appropriation to some sacred persons, and inaccessible to all others.
>
> (7. S12. 522–530, St. Paul's, 1627)

The matter of his linguistic elevation has led to observations of his resourcefulness and seriousness. This naturally leads to other features of his *selectivity,* especially his copiousness.

The standard we have been using would generally establish as elevated the more learned or specialized, and hence ideally more valid and reliable word. For Donne the elevated word is naturally to be found in the inspired word, from the Author of all being and meaning. The colloquial word in our sense may be the lower word in his sense because of its longer participation in man's fall from truth and loving concord. But there can be a kind of play back and forth between the hierarchies of human learning or technicality and of the ontological hierarchy, play admitting many variations from harmony to conflict.

> . . . call to minde Gods occasionall mercies to them; such mercies as a regenerate man will call mercies, though a naturall man would call them accidents, or occurrences, or contingencies. . . .
>
> (6. S8. 103–106)

Here not the most etymologically recondite term, but rather the most personal and relational is the most realistic.

For Donne, it would seem to be the personal language of Scriptures, or the Fathers, or the Prayer Book that a preacher's due care will oftenest bring him to. His own knowledge of Greek seems to have been very scanty, and even the best scholarship was unaware, until the early twentieth century, of how colloquial New Testament Greek was. But whether looking at the Greek of the New Testament or (with a much better trained eye) at the Hebrew of the Old, or Latin of the Vulgate, his eye often was on a metaphor or whole unit of meaning. So there is no contradiction when he asserts that "the Holy Ghost, in penning the Scriptures," was delighted "not with barbarous, or trivial, or market, or homely language." Rather the Holy Ghost showed delight with "not only . . . a propriety, but with a delicacy, and harmony, and melody of language; with height of Metaphors, and other figures, which may work greater impressions upon the Readers" (6. S1. 600–645). "Harmony," like the long sentences and the preoccupation with metaphor, seems to betoken Donne's passion for unifying. The recourse to "Fathers unanimly delivered" rather than "ragges and fragments . . . patcht together" (616–625) furthers that campaign. The preacher's engagement with the "eloquent and powerfull" language of the Bible and its "higher and livelier examples, of every one of those Figures and Tropes, which are collected out of secular Poets, and Orators" (639–645) will carry forward his own passionate concern with his subject at the same time that it urges involvement of his auditors. Donne contends that man should not "come to any kinde of handling of" the Scriptures "with an extemporall and irreverent, or overhomely and vulgar language" (8. S5. 621–25; similarly 5. S1. 312). It would seem no accident, then, that the sermons, for all their Old English-derived words, make scant use of that racy colloquiality which gives his poetry one part of its peculiar vigor.

For Donne, the substantively and morally most significant language was naturally that of "the Pen-men of the holy Ghost" (8. S5. 62), "that language in which God spoke, the Hebrew" (5. S1. 580–581; also 1. S9. 136–137). Occasionally St. Jerome's Latin can serve:

> . . . another feast, and another treasure are expressed, and *heightened* in two such words, as never any tongue of any Author, but the Holy Ghost himself spoke; *Inebriabit absinthio* [Lam. 3. 15], there's the feast, you shall be drunk with wormewood, you shall tast nothing but bitter affliction, and that shall make you reel, for you shall find no rest for your souls.
>
> (3. S1A. 450–455, English italics mine)

The "treasure" is presumably the "Life and Knowledge in every word of the Word of God" (8. S5. 56). The general tenor of the penitential message is "heightened" by a "Word" which is a vivid metaphor and which is imported from elsewhere in the Scriptures than the sermon's text. The height is maintained, it would seem, by the Latin translation, and hopefully by the preacher's temporal and logical development of the metaphor: "shall make you reel" because "you shall find no rest."

The whole procedure and the attention to the wholeness of the metaphor in particular attest the kinship with Augustinian notions of Christian teaching:

> The teacher will avoid all words that do not teach; and if he can instead find words which are valid and understandable, he will choose them; however if such do not occur to him (or exist at all), he will use words a little less valid, as long as the matter is taught and learned in its wholeness.
>
> (*On Christian Teaching* 4. 10) [26]

"Wholeness" (*integre;* and *integra* and *integris,* represented above by the two *valids*): it is virtually the pintle on which the whole

Donnean rationale of preaching turns, if construed to involve personal and relational integrity.

Of course substitutes must be found for the Hebrew, and for the Latin too (according to the English reformers), whatever may have been such language's intimacy with reality. There are several alternatives. In one place, four of them, given as successive glosses, constitute a paradigm of Donne's hierarchy of diction:

> And as the word imports, *Bechurotheica, in diebus Electionum Tuarum,* in the dayes of thy choice, whilst thou art able to make thy choyce, whilst the Grace of God shines so brightly upon thee, as that thou maist choose the way, and so powerfully upon thee, as that thou maist walke in that way.
>
> (2. S11. 25–29, and below, p. 194)

Here, the Hebrew word gives way: to a phrase in the Latin of the early Church, to a less resounding English translation of that, to a tentative, flat, prosaic echo, to the full metaphorical translation, with pilgrim "thou" acting by a combination of free will and grace.

So, as this among numberless examples suggests, metaphorical language has the greatest potentiality in the fallen world for equivalence to the reliability of unfallen language, whether in translation, imitation, or detached exposition—even, that is, when the original is not referred to. Some time later at Lincoln's Inn, Donne spoke in a compendious and expansively metaphorical manner again:

> doth not he that *pondereth the heart, understand it?* [Prov. 24. 12] where it is not in that faint word which the vulgar Edition hath expressed it in, *inspector cordium,* That God sees the heart; but the word is *Tochen,* which signifies every where to weigh, to number, to search, to examine; as the word is used by Salomon again, *The Lord weigheth the spirits* [Prov. 16. 2], and it must be a steady hand, and exact scales that shall weigh spirits.
>
> (2. S15. 238–244)

Notice that the term *vulgar* is used, when he might have said *Vulgate*[27] and thereby suggested somewhat greater institutionality and stability in the "Edition" he is criticizing. He shows regular awareness of both hierarchies of diction, the one he took to have been constructed by God, and the one constructed by man, and equal awareness of the energy that may derive from combining or counterpointing them. Flat, prosaic English, the "faint word," echoes the degenerate fallen world. Emotionally and intellectually energetic language, metaphorical or learned, strives toward regeneration:

> leaving that sense, as too narrow, and too shallow for the holy Ghost, in this place, in which he hath a higher reach,
>
> (3. S4. 115–116)
>
> When the Holy Ghost came upon Christ himselfe, after his Baptisme, there it is said, *He descended.* . . . But here [at Acts 10.44] the Holy Ghost is said to have fallen [on all who heard the word] which denotes a more earnest communicating of himselfe, a throwing, a pouring out of himselfe . . . as a fall of waters . . . as a Hawk upon a prey . . . as an Army into a Countrey . . . as that kinde of lightning, which melts swords, and hurts not scabbards. . . .
>
> (5. S1. 494–524)

The rare conspicuous colloquialism will help to present the fallen world in its gamy concreteness:

> . . . it is but going up another stair, and there's the *tother* Anabaptist. . . .
>
> (2. S3. 633; my italics)
>
> But these mysteries [of the Trinity] are not to be *chawed* by reason, but to be swallowed by faith.
>
> (5. S1. 462–463)

These examples, in context, reveal themselves as negatives: the unsociable company and vicious communion, which define by contrast divine positives: the company of the faithful and true Eucharist.

Language's divisions exhibit, for him, categories of being and action, and show moreover as marks of divine creativity; good composition becomes regeneration, a gradual restoration of the selfe as image of God.

> There is not a better Grammar to learne, then to learne how to blesse God, and therefore it may be no levity, to use some Grammar termes herein. God blesses man *Dativè,* He gives good to him; man blesses God *Optativè,* He wishes well to him; and he blesses him *Vocativè,* He speaks well of him, For, though towards God, as well as towards man, reall actions are called blessings . . . yet the word here, [*Eulogia*] is properly a blessing in speech, in discourse, in conference, in words, in praise, in thanks. . . .
>
> The Son of God is [*Logos*], *verbum, The word;* God made us

> with his word, and with our words we make God so farre, as that we make up the mysticall body of Christ Jesus with our prayers, with our whole liturgie, and we make the naturall body of Christ Jesus appliable to our soules, by the words of Consecration in the Sacrament, and our soules apprehensive, and capable of that body, by the word Preached.
>
> (3. S12. 98–139)

As metaphor draws together disparate elements and draws together the givens of nature and the evaluations of human willed activity, so language unites, as the characteristic passage above puts it, the private self concerned with a God partly within and the public self busy with the reintegration under God of the city disintegrated since that second Fall, of the Tower of Babel.

> A good hearer becomes a good Preacher, that is, able to edifie others. . . . it is not only the Preacher, that hath use of the tongue, for the edification of Gods people, but in all our discourses, and conferences with one another, we should preach his glory, his goodnesse, his power, that every man might speake one anothers language, and preach to one anothers conscience.
>
> (5. S1. 567–576)

On the other hand, absence of proper words is a kind of death in life and a sign of death by being out of society:

> *The dead doe not praise thee,* sayes *David;* The dead (men civilly dead, allegorically dead, dead and buryed in an uselesse silence, in a Cloyster, or College, may praise God, but not in words of edification, as it is required here, and they are but dead, and doe not praise God so. . . .
>
> (3. S12. 110–114)

There can hardly be a stronger emphasis on living outward than to say that one is languageless and indeed dead without hearers whose hearing will be integrated into social life.

Wrong words, in yet a different variation on the theme, are dangerous. In one place he rejects a translation of the Septuagint (at Psalm 144. 15) as "not the best, because it is not according to the letter" (3. S3. 43). Moreover, even if we did not know that Donne preached a series of sermons rectifying biblical passages "detorted" by the Roman Catholic Church,[28] we might well expect that the distorted or invalid word is for him another symbol of death in life, of degeneration entailing damnation. It is, in fact, a recurring image:

> for, those respects to them [the martyrs], the first Christian founders of Churches did admit in those pure times . . . not sacrifices to the dead, as they are made now in the Romane Church: when *Bellarmine* will needs falsifie *Chrysostome,* to read *Adoramus monumenta,* in stead of *Adornamus;* and to make that which was but an *Adorning,* an *Adoring* of the Tombes of the Martyrs.
>
> (2. S10. 237–245) [29]

Patristic Latin, or alleged patristic Latin, retains its linguistic elevation and is thus the more impressive in being damnable. To detort a saint is more shocking than to detort a lumber list.

Rectification and application, two of his usual lines of effort, become by contrast a performance more impressive and reassuring:

> . . . though it be a most absurd, and illiterate, and ungrammatical construction of the place that they [certain "Expositors"] make, yet there is a doctrine to be raised from thence, of good use. As God brought light out of darknesse, and raises glory out of sin, so we may raise good Divinity out of their ill Grammar;
>
> (3. S6. 371–375) [30]

Man salvaging is yet another pattern of man constructing the City of God among men.

In sum, we should avoid market words when we can take more authoritative words. Whatever we may need of wise passiveness in contemplative moments, as preachers in the pulpit or Christians in society, we need words; their absence implies estrangement from reality. Mistaken words betoken wrongdoing. These Donnean convictions and the practices in keeping with them have brought us to more basic issues of linguistic choice and to *validity.*

Donne flourished during a rather special time in the history of rhetoric, a time somewhat like our own. Services in reformed churches including the Anglican were to be conducted in a "language understanded of the people" yet—as we have heard Donne urge and practice—not without occasional touches of specialization.[31] And, more generally, a very uneasy balance of power obtained between proponents in that generation of the conviction that language is a part of creation, a component of reality glorious in itself, and proponents of the notion that language serves only as a beggarly handmaiden to some more fundamental reality. Hamlet's scorn of Osric's language, Gertrude's impatience with the little matter and much art of Polonius, Carew's praise of Donne for purging the muses' garden of pedantic weeds, and the muttering "doctrine men" quoted early in this section are only familiar instances of the movement against over elaboration, prosaic sing-song, decayed Spenserism, and the like. On the other hand, the campaign that eventually drove "eloquence" from the pulpit, drove polemic from "scientific" writing, and drove rhetoric and poetic into such supposedly harmless enclaves as Swiftian allegory and the heroic couplet—none of those battles had been lost by language in Donne's generation. The special way he responded to the prevailing ambivalence toward language and toward the unsteady relationships of words and referents harmonizes with his general behavior in his sermons and likewise his whole relationship with his congregation.

What are the ties that bind a word and its referent? If words are iconic, are parts of that to which they refer, then any word other than God's word, any name other than one given by Adam to a creature "according to its nature," is absurd, a kind of crazy nothingness. At the other extreme, is it *adequate* to say: "Words, as every one now knows, 'mean' nothing by themselves, although the belief that they did. . . was once equally universal."[32] Such a thesis makes good enough sense within a sufficiently careful delineation of what "by themselves" means (a care duly taken by Ogden and Richards). But an adequately careful notion of "by themselves" threatens to abstract words so utterly from lived experience as to become a useless fancy. If it does not do that, then such a thesis becomes in one of its implications a faith-assertion that God is either totally transcendent (indeed, a meaningless abstraction) or else has no special status in a universe of totally arbitrary words—a kind of multiple Manichaeanism fractionating divinity into the myriad pagan gods of place.

In the passage above from 3: S12, of 1621, Donne's procedure when using "some grammar terms herein" displays indeed "no levity" but a good deal of caution—postmedieval caution, one could say, noting his shyness of treating language as if it were iconic.[33] But of course this, too, shows Donne's profound kinship with his favorite Church Father. Augustine had written in his pamphlet *On Christian Doctrine* that readers "are undoubtedly to be preferred who remember the words less well, but who look into the heart of the Scriptures with the eye of their own hearts" (Bk. 4, para. 7) and "the life of the speaker has greater weight in determining whether he is obediently heard than any grandness of eloquence" (Bk. 4, para. 59).[34]

Later in the passage using grammar terms as metaphors for devotional action, Donne suggests a characteristically inclusive middle way and with his characteristic theocentric relativism. He says, "God made us with his word, and with our words we make God so farre, as that we make up the mysticall body of Christ Jesus . . . with our whole liturgie" (including prayers, sacraments, and preaching). God's Logos presents reality with absolute validity and reliability. Man's words are not the Logos. But they can be existentially adequate; they can be *oriented* toward the Logos and can help *orient* men in community toward the Logos. Earlier in his preaching career he had been even more explicit (in a passage quoted above for its generic implications):

> It is but little, that man is, proportioned to the *working* of God; but yet man is that creature who onely of all other creatures can *answer* the inspiration of God, when his grace comes, and exhibit acceptable service *to* him, and cooperate *with* him.
>
> (1. S7. 125–129; 1618; my italics)

In later years Donne would not "proportion" man directly to God even so ambiguously as here, but would proportion attribute to attribute (like sinfulness to mercy) or speak of quantity in contrast to infinity. But his early insistence on validity achievable through right orientation and on the public currency of language valid in that way—to that insistence he remained constant. And this middle stand on language, this stand of humble claims for its reliability and efficacy in the fallen world, but high claims for its status in community and its ultimate ends, guard this middle way against two extremes. At the outer extreme, a word or phrase has totally independent negotiability, as in irresponsible arguments from atomistic proof-texts or recent "novels" with unbound pages to be shuffled like cards. Extreme innerness retreats from language of shared meaning to private language to wordless "inner light" and depersonalizing isolation or depersonalizing noise or touch.

Within the middle way of Donne's era, Andrewes evidently committed himself more heavily than Donne to the iconic view of language. He occasionally treated the after-Eden verbal objectification of something as having a certain validity independent of its users' orientation toward God, as if it partook in large ways of its referent's nature. He might insist on groups of words as intrinsically *structural* figures of the entities or actions to which they refer. In the passage used earlier for statistics, Andrewes speaks of the speed the Magi made: "It was but *Vidimus, Venimus* with them;" the speed is not only the referential speed of the twelve-day journey, but St. Matthew's pace in getting the narrative from *saw* to *are come,* in seven Latin words: *"'vidimus enim stellam Ejus in Oriente, et Venimus adorare Eum.'"* Andrewes adds, *"Ecce Venerunt;* their coming hath an *Ecce* on it: it well deserves it;" he means not only the circumstances of the journey, but the collocation of the two words in Matthew's representation, as printed. Subsequently Andrewes comments, "We love to make no very great haste. To other things, perhaps; not to *Adorare,* the Place of the worship of God." The *Place* is, besides place on the ground, and event in auditor's life, and stage in Andrewes' line of argument, the location in the text of the word *Adorare.* All this implies that the Gospel text is iconic, is reality in several important ways. Though he might agree with Donne in prescriptions for Christian faith and works, his language on this point is less existential than Donne's. Donne seems most usually to treat even New Testament language as something which becomes real in the believer's cognition and action. In one passage, he remarks parenthetically that Adam named things according to their natures, but when Donne speaks of the *Sabbath* being named according to its nature, rest, he alludes to the nature of the day's proper observance, not to the word. The failure of iconicity, the breakdown in dependable relationships between words and their referents, goes with the fall of man and remains a feature of the Christ-killing world (1. S9. 359–364). Accordingly he attended to putting words and things and self in regenerate order, as long as he is "here, not in the School, but in the Pulpit; not in Disputation, but in Application:"

> the manifold promises of God . . . in his Word; and they cannot read, they cannot apply them, to them. There is Scripture, but not translated, not transferr'd to them: there is Gospel, but not preached to them; there are Epistles, but not superscribed to them.
>
> (1. S4. 429–430, 353–357) [35]

Donne may now and then suggest that the richness of meaning in a Scriptural word or passage cannot be justly represented by any single word or phrase in a more accessible language. But his sermons presuppose that the meaning can be born anew in English through metaphor and other resources. In another sermon, he speaks of confessing to prodigality:

> . . . there is, in that confession of mine, a Sermon, and a rebuke, and a reprehension to him, if he be guilty of the same sin; Nay, if he be guilty of a sin contrary to mine, For, as in that language in which God spoke, the Hebrew, the same roote will take in words of a contrary signification, (as the word of *Jobs* wife signifies blessing and cursing too) so the covetous man that heares me confesse my prodigality, should argue to himselfe. . . .
>
> (5. S1. 578–584)

And he goes on to postulate for the covetous man an argument to the effect that if an excess of generosity be a sin, an excess of non-generosity must be the more so. Again, language demands to be taken as action: a confession of excess is an action in a movement of dialogue wherein auditors must "take" and respond, "answer" with "service." And the relationships possible in "the language in which God spake" can be reformulated in some resource or situation of the English sermon. The reality is not so much *in* a bipolar Hebrew root or Scriptural text as it is *in* an analogy framed by preacher and lived in dialogue.

Even where the starting point is the word as a seen or heard thing, the attention is directed toward its significance in a pattern of human action and reaction:

> *Amen dico, verily I say unto thee* . . . so this *Amen* signifies *Fiat* . . . And this seale, this Amen, as Amen is *Fiat,* is always set to his *vae,* as his *vae* is *vox minantis;* whensoever God threatens any Judgement, he meanes to execute that Judgement as far as he threatens it. . . .
>
> (3. S6. 280–286)

Again, of the last part of Psalm 144: 15 ("Yea, blessed are the people, whose God is the Lord."):

> This blessedness then, you see is placed last in the text; not that it cannot be had till our end, till the next life. . . . But it is placed last, because it is the waightiest, and the uttermost degree of blessedness, which can be had, *To have the Lord for our God.* Consider the making up of a naturall man, and you shall see that hee is a convenient Type of a spirituall man too.
>
> (3. S2. 441–449)

He insists here that rhetorical climax exceeds the importance of structural parallel to referents or the importance of mere temporal progression. Such human rhetorical convention can accord not only with a spiritual end but with free individual evaluation ("convenient") and with mutuality ("our end, [I have seen and] you shall see"). The man in the social process of becoming regenerate can most likely make undeceived selection.

Words are in an obvious typographic or auditory sense things, but in ways more dynamic for Donne than markers in a row or weights in a balance or instances of degree. The quotation below is unusual for Donne only in its explicitness, as it identifies a dynamic substantiality of words akin to that of food or fresh water or seeds:

> It is the glory of Gods Word, not that it is come, but that it shall remain forever: It is the glory of a Christian, not that he hath heard, but that he desires to heare still. Are the Angels weary of looking upon that face of God, which they looked upon yesterday? And is not that *Alleluiah,* that song which is their morning and evening sacrifice, and which shall be their song, world without end, called still *A new song?* Be not you weary of hearing those things which you have heard from others before: Do not say, if I had knowne this, I would not have come, for I have heard all this before; since thou never thoughtest of it since that former hearing, till thou heardst it again now, thou didst not know that thou hadst heard it before . . . He that hath heard, and beleeved, may lose his knowledge, and his faith too, if he will heare no more. They say there is a way of castration, in cutting off the eares: There are certain veines behinde the eares, which, if they be cut, disable a man from generation. The Eares are the Aqueducts of the water of life; and if we cut off those, that is, intermit our ordinary course of hearing, this is a castration of the soul, the soul becomes an Eunuch, and we grow to a rust, to a mosse, to a barrennesse, without fruit, without propagation.
>
> (5. S1. 728–750)

Verbal knowledge must be *present* to the understanding to be real; knowledge and faith depend on constancy of exterior or interior rebroadcast to the consciousness, as he suggests by some terms different from those above, but even more kinetic though almost casual:

> . . . which we had occasion to say of the Joyes of heaven, in our Exercise upon the precedent Psalme, when we sayled thorough that Hemispheare of Heaven, by the breath of the Holy Ghost,

> in handling those words, *Under the shadow of thy wings I will rejoyce.*
>
> (7: S9: 613–616)

Words' referents, Scriptural words' referents, which are a region of heaven, accessible to that priest and congregation whose *exercises* are for those moments the *handling* of those words [36]—these conditions, like the need for constant hearing, seem to say that for men the ultimate mode of words' being is experiential, situational, dynamic.

Accordingly, later in the same sermon, the distinction between spoken and printed sermon has certain hierarchical features:

> And then, if I have done any good to any of Gods servants, (or to any that hath not been Gods servant, for Gods sake) If I have but fed a hungry man, If I have but clothed a naked childe, If I have but comforted a sad soule, or instructed an ignorant soule, If I have but preached a Sermon, and then printed that Sermon, that is, first preached it, and then lived according to it, (for the subsequent life is the best printing, and the most usefull and profitable publishing of a Sermon). . . .
>
> (7. S9. 659–664)

In a kind of mutual definition, the acted deed and printed word are taken to be normally the more conclusive because more consequential externalization (utterance) of the self. Or is that mainly so of the preacherly self?—a generic question for extended separate treatment. The acted deed of feeding or clothing seems to enjoy a freedom from the contingency attending the most fervent action of preaching or writing: the contingency that the words may not be so fervently heard or read. One remark in a letter even appears to concede the more precarious status to written words. He modestly acknowledged to the Countess of Montgomery "what dead carkasses things written are, in respect of things spoken" and intimated delicately as he sent a manuscript to her that it would have to be the "Spirit of God" which would make "a writing and a speaking equall means to edification" (2, p. 179).

In any case, different words can serve well enough for persisting things, with old words for recent models of old things—in context of preacher relating to hearers in terms of a Christ who is constant:

> And upon this Pelagian righteousness, it thought Nature sufficient without Grace; or upon this righteousness of the Cathari,

> the Puritans in the Primitive Church, that thought the Grace which they had received sufficient, and that upon that stock they were safe, and become impeccable, and therefore left out of the Lords Prayer, that Petition, *Dimitte nobis,* Forgive us our trespasses; upon this Pelagian righteousness, and this Puritan righteousness, Christ does not work.
>
> (7. S5. 680–687)

He similarly identifies old and new Sadducees, old and new Pharisees (9. S6), Catharists and Cathari, "Purifying Puritanes, and . . . purified Puritanes" (7. S13. 322–323).

Accordingly, too, a radical change in the life-world changes all meanings and even the relations of word to thing. The following sample from a phenomenological description (if one may put it so) of that situation illustrates Donne taking a stand beyond the rationalism sometimes attractive to Jerome, closer to the Augustine who pondered interfused cities of God and man:

> Now these two phrases, *Argui in furore,* and *Corripi in ira,* which we translate, *To rebuke in Anger,* and *to chasten in hot displeasure,* are by some thought, to signifie one and the same thing, that *David* intends the same thing, and though in divers words, yet words of one and the same signification. But with reverence to those men, (for some of them are men to whom much reverence is due) they doe not well agree with one another, nor very constantly with themselves. Saint *Jerome* sayes, *Furor et ira maxime unum sunt,* That this *anger,* and *hot displeasure,* are meerly, absolutely, intirely, one and the same thing, and yet he sayes, that this Anger is executed in this world, and this hot Displeasure reserved for the world to come. And this makes a great difference; no waight of Gods whole hand here, can be so heavy, as any finger of his in hell; the highest exaltation of Gods anger in this world, can have no proportion to the least spark of that in hell; . . .
>
> (5. S16. 491–504)

Finally, the existentiality of Donne's usage can give a nonreductive place even to the clothes metaphor, that recurring bugaboo of modern criticism:

> Saint *Paul,* in that former place, apparels a Subjects prayer well, when hee sayes, *Let prayers bee given with thanks;*
>
> (4. S9. 618–620)

Here we have words not as the clothes of (more essential) things, but rather words of personalizing engagement as a kind of thing complementing another kind of word/thing which otherwise would be guilty of savage nudity.

But an English expression may look different ways more directly than the preacher's word about prodigality, and with a minimum of existential contingency. Consider a word series like *desecration, consecration, obsecration,* where "the same root will take in words of a contrary signification." Or the signification may be ironically similar:[37]

> . . . they may be reduced, they may be seduced. . . .
>
> (3. S7. 241–242)

Referentially similar roots, by the agency of consonant English affixes, may suggest a process continuing:

> . . . this flesh, that is, I in the *re-union,* and *redintegration* of both parts, shall see God; . . .
>
> (3. S3. 789–790; my italics)

The process may be a kind of witty glossarial expansion:

> . . . a *de*facing, a casting of *d*urt in the *face* of Gods image. . . .
>
> (3. S7. 463–464; my italics)

He sometimes runs to a mélange of roots and referents and sounds:

> And this, (*spiritus Principalis*) as many Translators call a Principall, a Princely, a Royall spirit, as a liberall, a free, a bountifull spirit; If it be Liberall, it is Royall. . . . The very forme of the Office of a King, is Liberality, that is Providence, and Protection, and Possession, and Peace, and Justice shed upon all.
>
> (8. S10. 223–234)
>
> But this *Comfort,* a power to erect and settle a tottering, a dejected soule, an overthrowne, a bruised, a broken, a troden, a ground, a battered, an evaporated, an annihilated spirit, this is an act of such might, as requires the assurance, the presence of God.
>
> (3. S12. 536–539)

We notice that in this last example all the unobtrusively metaphorical, vestigially predicative modifiers accord not only with the general idea, a soul in need of comfort, but with the predication, "to erect and settle."

I have tried to pick examples which are interesting and brief but not atypically so. Certainly iteration or alliteration or assonance or like-endings appear on nearly every page of the sermons in one or more instances resembling an example in the foregoing two paragraphs. Clearly, too, many such instances carry on a lead of sixteenth-century prose, at hand to his congregations in Prayer Book doublets like "erred and strayed . . . devices and desires . . . declare and pronounce . . . pardoneth and absolveth . . ." The Renaissance rhetorical virtue of copiousness, one can murmur, watching him going beyond doublets to triplets or quadruplets or expanding into thematic reemphasis and variation including phrases. But mere copiousness might have come easier by spinning out antecedents and consequents and testimonies, or the like. Furthermore he risks—not *always* unscathed—the pedantry of sounding like Holofernes: "ripe as the pomewater, who now hangeth like a jewel in the ear of coelo, the sky, the welkin, the heaven; and anon falleth like a crab on the face of terra, the soil, the land, the earth" (*Loves Labours Lost,* IV, ii).

But historically Donne's listeners and readers have not seemed disposed to cry pedantry or regard a Donnean quadruplet as we do one by Holofernes or Armado. For one thing, the latter two worthies obviously belabor the obvious. A detachment of Donne's words, when they point at the same thing or a covey of closely related things, habitually sight both an important matter and one with some element of puzzlement or even mystery about it (like "a dejected soule"). Often the matter will be not a thing but a process, or a relationship, or an abstraction. Certainly *emphasis* is part of the effect in some way. Not infrequently a series may yield to description by some visual-spatial metaphor, like "overlapping" (as of successive transparent overlays on a city map). But a musical metaphor seems to me equally definitive: one word of a set will *resonate* more for one listener, another for another.

Ultimately then, his copious reiterations suggest both the multifarious appearances and names for truth in this world of flux and the multeity of men. For another thing, the movement from Old English-derived words to those derived from French or Latin or Greek emphasizes the speaker's power of choice, and how that power extends only as far as the speaker's knowledge. Moreover, since community under Donne's God depends greatly on language and greatly on choice, his tactic of choosing thesaurus-like clusters swells that theme.

A detachment of right names for identical or closely similar things can by a ready metamorphosis be set up as right and wrong names for a thing or as kindred misapprehensions. The congregation had been alerted to such ironies not only by contemporary literature, no doubt, but by occasional Prayer Book lections: "Not everyone who saith 'Lord! Lord!'" or "If the foot shall say 'Because I am not the hand, I am not of the body' is it therefore not of the body?" Once in a while Donne will make the point about misnaming by a quick flick as much of diction as of argument led by logic and referential meaning:

> Hee sees a *judgement,* and cals it an *accident.*
>
> (2. S3. 700)

The sound similarities of *declination* and *diminution* suggest a spread, a range of kindred errors in a sloth which would think of itself as tolerance.

> To be unsensible of any declination, of any diminution of the glory of God, or his true worship and religion, is an irreligious stupidity; but to bee so ombragious, so startling, so apprehensive, so suspicious, as to think every thing that is done, is done to that end; this is a seditious jealousy. . . .
>
> (3. S7. 448–453)

The four words, each with intensifying *so* prefixed, suggest a numerous progeny of that pride which would be thought zeal and the similar sound of *suspicious* and *seditious* confirms the likeness of direction.

Although it might well reward separate treatment, one other matter emerges so colorfully from just the quotations on these few pages that it demands some acknowledgment. This matter is at once formal, referential, and relational. I mean the intimations of play and game. Is there not about his partial paradigms of evaluation and his duplications and variations a taste of exuberance, of delighted *play?* My earlier remarks about choice and Donne's observably vigorous exercise of choice within the "rules" of lexical possibility and the array of topics presented by his chosen text all suggest aspects of *game* playing. Any such notion would only add to the sourness of "doctrine men," whose wish for edification is a request for *goods delivered* rather than some reorienting action of the *self.*[38] But clearly insofar as the Donnean sermon is a game it is a partnership game played in utmost seriousness (though not, of course, unwavering solemnity) with his congregation. Like a game it has large freedoms but is constituted by its rules, though these are humanly, historically assembled and freely sworn to. Like a good game it models at some aesthetic remove many kinds of human issue and conflict. Like a good game, the Donnean sermon compasses lively contingencies of damage and defeat, but those, too, under control as destruction and fatality are not, out there beyond the limits of game or walls of church. This declarer will not see a judgment and call it an accident, nor this team suffer from suspicion or sedition. At least not during the sermon, not during these "exercises" as he sometimes calls them.[39]

Truth may take many guises in fallen nature, depending on how fallen man veers from divine reality into life-worlds wherein one kind of distortion is inadequacy or invalidity or unreliability of language. But fallen man cannot abrogate divine reality, in Donne's conviction, nor even ignore it. He must seek it with unremitting care. The emotional atmosphere, insofar as one can generalize about such exceedingly diverse data, appears to be one of qualified assurance. Truth is not for Donne in the 1620s as it was in the 1590s atop "a huge hill, cragg'd and steep;" by the grace of God it may be found in the market place, perceived behind its stained or inadequate verbal masks, known and appreciated.[40] And the discovery comes not to the solitary pilgrim toiling his way up the mountain but to companions in the presence and dialogue of community:

> To that which is vulgarly said, *Loquere ut te videam;* speak that I may see thee; I do not see thee, not see what is in thee, except I heare thee preach: Let me add more, *Age ut te audiam,* do something that I may hear thee! I do not hear thee, not hear thee to believe thee, except I hear of thee in a good testimony of thy conversation.
>
> (4. S3. 818–823)

vii. Journeying—Metaphor, Subject, Action

The Donne who matured in a society wherein the biblical journey to the New Jerusalem (or Canaan or hill of the Lord) had been retransmitted by Augustine, Chaucer, lesser Fathers, doctors, and storytellers without number, the Donne who traveled on missions to Cadiz, the Azores, the Low Countries, and France, and presented himself "riding westward" on Goodfriday 1613, the Donne concerned with living from a fragmentary self outward through society to unity and certainty in God—committed himself wholeheartedly to journeying as fact and central symbol of human life. Earlier we glanced at some aspects of that as a general, generic fact. With some shift of emphasis and scope we may now appraise how the metaphor helps tremendously to furnish the life-world of the preacher, and by implication his hearers, and how it virtually makes the usual movement of the sermon from part to part.

Locally, the metaphor may develop simply as quotation, echo, and expansion of a biblical phrase like Leviticus 26.24, "If you walk contrary unto me, I will walk contrary unto you" (see 7. S14. 493–511). It can begin to take account of man-as-worker: "embrace a Calling and walk therein" (7. S5. 300). In short, he makes it render with experiential concreteness the essential Christian calling and way of life and end of man:

> Dost thou know every faire house in thy way, as thou *travellest,* whose that is; and dost thou not know, in whose house thou *standest* now?
> Beloved, to know God by name, and to *come to* him by name, is to consider his particular blessings to thee;
> (5. S16. 185–189; my italics)

Concurrently, a bit like Milton in *Paradise Lost,* he can take serious account of sin, evil, distraction, and destruction without collapsing into the Manichaean heresy that evil is a counterforce commensurate with God or evaporating into the Scholastic dictum that sin is nothingness:

> Sin is a fall; It is not onely a deviation, a turning out of the way, upon the right, or the left hand, but it is a sinking, a falling: In the other case, of going out of the way, a man may stand upon the way, and inquire and then proceed in the way, if he be right, or to the way, if he be wrong; But when he is fallen, and lies still, he proceeds no farther, inquires no farther.
> (6. S2. 248–253)

The foregoing few fragments stand for scores like them. As earlier remarked, the journey affords a consistent and inclusive (therefore unifying) allegory, a plausible matrix for typology, and familiarly concrete yet general terms for existential uniqueness, existential freedom, and the polar pair: existential limitation and divine transcendence.

At St. Paul's on Christmas 1622, he preached on Colossians 1. 19–20: "For it pleased the Father, that in him should all fulnesse dwell; and, having made peace through the bloud of his crosse, by him, to reconcile all things to himselfe, by him, whether they be things in earth, or things in heaven." He began: "The whole journey of a Christian is in these words; and therefore we were better set out early, then ride too fast" (4. S11. 1–2). The reconciliation or irreconciliation of all things to God Himself occupies much of the preacher's attention. It is the rationale for his referential and metaphoric language, and some of the best criticism of Donne in print has elucidated for us features of his imagistic language.[41] Notice, though, that explicitly in the citation at hand and implicitly throughout the sermons the reconciliation of things to Christ and persons to Christ takes place in a context of journeying.

Once he has established this basic metaphor (and any half-dozen of his sermons do that) many ordinary words—words often used lifelessly—can take life from the metaphor and give sustaining life to it. Words such as:

advance	go	run
ascend	got up	return
borderers	journey	sail
bring	let you in	step
carry	meet	strayed
comes	navigate	towards
contiguous	pace	transgress
course	path	transported
descend	perverted	tread
farther	proceed	turn
feet	progress	voyage
find	pursue	walk
		way

Hundreds upon hundreds of such words, interspersed with scores of explicit restatements of the metaphor, tend to make each sermon a stretch of the road in an on-going journey.

That journey proceeds through no desert place. Rather, the preacher's versions of himself and his auditors are jostled by an existential city continually presenting alternative selves and choices of direction and corporate challengers (the Papist or "Jesuited lady" or "tother Anabaptist") and individual Fathers or controversialists (historical or hypothetical) enunciating perennial compass readings, along a trail demarcated by the chosen text. Which is not to say either that the sermon form cannot acknowledge or that Donne cannot recognize that the crowd may be lonely:

> . . . woe unto that single soul that is not maried to Christ . . . but is yet either in the wildernesse of Idolatry amongst the Gentiles, or in the Labyrinth of Superstition amongst the Papists. . . .
>
> (3. S11. 380–385)

As he travels, the perspective of worldly things will constantly change and constantly he must turn or not, pause or accelerate; the journey metaphor preeminently insists on freedom, as much as it insists on dependence (to laws of nature, for instance, like gravity). With all that, it accords with good health, in any psychological or ethical sense we might care about, although the metaphor does not by itself prejudge the issue of health. It connects inner self and intentionality and exterior occasions and persons, connects auditory and kinesthetic experience with visual experience, spatial relationship, and the kind of analytic exposition instanced by map-making. The Christian journey-metaphor, in short, is antischizoid and at ease with the Incarnation in that.

Donne's handling of the journey metaphor tends to assimilate to his Incarnationalism the Anglican notion of a *via media*. Thereby he attests to a "way" which is existentially vigorous and in some sense inclusive.[42] The figure accommodates the secular world:

> Beloved, Christ puts no man out of his way, (for sinfull courses are no wayes, but continuall deviations) to goe to heaven. Christ makes heaven all things to all men, that he might gaine all:
>
> (2. S14. 655–657)

It can serve to organize interpretation of the Bible and liturgical practice:

> . . . betweene them, who make this place, a distinct, and a literall, and a concluding argument, to prove the Trinity, and them who cry out against it, that it hath no relation to the Trinity, our Church hath gone a middle, and a moderate way, when by appointing this Scripture for this day, when we cele-

> brate the Trinity, it declares that to us, who have been baptized, and catechised in the name and faith of the Trinity, it is a refreshing, it is a cherishing, it is an awakening of that former knowledge which we had of the Trinity, to heare that our onely God thus manifested himselfe to *Abraham* in three Persons.
> (3. S5. 345–354)

By such locutions he not only espoused a church trying to make its way between a painted church and a naked church (6. S14. 150–162), but touched hands, as in well-nigh uncountable instances, with a prominent series of Prayer Book formulations. In the service of Morning Prayer, the worshipper would himself say, "We have followed too much the devices and desires of our own hearts" and "lead us not into temptation, but deliver us from evil." The priest would pronounce the absolution with the phrase "turn from his wickedness" or (in the Communion service) "turn unto him." Later he would probably pray that the king "may always incline to thy will and walk in thy way" and that "all who . . . call themselves Christians may be led into the way of truth." In a Communion service, he would in the prayer of thanks after dispensing the bread and wine, ask that "we may . . . do all such good works as thou hast prepared for us to walk in."

Somewhat as the journey metaphor in sermon and liturgy tends to connect sermon with the multiple *actions* of Prayer Book worship, so he uses it for the better apprehension of history in a medium of coherent personal *actions*.

> Since God hath brought us into a fair prospect, let us have no *retrospect* back; In Canaan, let us not look towards Aegypt, nor towards *Sodom* being got to the Mountain; since God hath settled us in a true Church, let us have no kind of byas, and declination towards a false . . . .
> (3. S4. 668–671)

Canaan and the *mountain* are stages of the universal journey, just as *byas* and *declination* are degrees of defection from the Anglican middle way. Or, instead of alternative headings on a single typological road, an urban situation may figure as a veritable streetgrid by a typologically witty conflation:

> We need not put on spectacles to search Maps for this Land of the *Gergesens;* God knows we dwell in it . . . a Propheticall complaint by St. Augustine: we love the profession of Christ

> only so far, as that profession conduces to our temporall ends. We seek him not at the Crosse; there most of his friends left him; but we are content to embrace him, where the Kings of the East bring him presents of Gold, and Myrrh, and Frankincense, that we may participate of those: we seek him not in the hundred and thirtieth Psalme, where, though there be plenty, yet it is but . . . *plentifull redemption,* plenty of that that comes not yet; but in the twenty fourth Psalm we are glad to meet him, where he proclaims . . . *The earth is the Lords, and the fulnesse thereof,* that our portion therein may be plenteous: We care not for him in St. *Peters* Hospital, where he excuses himselfe. *Silver and gold have I none;* but in the Prophet *Haggais* Exchequer we doe, where he makes that claime . . . *All the gold and all the silver is mine.*
>
> (10. S2. 61–88, slightly repunctuated)

Typology as journey does three things. It fights typology's ordinary conceptual battle against the scary notion of temporal materiality as meaningless flux. There are meaningful sequences in it. Second, it obviates the numbing view that time has remorseless order, thrusting a past event ever farther away or isolating all events atomistically; history is vital; journeys—moral ones, at least—can be retraced. Events variously distant in mere chronology can have equally intimate presence, and decisive present relevance, the condition of experienced relationship.

Moreover, Prayer Book phrases and waystations in moral-typological geography like those above both draw from and give to the enormous vitality of medieval and later journey literature. Though Guillaume de Deguileville's *Pèlerinage de la vie humaine* no longer attracts the attention it received from the fourteenth through the seventeenth centuries,[43] the soul-building or soul-educating journey appears to continue as one of the liveliest myths in Western literature and thought. The thematic concerns and resolutions listed above would have further immediacy and apprehensibility for Donne's congregations because the journey metaphor was pervasive in literature, discourse, and thought.

But if Donne thumbed a well-strummed string with his journey metaphor, we should not suppose other ecclesiastics, any more than others writers, could make it sing as well. Edwin Sandys (1516?–1588), archbishop of York, tends toward flat exhortation or flat exposition, with facts and assertions ranged like fenceposts in the same middle distance of tone and generality. His subject in a paragraph on "Way" does not hoist him above his usual self, but he exhibits some openness to the metaphor's possibilities, though his mind is rhetorically less sophisticated than Donne's and accordingly more common, and his biblical citations by their variety and vigor contrast with his prose. He was preaching on Psalm 86.11: "Teach me thy way, O Lord, and I will walk in thy truth: O knit my heart unto thee, that I may fear thy Name":

> 9. The word WAY by a translation or metaphore in the Scripture hath sundrie significations. Sometime it is taken for doctrine, as *thou teachest the WAY of God truely/* Matthew 22 /; sometimes for religion, as when Saint *Paul* saith *I persecuted this WAY* / Acts 24 /; and again *According to this WAY which they call heresie, I worship the God of my Fathers;* sometimes it is taken for the course and order of a man's life, as in the words of the Prophet *Esay, The Lord taught me that I should not walk in the WAY of these people* / Esay 8 /; sometimes for the counsels and purposes of men, so *Elihu* meant it, saying, *His eyes are upon the WAYS of man, and he seeth all his goings;* The way which the Prophet heere would learne of God is true religion, the doctrine of his holy will in his word revealed, but chiefly the doctrine of the true Messias promised, the way of trueth it selfe, hee onely being the Way, the trueth, and the life, having given us an example that we should follow his steps who did no sinne. Now as God hath his way, so man hath his. *MY Wayes are not your wayes.* The wayes of Christ, and Antichrist, of the Church of God, and the Synagogue of Satan, of religion, and superstition, these are contrary to teach other. Christ saith of himselfe, *I am the way.* In the knowledge of this way Saint *Paul* gloryeth, *I esteemed to know nothing, but Christ Jesus, and him crucified;* and in the knowledge of this Way, the prophet desireth to be taught of God, *Teach me thy way, O Lord.*[44]

Yet Donne differentiates between human wayfaring and the aims, ends, and prescriptions of God or Christ or the biblical "secretary to the Holy Ghost" even when like Sandys he utilized a biblical metaphor of God's way or opposed ways:

> . . . for that which is less then these, he is as severe; *We command ye, Brethren, in the Name of the Lord Jesus Christ, that*

> *you withdraw your selves from every brother that walketh disorderly* / 2 Thessalonians 3.6 and 14 /. Where, *Calvin* thinks, (and I think aright, and many others must think so too; for a Jesuit / Cornelius à Lapide / thinks so, as well as *Calvin*) that the *Apostle* by the word *disorderly,* does not mean persons that live in any course of notorious sin; but by *disorderly,* he means *Ignavos, Inutiles,* idle and unprofitable persons; persons of no use to the Church, or to the State: that whereas this is *Ordo Divinus,* the order that God hath established in this world, that every man should embrace a Calling, and walk therein; they who do not so, pervert Gods order: and they are S. *Pauls disorderly persons.*
>
> (7. S5. 291–302)

Here again Donne delineates a middle way for himself and the listeners of his church between "notorious sin" and lethargy. One will get from here to the hereafter somehow. The choice to be made is between an *Ordo divinus* construed as if it were a ridge-line path and courses of sin or idleness construed as if they were thickets or miasmas on left or right. The dialectical activity is of interpretation and noting some recent agreements in interpretation. But the biblical text wherein St. Paul promulgated God's meaning, partly in terms of travellers' ways, that text remains a reference point essentially more firm and constant than the North Star.

Nor is this a fluke, his putting a journey's sequentiality at one with man's accumulation of knowledge or one man's accumulation of years, as one comes to successively broader views in climbing a mountain:

> We have a full cleernesse of the state of the soule after this life, not onely above those of the old Law, but above those of the Primitive Christian Church, which in some hundreds of yeares, *came not* to a cleare understanding in that point,whether the soule were immortall by nature, or but by preservation, whether the soule could not die, or onely should not die. Or (because that perchance may be without any *constant* cleernesse *yet*) that was not cleere to them (which concerns our case case *neerer*) whether the soule *came to* a present fruition of the sight of God after death or no. But God having afforded us cleernesse in that . . . .
>
> (5. S19. 186–195; my italics)

He is arguing for a right understanding of Psalm 6.5, "For in death there is no remembrance of thee," and again the biblical text stands as a fixed point of reference, while the history of interpretation unwinds as a sequential course of using or abusing growing knowledge. He has adjusted metaphors since writing to Sir Thomas Lucy (seemingly in 1607) of opinions "which . . . no Christian Church a this day, having received better light, will allow of" (*Letters,* p. 13).

But of course human journeys are in some senses reversible. Hence the figure can take account of man not only oriented from question or need to answer or fulfillment, but backwards:

> The best step, the best height in this world, is but the way to a better; and still we have way before us to walk further in . . . thou mayest contract a pride . . . and uncharitably despise those who labour yet under their ignorance or superstitions; or thou mayest grow weary of the Manna, and smell after *Egyptian* Onions again.
>
> (4. S4. 156–175)

Where Eliot tends to figure reality in terms of turning wheel of the worldly and still point of eternity intersecting with time in the Incarnation,[45] Donne proceeds quite differently. For Eliot's Becket, say, and in philosophical terms the still point, the Incarnation,[46] has unique importance, but the figure of a *point* implies a kind of statistical insignificance—roughly, very roughly, like comparing the datum of *one* citizen of Nazareth with the number of all citizens in history, or the years of Jesus's life with the years of geologic time. I wish not to underrate Eliot's devout irony in so doing, but to define by contrast Donne's invariable procedure in the sermons (and to some extent the *Essays* and *Devotions*).

viii. Markers and Reference Points

The shared and private existential worlds of journeying are *complemented*—in Donne's view of himself and his congregation—by a system of fixed references present in the Book of Scripture, the Book of Creatures, and to a lesser extent natural law as applied in the structure of civil law. Men travel through a biblical text or through the city or their lives—or through Church Fathers and biblical commentarists with gun and camera, it sometimes seems—with change to themselves and all their perspectives. But ethical locations may be surveyed and mapped with reference to the absolute cartography of biblical Egypt, Canaan, Sodom, and the like. Similarly, the biblical case-book of divine dealings with men remains at once absolute precedent and most royal prerogative. The relevance to life of fire, earth, air, and water remains constant, if ambiguous. Hierarchy remains a constant feature of universal order, like the structure of human law, even when flawed. Some of these data may have something less than absolute fixity about them, or even an element of the arbitrary, but like the North Star, bell-buoys, survey-markers, or mountain peaks they are quite reliable for the navigator.

The biblical text, then, serves as an inviolable matrix to the worldliness and timeliness of the sermon and the Scriptures, a kind of bureau of standards, continually referred to throughout the sermons. Mrs. Simpson estimated ten times as many citations from the Bible as from Augustine, the most-quoted Father (10. p. 295).[47] In the streets and houses of the intermingled fallen and regenerate cities, though, the true Bible may be as hard to recognize as the true church amid the merely visible ones.

The most reliable Father can mislead, obliging the careful preacher, behaving like any careful believer, to "pursue" a different path:

> S. Augustine, (who truly had either never true copy of the Bible, or else cited sometimes, as the words were in his memory, and not as they were in the Text) he reads not these words so, *supergressae super caput,* but thus, *sustulerunt caput* . . . S. *Augustines* is an useful mistaking, but it is a mistaking. But to pursue the right word, and the true meaning of this metaphoricall expressing, *supergressae caput.* . . . If they be above our heads, they are so, in many dangerous acceptations.
>
> (2. S3. 543–571)

The most reliable method may require enterprising adjustment. The literal sense of a Scriptural passage is always to be observed, but whereas the literal sense of Genesis resides in the *letter,* in Revelation as "in many places of Scripture," it is figurative (6. S2. 1–57). Similarly, a natural human tendency and a marked habit of Donne's, the push toward inclusiveness-in-unity, may require disciplined direction. In discussing the "light" of John 1.8, he insists that the literal coherence of the passage, "the *necessary sense*," requires understanding light to include Christ and the working of His Spirit in faith and grace; possible but lesser and so less necessary senses, such as light to mean "naurall reason" he rejects (3. S17. 141–193). Such explicit acts characterize his general practice. Neither Antiochene nor Alexandrian in any exclusive sense, he attempted to go a middle way assimilating into coherent pulpit discourse what was life-giving in both traditions of exegesis.[48] The principle of coherence appears to be a broader one than Augustine's (concurrence *"ad regnem caritatis"*): concurrence with a sense of God's historic dealing with men as a process challenging and often mysterious but generous, even to Redemption.

Again and again he will drive between "things which are made" and questions of significance and choice to insist on lining up with the company of faithful along an axis of view from origin-to-thing-to-eternal-God.

> *David* is a better *Poet* then *Virgil;* and with *David, Coeli enarrant, the heavens declare the glory of God;* the power of oratory, in the force of perswasion, the strength of conclusions, in the pressing of *Philosophy,* the harmony of *Poetry,* in the sweetnesse of composition, never met in any man, so fully as in the Prophet *Esay,* nor in the Prophet *Esay* more, then where he says, *Levate Oculos, Life up your eyes, on high, and behold who hath created these things;* behold them, *therefore,* to know that they are created, and to know who is their creator.
>
> (4. S6. 140–148)
>
> Employ then this noblest sense upon the noblest object, see God; see God in every thing, and then thou needst not take off thine eye from Beauty, from Riches, from Honour, from any thing.
>
> (8. S9. 69–72)

In short, his sense of Incarnation and Redemption tends to animate references to abiding features of life—dust, mountain, fire, day, cloud, sea—with the dynamism implicit by definition in immanent deity.[49]

A lesser but useful fixity and conclusivenes may be an attribute of legal analogy, legal metaphor, often even of individual legal words.

> *A verbo ad legem;* from a word suddenly and slightly spoken, to words digested and consolidated into a Law.
>
> (1. S2. 177–178)

But naturally the possibilities are ambiguous. On the one hand, Donne may note that God

> shewed man *his face* in the *Law,* and saw *Mans face* in the transgression of the law. . . .
>
> (2. S2. 701–702)

On the other hand, he develops a muted suggestion by St. Paul (1 Cor. 15. 50) into a long, legal discussion of the kingdom of Heaven as an inheritance. The passage (3. S4. 494 ff.) should be consulted in full, but it may suffice to note here that definition in legal terms of a clear title to the inheritance has the effect of being an absolute definition. "All" the nonvalid alternatives are considered and rejected: *purchase, gift, Covenant, Curtesie, Supererogation.* As this takes place, fraud in the legal sense becomes apparent as another face of fallen man and fallen collective man when fraud is conducted through institutional structures.

Whatever may have been the decorum of alluding to law in the presence of lawyers while he was at Lincoln's Inn, or whatever may have been Donne's temperamental affinity for the law, it seems to me apparent that he does use law terms and relationships throughout his preaching career in the general way described here. They are part of the fixed and constant world complementary to the journey, and they sometimes mark the difference between the two.[50] Death and resurrection are "Common Law, and no Prerogative" (3. S3. 594).

Some years later, he asserted that

> Of all Commentaries upon the Scriptures, *Good Examples* are the best and the livelyest; and of all Examples those that are nearest, and most present, and most familiar unto us; and our most familiar Examples, are those of our owne families. . . .
>
> (8. S3. 1–5; 1627)

The fact of persons being familial is a constant, like (though not altogether like) the Universal Transverse Mercator Grid System. The nature of anyone's family relationships can vary endlessly, like (and unlike) his relation to a particular set of grid coordinates. In the pulpit he relates himself to both, the constant given fact of being familial and the shifting options in what to make of that. Or the constant given fact of being placed among other works of God, and the countless options in what to make of that. The congregation may before the beginning of the sermon have sung Psalm 95, with its affirmations that "in his hand are all the corners of the earth; and the strength of the hills is his also. The sea is his and he made it; and his hands prepared the dry land." They might on occasion even have sung the optional canticle, "Benedicite, omnia opera Domini," with thirty parallel injunctions for works of the Lord to praise Him, works like "Showers and Dew . . . Lightnings and Clouds . . . Green Things . . . Whales . . . Children of Men."

ix. Growing Self and Society

With these observations on Donne's treatment of law, of need to praise creation, and of relation to familial status, we have reached the ground in which the volitional dynamics of journeying and fixed data meet and interact: lived relationship among persons. "Children of Men" constitute this third part of his referential world. So frequent are the Church Fathers and typical persons he cites and postulates and personates, their voices equal in existential weight (perhaps in statistical weight, too) his references to journey and transition on the one hand and to stability and permanence on the other. Even when he speaks of corners of the earth or works therein, he tends to speak in terms of persons apprehending and personal fulfillments as Divine immanence:

> And in these walles, to them that love *Profit* and *Gaine,* manifest thou thy selfe as a *Treasure,* and fill them so; To them that love *Pleasure,* manifest thy selfe, as *Marrow* and *Fatnesse,* and fill them so; And to them that love *Preferment,* manifest thy selfe, as a *Kingdome,* and fill them so; that so thou mayest bee all unto all; give thy selfe wholly to us all, and make us all wholly thine.
>
> (4. S15. p. 363)

"And fill them so;" he proposes that God be found in the world and its furniture. Sensory appearance and ultimate meaning need not be antagonistic, any more than the present need be a tyranny thrusting the biblical world irretrievably farther away in a relentless chain of historical events. But in either case good coherence requires both will and grace.

Donne's rationale in filling his sermons with voices may be further characterized by a kind of triangulation. Wallace Notestein has succinctly observed about that generation's Puritan preachers: "These men did not discuss the abuses of the time, enclosures, patents of monopoly, and corrupt administration. They stuck close to the Bible and what it taught; they were concerned with election and grace, and with man's duty. About heaven and hell they had less to say than might be expected."[51] In somewhat ironic contrast, John King, the bishop of London who had ordained Donne, preached on 26 March 1620 at Paul's Cross "on behalf of Paules Church," more or less on Psalm 102. 13–14, an extensive text which includes the phrase "For thy servants take pleasure in [Zion's] stones." King James, rarely present either in the cathedral or at Paul's Cross, was there; and the bishop praised his monarch according to Renaissance norms, which is to say more effusively than was Donne's practice. Bishop King also praised and described London as the gem of the ring, eye of the land, apple of the eye, favored in comparison with contemporary Prague or Rome, and so on. A contrast begins to emerge here, a third direction which seems to me impressive in Donne. Enclosures and patents of monopoly are no longer urgent alarms to us, but material abuses and bad faith afflict us daily. Donne anatomized not the destructive instruments but the destructive personal relationships, such as squeezing another man economically or giving false witness. Even so he attended vastly less to hellish failures or abuses of relationship than to heavenly community. He was as concrete as Bishop King, but his orientation was away from impersonal travelogue toward a mode of personalized generality that might be called perennial lived experience.

He drove between a historical, particular political event and Aristotelian causes to insist in a sermon on "the Powder Treason" that personal responsibility must not be obscured by erring opinions in the market place:

> In these divers opinions which are ventilated in the Schoole, *how God concurreth to the working of second and subordinate*

> *causes,* that opinion is I think, the most antient, that denies that God *workes in* the second cause, but hath onely *communicated* to it, a power of working, rests himselfe. This is not true; God does work in every Organ, and in every particular action; but yet though He doe work in all, yet hee is no cause of the obliquity, of the perversenesse of any action.
>
> (4. S9. 579–586)

But he will equally insist that a disfurnishing of one's life-world, a disaffiliation even from erring brethren, cannot be effected by recusancy or some "fugitive and cloistered virtue."

> God hath made all things in a *Roundnesse, . . . this earth . . .* the round convexity of those heavens . . .and then a Circle hath no *Angles;* there are no *Corners* in a Circle. Corner Divinity, clandestine Divinity are incompatible termes; If it be Divinity, it is avowable.
>
> (7. S16. 131–137)

But what of the many defaced images of God, those otherwise-oriented eyes, those less-than-absolute voices that crowd the panorama and swell the antiphony in the sermons? Sometimes he moves among them like a man in the central civic square, trying all things and holding fast to that which is good, in the cause of some new City of Grace:

> Fathers (truly I think more generally more unanimely then in any other place of Scripture) take that place of *Ezekiel* which we spake of before, to be primarily intended of the last resurection, and but secundarily of the Jews restitution. But *Gasper Sanctius* a learned Jesuit, (that is not so rare, but an ingenuous Jesuit too) though he be bound by the Councel of Trent, to interpret Scriptures according to the Fathers, yet here he acknowledges the whole truth, that Gods purpose was to prove, by that which they did know, which was the generall resurrection, that which they knew not, the temporall restitution. *Tertullian* is vehement at first, but after, more supple . . . and then the truth satisfies him, for it doth signifie both.
>
> (4. S1. 573–589)

Meanwhile the Anglican word in the metropolitan Jacobean life-world may be assailed, like Eliot's Word in the desert, by voices scolding, mocking, or merely chattering. The preacher may notice a contentious faction:

> It is no wonder to see them who put all the world, into differences, (the Jesuits) to differ sometimes amongst themselves.
> (3. S7. 187–188)

His wry stroke warns his listeners away from stirring up strife and momentarily reduces the redoubtable Jesuits to absurdity.

Similarly he may sort out the true identity of manners, mores, and arguments in the city to reveal that "they" are reducing traditional significations:

> There is a snare laid for thy wife; Her Religion, they say, doth not hinder her husbands preferment, why should she refuse to apply her self to them? We have used to speak proverbially of a Curtain Sermon, as of a shrewd thing; But a Curtain Mass, a Curtain *Requiem,* a snare in thy bed; a snake in thy bosome is somewhat worse.
> (4. S4. 234–239)

Here "they" have reduced conversion to domestic comedy, if not boudoir farce. But taking an element of ultimate reality with insufficient seriousness can be dangerous. If the self is not fulfilled in relationship to the true and good Other, then the self fractures amid semi-communions and sesqui-communions (3. S17. 822–823), or semi-gods and sesqui-gods (8. S5. 490–500).

> For, Gods eye sees, in what seat there sits, or in what corner there stands some one man that wavers in matters of Doctrine, and enclines to hearken after a Seducer, a Jesuit, or a Semi-Jesuit, a practising Papist, or a Sesqui-Jesuit, a Jesuited Lady;
> (7. S13. 119–122)

The rhetorical figure in those last three instances we recognize readily as *reductio ad absurdum*. But Donne has pushed it toward personal life and toward concreteness, so it comes out as fractionation into frivolity. That the other instances of satiric diction or manipulation in the two paragraphs above and throughout the sermons accord with these three should not surprise us. He attacks ways of life he regards as divisive or denigrative or cacophonous. His passion was for exaltation and unity in a divine harmony, a "Quire of Saints." The power and resourcefulness of that passion suggests both his genius and his limitation. After all, convenience and even graciousness may sometimes prescribe taking one day or one thing at a time.

But while being mastered by the preacher's wit, the dividers and reducers and distorters of meaning contribute to larger movements of definition and affirmation. Donne's analytic procedure of identifying main courses and byways available for every man may bring the listener to turn on himself whatever self-righteous hostility he initially felt in connection with a scare-word like *Rome* or *Jesuit.* He does not excommunicate nor anathematize persons or groups in his sermons, not even "Atheisticall enemies" or "Papisticall . . . Schismaticall . . . [or] sacrilegious enemies" (3. S12. 32–43) though he regularly speaks of persons excluding themselves from man or God. Insofar as his rhetorical management of, say, Jesuits leaves them alive and serving purposes of definition *ad majorem dei gloriam* or *ad regnem caritatis,* that management represents a way to love them. He assumes as well as the Augustine of the *Enchiridion* that not to love another person for God's sake is necessarily to love him for one's own (Chaps. 20, 30, 31).

Still, most in Donne's congregations would have resisted considering themselves Jesuits even by analogy. He ordinarily takes a nearer way: *you,* or *I,* attending to events, or acting eventfully, will thereby furnish a life-world. That life-world has an exteriority and interiority always as close as the convex and concave of the same curve, has a boundary which is a barrier but a permeable one, like a hedge. Its furnishings are human attitudes and responses no less than flora and lights. The significances of *things* in alternative life-worlds can be variant or even antithetical, depending on the arrangement of or attitudes toward those same things. Years before, in a moving letter to his friend Rowland Woodward, he comments ruefully that his muse

> . . . to too many hath showne
> How love-song weeds, and Satyrique thornes are growne
> Where seeds of better Arts, were early sown.

But, he avers in the soberly hopeful second half of the poem,

> . . . wee, If wee into our selves will turne,
> Blowing our sparkes of vertue, may outburne
> The straw, which doth about our hearts sojourne. . . .
> Wee are but farmers of our selves. . . .[52]

By the time his preaching career was underway at Lincoln's Inn, there could be no doubt of his familiarity with meditative arts, with polemical and homiletic arts, with political and personal vicissitude, and with the systole and diastole of retirement and emergence. At Lincoln's Inn he presents the self as oriented outward as much as inward, even when developing the same metaphors he had used to explicate inner life in the Woodward letter. Any man may be a farmer of himself, for instance, with regard to his anger, which is a thornbush

> . . . not utterly to be rooted out of our *ground,* and cast away, but *transplanted;* A gardiner does wel to grub up thornes in his garden; there they would hinder good herbes from growing; but he does well to plant those thorns in his hedges, there they keep bad neighbors from entring.
>
> (2. S2. 179–183; probably 1618)

The sparks and flames of virtue glow with augmented variety in a sermon of (probably) 1622, on Romans 12. 20, "Therefore if thine enemy hunger feed him, if he thirst give him drink; for, in so doing thou shalt heap coals of fire on his head."

> The Holy Ghost hath taken so large a Metaphor, as implyes more then that. It implyes the divers offices, and effects of fire; all this; That if he have any gold, any pure metall in him, this fire of this kindnesse will purge out the drosse, and there is a friend made. If he be nothing but straw and stubble, combustible still, still ready to take fire against thee, this fire which Gods breath shall blow, will consume him, and burn him out, and there is an enemy marred: If he have any tendernesse any way, this fire will mollifie him towards thee. . . . If he be waxe, he melts with this fire; and if he be clay, he hardens with it, and then thou wilt arme thy selfe against that pellet. . . . yet this fire gives thee light to see him clearely, and to run away from him, and to assure thee, that he, whom so many benefits cannot reconcile, is irreconcileable.
>
> (3. S18. 378–403)

The exposition of the *range* and *contingencies* of presence distinguish this, I think, above most other Renaissance poets and preachers who could well enough spin out multiple "applications" or implications of a metaphor. Concrete acts of charity here materialize from the fire-flakes of "God's breath," the *hagia pneuma,* the Holy

Ghost, which is by definition an epitome of intimacy; we are reminded of a warm foundry and the space of friendship, stubble field and the barren openness of enmity, the active and passive closeness of human interaction, the peculiarly specialized presence and space of developing single combat, the ambiguously vast yet close space of partly lit flight.[53]

When his wit, which shows something of his freedom, develops several implications in a Scriptural metaphor, he is aligning in this way his own freedom with his listeners' freedom to restructure or refurnish their lives, since their freedom requires awareness of different choices and consequences of choice. Much of a sermon on Psalm 38.4 he devotes to how "mine iniquities" may be "gone over my head" in five several ways (2. S3).

So then, the multiplicity of voices and attitudinal "positions" which Donne acknowledged in society could be articulated by allowing the body of faithful an identity partly by contrast with self-professed outsiders; the antiphonies within the fold could be marked off by the buzzing cacophony of outside voices. Similarly, the harmonious multiplicity of things and implications in Scripturally grounded truths (as above) parades beside opposites and irreconcilable meanings when his attention turns to fallen wills.

One has to say something like *wills,* because although one soon notices that Donne's sinners become less and less free (like Milton's fallen angels), still they are too free and too dynamic for their doings to count simply as error, simply as lapses in understanding. In any case, he habitually presents graceful and dis-graced ways of life tending toward polar opposition. This appears in matters of perception, for instance:

> The habituall, and manifold sinner, sees nothing aright . . . He hears nothing aright; He hears the Ordinance of *Preaching* for salvation in the next world, and he cals it an invention of the State, for subjection in this world.
>
> (2. S3. 699–703)

A sinner's perception may go a kind of rake's progress from suspicion to more or less neurotic exaggeration to what might be either synaesthesia or delusion:

> Hee shall suspect his Religion, suspect his Repentance, suspect the Comforts of the Minister, suspect the efficacy of the Sacrament, suspect the mercy of God himselfe. Every fit of an Ague

> is an Earth-quake that swallows him, every fainting of the knee, is a step to Hell; every lying down at night is a funerall; and every quaking is a rising to judgment; every bell that distinguishes times, is a passing-bell, and every passing-bell, his own; every singing in the ear, is an Angels Trumpet; at every dimnesse of the candle, he heares that voice, *Fool, this night they will fetch away thy soul;*
>
> (2. S2. 456–465)

Of course he takes frequent care to present the antithetical divergence of graced and disgraced ways of life controlling perception, in the whole range of life from deepest interiority to most transcendent relationship, and from the most immediate instant to time under the aspect of eternity.

> Thou seest a needy person, and thou turnest away thine eye; but it is the Prince of Darknesse that casts this mist upon thee; thou stoppest thy nose at his sores, but they are thine owne incompassionate bowels that stinke within thee; Thou tellest him, he troubles thee, and thinkest thou hast chidden him into a silence; but he whispers still to God, and he shall trouble thee worse at last, when he shall tell thee, in the mouth of Christ Jesus, *I was hungry and ye fed me not:*
>
> (3. S5. 121–128)

Here, an occasion of sight has been used for blindness, occasioning a confusion of what is truly *his* and *thine,* in turn a silence and adversive communion, in turn a brief *now* incompatible with a *then* which may entail eternity.

Similarly, in his imagery of family relationship, which he liked for its concreteness, personal immediacy, and universality, Donne can present wifehood in a variety of antithetical ways. It can be the relation of bodily "sensuality" to the soul (3. S2. 150) or antithetically the resurrected body to the soul (3. S3. 789), or, opposed again and shifted toward action in society, the sin of early life and that of later life as first and second wives (5. S1. 220).

A prominent point of his attention, again and again, has to do with sin in society as destructive activity which makes living space hectic and deathly:

> . . . a disease that carries another disease in it, a fever exalted to a frenzy; It is . . . a spauning sin, a sin of multiplication, to sinne purposely, to lead another into tentation.
>
> (3. S7. 34–36)

Or living space metamorphoses with a kind of collapse:

> Have we not seen often, that the bed-chambers of Kings have back-doors into prisons. . . .
>
> (3. S12. 190–191)

Or, in another variation on developments in a bad ambience, a kind of unliveable attenuation:

> . . . rooted in some *one* beloved sin, but derived into infinite branches of tentation.
>
> (2. S1. 487 ff.).

One of the sermons' very rare personal anecdotes has Donne lodging "at *Aix,* at *Aquisgrane*" in a household of mutually hostile Anabaptists:

> And I began to think, how many roofs, how many floores of separation, were made between God and my prayers in that house. And such is this multiplicity of sins, which we consider to be got over us, as a roof, as an arch, many arches, many roofs: for, though these habituall sins, be so of kin, as that they grow from one another, and yet for all this kindred excommunicate one another, (for covetousnesse will not be in the same roome with prodigality) yet it is but going up another stair, and there's the tother *Anabaptist;* it is but living a few years, and then the prodigall becomes covetous.
>
> (2. S3. 656–664)

And he comments: "As S. *John* is said to have quitted that *Bath,* into which *Cerinthus* the Heretique came, so did I this house."

But alternatively, Donnean imagery can insist that the continuous choices and changes of journeying may metamorphose into a constant life of divine order.

> There is but one; But this one God is such a tree, as hath divers boughs to shadow and refresh thee, divers branches to shed fruit upon thee, divers armes to spread out, and reach, and imbrace thee. And here he visits thee as a *Father:* From all eternity a *Father of Christ Jesus,* and now thy Father in him, in that which thou needest most, *A Father of mercy,* when thou wast in misery; and a *God of Comfort,* when thou foundest no comfort in this world. . . .
>
> (3. S12. 78–85)

The movement reverses the Ovidian, Dantean, Spenserian metamorphoses *into* a tree. This kind of event, noted by the preacher, depends on the assumption that:

> this, where we are now, is the suburb of the great City, the porch of the triumphant Church, and the Grange, or Country house of the same Landlord, belonging to his heavenly Palace, in the heavenly Jerusalem.
>
> (3. S13. 524–527)

And the travelling believer in such a country will not only be reminded of the glorious tree-Father that he may encounter in life (as in that sermon) with an almost dream-like unexpectedness, but will be reminded of more volitional programs for doing and being. In a sermon exhorting the Society of Lincoln's Inn to build their new chapel, he comments

> except thou build a house for the Lord, in vaine dost thou goe about any other buildings, or any other businesse in this world. I speake not meerly literally of building *Materiall Chappells* . . . but I speake principally of building such a Church, as every man may build in himselfe. . . .
>
> (2. S10. 341–346)

Some years later he put the matter again in expanded terms of being and doing, from the roots of the self's interior life to the branches of social relationship:

> The pure in heart are blessed already, not onely comparatively, that they are in a better way of Blessednesse, then others are, but actually in a present possession of it: for this world and the next world, are not, to the pure in heart, two houses, but two roomes, a Gallery to passe thorough, and a Lodging to rest in, in the same House, which are both under one roofe, Christ Jesus; The Militant and the Triumphant, are not two Churches, but this the Porch, and that the Chancell of the same Church, which are under the Head, Christ Jesus; so the Joy, and the sense of Salvation, which the pure in heart have here, is not a joy severed from the Joy of Heaven, but a Joy that begins in us here, and continues, and accompanies us thither, and there flowes on, and dilates it selfe to an infinite expansion, (so, as if you should touch one corne of powder in a traine, and that

> traine, should carry fire into a whole City, from the beginning it was one and the same fire) . . . .
>
> (7. S13. 560–573)

"To an infinite expansion"—a paradox, of course, like Milton's "distance inexpressible by numbers that have name," but Donnean in looking to a heaven of largeness even as it is traditional in that it portrays heaven paradoxically. Donnean, too, in reminding us of the fallen world of wars and rumors of wars even as he celebrates the traditional Christian notion of love as freedom. Most essentially Donnean, probably, in the extraordinary juggling of the world's multeity with a constant conviction of the imperially unifying power of blessedness.

x. Action

Donne's pulpit is a worthy pavilion, but cannot, anymore than Shakespeare's Globe, hold the vasty fields of Egypt. Nor can he cram within this wooden **O** the very casques that did affright the air at Jericho. We have taken some account of him furnishing by words and referents the world of his listeners' attention and concern. We know that the world is both for better and for worse coextensive with church-space only at occasional moments. We see that he cites Church Fathers, biblical persons, and sometimes latter-day controversialists, and so recognizes and deals with them in the pulpit. But our contention that the sermon is dramatic need not rely on exaggerated claims that such rhetorical dealings are equivalent to bouts of friendly drinking or hostile swordplay in the theatre, even though he asserts "Rhetorique will make absent and *remote* things *present* to your understanding" (4. S2. 900–901, my italics). Rather, the sermons do present noteworthy action, apparent for our examination if we go back to the fundamental situation of preacher facing congregation in the context of Prayer-Book worship, which is a context of dialogue. Talking to anyone is an action. Talking—trying to talk—at once to each of several persons in a group differs considerably from the action of swinging a broadsword, but nevertheless takes place as action. We have already begun to qualify and refine that too-inclusive definition toward useful distinctions. He acts by talking in words conspicuously careful, we say, careful for the precision often concurrent with elevation, careful for the variety of auditors which may be accessible through copious equivalencies, careful for words as things with phonic kinships and equivalencies, and problematical relationships to saving Truth in this fallen world.

All his words are actions and reactions toward his chosen text, but they are even more vigorously directed toward his congregation. In their course, he shifts his own ways of being-toward-the-world and being-toward-his-hearers, thereby nudging them to some shifts of ground and changes of heart. Andrewes by his tactics says "Scriptural texts are puzzles, but I am an explainer." Donne says "This text challenges us, as I will show you, and we will respond, perhaps not well but as entirely as we can."

This, too, represents something of a middle way, and a forward station on it. Increasingly vital universities and the work in England of the Dominicans (from 1221) and the Franciscans (from 1224) had given currency to Latin handbooks on the arts of preaching and to norms of preaching that drew shape and substance and vigor from schematization, formal argument, citation of authorities, employment of concordant scriptural passages, and a wide range of exempla. By the generation of Andrewes and Donne, a new round of reform was afoot: against inevitable relapses into pious platitude or general rumination on general topics (as in the *Book of Homilies*), excessive dependence on "neoteric" authorities,[54] or on exempla, or the like. But the Puritan tendency to turn worship into "a purely *mental* activity," or the Ramist schematization proposed by a rhetorician like Bartholomew Keckermann could threaten to turn the sermon into a lecture.[55]

But we are "not upon a Lecture, but upon a Serman" (2. S15. 352), Donne always insists, making a distinction he cares more about than Andrewes does. Not that he will avoid logical argument in forms deductive or demonstrative:

> Thus far then we are directed by this Text, (which is as far, as we can goe in this life) To prove to our selves, that we have *faith,* we must prove, that wee need not the *law;* To prove that *emancipation,* and *liberty,* we must prove, that we are the *sonnes of God;* To prove that ingraffing, and that *adoption,* we must prove that we have put on *Christ Jesus;* and to prove

> the apparelling of our selves, our proofe is, that *we are baptized* into him.
>
> (5. S7. 62–68)

But that sermon does not conclude with a Q.E.D. at that point; rather, it explores the nature of baptized life through more than five hundred lines following.

Or, in a mode slightly different from demonstration, a declarative sentence may with a touch of urgency remind the hearer of self-development by education, including education by a sermon:

> . . . so must a Christian also *labour to grow* and *to encrease,* by speaking . . . asking . . . and farther informing his understanding, and enlightening his faith. . . .
>
> (2. S10. 703 ff., my italics)

"We grow and change by learning more about ourselves, and particularly in learning about the relation of ourselves to what lies beyond ourselves." So he seems to say, and such a learning process might be called dramatic, yet closely analogous terms about such "labour to grow" could be construed to include a lecture on the biophysics of cosmic rays, which Donne would probably not account personal or crucial enough to be dramatic. The whole sermons which conclude this book present sermonic drama in the sense of personal debate, development, inconstancy even, as suggested by the following description:

> This very scruple was the voyce and question of God in [Peter]: to come to a doubt, and to a debatement in any religious duty, is the voyce of God in our conscience: And *facile solutionem accipit, quae prius dubitavit,* sayes S. Chrysost. As no man resolves of any thing wisely, firmely, safely, of which he never doubted, never debated, so neither doth God withdraw a resolution from any man, that doubts with an humble purpose to settle his own faith, and not with a wrangling purpose to shake another mans. God rectifies *Peters* doubt immediately, and he rectifies it fully; he presents him a Book, and a Commentary, the Text, and the Exposition: He lets downe a sheet from heaven with all kinde of beasts and fowles, and tels him, that *Nothing is uncleane* . . . [a] visible Parable.
>
> (5. S1. 104–118)

Typically, as here, he will doubt in concert with someone, St. Chrysostom or another, whose voice will be part of the situation, since his Latin will be briefly echoed. Similarly, he will often suggest that here and now his own or his listener's doubt may not be rectified so immediately as in the biblical life-world, for all his efforts to provide commentary, exposition, and parable. Yet as we may also come to see more clearly in following chapters, the distance from here to biblical situation remains primarily existential and thus subject to renewal of closeness, rather than unyieldingly temporal or geographical or anthropological.

> . . . let us be ashamed and confounded, if *Job,* a person that lived not within the light of the covenant, saw the resurrection more clearly, and professed it [Job 19. 26] more constantly than we doe.
>
> (3. S3. 360–363)
>
> And when we have paced, and passed through all these steps, we shall in some measure have solemnized this day of the Resurrection of Christ, and in some measure have made it the day of our Resurrection too.
>
> (4. S14. 47–50)

To talk and listen together through any such sermons as these will be to do something to one's self. Or so he asserts. Before identifying some of the actual movements of that asserted larger action, we may notice in passing the dissonance and consonance of two quite disparate observers when they describe such discourse as might include sermons. Harvey Cox, for instance, adduces a different pair of actions, with antagonistic meanings: "That the pragmatist works at his problems one at a time testifies to his belief in the order of things. Conversely, it is a mark of unbelief in the ontologist that he must always scurry about to relate every snippet to the whole fabric." [56] Donne, we have begun to see, does both. Picking a single biblical verse and (still more) taking its significance a word at a time amounts to working at problems one at a time in a spirit of hope. In complementary fashion, the sermons often end on a contingent note of proposal or petition that we *may* be subsumed in a cosmos of divine power or mercy or even a sea of Christ's blood. Though any such petition betokens a certain anxiety for ontological whole cloth, we should keep in mind the existential freedom Donne's particular variations tend to emphasize. Christ's blood, for instance, may be a sea for him who is buoyed up by it and whose world is encircled by it, the same man who earlier weltered in some different sea.

But another recent writer has drawn from surprisingly diverse contexts a thesis about the compatibility of philosophy, poetry, and dramatic action, a thesis remarkably close to Donne's procedure:

> It is when one (as with Dewey) considers "experience" as a general, global concept, or (as with Heidegger and Merleau-Ponty) as an attitude of concern toward a world "lived from the inside" that one finds not only that it develops in time, but that it has an emotional and an episodic character which can only be described as dramatic. The dramatic poet merely adapts for his specific purposes those structures of lived experience which are common to us all.[57]

Yet other kinships begin to emerge when we notice Donne's numerous verbs of making, doing, and moving—often transitive, often metaphorical. Josephine Miles has observed that the language of his poetry and the Donnean poetic tradition is "vocative, predicative, abstract," and "is also Chaucerian, Tudor, metaphysical, romantic, and modern; it belongs to all those poets who, whatever the peculiar materials of their day, tend to emphasize the materials of controlled process in thought and speech as distinguished from the data of sense and status."[58] Perhaps such process further reveals the pragmatist taking things one at a time. However that may be, the *syntax,* as everyone agrees, tends to put everything together. "And with occasional stretches and strains of the anxious ontologist," we might say, in deference to the Cox formula. Yet . . . Familiar words and grammatical practices are given to us and are necessary for us to adopt if we would be understood by another; but Donne's energetically agglutinative syntax betokens his freedom and wit. He will not often pause to embed an analytic qualification in the middle of a clause in the manner of Henry James. About as seldom will he cast off as extraneous those sentence-elements missing in the familiar elliptical tags of Andrewes. Rather, he drives on unwearyingly to a vision inclusive by addition; or, more strictly, not a vision so often as a state of life. In a sentence which illustrates the pattern, he himself states one reason why:

> *Knowledge* cannot save us, but we cannot be saved without Knowledge; Faith is not on this side Knowledge, but beyond it; we must necessarily come to *Knowledge* first, though we must not stay at it, when we are come thither.
>
> (3. S17. 404–407)

"We are come thither"—not a bigger bank account of knowledge, but a new ground of being.

The steps by which he conducts himself and those in step with him to the "thither" of each sermon are subject each step to its own distinctive description, as the following accounts of whole sermons will suggest. But there are typical relationships. If we tabulate some here, the list will help to substantiate both his forcefulness and his direction in moving his listeners with himself to ground existentially different from where they began.

Donne's vocation, to "exhibit acceptable service," was to be not door-keeper in the house of the Lord but preacher. No more insistently urgent version of himself rings through the sermons than his acknowledgment that our distinctively human fidelity demands of *him* that he preach. It may be *service* exhibited in ambiguous ways to carry on the work of God, exhibited faithfully like the "Juggler of Our Lady" in the old tale, or exhibited with imperfect fidelity (as he occasionally acknowledges), or exhibited as a spectacle to churchgoers whose attentions remain elsewhere. But *vae mihi si non,* he says in the words of St. Paul (1 Corinthians 9.16). He says it at least 22 times in the 160 sermons.[59] The rewards of his preaching cannot be affirmed without conditions and contingencies, he knows, though we will observe one of his sanguine gestures in that direction in a moment. But he can regularly affirm to his various congregations his deep faith that to fall from man's calling as a promise-keeper is misery.

Of course the cry "Woe unto me if I preach not the Gospel" implies pressures and temptations working against that service.[60] Donne will occasionally stand with his congregation and a little apart from his preaching function and one special type of listener:

> Nay how often is the Pulpit it selfe, made the ship, and the Theatre of praise upon present men, and God left out? How often is that called a Sermon, that speaks more of Great men, then of our great God? . . . and when I have spent my selfe to the last farthing, my lungs to the last breath, my wit to the last Metaphore, my tongue to the last syllable, I have not paid a farthing of my debt to God; I have not praised him, but I have praised them, till not only my selfe, but even they, whom I have so mispraised, are the worse in the sight of God, for my over-praising; I have flattered them, and they have taken occasion by

> that, to thinke that their faults are not discerned, and so they have proceeded in them.
>
> (4. S12. 166–211)

The movement here ends by turning back to judge himelf more harshly than he judges them. His listeners are cautioned, though.

He may stand with his congregation a little apart from his subject-matter:

> . . . my spirituall appetite carries me still, upon the *Psalms of David,* for a first course, for the Scriptures of the Old Testament, and upon the *Epistles* of *Saint Paul,* for a second course, for the New: and my meditations even for these *publike exercises* to Gods Church, returne oftnest to these two. For, as a hearty entertainer offers to others, the meat which he loves best himself, so doe I oftnest present to Gods people, in these Congregations, the meditations which I feed upon at home, in those two Scriptures.
>
> (2. S1. 6–13)

Here the pulpit becomes remarkably equivalent to "God's board" (because of the dual ministry and because "man does not live by bread alone"). The minister is one with his listeners in being a meditator, but the preaching function differentiates him, too, in making him like Chaucer's Franklin, "St. Julian . . . in that contree." "Accept a loving and life-supporting gift, or reject that" is the choice his rhetoric puts them in the position of having to make.

Or he may stand with them a bit apart from elements or doings in themselves.

> . . . for, as God was well pleased, with the widowes two farthings, so is the Devill well pleased with the negligent mans lesser sins. *O Who can be so confident* in his footing, or in his hold, when *David,* that held out so long, fell, and *if we consider* but himselfe, irrecoverably, where the tempter was weake, and afar off?
>
> (5. S15. 176–181)
>
> The heart of man is *hortus,* it is a garden, a Paradise, where all that is wholsome, and all that is delightfull growes, but it is *hortus conclusus,* a garden that we our selves have walled in; It is *fons,* a fountaine, where all knowledge springs, but *fons signatus,* a fountaine that our corruption hath sealed up. The

> heart is a booke, legible enough, and intelligible in it selfe; but we have so interlined that books with impertinent knowledge, and so clasped up that booke, for feare of reading our owne history, our owne sins, as that we are greatest strangers, and the least conversant with the examination of our owne hearts. . . . a whole bundle of those things, which we are bound to beleeve in the Apostles Creed; And . . . beleeve this, this, that God hath established meanes of salvation here, and *He that beleeveth not this,* that such a Commission there is, *shall be damned.*
>
> (5. S13. 115–138)

In these last four illustrations, as generally in the sermons, he concerns himself with relationships, not with abolishing differences. In the last citation he finally stands with like-minded listeners apart from a group differentiated by the Scriptural *damned* and by the Scriptural third-person discourse (in Mark 16.16, the text of the sermon). He attends to traffic through gates in the walls and encounters along the journey rather than to levelling walls or merging with others. He would surely applaud Marcel's formulation of the fundamental reason: "there is no real community [if] there is no real plurality, no distinctions acknowledged as such."[61]

Though he acknowledges distinctions as generously and gracefully as any Renaissance Anglican, he can just as deftly acknowledge also a kind of devotional symbiosis, as in this:

> The Son of God *is Logos, verbum, The word;* God made us_1 with his word, and with our_2 words we_2 made God so farre, as that we_2 make up the mysticall body of Christ Jesus with our_2 prayers, with our_2 whole liturgie, and we_3 make the naturall body of Christ Jesus appliable to our_2 soules, by the words of Consecration in the Sacrament, and our_4 soules apprehensive, and capable of that body, by the word Preached.
>
> (3. S12. 133–139; edited for convenience)

The *us* numbered 1 seems to mean "all of us." The first-person plural pronouns numbered 2 seem to refer to those (including the preacher) united in the visible, practicing, liturgical church. "We_3" apparently means "we of the priesthood," and "our_4" refers at one and the same time to speaker and auditor. Yet obviously the passage as a whole affirms union of God and man: a union perennially coming hither as Incarnation and going hence in sacramental orientation of the self in receptivity and commitment.

Or he may be more emphatic about his separation (*in* pulpit and *in* priestly calling); but typically charity of tone or parallelism of argument will call his congregation to a kind of parallel situation:

> But this Preacher [the penitent thief, in Luke 23.40] leaves all the rest, either to their farther obduration, or their fitter time of repentence, if God had ordained any such time for them: and he turns to this one, whose disposition he knew to have been like his own, and therefore hoped his conversion would be so too; for nothing gives the faithful servants of God a greater encouragement that their labors shall prosper upon others, then a consideration of their own case, and all acknowledgement what God hath done for their souls . . . We have not that advantage over our auditory, which he had over his, to know that in every particular man, there is some reason why he should be more afraid of Gods judgments then another man. But every particular man, who is acquainted with his own history, may be such a Preacher to himself, and ask himself *Nonne tu,* hast not thou more reason to stand in fear of God then any other man, for any thing that thou knowest?
>
> (1. S6. 405–421)

The seeming parallels converge: he stands with them in their *essentia* as fallen men, dying thieves, each partly a scoffer at the Crucifixion. And *if* they are confirmed in their *essentia* as regenerate man, *then* he will stand with them as heirs through hope. At the end of the sermon, he reiterates "it is all our cases," then rises himself to speak "in the midst of us" the words Christ "takes into his own mouth now, the words which he put into the thiefs mouth then, and more." In these last two citations, as in 3. S16. 540–553, quoted in Chapter 1, and again and again throughout the sermons, we can observe a rhetoric of coalescence. For that, too, Marcel can speak as a gloss:

> Literally speaking, we communicate; and this means that the other person ceases to be for me someone with whom I converse, he ceases to intervene between me and myself; this self with whom I had coalesced in order to observe and judge him, while yet remaining separate, has fused into the living unity he now forms with me. The path leading from dialectic to love has now been opened.
>
> (*Creative Fidelity,* p. 33)

We see throughout the sermons a drama of changing selves: the preacher as High Priest or Everyman Fallen or Everyman Redeemed or Pilgrim or Explorer or Teacher deals with his listener as individual or corporate identity, fallen or regenerate, resistant or zealous—now one articulation of self and hearer, now another. Thus he dramatizes the mystery of simultaneous persistence and change in the self. Thus he answers the Prayer Book's call to "newness of life," to "sing a new song," at the same time that he witnesses to the requisite reliability and endurance of the self. (The traditional notions of freedom, responsibility, sin, penitence, and hope for a sinner to "turn from his wickedness and live" presuppose some continuity in the self, or else they would all be hollow absurdities.) Indeed, perhaps speaking in many voices, many situations, while remaining a recognizable self, represents the most general "middle way" he goes.[62] Because without freedom life lacks dignity and ultimately meaning; without endurance, without promise-keeping fidelity, the self evaporates into atoms or absurdity (see, for example, 8. S15 on "the law of Liberty").

Atop all that has gone before, we can now make brief observation of changing selves in changing relation to the world and then make concluding observations about the sermon as symbolic in its delivery and reception. In the light of passages just now cited from Donne and Marcel and remarks just made about freedom and endurance, we can mark by a later man's differences some of Donne's finesse. John Bramhall was one of the Anglicans justly celebrated by Eliot in *For Lancelot Andrewes*. He preached in Dublin on 23 April 1661, "being the Day appointed for His Majesties Coronation," on Psalm 126 in the six verses of which "Zion celebrates the return from exile."

Where Donne began a sermon on a psalm by offering himself as one feeding the hungry with the food he likes best himself, Bramhall in an equally traditional metaphor offers to afflicted persons some tested remedies of "the best Physician." David is good because he "speaketh experimentally [that is, experientially] . . . both for soul and body." His third paragraph opens the subject with something like Donne's emphasis on existential life-world:

> There are two sorts of captivity, corporal and spiritual; both are bad but the latter ten times worse. In a corporal captivity the Tyrants are external, but in spiritual captivity they are internal, in our bosomes and bowels. There the stings are sharp; but nothing so sharp as the stings of a guilty conscience. Corporal

> Tyrants may dispossess us of our wealth, our life, our liberty; but spiritual deprive us of our souls, of Gods image, of eternal blessedness. There, one or two members do sinful and slavish offices; but here all our members are weapons of unrighteousness. Corporal captives have but one Master, but spiritual captives have many Masters, Pride commands to spend and covetousness to spare . . . Corporal slaves have hope to escape by flight, but in spiritual captivity no flight can help us, unless we could flie away from our selves.[63]

He is preacher and priest to his congregation and intermittently one of them. Yet two features of this passage contrast with Donne's practice. Most conspicuously, his tendency toward balance and antithesis needs but a Dryden "to tag his verses" and we would have neoclassic couplets, with less violence done to Bramhall's prose than was done to Donne's satiric verse by Pope's "translation." We have glanced at Donne occasionally striking a balance in his sermonic prose or pushing contrasts into antitheses. But his preoccupation with process and change, with "the whole journey of a Christian," with the "fair way" *between* Nicolaitan heresy on the left hand and Tatian on the right, or the like (rather than their antithetical relationship)—all these activities tend to subordinate the relatively static figures of balance and antithesis.

The second contrast with Bramhall may be both less obvious and more important. He says *"a* corporal captivity" and *"may* dispossess" and (twice) "captives *have"* and "unless we *could* flie away from our selves." He also says "our bosomes . . . our life . . . no flight *can* help *us,"* but still there is an air of the hypothesis about Bramhall's exposition. Donne's delineations of alternatives and sense of himself and listeners are characterized by more consistent personal presence, perhaps because he knows we *can* "flie away from our selves."

In a wedding sermon, he marshals a whole series of inhumane options in shifting antitheses which define different features of a *constant* middle ground:

> Between the heresie of the Nicolaitans, that induced a community of women, any might take any; and the heresie of the Tatians that forbad all, none might take any, was a fair latitude. Between the opinion of the *Manichaean* hereticks, that thought women to be made by the Devil, and the *Colliridian* hereticks that sacrificed to a woman, as to God, there is a fair distance. Be-

> tween the denying of them souls, which S. *Ambrose* is charged to have done, and giving them such souls, as that they may be Priests, as the *Peputian* hereticks did, is a faire way for a moderate man to walk in. To make them Gods is ungodly, and to make them Devils is devillish; To make them Mistresses is unmanly, and to make them servants is unnoble; To make them as God made them, wives, is godly and manly too.
>
> (3. S11. 48–60)

The living space of a man's relationship with his wife may be crowded. But even in this unusually schematic formulation, there will be a "fair way" for any man, even as his shifting preoccupations may face him toward successively different adversities.

Preaching action may on occasion transform misdoers:

> . . . if God lead me into a Congregation, as into his Arke, where there are but eight soules, but a few disposed to a sense of his mercies, and all the rest (as in the Arke) ignobler creatures, and of brutall natures and affections, That if I finde a licentious Goat, a supplanting Fox, an usurious Wolfe, an ambitious Lion, yet to that creature, to every creature I should preach the Gospel of peace and consolation, and *offer* these creatures a *Metamorphosis, a transformation, a new Creation in Christ Jesus,* and thereby make my Goat, and my Fox, my Wolfe, and my Lion, to become *Semen Dei,* The seed of God . . . .
>
> (7. S4. 616–625)

Such convertibility of misdoers may be reassuring. But the proportion, "eight soules" to all the self-dispossessed "ignobler creatures," must seem cautionary, like the way of a marrying man among Manichaeans and Colliridians. Some listeners or preachers might indeed say "from me to Thee's a long and terrible way,"[64] yet Donne usually in these matters as in others maintains a tone of guarded, humble assurance:

> . . . let every man take heed of Excommunicating himselfe. The imperswasible Recusant does so; The negligent Libertin does so; The fantastique Separatist does so; The halfe-present man, he, whose body is here, and mind away, does so: And he, whose body is but halfe here, his limbes are here upon a cushion, but his eyes, his eares are not here, does so: All these are selfe-Excommunicators, and keepe themselves from hence. Onely he

> enjoyes that blessing, the want whereof *David* deplores, that is here intirely, and is glad he is here, and glad to finde this kinde of service here, that he does, and wishes no other.
>
> (7. S1. 303–312)

The company of persons with a common orientation toward transcendence will be *there,* he seems to assume, even if the self proves inconstant or wayward.

He appeals to that company by interpreting his chosen text in "applications" oftentimes to both Old and New Testament matters, but always to "all our cases." But a lecture might do that. No usual lecture, though, would deal with space, time, allegorical Egypts or churches or the like, so as to establish a continuity of the architectural interior housing the audience with the exterior landscape and a continuity of the self's interior with the selfhood of others. As the notes above on changing persons concur to suggest and as the complete sermons to follow document more emphatically, the Donnean sermon *models* involvement with society. Occasional references to London or Rome or Spanish match or royal prerogative are only one level of particularity in that model of involvement, and they represent a level too limited to engage him much. Social-involvement-as-sermon moves in step with its context of group dialogue in Prayer Book worship, and—in its rationality—with the traditional association of reasoning with public discourse. And the social quality of the sermon takes some of its temper and definition by contrast with its particular complement in the normal human systole and diastole of public/private:

> . . . we begin, (if wee will make profit of a Sermon) at Prayers; And thither wee returne againe, (if we have made profit by a Sermon) in due time, to prayers.
>
> (7. S12. 455–457)

Typically, he takes his text as a kind of challenge by the Holy Ghost. He once preached on James 2. 12: "So speak ye, and so do, as they that shall be judged by the law of liberty." Near the end of his division he comments "our Text is an Amphitheater. An Amphitheater consists of two Theaters: Our Text hath two parts, in which, all men, all may sit, and see themselves acted" (8. S15. 75–77). The remark is unusual only in its explicitness. He normally responds to "the Holy Ghost's" challenge by text and his church's challenge by liturgy—and in both of those life's challenge to integrity of self—

with a challenge to himself and listeners by explication (against conflicting interpretations) and by metaphor (with its tense fusion of likeness and unlikeness) and role-making. That last tactic, to which we have already given some attention, seems to have something to do with accessibility and availability to that God who is always for Donne among many things the Master of Changes.

> God will speak unto me, in that voice, and in that way, which I am most delighted with, and hearken most to. If I be *covetous,* God wil tel me that heaven is a pearle, a treasure. . . . God will make a *storme* at Sea, or a *fire* by land, speake to me, and tell me his minde, that there is no safe dependence, no assurance but in *him*. . . .
>
> (10. S4. 267–276)

Thus, the preacher and his congregation are to his chosen text as man is to God in the world at large. Hence going through the sermon (as preacher or communicant) to come to terms with its challenge is a symbolic action. Appropriately, too, the priest who should "preach the true and lively word" somewhat *as* he "rightly and duly administers the sacraments"—such a preacher should be heard by a communicant somewhat *as* he receives the Eucharist:

> What the bread and wine is, or what becomes of it, *Damascen* thinks impertinent to be inquired. He thinks he hath said enough; (and so may we doe) *Migrat in substantiam animae;* There is true Transubstantiation, that when I have received it worthily, it becomes my very soule; that is, My soule growes up into a better state, and habitude by it, and I have the more soule for it, the more sanctified, the more deified soule by that Sacrament.
>
> (7. S12. 756–762)

Coming to terms with the Scriptural challenge is likely to involve one or more of several progressions. Often it is from fear to knowledge to love, "for, *the fear of God is the beginning of wisdom,* but the love of God is the consummation, that is, the marriage, and union of thy soul, and thy Saviour" (1. S5. 280–282). Or it may be from ignorance to knowledge to faith, for "faith is not on this side Knowledge, but beyond it" (3. S17. 405). Or from perplexity to resolution to assurance, "and so leave you in that, which I hope, is your *gallery* to heaven" (6. S7. 549–550). Or from anxiety to generosity and humility: to Father, Son, and Holy Ghost be ascribed

"All Power, Praise, Might, Majestie, Glory, and Dominion, now, and for ever. Amen" (6. S12. 750; 7. S14. 753).

By the end of a good sermon, he has kept the faith of his calling by making himself present to an issue of ultimate significance as he develops it from biblical context or topical context to life context. He has vigorously challenged his listeners to participating presence by making them dependent upon his (and their own) active course through thickets of conflicting choices attending the issue. He has shown his listeners a way through to a response that can unite them all in more abundant life. To see all this taking place, it is necessary to see whole sermons, to which we now turn.

Part II
Single Sermons

3

FROM THE EXTREMITY: THE SERMON OF VALEDICTION

The "Sermon of Valediction" has some special attractions, at the same time that it is typical in some of its ways and strengths. It comes to us trailing the cloud of an early manuscript version (available as "Appendix B" to Volume Two of the Potter-Simpson Edition). The contrast between the two versions argues that here his notions of sermon action and his craftsmanship had liberty to make full contribution to the challenge of a demanding text and a demanding situation.

Ecclesiastes has long been a source-book and prize exhibit in the tradition of crying "vanity and vexation of spirit" (Ecclesiastes 2.12), or announcing the decay of the world. Donne treated at length the decay of the world in his 1611 "Anatomy."[1] But he did not *preach* the uncomfortable words of that pseudoexistential *angst* which glibly locates all corruption "out there." Even two sermons on the text "Wo unto the world, because of offences" (3. S6, S7) end with both insistence on the continuity of the exterior world and innermost self and with reassurance. In the first we are invited to recognize "that it was well for thee, that there were scandals and offences;" in the second we are invited to "overflowing charity." Similarly, an early sermon on Ecclesiastes 8.11 opposes "defamations" and celebrates penitence (1. S2).[2]

Moreover, in this valedictory he eschews his frequent practice of "placing" his text in its biblical context. Thus, he develops the sermon from one verse, Ecclesiastes 12.1, sufficiently different in temper from its context to have occasioned suspicion that the biblical text is contaminated.

The sermon marks a rather specially symbolic occasion. His revised lines mark that occasion no less than the lines of the early version. He kept the unusually personal subtitle: "A Sermon of

Valediction at my going into Germany, at Lincolns-Inne, April 18, 1619." He was wishing farewell, because vicissitudes of health or travel or enemy action might almost expectably take his life while he accompanied Viscount Doncaster's embassy to Germany.[3] The situation is an extreme one: what choices shall be final choices? What shall be dismissed as self-indulgence and what embraced as unselfishly self-fulfilling? How shall this relate to the man who is a preacher and his brothers in Christ who are his congregation? Donne himself began a Whitehall sermon on Matthew 9.13 (in 1626) with the remark that "first, we consider the occasion of the words, and then the words themselves, for of *these twins* is this Text pregnant" (7. S5. 71–73), my italics).

The sermon begins in the earth, in mines, and ends in Heaven. It begins judiciously and ends committedly, in a powerfully controlled manner, even passionately. It initially treats its auditors as relatively casual bystanders, *disjecta membra* perhaps, and ends taking them as followers and partners in caravan, members incorporate of a mystical body with Christ as head. These features are all generally characteristic of the 160 surviving sermons. A significantly large number, some 38, of those utilize a text which takes the form of an injunction, none any more tellingly than this one.

Yet he begins almost deferentially, presenting for consideration two things, saying not "we must consider" or "you will" but

> Wee may consider two great virtues, one for the society of this life, Thankfulness, and the other for attaining the next life, Repentance; as the two pretious Mettles, Silver and Gold: Of Silver . . . there are whole Mines, books written by Philosophers . . . of this Gold . . . there is no Mine in the Earth . . .

The simile of silver and gold invites a kind of measured, rational apprehension. It has a certain vividness, sensory and intellectual, and we hold for further consideration, perhaps, the implication that the philosopher is a sort of alchemist who *creates* thankfulness—that all we need to do is enrich ourselves by lifting it from his book, grasping it, or dropping it. But we are not in much danger of becoming lost, nor are we likely to feel challenged so abruptly as by those familiar similes of "two soules . . . Like gold to ayery thinnesse beate. . . . two . . . as stiffe twin compasses are two." To say nothing of such daring metaphoric identifications as: "She is all States, and all Princes, I" The dilute, repetitious progress of the opening lines (obscured by selective quotation) even suggests that he does not count on very alert attention.

We note, though, the slightly loaded word *society*. Spoken by an able Latinist, in a context of dialogic, Prayer-Book worship, to "The Honourable Society of Lincoln's Inn," it carries more than a usual overtone of intimacy. Then, suddenly, a curious thing happens:

> this *Gold* is for the most part in the washes;
> this repentance in matters of tribulation;
> but *God* directs thee to it in this Text . . . .
> (my italics)

"Materials on this topic are scattered, but you'll be interested in one short article by God." Perspectives of an enclosed egocentricity and alien world begin to yield to perspectives open toward salvation, the major movement and drama of this sermon. Further, one notices on brief reflection how dynamic a thing repentance becomes in this formulation. Although "the washes" may seem more diffuse than a mine, they are ceaselessly active, and moreover silver and gold alike are always—in the sermons—to be coined and so made current. All this implies that human identity requires worldly involvement and perhaps less clearly suggests something apparent enough elsewhere: the Donnean sense that true society is a face of divine immanence.

At this point in the sermon, the heavenly equation is drawn reassuringly and simply as a logical closed system.

> remember now thy Creator before those evill dayes come, and then thou wilt repent the not remembring him till now.

The command produces remembrance, which produces repentance, which produces salvation. But the thrust is toward wider implications, a larger universe of discourse. In the movement of syntax and diction, there is an example of movement toward metaphor as he advises all to use the back of their brain (the memory's supposed location) now, not at life's end:

> hindermost part of the brain . . .
> hindermost part of thy life . . .

Here the not-quite-parallel phrases move from literal to metaphorical in a concern which expands from physiological divisions to consideration of the whole man and his lived experience. The parallelism in the sequence tends to give *thy life* significance just as coherent and concrete as *the brain*.

As an alternative to remembering only at life's end or not at all, the respondent may remember "now, *in die,* in the day, whil'st thou hast light, now *in diebus,* in the days, whilst God presents thee many lights, many means; and *in diebus juventutis,* in the days of thy youth, of strength. . . ." Light figures in the conventional sense of enlightenment, and hence an accessory to "means;" but no less does it figure *means* themselves, although not the whole armory of "means." Further, remembrance and whatever remains of the suggestions of enlightenment stand in a relationship of poetic equivalence to *action,* almost as much as to say "thy truths are thy doings." Such a sentiment would accord with the earlier implication that repentance is a species of action, but would be uncharacteristically abrupt and mechancial for Donne. Nevertheless the formula may serve for expository convenience and to schematize what in this as in others of his best sermons he gradually dramatizes.

His division of the text, then, has blocked out some chief metaphoric directions. As a sort of overture, its value to auditors is plain. The steps it foreshadows will be of substantial extent when they occur. Yet even this segment does not lack independent vitality sufficient to justify its part of the whole work. We may notice one extraordinary passage particularly:

> And as the word imports,
> [1] *Bechurotheica*
> [2] *in diebus Electionum tuarum,*
> [3] in the dayes of thy choice,
> [4] whilst thou art able to make thy choyce,
> [5] whilst the Grace of God shines so brightly upon
> thee, as that thou maist choose the way,
> and so powerfully upon thee,
> as that thou maist walke in that way.

Here we are presented not merely another quotation from the Vulgate, with a conventional gloss, but the original Hebrew and four glosses. As I argued in Chapter 2, vi, they form a sort of hierarchical emblem, suggesting the presuppositions and method of the entire sermon. *Bechurotheica,* as a transliterated Hebrew word, reminds us again of the sermon's oral dimension and of a community of voices enduring in history. As we saw, it represents the height of diction, the limit of theological resonance, the most valid and reliable relation of word and thing (since nothing outside Scripture could so securely claim to be the language of the Holy Ghost). It is translated into Latin, a slight dilution and descent, but still the language of the early Church and many of its Fathers. Then, as reiteration of the word *electionum,* in "choice . . . choyce," insists on the option of salvation, the two English glosses move the scene into the workaday language of the city. The succinct phrase, "in the dayes of thy choice," and the flat, prosaic, relatively tentative "whilst thou art able to make thy choyce" bring us down to the fallen world. The fallen world is ground for controlled optimism, however, as we would expect in this atmosphere of Anglican orthodoxy. The last, the artistic and creative translation, gives the hint of regeneration. The ordinary day of clock and calendar can give way at any time, it implies, to a sunlike source of loving, directing, encouraging light which will shine as long as necessary for the willing pilgrim to journey to salvation. Not grace as polemical abstraction nor as theocentric determinism, but rather as a medium of free life.

Thus Donne's commitment to freedom of the will characteristically appears not as a dogmatic and reductive assertion of equivalence ("Will is free") but as an inextricable element of lived experience. Moreover, the sermon qualifies and extends itself, as it will do again and again. The early summary statement that "the Holy-Ghost takes the neerest way to bring a man to God, by awaking his memory" becomes the introduction to a prerequisite of that pilgrimage, thoughtful and deliberate choice. This concept has a corollary: that failure to make the pilgrimage results from internal and external failures of the self, not from predestination or any other mode of determinism. In *awakened memory,* the term for harmonizing the paradox of grace-with-choice has been given. But its definition requires more time. We get just a glimpse of the depressed area where failure resides, the domain of fallen men, busily laying up treasures on earth, intent only upon the Creature, and therefore needing to "Remember the Creator." The renewal of that injunction closes the division, not only as a repetition but as a mark of new ground won, because now the idea of possible disobedience is more vividly present to us than when we were confronted with an apparently closed logical system. Thus he begins here the process so typical of his best sermons: the concurrent consideration of boonful and baneful alternatives in a world of *radical* freedom.

Since disobedience comes easy for anyone, the preacher, in an agile demonstration of care, marshals a panoramic definition of that *memory* we are enjoined to. The paragraph is long, heavily furnished, and wide-ranging.

In a sermon probably predating this, he remarks, "The art of *salvation* is but the art of *memory*" (2. S2. 52). A recurrent feature of his structures is the progression through reason to faith. Just as he began by proposing the matter of repentance in relation to, but apart from, the matter of thankfulness, so here he narrows the focus by proposing memory in relation to, but apart from, much that stands ranked opposite: "forgetfulness and neglect."

Memory is established as a necessary action first by the logic of elimination. "All" the alternatives appear defective. The understanding *by itself* is wittily shown to lead Jews into behaving (seemingly) like short-change artists and the Roman Catholics like (perhaps) myopia-sufferers, some Protestant Christians, (whether hierarchy-oriented *or* congregation-oriented) like astigmatic viewers of ecclesiastical polity. Similarly, the will, when oriented towards itself, appears in strident inanities of uncharitableness and stammering insecurities about its own freedom (Jesuits vs. Dominicans,[4] will vs. grace). Of intellect, will, and memory, the interior trinity of Augustinian analysis and Renaissance faculty psychology, there remains only memory.

We could describe him as contrasting the freedom of self-realization in a great social cosmos with the restriction of functioning in terms of intellect or will. Prophesied deliverance means something less general to Jews, Antichrist something less general and less concrete to "Papists." But *remembering* can unite in significant measure of congeniality all peoples and faculties in "this issue," "a thankful acknowledgement of [the Lord's] former mercies and benefits."

Memory here associates itself with action and closely associates the Old Testament with the New.

> *I am the Lord thy God which brought thee out of the land of Egypt;* He only presents to their memory what he had done for them. *And so* [my italics] in delivering the Gospel in one principal seal thereof, the sacrament of his body, he recommended it only to their memory, *Do this in remembrance of me.*

In one case, the hugely symbolic journey is the subject *of* memory; in the other action is involved with and animated *by* memory; in *both* cases, God is known by action and known in terms of liberation and bounty. Donne cites a metaphor of St. Bernard ("that father of Meditation" 3. S5. 402):

> The memory . . . is the stomach of the soul, it receives and digests, and turns into good blood . . . .

After this ambiguous "blood" and phrases on the Eucharist quoted above, he returns to develop Bernard's metaphor. "St. Bernard calls that the stomach of the soul, we may be bold to call it the Gallery of the soul, hang'd with . . . pictures of the goodness and of the mercies of thy God to thee." The organic metaphor propounded by the meditative saint yields to a less deterministic and more social and diversified metaphor with the seventeenth-century preacher. Both formulating a gallery and touring it imply a labor of love in a wide latitude of choice. The results may be no less dynamic: God may shine upon the previously "beclouded" pilgrim understanding and straighten out, "rectifie," the previously turned-aside, "perverted" will.

At this point the symbolic extension of the imminent "going into Germany" can scarcely wait longer for at least summary notice. This sermon moves as pervasively as any and more conspicuously than many in the terms of that baptized archetype, the journey of life to a promised land. In this as in other of his surviving sermons, wayfaring shifts now and then into terms of another mode, another medium than the solitary or comradely walk. Donne, with a naturalness both of contemporary Britain and Christian tradition, shifted to notions of pilgrimage as voyage. Here we are given the ark of Noah in a grammatical structure of equivalence with "Gods protection" "in both captivities, in infinite dangers." Later, among a bill of acts of the antichristian apostles, "the Navy" of Spain figures as a sort of anti-Ark in a muted instance of such concrete antitheses as mark his sermons' ethical-psychological landscapes now and again. The structure might be called the "vile antithesis"—sea of troubles/sea of mercies, sea of sin/sea of redeeming blood, consuming fire/refining fire, and the like.

Here, at the end of the massive paragraph on memory, "every man" in the self of graceful rememberer moves from (implicit) stasis and desiccation to *branch, navigable river,* "and endless Sea of Gods mercies." In a sermon perhaps less than two years later, he presents a protean ark of church, state, and self in political and ecclesiastical seas of Roman threats (on Matthew 18.7, 3. S7. 481–527). The individual terms of such patterns were venerable and commonplace enough.[5] Donne wields the well-worn terms with a kind of agility hard to isolate and difficult to schematize and which his contemporaries, similarly hard put to define labelled with their multipurpose term *wit*. But as we shall see, other witty preachers were not so humanely personal and socially relational.

Almost a hieroglyph of the Donnean mode appears in the tense counterpoising of the expansive, then accelerated, then slowing cadence at the end of "Memento." Two elements besides the pacing call for notice. First is a structure more frequent in Donne, Shakespeare, and the metaphysical poets than in other poets then or since: imagery of quasi-mathematical proportion. In this case, the well-placed picture portrait is to the viewer as God is to the rememberer. Note the implications that God must be deliberately encountered, that human ideas of God are made things and hence relative but may nevertheless suggest something not relative. Moreover, note that the terms are for his seventeenth-century island-dwelling audience familiarly experiential, the parallels and cadences climactic and urgent. In dramatizing the act of remembering thankfully, he avoids two obvious pitfalls: terms that are sensuous and passionate, but hopelessly private, and terms public but vague or static. He has the spectacular public process or the general yet concrete event (Reformation, Armada, Powder Plot),[6] and he has the leaves in the "bosome book" of "every man," detailed and concrete, individual for each auditor yet universal, a part of every auditor. Donne posits at the last a typical figure particularly plausible for Lincoln's Inn: the devout Christian working his way student-like in the privacy of his own energetic meditations from the immediate page of his own day, "that little branch" to the organon, "the great and endless Sea of Gods mercies towards him, from the beginning of his being." He is of course another figure of living from the center outward, creating himself by the grace of the raw material given him.[7]

The logical activity of the sermon goes on in the third paragraph, "Nunc," as definition of a basic term, as in his previous paragraph. "Now" is defined, along with time itself, as relative to each person and to eternity, which circumscribes temporal and cognitional human limitations.

But such defining as that integrates readily with the more profound continuing social action of the sermon. The preacher responds here to the injunction to remember by remembering items of his Creator's life in human experience, which entered the preacher's own experience through his ministerial training. Thus he remembers as part of exhorting to healthy life and action. Further, he shows the terms of his historical knowledge—first ears of grain, first loaves, first fruits—expanding by relational analogy to yield a symbolic revelation for any man: *"primitias panum* . . . when thou hast kneaded up riches . . . thy *Easter,* whensoever thou hast any resurrection . . . thy Pentecost, when the Holy Ghost visits thee . . . thy fal . . . thy winter . . . thy death." Notice the elasticity of the distance between tenor and vehicle in these metaphors; "thy Pentecost" might be a moment in winter, the calendar festival, or half a lifetime. Finally, he has moved from announcing "we consecrate all his creatures to him, in a sober and religious use of them," to the definition and reminder that "thy business is to remember." He has in fact busily used raw material from the past to fashion a program for liberation from time.

As we have already had occasion to see, he takes the historical account of Hebrew practice, already half-metaphorical in its pastoral quality, and employs metaphorical verbs in particular to limn a figure of the self in a divinely prescribed yet individually determined time-cycle. Of the third offering of first fruits, the offering from "all their Fruits and Revenues," he first wrote:

> and this was very late in Autumne,
> in the fall,
> about September.

Revised, this reads:

> but this was very late in *Autumn,*
> at the fall of the leaf,
> in the end of the year.

The oral stresses now fall on the important words, one of which, *leaf,* adds a sensory dimension absent before, and the series ends with the symbolic "end of the year," rather than an anticlamactic station of the calendar. This suggestion of time, decay, and death soon precipitates a warning to act before a gradual falling away of the self's name and calling and time.

That image of self-abdication ("Lethargy") and the spur of limitation, whether an angel to "swear, that time shall be no more" or (a few lines later) Christ to say "Fool . . . this night they will fetch away thy soul," make the middle of the sermon intensely vigorous. Six paragraphs of willfully dynamic remembrance transport us from an image of family portrait galleries and bosom books to panoramas of the seven days of creation and world-wide latitudes of choice.[8]

Between paragraphs attending to the "now" and the "in the days" of Ecclesiastes 12.1 Donne has constructed a paragraph which is mediatorial in ways that are partly logical. This fourth paragraph on daytime substantially differentiates the nows earlier defined into those with a daylight and ultimately Heavenly future and those of the night which is finally eternal. The notion of "In Die," in turn, includes the subsequent notions of "In Diebus." The punning verb *travails,* "travels, works, suffers," opens up some implications of the scene:

> To him that travails by night a bush seem a tree, a tree seems a man, and a man a spirit . . . .

In this night of degenerating man, the familiar Spenserian-Shakespearian contrast between seeming and being is inevitable, is commonly a downhill course. The terminus in that direction is not Milton's "bottomless perdition" but a sort of revised lethargy, articulated in a highly formal still point of the sermon.

> A wretched covetousness,
> to be intruders upon the Devil;
> a wretched ambition,
> to be usurpers upon damnation.

This still vision immediately gives way to tense process and change, in a brief summary acting simultaneously as contrast and consolation:

> God did not make the fire for us; but much less did he make us for that fire; that is, make us to damn us.

Concrete groups of men (Medes, Persians, Ninevites) show that human reality sometimes banefully accords with human appearance, while divine appearance and reality may be gracefully inconsistent:

> we may see the day break,
> and discern beams of saving light,
> even in this Judgment of eternal darkness . . . .

We have been led a rapid pilgrim journey from day, through night of self-questioning on earth and night in Hell, to a new day.

In the Donnean life-world, the quintessential new day, the primary day of the many days by which "to see and remember" God, remains always the day of "the light and love of the Gospel," anyone's day of first turning toward Incarnation and Redemption.

Hence the Creation story that follows becomes for Donne not quite so much the microcosmic allegory of maturing consciousness that it was for Milton in Book Seven of *Paradise Lost,* but rather a typological allegory of "our regeneration."

Exposition of the second day parallels in some respects the earlier division of the present into moments now dark, now light. Here the division between waters and the firmament asserts a distinction between the firmament of the self in its communal life-world and waters of revealed mysteries below, unrevealed mysteries and non-validated speculations above. Here, too, the inevitable thematic comparison with Milton comes closer; with something of Raphael's assurance (though with a sprinkling of first-person plural pronouns), the priestly voice counsels keeping to ways of belief ecclesiastically close at hand somewhat as the angelic voice counsels "joy thou In what he gives to thee . . . Think only what concerns thee and thy being" (*Paradise Lost* 8. 170–174).[9]

The priestly address shifts then to the very basic petitionary ground which can support relationships of command, request, prayer, or even speculation. "Let it be . . . ," he says several times in the seventh paragraph, as he wittily glosses ways in which contrasts of the fourth, fifth, and sixth days may be constructively lived by the remembering believer. It seems the sunlight of prosperity and darkness of adversity, the dejection of creeping things and exhilaration of flying things, the dignity of soul and the indignity of dust may all be mediated by the presence of the Creator, whose presence through this lively Augustinian mode of memory can "perfect" temporal and ecclesiastical Sabbaths in "a spiritual Sabbath, a conscience of peace, by remembering now thy Creator." And with that stroke the preacher comes full circle with "the week of thy regeneration" and connects the symbolic time of the "week" with the present literal time of the congregation and summarizes imperatively.

He has defined and demonstrated a faculty and a time, memory in a creative sense and "nowadays" in several symbolic senses. It remains to gloss capability, which paragraphs eight and nine, *Juventutis* and *Electionum,* engage to do.

Lexically defining two meanings for *Bechurotheica,* rhetorically the two paragraphs move in a complementary sequence. The first presents itself as vividly, diversely concrete, in a manner that is moderately general by virtue of being historic and civic: we hear of David's prayer, Job's remembrance, how "we were" and how "we are," "*Tobias* comfort," Basil's aggressive question and Augustine's formula. The sum of these things includes a relative sense that younger is easier than older and a sense of the radical contrast between the "infirmities" of childhood and age as opposed to the ambiguous "strength of youth." [10] Horse, chalice, and clock, as metaphoric vehicles in the first of these two paragraphs all insisted on the potentially honorable physicality of pilgrim journey. Now, in "Electionum," the physicality continues in heats and markets and bells. But the antithesis of infirmity and strength widens into antithesis between death and life, dying life and eternity with the Ancient of Days. The general civic and historic instances give way to the altogether universal but utterly personal necessity of crucial choice and the concurrent fact of fleeting power of choice.

Donne explicates a biblical text in each of his sermons and so do many of his contemporaries in theirs. That practice was not so common either half a century earlier or half a century later, as the admired sermons of a subsequent Reader at Lincoln's Inn, Geoffrey Tillotson (later Archbishop of Canterbury), illustrate. The practice might well have continued in better repute had there been a continuing line of preachers with some of Donne's ability to anatomize much of his congregation's life-world in his explication of a text. Here, at the beginning of the final four paragraphs of the sermon, he recapitulates how he has brought us to the climactic topic: "This is then the faculty that is excited, the memory; and this is the time, now, now whilest ye have power of election: The object is, the Creator."

Remembering the Creator is no mystic's contemplative separation from mundane reality. Rather, it is a rigorous, constant apprehension of lived experience and an energetic clearing away of obstacles. The preacher dramatizes the action, freeing a scriptural passage of a disorderly interpolation. From John 7: 39 ("The holy Ghost was not *given,* because Jesus was not glorified"), he rejects the word *datus,* represented in the Wiclif, Rheims, and Authorized (and New English) Versions, and adopts the reading given by the Biblia Sacra Sixti Quinti and represented in the Tyndale, Cranmer, and Geneva Versions. That argument, the statement just before it that "what God hath done for us, is the object of our memory" and the statement after the argument, explaining that the Holy Ghost "hath no being to us-ward, till he works in us"—these bits together exemplify as neatly as anywhere in the sermons his toughmindedly existential insistence on life-issues.

He forthrightly extends the principle and the demonstration to include his usual theocentrically telic dynamism, in a metaphoric summary of the recommended journey:

> *Remember the Creator then,* because thou canst remember nothing backward beyond him, and remember him so too, that thou maist stick upon nothing on this side of him, That so neither *height, nor depth, nor any other creature may separate thee from God;* not only not separate thee finally, but not separate so, as to stop upon the creature, but to make the best of them, thy way to the Creator. . . .

He offers here no royal progress with standing houses, it seems, but a pilgrim way which is an uneven *via media,* with traps of materialism and presumptuous speculation. Yet, remarkably, he can maintain the double vision of the solitary pilgrim rememberer (even visibly isolated by the pulpit) and of the community of appraising viewers: *"We,"* he says, "see ships in the river" (one ship for John Donne, soon enough), "we see men" but *"remember the Creator,* and get thither, because there is no safe footing upon the creature, til we come so far."

God, seen now as "thy Creator," looms very large, so large that in definition by exclusion ("Who so faithful? Who wiser, better, *nearer?"*), the world of fallen man gets successively reduced. At this point in paragraph eleven, one of the most interesting examples of revision occurs. First, he wrote:

> soe what degrees or titles soever a man have in this world, the greatest of all is the first of all, that he had a being by Creation, for the distance from nothing to a little is *infinitely* more, then from that litle to the *best* degree in this life. . . .
>
> (2. Appen. B. 524–527, my italics)

He altered this latter part to read:

> the greatest and the foundation of all, is, that he had a being by creation: For the distance from nothing to a little, is ten thousand times more, than from it to the *highest* degree in this life. . . .
>
> (my italics)

I demurred at first, thinking Donne had lost hold of the logical fact and lapsed into casual hyperbole. But more is in the second version. Of course dividing a number by zero gives infinity; dividing a large number by a small number gives a number; even if it is a large number, infinity is infinitely greater than any rational number. The trouble is that one order of infinity cannot be comprehended by the senses and emotions any better than another order of infinity. They remain abstract counters. It is part of one preacherly problem in miniature: how to make real, to a listener, things which by definition exceed his human faculties of comprehension—things like omnipotence, omniscience, eternity. Characteristically, Donne picks a concrete analogue which can be apprehended in some way and which he can make point toward the supernatural truth. The figure *ten thousand* conveys more of the quality of that largest gathering of units into coherence, absolute creation, than the uncompromising abstraction of the early version.[11]

Moreover, the revision puts the passage clearly and coherently into its context, a delineation of the scale of creation, and the point on it which the congregation has reached. The earlier question, "who so faithful, wise, good, and near as our Maker?", and its unmistakable answer, "No one," leads emotively, whether it does or not logically, to the question, "What, without Him?", and the answer, "Nothing." Thus he invites awareness of the whole scale and defines our position as permanently elevated well above the nether end, even though the highest degree here is below the Chorus of Heaven.

> To end all, that being which we have from God shall not return to nothing, nor the being which we have from men neither.

As usual, Donne's summary adds a new element, in this case the idea of social influence as creative. He immediately makes the concept concrete and institutional:

> so those Images and those impressions, which we have received from men, from nature, from the world, the image of the Lord, the image of a Counsailor, the image of a Bishop . . . .

Misapprehensions and misjudgments by men of a lord, counsellor, or churchman aggravate and further his misdoing, as a result of which he willingly descends (not "falls" or "sinks") into the abyss. Accurate recognition of fellow pilgrims thus becomes another responsibility.

Although a man's creative journey through time justly cannot proceed to one extreme, nothingness, it mercifully can proceed, his argument goes, to the New Jerusalem, the other end of the scale of creation. The final paragraph orients attention toward that goal, having delineated the path and illuminated pitfalls along the way. In reinvoking remembrance, he speaks of making up a circle. Remembering God has appeared to be to love Him and to love, properly, the self and now, in keeping with all, the neighbor as the self. The exposition may have closed where its terms began, like a circle, but in another sense has carried the argument and "the understanders" somewhat like Yeats's famous ascending spiral stair.

> Now, to make up a circle, by returning to our first word, remember: As we remember God, so for his sake, let us remember one another.

Remembering others in a decorously loving and thankful manner leaves "the society of this life" in its proper place, subservient not to personal "conveniency," but to God. The activity of remembrance, mainly rational at first, has become a sacramental activity of self-creation in a context of charity and humility. Accordingly the preacher has moved from his diffident opening optatives to a species of contingent imperative—"We remember God, so . . . let us remember one another"—to something of compassionate command and benign contingency:

> In my long absence, and far distance from hence, remember me, as I shall do you in the ears of that God, to whom the farthest East, and the farthest West are but as the right and left ear in one of us; we hear with both at once, and he hears in both at once;
>
> . . . .
>
> And so as your ears that stay here, and mine that must be far off, for all that distance shall meet every morning, in looking upon that same Sun, and meet every night, in looking upon that same Moon; so our hearts may meet morning and evening in that God, which sees and hears every where. . . .

Somewhat as the ten thousand pointed toward infinity and the miracle of creation, the ears and eyes now are pointers toward omniscience and omnipresence, domesticating those attributes of God without reducing their majesty and simultaneously associating human ears and eyes with immanence.

Since the pilgrimage is one of shared commitments, men becoming regenerate are spiritually together in the Divine consciousness, in the sunshine of prosperity and grace, as in the moonlight of the

Good News. The society of men, first an unknown, then a perversely aggravating quantity, now is a regenerating one, taken in terms of its opportunities for humility and charity. Hence the preacher has double reason for the assurance of his *shall's* and his *may*. They are self-restrained proposals put to his auditors in their Christian *essentiae,* as regenerating men. He has been able "to make the best of them" his "way to the Creator."

In this advanced context, a reference to sins of the preacher's youth would be substantively redundant and tonally and rhetorically irrelevant. Donne omitted just such an allusion (2. Appen. B. 564–565) in making his revision.

> and may come to him with my prayer that what Paul *soever* plant amongst you, or what Apollos soever water, God himself will give the increase: That if I never meet you again till we have all passed the gate of death yet in the gates of heaven, I may meet you all, and there say to my Saviour and your Saviour, that which he said to his Father and our Father, *Of those whom thou hast given me, have I not lost one.*

The preacher, *knowing* himself more closely than he knows others in the context of human tendencies and delinquencies, judges himself one of the least. But dejection is destructive and mistrustful of the mercy offered to penitence, Donne always insists. So in dedicating himself in his apostolically ordained status to continuing the work of salvation, he can rank himself in a line of Pauls and Apolloses. It is a yet more intense expression of charity that he can envision entering the Presence as the very *essentia* of a minister, divested of self (almost as if he were shedding his personal life for his friends), speaking not his own words but those of Another. Having come so far, he can envision the antitheses of Heaven and the fallen world in a distant perspective, quite close together; he can see old distinctions metamorphosing into truer unities. The gate of death stands very close to the gates of Heaven, rhetorically, chronologically, and symbolically. *My* and *your* become *our*.

That he is setting out cannot be doubted. We naturally keep in mind the facts of John Donne's situation: his ill health, the impending expedition's possible dangers, his expectation of death abroad. But we should not allow our knowledge of Viscount Doncaster's companion to blind us to the behavior of the rhetorical personage, God's lieutenant, whose pulse, like that of Henry King's grieving speaker and like every man's, beats a soft drum, timing a march to the grave. He then speaks of "this Kingdome of peace," of "those Kingdomes," of "sword of Justice," and "necessary defence," a final genuflection to Augustine and his theory of the just war as much as to James I's England. The quotidian particular world is fading out of view as his attention focuses on the profounder reality. Nothing in mundane life now has the substantiality of the figure of Christ, of the sea of His blood, of the *hagia pneuma,* "the spirit of God that. . . . shall blow away all contrary winds of diffidence or distrust in God's mercy."

> where we shall be all Souldiers of one Army, the Lord of Hostes, and Children of one Quire, the God of Harmony and consent. . . .

This harmony begins to reconcile the disparate elements of the intellectual landscape through which the pilgrim moves—the Hebrew heritage (suggested by *Paul* and *Allelujah*), the Greek (by Apollos), the Latin (by *Gloria in excelsis*). The ramifying disputes of princes, *Jews, Christians, Papists, Jesuits, Dominicans, Scholastics, Conformitants, Refractories,* fall to one side of a new division, tend almost to fall out of sight (but never entirely) below a new differentiation, the contrast with the praise-hymning choristers of "the God of Harmony and consent."

> where all Clients shall retain but one Counsellor,
> our Advocate Christ Jesus,
> nor present him any other fee but his own blood,
> and yet every Client have a Judgment on his side,
> not only in a not guilty,
> in the remission of his sins,
> but in a *Venite benedicti,*
> in being called to the participation
> of an immortal Crown of glory. . . .

The army, the choir, and the *procès* have assured us successively that there will be subordination, but without loss of community, variety of part, or individuality. At the same time, the laws of Medes and Persians and the local efforts of law students and counsellors to promote human order (and their own welfare) fall alike into contrast with the unity of absolute justice, tempered by absolute mercy.

As absolute mercy implies absolute charity, the focus of this creative remembrance shifts to the creative atmosphere of Divine love. The preacher's selected aspects of life in the Presence trace a deepeningly poignant comment on life amid the conflicting claims of a fallen world, a comment tending to overrun prosaic schematization, as it modulates through zeal, compassion, humility, and charity:

where there shall be no difference in affection,
nor in mind,
but we shall agree as fully and perfectly in our *Allelujah,*
and *gloria in excelsis,*
As God the Father, Son, and Holy Ghost
agreed in the *faciamus hominem* at first;
where we shall end,
and yet begin but then;
where we shall have continuall rest,
and yet never grow lazie;
where we shall be stronger to resist,
and yet have no enemy;
where we shall live and never die:
where we shall meet and never part.

For all the shadows cast on the fallen world, by these final cadences, they are apt to seem remarkably buoyant. They should not be depressing to members of the modern audience who do not think of themselves as Christian, and certainly not to those who do. He has written a sober, older, and some would say richer "Valediction forbidding Mourning." He tells his charges how they shall be apart and how they may be together. He dramatizes a community of responsibility and commitment and trust, which may be taken to model truly loving community in general.

This expositon of Donne's sermon may be otherwise summarized and amplified by the contrast of a contemporary sermon on the same text by Henry Smith, a Puritan. Though he may not have ever preached the sermon, Smith published it under the title "The Young Man's Taske," in a collection in London, 1622.[12] Four brief excerpts will show several of the most important differences.

Warming up to what eventually becomes rather strident exhortation about "the Young mans Taske," he makes a strange claim:

> Let him remember his Creator in the dayes of his youth, and all his life shall run in a line, the middle like the beginning, and the end like the middle; as the sun setteth against the place where it rose.
>
> (p. 216)

The claim is easily made and appears more flatly and schematically than anything in even the early part of Donne's sermon. The "line" running indiscriminately from one age of man to another contrasts with the "circles" Donne draws in his "Valediction forbidding Mourning" and from beginning to end of his sermon of valediction. Most of all, Smith takes the text and time and living space in a flatly literal or else merely geometrical way that is impoverished in comparison with Donne. For instance, he says with regard to time and materiality:

> Thus like bad borrowers, when our day is past already, we crave a longer, and a longer, and yet a longer, till we be arrested with death: so the prince of creatures dyeth before he considered why he lived: for as no discipline is used where Christs discipline is neglected, so no time is observed, where Gods time is omitted. It is an old saying; Repentance is never too late: but it is a true saying; Repentance is never too soone. . . . For God requiring the first-borne for his offering, and the first-fruits for his service, requireth the first labours of his servants, and (as I may say) the maidenhead of every man.
>
> (p. 220)

The silly metaphor at the end makes no unfit counterpart to the silly assertions in Euphuistic singsong at the beginning. Smith is rarely so bad, but that passage alone could demonstrate, if demonstration were needed, that the raw *material* of this or other Donnean sermons does not assure good sermons. But if Smith has no Donnean sense of the elasticity of time and space, he can report with verve from another front: not the Pisgah-sight of bad existential options, but a close-to-the-ground communiqué from some arena where choice is obscured by mechanical sequence of events:

> Many masters of Israel, Maiors, Aldermen, Sheriffes, Justices, Baylifs, Constables, Gentlemen, know no more what it is to be borne again, then *Nicodemus* which came by night. . . . All their Tearmes are vacations, all their religion promises, and all their promises hypocrisies. In stead of catechizing their children as *Salomon* teacheth them, they catechize them to hunt and hawke, to ride and vaunt, to ruffle and sweare, to game and dance, as they were catechized themselves, lest the child should prove better than his father; and then hee is qualified like a gentleman. Is this to seeke the Kingdome of heaven first, or last,

> or not at all? Woe to the security, woe to the stubbornnesse, woe to the drowziness of this age. The thiefe commeth at midnight, and wee sleepe till the dawning of the day: we let in Satan before we bid him avoide: we sell our birthright, before it come to our hands: wee seeke for oyle, when our lampes should burne: this day passeth like yesterday. and to morrow wee shall spend like this day. So he which should have the first fruites, can get no fruites, because we marre the ground before we sow it.
>
> (pp. 226–227)

The gentlemanly catechizers are a good stroke, fit company for Fielding's lawyer "alive these four thousand years at least." But the fulmination dissipates itself —as Donne's almost never does—on a high abstraction: *this age*. Even the *we* in subsequent parallel clauses has a vague generality of reference crude beside the care of Donne's personal definitions and conjunctions.

Finally and not implausibly, Smith concludes by urging the believer who has remembered his Creator early in life, literally early, to remain faithful to Him late in life.

> The Vine would not leave her grapes, nor the Olive her fatnesse, nor the fig tree her sweetnesses to be a King, but the bramble did; he is not a vine, nor an olive, nor a fig-tree, but a bramble made for the fire, which leaveth his righteousness to become worse. He which is of the Church will say with the Church, *I have washed my feete: how should I defile them again?* Let the dog turne to his vomit, and the swine to their wallowing: but hold thou on thy sacrifice like Abraham, to the evening of thy life, and a full measure shall be measured unto thee, as thou hast measured thy self. Unto which measure without measure, the Lord Jesus bring us. FINIS

That biblical plants *chose* on certain occasions does not relieve vegetable imagery in general of mechanistic implications, which probably is one reason Donne uses it with greater tact. Somewhat similarly, his references to Hell are usually in the middle of a sermon, not at the end where they would tend to register as a crude threat, especially if materialized in terms of fire. But then Smith's *measures* are material, too, for all their vague generality. Righteousness is not a way of life but a thing, grossly material in contrast to Donne's exquisitely humane closing cadences about Heavenly community.

❦ 4 ❦
OF DISTANCE AND DISTRACTION: THE THIRD SERMON ON JOHN 1.8

The fascination of this biblical text can inhere in our sense of light's superiority to darkness, or the Renaissance hierarchy of the senses, or more recent arguments about the preponderant importance of the visual, or apprehensions during any generation that the night is coming wherein no man can work. Donne accepts this text as an invitation to explore any man's possible role as mediator. To be *sent* from some solitary place of solemn commissioning to bear witness in a crowd, to carry out that difficult trust faithfully—these are the main considerations in this sermon.

He begins with a brief but oddly rich introductory paragraph. He makes the conventional approach to the practical and problem-solving disposition of his auditory in the usual brief outline, or in this case a division of the text into two topics, with two subdivisions in part one. We do not hear until the beginning of part two that it contains three subdivisions. And there is the note, not unusual with Donne, of a kind of concern hard to identify specifically as compassion or diffidence or sympathy: "The third time I have . . . I must not say *troubled* you . . . with this Text." This third of three sermons on this text will examine John's "office" and treat the *luminescence* of Christ and the *person* of John as something like antecedent action. Most suggestively, perhaps, the preacher's own office will be to serve and edify and *entertaine* the auditory with something they shall thereafter "by Gods grace" *have.* He has himself mediated in this way on this text at Christmas and in *"Midsummer* . . . upon his *owne* day" and now late in Trinity season.

The next two paragraphs illustrate another variation on a characteristic Donnean expository movement, the removal and return. The preacher stands alone in the pulpit and with an intellectual coolness symbolically similar to that physical situation moves topics about somewhat in the manner of furniture. There are classes or clusters of persons *placed* like objects: Ambrose and his abstract or general reasons, Gentiles who are weak in understanding, others weak in faith, others "perverse" (metaphoric term!) in their "course of life." Nominally Donne has the auditory with him in this act of furnishing the intellectual scene with comfortable sparseness and coolness. He says *we* and *us* because he represents his audience in the fashion of a man among men, because their cognition will have been with him at least this far in the exposition, and as usual because the liturgy in preceding moments of this service has made them a community. The gospel was "amongst us . . . established," he reminds them. But an ambiguity is developed, to be resolved in succeeding paragraphs. Even as the preacher has said *we* "are *asleep*" and has introduced "the *preacher*" as a kind of institutional, general third-person figure not yet identified or commensurate with this speaker himself, he heats up the discourse. Both syntax and imagery assume greater urgency and immediacy with the description of the preacher's office as "shaking the soule, troubling the conscience, and pinching the bowells, by denouncing Gods Judgements."

Accordingly the analytic emphasis of the second paragraph gives way in the third, on behalf of unbelievers. It gives way to a relentless reflexiveness about persons hearing sermons and having audits with God and coming *hither* and being here and being hearers.

That *immediacy* persists in the next two paragraphs on the unconfirmed and the inconstant. He invites any hearer to look at a neighbor: ". . . how often may you surprise . . . a man, whom you thinke directly to look upon such an object, yet if you aske him the quality or colour of it, he will tell you, he saw it not?" He symbolically places himself among the uncertainly confirmed or uncertainly constant ones in the congregation: "We may pore upon *books,* stare upon *preachers,* yet if we reflect nothing . . . we shall still remaine under the increpation . . . of Saint *Paul,* out of *Esay, Seeing yee shall see, and shall not perceive*" or "we put ourselves in such a position and distance from this light, as that we suffer dark thick bodies to interpose." Little by little, of course, exploring these psychological stations of increasing acquaintanceship presses the communicant to "reflect" upon the preacher or a neighbor at a near "distance" and see himself. Thus the literal presence of each communicant to himself, to his fellows, to the preacher and to the gospel challenge in the church has begun to open out into a model of his psychological postures anywhere. Donne's summary at this point characteristically introduces a related idea for further development, the conception of the literal time at the sermon as a symbolic time: ". . . thinke not that thou hast heard witnesses enow of this light, *Sermons enow,* if thou have heard all the points preached upon, which concern thy salvation. But because new *Clouds of Ignorance,* of Incredulitie, of Infirmitie, of *Relapsing* rise every day and call this light in question, and make thee doubt whether thou have it or no, every day, (that is, as often as thou canst) heare more and more witnesses of this light." "This light" is associated with day, though not the same as day, and day is associated (as in the Sermon of Valediction) with choice.

Prayer-Book worship features an ongoing dialogue which has the preacher talking to communicants and himself and each communicant answering and reflecting on the dialogue and his neighbor and himself. This sermon amplifies that process and contends against incredulity, infirmity, and relapsing. Such a dialogue involves continual creation. Accordingly, the "other branch of this first part" develops as an instance from the symbolic time of biblical history scaled to the literal hourglass time of the sermon to serve the symbolic "every day" of each communicant.

That symbolic every day gets further definition in the thronging hurry of paragraph seven, definition in an existential situation of dialogue. The temporally somewhat atomistic testimonies "from *himselfe,* from the *Father,* from the *Angel,* from the *star,* from the *wise men,* from *Simeon,* from *Anna*" would not suffice. "For, beloved, we must have such witnesses as we may consult farther with." And, again characteristically, Donne keeps alive an edgier counterpart argument: that if Christ needs the continuing witness of men, even more must there "be that done by us, which must make men testifie for us."

What follows would probably have been called a digression twenty years ago: paragraphs successively on the whole Bible, on the "severall books of the Bible," on the sense of particular passages, and on Jeromian or other expert interpretation of difficult passages. Yet if right testimony of men must establish Christ with men and just testimony of men must confirm every man's sense of himself, what more thematically relevant and dramatically apposite than the kind of cross section running from general and remote in time or place to particular and near at hand, a cross section of "humane arguments" and the testimony of men? If "every Christian is a state, a common-wealth to *himselfe,* and in him, the Scripture is his law," then the status of that Scripture and continuing arguments about it are good part of both structure and substance in that state.

Donne exploits the constancy of the Scriptures as an arresting contrast to the vicissitudes of interpretation. He does not outline the argument so much as he dramatizes it: he has, on the one hand, Scripture constantly accessible to those who will scrutinize it by "the Analogy of *Faith*" in reverence and charity or perhaps constantly inaccessible because reserved "till the time come for the fulfilling of those Prophecies;" on the other hand he has doubts and distortions, reductions of the Holy Ghost from time-redeemer to "time server," reductions of His people from seekers after light to heretics coveting darkness.

The long, long paragraph on conscience (numbered 12) celebrates by its sympathy the vitality of that "Judge" in everyman's state as that conscience and state have endured enthrallments and liberations. A casual reading may well take it as another variation, slightly stern and civic, on the Christian theme that in love is freedom. Clearly Donne rejects mandatory auricular private confessions; he disdains the unexamined conscience; he seems to suspect the scrupulosity of modish casuistry as a holier-than-thou pose. But the density and resonance of the passage resist attempts to confirm and refine that appraisal.

The passage stands at the heart of the sermon organizationally and midway in the sermon's time-span of delivery. Moreover, the preacher has led us step by step from cool considerations, temporally or spatially or psychologically distant, to more intimate ones. We have considered two other sermonic occasions in the Church calendar, some intellectual and psychological issues somewhat distanced by meteorological imagery, the Bible as a disputed thing in history. But those last have brought us to the crucial, innermost ground of decision, the inner self resolving any particular issue of *faith* or *manners,* of epistemology or ethics we could say. The critical point in his argument is that any such judgment of what is real or what is right to do can be free and valid and reliable—can be truly human—only as "a debated, and deliberate determination," and that implies consciousness. Present-day arguments over collective memories and archetypes or Freudian tropes and syndromes are in a sense obviated by such an assessment of the subconscious as subhuman. Similarly, for abdication of the inner debate, Donne uses the more-

or-less symbolic instance of parochial papacies, as a "butchery of the conscience" and "an eddy . . . a whirlpoole." These images say only a little about the *mechanism* of the inner abdication, less about its *origins,* though they offer a Roman Church fallen off from primitive purity as one particularly threatening current agent. But they say plainly that the fundamental bondage of man relates to solipsism, whether in the "stupefied" conscience that "admits no search" or the conscience bound to human confessor like a binary star. Elsewhere in the sermons, solipsism is developed as an image of hell. Here in a sermon on what witness to Christly light means, the exposition naturally deals with directions that the self can follow unswervingly. The technique defined here for such channeling is Donne's usual one, self-effacingly attributed to "the holy Ghost" who "directs us to that that is nearest us, to . . . testimony of man, that instrumentally, ministerially works . . . beliefe in men."

He reminds the communicants that they "think it no *diminution"* (my italics) of themselves to consult a lawyer or physician. So it would be no more a diminution to consult divines or men of similarly good parts as to Scripture and its application in our "conversation." The extension of the self, then, out of bondage into a liberated, larger life, would seem to consist in breaking the mirrors of solipsism by importing the godly Other. The subject-object split is idolatry of an other which is taken as a hypnotizing image in a darkened room. And any such self-butchery or eddy is forestalled by taking the other as not an image but as a voice, and answering and questioning its origin and direction in a kind of dialectical antiphony whose resolutions are new syntheses. By these means and terms the old notion of love as freedom finds elaborated expression.

According to the usual systole and diastole of the Donnean sermon, the impassioned intimacy of tone and imagery and referential meaning in his paragraph on conscience yield to a somewhat contrasting mode of expression as "we passe to our dogmaticall part, what his testimony was." The transition's abruptness may seem startling in its general civic externality: "Princes which send Ambassadors, use to give them a Commission." But the commission of Ambassador John comes from the pre-Incarnational Isaiah and unites him with this latter-day John and other post-Incarnational ambassadors of devotion: " 'To Prepare the way of the Lord, to make straight his paths'," and the New Testament fulfillment "that therefore 'every valley should be exalted, every mountaine made low.' "

These terms of Isaiah's and Mark's phrasing will give John Donne warrant for free movement over both civic realms and neo-Spenserian landscapes within the self.

In keeping with that exploration, earlier metaphoric references to ways and eddies continue in explications (in paragraphs 15 and 16) of the "crooked channell" and sensory inlets and straightened ways. The counsels of the preacher likewise range analytically in extended space and time: "apply that way, in which he hath gone to others, to thyself;" "Watch the way . . . in which he comes oftnest to thee." In these terms civic and autobiographical history are alike media of self-realization. Complementarily, he comes at the end of this subsection to exhort intensive constant commitment in time and the exhortation gains much of its passion from his technique of iteration: *"embrace* him in those meanes, and *alwayes* bring a *facile,* a *fusil,* a *ductile,* a *tractable* soule, to the offers of his grace, in his ways" (my italics).

The synthesis of these elements of extensiveness and intensiveness "reaches to" a new kind of extension, explored civilly, psychologically, universally in terms of "Let every valley be exalted" (para. 17) and that in turn in the countering debatements of "every mountain must be made low."

Initially, the preacher's bidding so boldly combats abstraction of a fairly simple kind that one might be tempted to hear a proto-Wordsworth scolding early Coleridges for having "no regard to this world, to your bodies, to your fortunes, to your families." But by the time Donne has renewed the biblical, patristic, and Prayer-Book metaphor of the soul's and body's relationship as a *marriage* and has mapped a considerable range of biblical mountains, other orientations begin to emerge. Each mountain in this range is a spiritual height which affords ascent from a fallen world's obscurities and distractions to view some sector of Divine Reality, some feature of a truer life.

Since the medium of these "mountains" is human nature rather than topographical nature, the mountain path, a readily available element in the metaphor, becomes a dramatic reminder of the profundity of human freedom. The mountain path is a straight and narrow two-way street leading, we may suppose, about as fast as any such street to divergent and incompatible worlds, depending on the direction chosen. The valley, in this configuration, is a place of cabined, cribbed confinement: "Sinne hath diminished man shrowdly, and brought him into a narrower compasse. . . ."

To this range of mountains which can afford Pisgah-sights of the ultimate promised land, Donne has counterposed an antithetical range, "our mountainous, and swelling affections, and passions." That paragraph (18) would seem to style the self as an impassable jumble when passions and appetites become their own ends rather than means of approaching the New Jerusalem.

But an alternative kind of ground provides not so much by synthesis as by exclusion another way to a holier city. That way is first defined (para. 19) as a desert "of solitude, and retirednesse" antithetical to "a tumultuary place . . . of distraction." This sounds like the *via negativa* of St. John of the Cross. That "Negative Way" has always had contact with the Anglican liturgy through such texts as Psalm 46 and its injunction to "Be still and know that I am God." In recent years the fine translations John Frederick Nims has made of St. John of the Cross and Eliot's "Ash Wednesday" have made this connection more apparent.

But what more surprisingly claims our attention here is the alacrity with which Donne transforms the notion (not improbably his from St. John) of "emptying" the self. It becomes not quite the self as empty vessel to receive grace, but rather the self as *integrated* being the better able to execute some divine commission: "I am here, not where the affairs of the world scatter me, but *here . . . command what thou wilt.*" As alternative to the self not overfilled but instead centrifugally *scattered,* we are offered a desert sufficiently solitary whenever "God and a good soul are met." Court, army, or fair are deserts *relative* to the nondistractability of the believer's devotion. Oddly, the sermon which endorses consort and concert with duly established authority leads its auditors through warnings against letting authorities eclipse God and brings them to a desert.

The "we" who publish the Lord's commission are ambiguously the ordained priesthood or the priesthood of all believers. Accessibility to "the way of the Lord" endures as the criterion of civic structuring, almost of architectural structuring. Such accessibility rests, we are made to understand, partly on the configurations of man's most private interiority, but extends without break into the most public and verifiable history: "A good life inanimates all." The preacher concurrently exemplifies faithfulness to one's own commission, to the commission which is in his own case to preach repentence and readiness for the sacraments, to his brothers as well as to himself.

This dramatization and self-dramatization increasingly gathers together the substance of the sermon. Donne brings down a series of mountains, beginning implicitly with himself (the illustrious preacher thanks to *reflected* light, he always insists). Other eminences, whether a papal mountain or sectarian hills, are connected by trails of preachers and believers.

To the latter the focus gradually shifts, as earlier when he drew an analogue of the self hindered but not totally without freedom among the badlands of its own passions. Here in the more social vision, preachers and believers *transgress* or go *farther* or *advance ends* or promote peace *all the way*. In all his sermons, but rarely as explicitly as here, Donne defines the great end of all this: an inclusive and dynamic divine order. That order might well in many a personal case make *some* truths irrelevant (truths of the new science, say) and some "mistakings" inconclusive, "but obedience to order is necessary, and all disorder pernicious." Donne's most private thoughts on the status quo remain by definition beyond our cognizance. He might have acknowledged as quickly as we that by itself the remark just quoted can be taken in the spirit of the Elizabethan Homily On Obedience. But Donne's conclusion to the whole paragraph invites no complacency whatever:

> we confesse . . . *our own parts,* our *owne passions,* the purpose of great persons, the purpose of any State, is not Christ; *we preach Christ Jesus, and him crucified* /1 Cor. 1.23/ and whosoever preaches any other Gospell, or any other thing for Gospell, let him be accursed.

The implications of such a stand for, say, kingship took some generations to work out, in ways often bloody. We know, too, that our own society, secularized in some ways which Donne might not have applauded, has blossomed poisonously with neo-Gnostic cults of parts, passions, purposes of state and "other Gospell." Not Milton himself was ever more practical and emphatic in rejecting all false gods than this life-worn figure speaking with the voice of Paul, amid a troubled English generation.[1]

The language of the three final paragraphs suggests the liturgical language of bidding to communion and administration of it. Certainly the office of Holy Communion would provide an altogether fitting close, recapitulation, and comment to this sermon. But in any case these three paragraphs of themselves provide a final movement from social extension to personal intimacy to intensified community, and this on a climactic level of reassurance.

He marshals data of Old Testament prophecy and New Testament witness. He defines the Christ currently present to memory, understanding, and will by exclusion of non-Christs (and a Christ equivalently present to sight, touch, taste, and smell, if the bread and wine of eucharist are present, as I think). This self-collectedness in the presence of Christ refines the emptying of selfishness called for earlier. This proceeds by a transition from *there* in biblical history to "*here* he . . . cries to you . . . *Here* he bleeds in the *Sacrament,* here he takes away the sinnes of the world. . . ." (first italics mine).

That in turn seems to generate vigorous and searchingly personal reassurances to any auditor diffident about his own acceptibility. And the reassurances make palatable a final injunction which might otherwise fall on defensive ears, the injunction to complement the words, doings, and sufferings of the self as known to the self by being a witness for Christ "to one another," the perennial return from the desert of self to society.

It can be seen in retrospect that the preacher has exemplified the dramatic witnessing he enjoins on his auditors by enacting at large a Christly pronouncement he quotes in this climactic paragraph:

> the Spirit of the Lord is upon me, to preach the Gospell to the poore, to heale the broken hearted, to preach deliverance to the captives, and the acceptable yeare of the Lord.
>
> (Luke 4.18)

This text has been taken to prescribe any proper Christian preaching as well as to summarize the church's conventional functions of prophecy, social work, and teaching (kerygma, koinonia, diakonia).

This sermon's action and imagery seem to define "the acceptable yeare of the Lord" as a figure of existential order, a pattern of "days" commensurate with a segment of the good journey, commensurate with an act of witnessing.

Another partial and general definition of the Donnean action emerges from the contrast with a sermon preached and published in 1609 by Antony Wotton "of Alhallowes Barking Church, London." From his *Sermons upon a part of the first Chapter of the Gospell of St. John* this is number six, John 1, verses six through eight. It runs from page 252 to page 304. I quote from pages 301 and 302, where he finally turns to the eighth verse, and I then quote the closing lines of the sermon. Briefer quotation, without these page references, might leave a reader with an impression that the man is laconic.

In the meane while, let us proceede with that, which followes. *Hee was not the light, but was sent to beare witnes of the light* /Ver. 8/ Where the Evangelist describes the office of *John,* by denying that, which is contrarie unto it, and repeating the substance of it. He denies him to be the light, he tels us againe, that *hee was sent to beare witnesse of light.* This later point hath been expounded, and inlarged. If the time, which is almost past, will give mee leave, perhappes a word or two shall be added. In the handling of the former, I will speak shortly to these two points; that *John* is not the light: why our Evangelist addes this caution, in the describing of his minestry. For I hold it altogether needlesse, to show that *John* as hee, of whom this *being the light* is denyed. There is no man, but upon the reading of the text, discerns as much. Neither is it greatly needful, to inquire in what sense John is denied to bee the light, seeing our Saviour professeth of him, that *Hee was a burning & shining Candle* /John 5. 35/. A Candle may be without light; & a burning Candle may give very little light, that it shal be very hardly perceived, but a shining candle is light indeed. It may bee overwhelmed under a bushell, and so hid, not from shining, but from being seene to shine; but *John* spred his light round about, that as it followes in the same place, *the Jewes (for a season) would have rejoyced in it/* Cyrillus in Joa. lib. 1. cap./ But this doubt is easily satisfied. *John* was a *light:* but not *the light.* What is a Candle to the Sunne? But the difference was greater, and of another kinde. The light shineth of it selfe by nature, as the Sunne dooth. A light is like the Moone, which shineth indeede, but by a borrowed brightnesse received from the Sunne, which is the fountaine, from whence all that light streames. So was the Baptists light. so were the Apostles the light of the worlde/ Mat. 5.14/. Not shining of themselves, but delivering abroade, as a glasse doth from the Sunne by reflection, the light, which Christ the true light powred upon, and into them, for the inlightning of others. John showed [the Jews] Christ, but in his beginning oneley, before he had made any proofs of his divine power, in teaching; and working miracles. We have the knowledge of all those wonders, and the distinct understanding of the nature, and course of his mediatorship. We have beene made acquainted with his sufferings of our sin, his triumphant resurrection, and glorious ascension. And shal we neglect so many, and so worthy points? Nay rather, let us stirre up our-

> selves both to learne, and beleeve, that wee may attaine to the ende of our faith, the salvation of our soules, through our Lord & Savior Jesus Christ: to whome with & c.

The man is not laconic, he is dull. He tells what he will do and then does little. Donne, even when he is telling in the division of a text what he will do, does more. I don't believe Donne ever sounds as avuncular as Wotton does here, scoring easy points and pushing over straw men. Wotton on the light of John and apostles and Christ is in a sense dully literal, even when he is most figurative. There is not the action of Donne's passion for integration and conviction of "concinnity" in the universe. Moreover, Wotton's candle and sun negate an opportunity Donne seizes through images of sun and illuminated mountain tops, the opportunity to insist on twin mysteries of grace and free will. Finally the rationalistic and privatistic emphasis of Wotton's conclusion contrasts strangely with Donne's existential and communal commitment.

❦ 5 ❦

STEWARD TO THE AILING CITY

Psalm 63.7 Because thou hast been my helpe, therefore in the shadow of thy wings will I rejoice. The second of my Prebend Sermons upon my five Psalmes.
Preached at St. Pauls, January 29. 1625 [1626].

Sometimes Donne opens abruptly by dividing the text for his sermon into the subsections he intends. Other times, and just as conventionally, he first places the text in its context of chapter or psalm or even whole book of the Bible; or he opens with some arresting intellectual proposal. Here he begin by placing the text secondarily in its biblical context, but primarily in the life-worlds of the auditors congregated before him. His metaphors accumulate to argue the relevance and dynamism of the text: psalms are not so much objects to be examined as active allies for the internal self, whether as special food for special need (manna) or as ointment or balm or "Searcloth." He quickly canvasses individual and universal categories in asserting that David "fortels what *I,* what *any* shall *doe,* and *suffer,* and *say"* (my italics). Accordingly, in a roughly logical corollary, some of those psalms are voices addressing imperial commands to all or any *affections, occasions,* or *necessities.* The substantiation, for this psalm and this verse in particular, of so large a claim engages the priest and congregation in twenty-seven following paragraphs that search tensely and soberly how far and how near, how much and no more—the verse's whole scheme of implied relationships. The final suggestion of the verse's momentousness divides the text "here the whole compasse of Time, Past, Present, and Future." But as usual even Donne's paragraph of division offers something more provocative than mere outline. Human vicissitude, he remarks, contrasts with the "Circle" of Divine perfection and constancy.

But the vicissitudinary world becomes the substance of the next two-fifths of the sermon, paragraphs three through twelve. David's "Wilderness of Judah" becomes not a deserted arena wherein interior options are exposed by debate between a humanly superlative figure and a diabolical one, as in *Paradise Regain'd,* nor the interior place of submission to God, as in the third sermon on John 1.8. Rather, David's wilderness is made to manifest itself for Donne's city congregation as the overcrowded *civitas terrena* of western man. The section might easily have unfolded as mere lecture, as an impersonal catalogue of afflictions along with theological argument for the primacy of the spiritual over the "temporall." In two ways, though, he has made it dynamic literary expression: he has personalized it with question and exclamation and has animated it with the evaluative activity of two virtually mythic metaphors.

First, he explicates that world which is too much with us as *weight.* At least three things are noteworthy as his crowd and press of biblical references develop the conventional notion. First, he "counterpoises" the image of crushing weight with one of his characteristic antithetical images. In paragraphs four and seven the particular heavenly consolation invoked is the mystery of "Pondus Gloriae, an *exceeding* weight of eternall glory" (my italics).

Secondly, he invokes all the significance he can for the metaphor of bad heaviness. For one, he commits himself to it, as akin in the antithetical way just described to the "blessed Metaphore, that the Holy Ghost" gave Paul (of *Pondus Gloriae*) *rather* than to David's metaphor and Solomon's, of *"vanity* and *levity."* For another, he marshals one of his phalanxes of synonyms, which imply that a *meaning* persists throughout changes in lexical, and by association social, substance: "all is waight, and burden, and heavinesse, and oppression."

Finally, in the phrase placed climactically at the end of paragraph four, he concludes that without that "counterpoise" of future glory, "we should all sinke *into nothing*" (my italics). The assertion is not physically illogical; it is a paradox akin to that Miltonic touchstone "down to bottomless perdition." The legions of Milton's Lucifer reached a situation in which they can indefinitely fall further. That physical and logical paradox may be resolved psychologically. So it seems to be here, as a sinking into that existential nothing so often signalled in literature—and apparently in psychological case-histories—by imagery of engulfment, drowning, entombment, implosion. The most persuasive and illuminating modern account I know of existential pressure felt as crushing occurs in R. D. Laing's *The Divided Self*.[1] The state of oppression then, where "sin is certainly, sensibly a burden" and where many faint "under a sand-hill of crosses," must be evaded. To present open roads out will be the action of this sermon's second half.

The composition of that second half relates to the third remarkable fact of this four-paragraph exposition of weightiness in worldly afflictions: Donne's restraint and vigorous sense of proportion. He could go on longer. He had. Beyond doubt one of the few explorations of engulfment more extensive and impressive than Laing's was Donne's own, succinctly in this sermon and throughout three sermons at Lincoln's Inn some years earlier on the text, "For mine iniquities are gone over my head, as a heavy burden, they are too heavy for mee."[2]

Here somewhat more than there—and who can appraise the contribution of the text at hand relative to the intervening years of experience and meditation?—Donne presents more emphatically the phases of distress and the structure of liberation and emphasizes them as elements of action.

> One may find oneself enlivened and the sense of one's own being enhanced by the other, or one may experience the other as deadening and impoverishing.
> The main manoeuvre used to preserve identity under pressure from the dread of engulfment is isolation. Thus, instead of the polarities of separateness and relatedness based on individual autonomy, there is the antithesis between complete loss of being by absorption into the other (engulfment) and complete aloneness (isolation). To turn oneself into a stone becomes a way of not being turned into a stone by someone else.[3]

Whatever the claims to adequacy or exactness of Laing's formulation as represented above, it elegantly glosses the order of Donne's presentation. Slings, arrows, and other more or less overwhelming impingements of outrageous fortune[4] have been defined as the usual situation. What Donne calls spiritual afflictions he defines in effect as destructive or sterile articulations by the self of its own posture towards reality. It is precisely in imagery of stoniness that Donne argues "these spirituall afflictions" may "grow out of temporall . . . out of worldly calamities" (para. 7). Pliny's lithosperm, and the visions of Ezekiel and St. John, all attest more or less directly to the self's defensive ability to petrify itself (para. 8).

By the switch of inner-to-outer familiar to many English readers in Spenser, the stony heart optional for any man becomes ambiguously a "precipice" off which he may fall or part of a landscape of stony hearts which make for the pilgrim "slippery sliding into that bottomlesse depth" (para. 10). But in setting up this measure of convertibility between inner and outer in paragraphs nine through eleven, he not only shifts attention somewhat further along the train of consequences but also moves the sermon toward livelier alternative courses of action. Addressing God in the voice of everyman, he speaks against the self being overcome irremediably; then he turns in paragraph ten back to the particular case of David. David's situation he defines essentially as alienation, remediable alienation; our partly similar case is more eligible than David's for the reassurance of Christ's words that we are worth more than many sparrows.

The preacher thereupon dramatizes "Mustering of our forces" in himself, "whose whole service lyes in the Church," and for his congregation who as the company of faithful people equally "dwell in the Church." By a power of wit he translates the inner-outer equation into a series of turns on the polarity of private and public. He contends (para. 12) that life is "people's work," is liturgy around altars and charitable relationship among the company of faithful people in the church militant at large.

These dramatic and existential considerations mute somewhat the terms of what some contemporaries might have presented as plain argument, a more exclusively logical exposition: "spiritual afflictions, as previously defined, materialize internally a failure of community; the church is the chief materialization of community; therefore the church ought least of all things to be denied (by legal-ecclesiastical procedure) to any eligible (a) other person or (b) self." But here familiar shards of society and fragmentations of the self are posed against joyous fulfillment in community, in an existential and dynamic continuum. Once again Laing can helpfully delineate the negative extreme, toward which Donne merely glances:

> The more one attempts to preserve one's autonomy and identity by nullifying the specific human individuality of the other,

> the more it is felt to be necessary to continue to do so, because with each denial of the other person's ontological status, one's own ontological security is decreased.[5]

The positive end may well stand in Donne's own words that conclude paragraph twelve:

> Onely he enjoyes that blessing, the want whereof *David* deplores, that is here intirely, and is glad he is here, and glad to finde this kinde of service here, that he does, and wishes no other.

Part two, in paragraphs thirteen through sixteen, similarly makes a rational argument of fundamental significance and warns against psychological consequences with sympathetic urgency. The argument depends on a thesis which is taken as an assumption. That in itself suggests something of Donne's healthy ego-strength, because the assumption is one that goes something like this: the observable order and regularity of the universe is fundamental, not happenstance; it holds generally, whatever the local disorders. On this foundation, he can work during nearly the whole extent of part two in terms of the following argument: (1) human life, lived experience, moves in every situation *from* some past *toward* some related future; (2) anyone's past-from-which is at any time significantly ambiguous and contingent and a matter of choice; (3) the past of God's doings with us is the most valid and reliable and verifiable past anyone can choose; (4) that past must furthermore be the most predictable as to subsequent parts ("He being perfect will do as He has done"). As a familiar and practical matter, this disparages "enthusiastic" Puritan prayer and worship, of course.

But to the *thens* and *therefores* of such argument we may well notice a humane antiphony of words difficult to schematize so neatly. One item is the pervasive suggestion that the good life must be furnished with history or equally that history rightly selected and remembered endows life with milk and honey. A squad of Fathers making of biblical words "which we read otherwise" a way to devotion suggest semidramatically the diversity of some distinct life-worthy paths and some perverse and idiosyncratic paths leading to isolation. Among the latter the "extemporall" in faith or preaching or whatever appears to be a fragmentation of the self in *time*. That in time, like any fragmentation of the self away from communal relationship in *space,* has no particular stopping place this side of atomistic, solipsistic isolation. Even if an enthusiastic outpouring transported preacher and hearer alike, the trip for each would be private, in Donne's view. Presumably we can attribute to contention against such privatism those touches in paragraphs seventeen and eighteen like the celebration of the past tense's status in Hebrew and the attention to existential nearness for his congregation as marked by phrases like "nothing more availably" and "surest way, and the nearest way." True community is not easily come by. Titillating pseudocommunity is.

The remarkable composite argument from the kind of perception attendant on faith (in combination with probability), the argument that "God will do as He has done, to my benefit," leads to the transition of insisting on the concurrence of will, faith, and grace. That insistence, faintly dramatized by the emphatic declarations of the nineteenth paragraph, leads to a carefully limited showing forth in the twentieth of the preacher as a new David. He does the things he quotes and describes David as doing, and he "proceed[s] to *Davids* confidence for the future."

Those proceedings establish for his presumed auditor the present reality of a possible future and the problematical character of any future. Part three, the last eight paragraphs, also involves casting the Christian everyman of the congregation as something of an antitype of David. Concurrently Donne reinforces the congregational situation, the sense of presence, with a remarkable sequence of variations on the imagery of viewing, of bodily movement, and of living space.

Something of a conventional generic literary motif materializes in the first paragraph (para. 22) of the section on *umbra alarum.* The passage on a God who needs no defensive arms really defines Him as the hero who subsumes and transcends epic norms. At the same time, He seems to be presented there and subsequently as One who raises men to epic status, even to potentially epic stature. It is hard to know how far to press this matter, because his references to "Poets" and "their great Heroes" will mean much less to some in a given congregation than to others. Yet a journey and voyage to both hemispheres of heaven, with frequent opportunities to *decline* or *rest* or *ascend* or *stray* or be cast down before entering the hemisphere of glory, surely such a journey needs no more than the touches of epic naming and quintessential combat here to claim epic status.

Perhaps not every reader will allow that claim. Similarly, some will prefer not to consider as epic (or folk-tale or romance) ordeals the admissions of being *touched* or *pinched* or *wounded* (para. 23), the threat of being *shaked, disinherited, excommunicate, devested, annihilated* (para. 24) as opposed by pledges "to preserve me in my being" (para. 24), "never . . . to forsake my selfe" (para. 20). In any case, the preacher does describe a journey in which the self can *persist* despite constriction and impairment, can enjoy the good press of God's imprinting, and in moving from river to ocean and intermitted joys to eternal joy enter precisely a larger and more abundant life.

The preacher is everyman among the priesthood of all believers by the end of paragraph twenty-five; and we should recall he had insisted earlier in the sermon that humanity and self-hood and joy oppose excommunication. Thus his invitation to joy, which dramatizes some hopeful and charitable attitudes naturally part of a joyous life-world, appropriately includes notice of everyman's local and familiar adversity, the city's malaise (para. 27). At the start of the very passage labelled *Gaudium,* we are reminded of two afflictions in the city. The disease he calls new, and which always seems to be called new, he characterizes with enough syntactic awkwardness and hesitancy in diction to suggest was really unfamiliar.[6] His target seems to be that carelessness that reduces groups to uncommunal crowds, the Lucretian closeness of mere independent atoms hurrying and knocking in space. Consistent with this and with all he has said before is the complication he has observed and which he describes so generally and forthrightly that he appears to assume his auditors know it well: the melancholy of the excommunicated and therefore attenuated self. Disease imagery in Renaissance literature as in medieval and patristic writings frequently defined sin, we recall, and this sermon followed within three years Donne's serious illness of 1623 and his allegorical treatment of it in *Devotions upon Emergent Occasions.*

So the preacher must be taken as a representative "I," associated by a right memory of God and by faith in God, with a company of similarly minded communicants, in a journey of discovery which need not leave the physical clutter of afflicted city to range comfortably in the existential hemisphere of joy and even cross to the hemisphere of glory. He gives in his final lines some attention to the gorgeously free and agile speed of that crossing. The speed he describes recalls a similar description in *The Second Anniversary.*

But here he insists quite differently that heaven is with us for those who have the life-world to know it, and he sees the religious death as furnished with *faces,* faces of *Death, Devil,* and *God* (represented, perhaps, in any "one of the least of these persons"), in contrast to the cosmological matters that crowd his lines on Elizabeth Drury. His own surety and health would seem to have gained enough to collaborate in a prescription for his city.

❦ 6 ❦

TASK-FORCES: THE SERMON ON FISHERS OF MEN, AND CONCLUSION

i. Exposition

Donne preached his basic sermon on Matthew 4. 18–20 at the Hague on 19 December 1619, and evidently it was well received then.[1] We may ask how his "short notes" for that might have compared with "these two" sermons into which "in my sicknesses at Abrey-hatche in Essex, 1630 . . . I digested them." We are unlikely ever to know exactly, since no foul papers have come to light. But some few points may be noted. To a noble congregation on a state occasion, he preached from "short notes." And naturally so: an illustrious preacher of his generation would no more have been tied to a text fully written out than would a bardic singer of tales have required a written text. The ordinary Renaissance training in copiousness, a preacher's practice in fluency, and Donne's habitual meditation in advance on his sermon material—all that suggests something like a list of paragraph topics. Certainly such a list would have sufficed. But there are fifty-seven paragraphs in what we have, a generously large number for a pair of his usual sermons, although some of the fifty-seven are very short transition paragraphs. Similarly, the double-sermon's length approximates that of each of his two longest surviving single sermons, and both of those were marathon performances for open air occasions that were almost as much civic as ecclesiastical.[2]

With the Sermon of Valediction, we saw labor of the file and of very local rearticulations; the revision was only seven-eighths the length of the original. Here, where he has had eleven years to rethink the gospel incident and sermon, he ends by expressing himself in half again as much, perhaps even twice, the length. The thought which Donne has here "digested"—that is to say both remembered and converted—into a sermon on work would seem to be thought and experience from the greater part of his preaching career.

For all the doctrinal orthodoxy and rhetorical conventionality of Donne's sermon on "fishers of men," his achievement here bears definition by comparison as well as it does elsewhere. And it seems fairly likely that he preached—or at least "digested"—on this text after acquaintance with a sermon on it by Latimer.

Probably the finest preacher in sixteenth-century England, Master Hugh Latimer (1485–1555), Bishop of Worcester, was burned at the stake with Archbishop Cranmer during the Marian persecution. His *27 Sermons* "Preached . . . before King Edward" were published in 1562 and several subsequent editions. They include one preached on St. Andrew's day, 1552, on fishers of men.

Latimer wrote some of the most pithily energetic and concrete English prose of his century. The movement of his sermon may fairly be gauged from his very numerous and substantial marginal hangers and his final paragraph, which follow:

The Apostles fished after men.
Why Christ called fishers to be Apostles.
The office of prelates
The doings of prelates
The reward of negligent prelates
The miraculous doing of our Saviour Christ.
John the Evangelist was a disciple of John Baptist.
The apostles were divers times called.
Marke this ye that chuse officers [exhortation to pray].
A good wish and profitable.
A lamentable thing [of buying and selling offices].
Ambitious men should not live in a common wealth.
Officers should be sought.
An officer must hate covetousnesse.
Jethro would not allow our officers.
Clergymen must not flatter for benefices.
Mark this ye that buy patronages.
The Apostles come not before they were called.
John Baptist sued for no benefice.
God looketh upon low things.
God saw Joseph in the prison.

Moses was a shepherd.
Saule sought not to be made king.
Marke the end.
David was a shepheard.
Jonas was found out.
God will punish the ambitious.
An horrible ensampel [Cozath, Dathan, Abyram].
The hurt that cometh of ambition.
Ambition lost the Rhodes.
God defendeth them that he calleth to office.
The cause why Paul was so often delivered.
Hunting and hauking is not the chiefe poynt of great mens calling.
The chief point of a serving mans office.
One special vocation must be followed.
A note for the spirituality.
Abraham did follow his calling.
The man that hath but a general may not follow his example that had a special vocation.
No man may preach except he be called.
The right holy dayes worke.
All Adams children must labor.
Labour is the ordinary meane whereby we live.
God will encrease our labor.
Two things to be noted in St. Paules workes.
A preacher may speak by hearsay.
Rub a galled horse and he will kick.
A terrible saying to all princes.
A great number is meant when we speak by the universal.
Restitution of Two Sorts.
Some think that their increase cometh of the devil.
The devil is not worth a goosefeather.
Many set their soules behind the door.
He that hath much must accompt for much.

Now to make an end, I desire you let us consider our generall vocation, that is to say, let us labour, every one in that estate wherein God hath set him, and as for the increase, let us looke for it at Gods hands, and let us be content with that which God will send us: for he knoweth what is best for us, if we have *Victum et Vestitutum, Meate,* and *drinke, and clothes,* let us be content withall, for we cannot tell how soone death

> will come, and make an end of all together. For happy shall he be, whom the Lord when he commeth, shall finde well occupied in his vocation.
>
> And if we have speciall vocations, let us set aside the generall, and apply the special points of our vocation, rather than the accidents, and let us labor in our calling, and yet not think to get anything by it, but rather trust in God, and seeke the increase at his hands: let us looke for his benediction, then it shall goe well with us, but above all things beware of falsehood, for with falsehood we serve the devill. But as I told you before, I feare me the Devill hath a great number of servants in *England*.
>
> Almighty God therefore give us grace so to live here in this world, and to apply our businesse in such wise, that hee may be glorified amongst us: so that we may finally come to that felicitie which he hath prepared for us.

. . . .

Latimer has a sure touch with concrete detail, yet the world's plenty tends to seem more a miscellaneous collection in his sermons than in Donne's best. Latimer seems to feel an obligation to conceptual reality; at least the topics in his marginalia quoted above owe relatively less to the experience of the biblical text, relatively more to conceptual considerations, than is the case with Donne. To exaggerate a little for clarity, there is with Latimer a thinness, almost a gap, between the concrete and the conceptual. Donne's discernment of implications and lived experience and social historical presence leaves no such gap. Donne's provocative *paragraph* on the Gospel as a net may be compared with Latimer's bare *phrase* "The Gospel is the Net."

Both the shape of things to come and an instance of the abuses that fueled the mid-seventeenth-century revolt against pulpit eloquence can be found in "Fishers of Men, A Sermon Preached at Mercers Chapell on Mid-Lent Sunday the 26 of March 1609," by John Rawlinson, who dedicated the slender little quarto to Sir John Egerton (in whose family Donne was a warmly received friend). It is neither necessary nor profitable to speculate whether Donne had read it. Rawlinson mentions at the outset "having elsewhere commenced the handling of this Scripture." "The words," he goes on, "may be quartered into foure parts." But only after they have been hanged and drawn; we are far from the "branches"

Donne typically saw in his texts or saw growing or running out of them as significance and implication. Rawlinson divides and subdivides differently: first, "The calling" which was *"Externall"* (Christ's voice) "and *Internall"* (Christ's grace); second, *"The Caller* . . . Affectus" and "Effectus;" third, the *"parties* called . . . *Number:* They were Two . . . *Consanguinitie* . . . *Condition* or *Qualitie: poor, ignoble ignorant"* and upon these three divisions, Rawlinson tells us "I spent my *former discourse"* (p. 3).

So this (apparently) second sermon on the text will deal with the fourth "part" or division: *"Function* or *Office* . . . Their *Dignity* . . . *Diligence* . . . *Discretion."* When Rawlinson further says he will speak "First of the *Metaphor;* And then of the *Matter,"* we may sniff an almost Manichaean dualism. So arrogant a suggestion by example and precept that reason and mechanics are real, whereas metaphor is flummery, seems to prefigure the Royal Society almost typologically.

But Rawlinson then does something that Archbishop Tillotson or other Anglicans of Bishop Sprat's generation would not have done. He lavishes the next thirteen pages of this forty-page sermon on the metaphor. Why? Presumably because "it is the usuall practise of our Savior to speake of spirituall things as if they were corporall, *Ut ad excellentiam divinarum rerum per corporalia hominis attolat* (saith *St. Hilary/* liber 6 de *Trinitate/*) that so he may raise our groveling and earth-creeping affections to an higher levill, and weane them from corporall and temporall things to the consideration of things spirituall" (pp. 4–5). Moreover "our Saviour in this place [doth] teach us to alienate our thoughts from earth to heaven, from things temporall to things spirituall . . ." (p. 6). Finally "Not a *Metaphor* thorowout the whole volume of Gods booke that more willingly dilates and spreads it self into an allegory" (p. 7). Donne occasionally translated Church Fathers as expansively as Rawlinson did here, but his additions are not in the vein of "groveling and earth-creeping," nor does the tenor of his sermon on this fisher text run in that vein, even when he says a man is a ship necessarily running in the world-sea, but by means of sails that are above it. His metaphor, in short, is less dualistic.

How dualistic Rawlinson can be appears in the atomistic, arbitrary discord of his *"semblances* wherein *men* accord with *fish."* He remarks "I will name but some few of many." (p. 9):

1. multiplication
2. "fish . . . *swimme* thrice . . . in *water,* in vinegar, and in wine"
3. "without the pure *element of Gods word* (the *water of life*) . . . we die."
4. "As *brine* keepes fish from *putrefaction:* so the . . . *brinish waters of repentance* . . ." (p. 10)
5. onely . . . *cleane* . . . which have finnes and scales . . . the coat-armour of patience, and the finnes of joy and cheerfulnesse to spring up to God-ward.
6. "as *ichthues ichthuophagi,* so *anthropoi anthropophagi*
7. "billow beaten, yet faint not"
8. "So must we when wee are *wounded with sin,* repair to our Saviour Christ *the true tench,* the *Physitian* . . ." (p. 12)

"And yet this *difference* I find between them. . . . For fishes are taken that they may be devoured by the *jawes of men;* but men are taken that they may bee *delivered* from the *jawes of hell*" (p. 13). A generation after Euphuism and two generations before the flourishing of the neoclassic couplet, Rawlinson acknowledges the inevitable discontinuity of a metaphor in an antithesis more syntactic than substantial, but stout enough to dissipate many of his own previous metaphoric terms.

His paragraph on the *net* even better illustrates his difficulty, compared with Donne, in appreciating how life-issues change or persist in differing life-worlds:

"5. *Rete, verbum.* The Net is not any materiall Net, like that in *Suidas,* which one cast over another while they were in single combate together, and when he had ensnared him in his net, slew him. Nor such a phantastical, imagery Net, as is Purgatory; which *Szegedin* cals *Amplissimum rete ad capiendas animas* /Spec. Pont. Rom.[3]/ A most spacious Net to intangle souls: Nor such a *bloody spiritual Net* as the Prophet *Micah* speakes of chapter 7 *All lie in wait for blood: every man hunteth his brother with a net.* But it is *Sagena,* that sweepe net, which our Saviour brought downe from heaven, even the *glorious Gospel* of Jesus Christ, catching whole nations at a drought: that *Net,* wherein men, who are plunged in the darksome holes of ignorance, and muddy cares of this world, are

> drag'd and drawen out to the light of truth, and love of supernall things.
> Or (as St. Bernard hath it) *Nassa ecclesia est:* The weele is the Church of God: *Quae licet hominis certis legibus et ceremonies retineat;*[4] which though it keepe men under certaine lawes and ceremonies, yet it so keeps them under, that it also secures them from being swallowed up of other mighty sea-monsters, such as are heretikes and schismatikes." (pp. 15–16).

Rawlinson is no dolt. His marshalling of observations in a suspenseful definition by contrast resembles tactics Donne uses. But (no reproach to St. Bernard), Rawlinson has little to offer in lively positive definition. He turns soon after to what he evidently regards as the *real* work of the sermon: "And so I come from the *Metaphor,* to the *Matter* it selfe, including (as I told you) three remarkable points" (i.e. preachers' dignity, diligence, discretion).

Rawlinson turns with relief to literal points for his final twenty-two pages. When he has not been merely casual, there has all along been and continues to be a literal base and rudimentary logical articulation to his metaphor. Things which are equal to the same thing are equal to each other: if ministers and heavens "declare the glory of God" (Psalms 19.1), then ministers "are *Coeli*" (p. 23); if repentance betokened by salt tears preserves men and brine preserves fish, then tears are brine and men are fish-like (p. 10). But of course the psalmist's heavens *declare* in a more dramatic, less propositional way than the Rawlinsonian preacher, and "brine" is a destructively ambiguous term, and the senses in which men might be said to "swimme thrice . . . in *water,* in *vinegar,* and in *wine*" (p. 10) are too existential to submit to the control of Rawlinson's resources. Recognition that metaphor can materialize for discourse the urgencies shaping life for speaker and auditor, urgencies otherwise elusive to their mutual understanding—that recognition transcends his rudimentary sense of metaphor as fancily packaged identities or playful naming.

Rawlinson, though a less engaging prose speaker and sermonizer than Latimer, represents no mere straw man but rather the substantial norm from which Donne stood out. An instance to substantiate that not-altogether-provable thesis may be briefly cited. Jerome Phillips published "The Fisherman. A sermon preached at a Synode held in Southwell in Nottinghamshire" (London, 1623). The title page lists eight thematic topics developed in the sermon "with other points of moment." None are terms of the Scriptural text, though the sermon does develop in two parts, "1. Calling; Follow me" and "2. Qualifying; I will make you Fishers of men." A moment late in the sermon, and its final moment, show three noteworthy features of Phillip's discourse: first, the bondage to the physical referents of words, second, an accompanying penchant for unanchored abstraction, and third, a related feeling that if metaphor should be avoided, then perhaps the wholeness of lived experience can be communicated in such mechanical arrangements as euphuistic syntax:

> The second qualitie in Fisher-men, is Painfulness. Fishing is a painful trade. As *Peters* Trade of fishing for fishes of the Sea was painfull, in the sweate of his browes: so this his trade in fishing for men is as painfull, in the seate of his braine. . . And the hungrie flock of Christs fold expect their food from them that are their Pastors: they must therefor with all diligence give them their meate in due season. [p. 18]

> Wel, the Calling is a good Calling, good enough for any man, and too good for any man that thinks it not goode enough. . . . It is the sinne of this age to make their Priests meaner than the meanest of what tribe soever he be: if he be a Priest once, that is an attainder of his blood, (in the estimation of some;) and if he be nobly descended, an abatement of his Gentry; so is this high Calling dishonoured and disesteemed. God grant this sinne be not layed to the charge of this generation. [pp. 25–26]

Not a contemptible speaker, Phillips, yet it would be hard to find in any paragraph of Donne's sermons such a clot of reified abstractions as *age, tribe,* and *generation*. Donne nearly always has a consistency, agility, and congeniality in managing first and third person relationships which Phillips misses through weakness of talent or strength of self-interest. And Donne on fishers as in his many other good sermons not only responds to the successive invitations and opportunities of his text, but orchestrates them to a conclusion emphatic or even climactic in terms of lived experience. Phillips's anticlimax can fairly be said to foreshadow generations of sermons that would abhor "mere enthusiasm" and end with no more (and no less) resonant a move than placing the final term of an argument.

If earlier structural analyses have been faithful, and if the early assumption of a certain homogeneity throughout the sermons was realistic, then this fourth structural analysis ought to require less elaboration. Concentrating here on somewhat general features of Donnean procedure ought to help bring this study to a logical and thematic conclusion.

This text is unusually long for Donne, though a bit less so for his contemporaries. It is mildly unusual, too, for him, in being a complete incident with beginning, middle, and end. His opening paragraph places the text not in Matthew's gospel, nor even in a New Testament context, so much as in a general thematic context. Everyman's work, it seems, can at its best be Christly work on behalf of the good community, in opposition to that community's adversaries. Regular attention to a variety of adversaries gives drama and pungency to these two sermons (as to the previous three) which we are likely to miss in his sermons which heed adversaries less.

Although he rewrites to compose a sermon which perhaps he never did preach, he carefully writes not an essay but a sermon which *might* be preached. He divides the text into considerations for "now" and a second portion "impertinent . . . to open . . . because . . . this day we shall not come to that part." But by the end of that paragraph of division, he has challenged his audience, more explicitly than in his opening paragraph, to undertake recognition of two life-worlds. There is a realistic non-Christian one: "they were fishers . . . they might not have usurped upon anothers Calling." And there is a new creation in Christ: "they did somewhat more . . . Their preferment." The preacher will speak of his own vocation as priest, but equally of every believer's vocation to the Church Militant, as the paragraphs below will try to show in the simplest general account I can frame of the sermon's observable features.

His sermon finds in his chosen text the challenge "how can my work be other than self-seeking?" and "how can I labor toward the reign of love?" He works to make his explication of the biblical example an unselfish proceeding. In these terms, the otherwise puzzling elements of paragraph three make sense. There is antecedent action noted because Christ like any man creates not from nothing but from raw material. A substantial parenthesis: "that other Disciple . . . because he is not noted to have brought any others but himselfe, is not named in the Gospel." This seems a particularized and dramatic presentation of Donne's conviction that self-realization involves work, and work with other persons, and somehow work with God. The auditors of this sermon are not "well enough preached unto" unless they respond by orienting themselves to such a three-party relationship. That may be a humbling consideration to the preacher. The mysterious ways of who shall be first, who last in the divine order, are another. "Our adversaries of the Romane heresie," who "racke every passage of Scripture," exemplify labor of self-seeking, self-promotion, uncharitable in giving the humble Andrew less than his due.

With no little agility, Donne modulates from arguable interpretation to straightforwardly acceptable description of the Sea of Galilee. The *variety* of his concreteness here might well strike us first: nomenclature and geography, a local parallel, fish stories, gazetteer and résumé of great events on the lake. Yet his economy and restraint invite reflection. He has made the lake a potential symbol, fused for detonation forty-eight paragraphs later.

But now scene-setting yields to something like modern expositions of a dramatist's rationale of characterization. The next two paragraphs (4 and 5), on the unschooled fishermen, have a complementary relationship to one another. The first is philosophically oriented and might speak particularly to any auditor who was feeling inadequate, not least because it controverts the belittling argument of Julian the Apostate. But the concluding remark in the present tense—"Christ excuses no mans insufficiency"—works against complacency, urges on the auditor that tense alertness pervasive in the Donnean sermon and its world. The following historical paragraph, with its analogues, reinforces this example of Donne's usual insistence that relationship outranks mere substance: these insufficient men, "weake instruments," are given fulfillment beyond expectation through power of the divine relationship and in the cause of gathering "all Nations."

The paragraph following (para. 7) might be merely a mechanical carrying of the foregoing into New Testament terms except for two things near the end. One is the less-than-mechanical ink-horn syntax of the sentence with double-decker parentheses, perhaps evidence of "Lucubrations and night-watchings" beyond the normal wakefulness of Donne's editorial eye. The other is the modest disclaimer to the effect that some penitents' restoration of "ill-gotten goods" might preach "a better Sermon than ever I shall." As with most such formulae, there is an open end; Donne believes a good sermon *can* provoke penitence.

With another remarkable shift, the argumentative structure and somewhat polemical tone of the paragraphs on "why He chose fishermen as instruments" (para. 5–7) modulate in eight and nine. He stops arguing and *meditates* on the fitness of these men. Donne regarded sermons as public exercises, meditation as a private exercise. Here he models in the pulpit the application of a Christly doing to the self. The analogies of "cunning Lapidary" and "cunning Statuary," the vividness of "rough-cast with foame, and mud," the reiteration of "his owne bowels, his owne eternall bowells" all reinforce the *presence* of the mystery of a man's being called to surpass himself. The "our" is the plural of the priesthood, of this preacher moving his attention from the pole of fitness for God to fitness "to our present auditory . . . to them." He talks almost as if to himself. But by the end of the following paragraph (para. 9), he has applied himself to the listeners' situation and that situation to himself. The final "we" who consider "fitnesse . . . in the Minister" are the whole household of faith.

Accordingly, he can resume dialogue in the ensuing three paragraphs. The withdrawal and return brings him to his congregation reminding ("as wee told you") and explaining and enjoining with either joint particularity ("we must make account to meet stormes") or broad generality ("A man must not leave . . . A man must not be").

Another feature of his remarks on the *for* of "for they were fishers" is the celebratory aspect. He celebrates internal consistency, men holding to what they know and care for and can do, and external responsibilty, unsentimental charity in continuing action. The opposite of that, which he delineates as the enemy, appears naturally as a kind of novice dabbling, cheeky angling by "men that are not fishers in that Sea." The point should not be degraded from its status in this sermon and Donne's sermons in general to the level of an Elizabethan commonplace. Donne says not "a man should know his place and stick to it," but rather "a man must serve his calling, must be faithful to the mode of life in which he is himself." The celebratory note recurs throughout the two paragraphs on "two together" (para. 13 and 14).

But gradually celebration thins out to a kind of earnest appraisal in the paragraphs on "two brothers, not kindred to him" (15 and

16). In retrospect, this section of half a dozen paragraphs or so in the middle of this first sermon has some qualities of a survey, almost a walking survey of partnerships available in daily city living.

Celebration recurs, but somewhat indirectly, as Donne praises the alacrity of the brothers. It appears in the thoughts of an alternative kind of man, wont "to consider that it was well for him that he was got out of *John Baptists* schoole, and company, before that storme, the displeasure of the state fell upon him . . . ." The colloquial vigor there, the knowing role-call of mental faculties of "contemplation . . . example . . . apprehension . . . sense," the urbanity in noting "a false Method in this art of love" all these turns of diction continue to accommodate Galilean shore to London strand.

Julian the Apostate reappears (para. 18), associated with a species of sophist rhetoric which defines by contrast the rhetoric of Jesus. Apparently too it defines Donne's rhetoric in this double sermon by a contrast similar in degree although quite different in kind. Jesus said little; Donne and the sophist must say much. Instead of the "way of Rhetorique" that aggressively imposes disorientation in order to supersede all "former apprehensions and opinions," Jesus—we are given to understand—spoke and acted with irreducible simplicity: the simple command. Donne acts and speaks with great complexity through the fifty-seven paragraphs of this double sermon, but with great gentleness, building with exquisite deliberation, modifying rather than superseding, extending rather than setting aside, orienting rather than disorienting. Not at all surprisingly then, this paragraph concludes with a historic doctrine about orientation, a quite Augustinian definition of the *true* "art of love." as to "love God for himselfe, and other things for his sake."

Very much in the vein of Augustine's *Enchiridion, on Faith, Hope, and Love* or his *On Christian Teaching,* Donne continues in the paragraphs on Andrew and Peter leaving their nets (19 to 22). These remarks come at us as quiet, communal pondering on the practical limits and practical implementing of so imperial an invitation, whether beside Galilee or Thames. *We* and *thou* and *thy* and *our* mix easily. "They" are visible, as usual, but here as idolaters some distance down the shore, no urgent threat. Or at least not to treat them as threatening implies here the preacher's trust that he and his congregation are together in respectful apprehension of Andrew and Peter's faithful example.

At this point, the conclusion of his first sermon of the pair,

Donne issues another invitation of his own: "But still consider." And the monarch of wit thereupon goes a progress of some agility. There is the implication stated in his gloss, the implication invisible save to the sympathetically imaginative eye, that they "did but leave their nets, they did not burne them." There is the vigorous sequential extension of vehicle and tenor, from nets as nets, to nets as *"things* which might entangle them" (my italics), to nets as uncharitable attitudes, as secular power, as, finally, any misdirected attention. Along the way we may be overtaken by an odd sense of *déjà vue:* "But (which is strange) you fish for a net, even that which you get proves a net to you, and hinders you in the following . . . ." "For thou thy selfe art thine own bait; / That fish that is not catch'd thereby, /Alas, is wiser farre then I/."[5] The trope of angler angled was not original with Donne, perhaps not even the variation of net-wielder netted. But no foil to this late "Baite" could be any more apposite than Donne's own early one. The ultracitified speaker of the early poem, who plays fast and loose with the pastoral convention in getting to his final note of worldly-wise wryness, differs obviously from the multiple elements of sober Christian Donnean self-hood poured so extensively into this sermon. Yet there remains an element of thematic similarity: the seducer seduced and assenting to the new state of affairs. In the poem the tone and elegant imagery (contrasted with rude country imagery) make the action a parody-tragedy in miniature;[6] here in the sermon we have a side glance at real tragic action rather than a parody of it. In any case, his paradox of lightness being most weighed down resolves itself in the by now familiar primacy of relationship over mere substance. Right relationships are the life-world of men serving God among men. That life-world is canvassed as to similarity between rich man and poor man, as to wholeness between interior and exterior, and as to continuity between now and later. In a ringing conclusion to this sermon and a thematic overture to the following one, the polarities in each instance are reconciled by the enormous command: to follow.

He begins the new sermon with a subtle combination of division by grammatical parsing and division into thematic topics. And it notes for subsequent use some of the main reference points in the new creation. The preacher elevated in the pulpit is in the trying dramatic position of calling his congregation to follow him on a tour-by-attention that will explore through paragraph after paragraph the features of humility and pride and leadership and subordination, all variously worthy and unworthy.

Interestingly, he begins the body of the sermon with one of his uncommon treatments of a biblical phrase as if it were statuary, beginning in this case with the first word as the head. He claims a kinetic effect: the word *sequere* makes on us "an impression of Humility." But even though the paragraph comes full circle to reiteration of *sequere*'s initial position as a sign and warning of pride's primary status, the assumptions and implications of the discourse have quickly burgeoned beyond the mechanical and iconic. Even *sequere's* "Impression" on us depends here on its referential meaning (rather than, for example, its softness of utterance). There is the conscious choice not to "enlarge" our "consideration" by putting "our meditations upon the whole body" of pride. More than that, we are offered a definition of pride with a different focus and different terms: "there is not so direct, and Diametrall a contrariety between the nature of any sinne and God, as between him and pride. . . ." Here touch and sculpture give way to a different kind of analogy, seemingly a line, perhaps the diameter of a circle. Clearly existential relationship has become the focus of attention again, in alternation with a metaphor emphasizing physical presence.

The first of the six paragraphs on pride's contrary relationship to God, the first of a dozen anatomizing pride in the human life-world, promises to *"exalt* that consideration." What kind of celebration this shall be, we may be slow to decide. Certainly we can be caught up by a kind of exuberant vitality in calling the roll of Old Testament metaphors for God's mood or nature. All these miniature incarnations naturally indict by implication the fallen city: "for the better applying of God to the understanding of man, the Holy Ghost impute[s] to God these excesses, and defects of man. . . ."[7]

Having put the essential concepts in order with the distinction (in paragraph four) between pride and legitimate self-respect, Donne can set them in motion and attend to the process of action, which he does in paragraph five and generally on to the end of the sermon. He must, because "There is no standing at a stay." Note that changefulness, so apt to be threatening or baneful in, say, *The Faerie Queene,* more typically here and throughout Donne's sermons figures as hopeful and endlessly diverse opportunity. Time-as-change forms the matrix, almost the medium, of regeneration. Hence the relation, in affection and in time, of parent to child must include leaving to them not only "possessions and maintenance" but [by training and example?] vocation and calling."

The Donne whose deepest impulse moves him to unify and synthesize and harmonize turns to exclude and distinguish in paragraph eight. But even this extraordinary move gets prepared for in ways that differentiate it from the totally uncharitable (and therefore disorientingly antisocial) rhetoric which he earlier stigmatized by association with Julian the Apostate. He has distinguished (para. 7) between a poor man of good conscience and a rich man who has good conscience but inhabits a somewhat constricted life-world, a "sphere and latitude of envy." The distinction resembles as to degree others between ways of community and adversive ways. But the point is a radical one that he insists on when he removes the translators' word *suffer* from Psalm 101.5: "'Him that hath a high looke, and a proud heart, I will not . . . suffer him.'" The "Originall . . . abrupt breaking off on Gods part, from the proud man . . . froward departing from him" argues that he and God "can meet in nothing." Reconciliation's works, it appears, have a boundary with radically alien and irreconcilable worlds. The dynamics of someone escaping, by grace or recognition or penitence, into a new world of community engage a good deal of Donne's attention elsewhere. Here he attends to what men can do in "the worke of God" and what not, the omnipresent and crucial distinction between *civitas terrena* and *civitas dei*.

He indicates by a series of living tableaux (para. 9, 10, 11) that no circumstance has any natural immunity to pride, that no place offers sanctuary. The first of these redefines the issue "how shall I work?" in primeval and structural terms. The new-made angels were not to seek themselves places, as fallen men must do, although some would lose the place they had. The issue of work to do, and how to do it unselfishly, appears for them congruent with the whole panorama of what to do and how to look back and look forward and how to keep relating. Their work, the preacher notes succinctly, was to look back with "praise . . . for their Creation" and look ahead with prayer for "Sustentation . . . Confirmation" and "farther relation . . . to God."

Between the solipsistic "radicall pride" of the angels who fell through "proud reflecting upon themselves" and the existential roll call at the end of paragraph eleven stands a *range* of abuses.

There are misuses of comparative position for self-aggrandizement and destruction instead of the glory of God (para. 10). And more particularly, we are reminded that company and demeanor and clothing and office and means—all instruments for maintaining right relationship with God and man—all can be turned to prideful reflection. We are reminded that such abuse can take place in church or nunnery as well as elsewhere, and our awareness is thereby awakened to the Donnean conviction that no space is inherently or irresistibly sacred space.

In paragraphs nine through fourten we are presented not only the three-paragraph range from primeval status to existential relationship, but with and beyond that another sequence: a thorough logical anatomizing yields in fourteen a colloquy. He has posited the "follow" of Christ's command as opposed to arrogant venturing, which can define such following by contrast, and which the congregation apparently should be further trained to recognize. The anatomizing which will warn and train them begins (para. 9 and 10) with the ontological "earliness" of prideful venturing, antedating the world of human time and relativity. In Paradise, the initial world of human time and growth, the bad crop grew early and omnipresently (para. 11). The *constancy* of that growth, whether a bad catch (like unpalatable fish) or a malign plant (branching evergreen in para. 13), provokes witty glances at the range from affectation in ranking cradles to the surrealism of Jacob seizing Esau's heel in the womb (para. 12) and the absurdity of larger-than-life disbursements for tombs.

The colloquy on the earliness and lateness of "this infectious disease of precedency" (para 14) appropriately opens positively into Christ's challenge to follow *me*.

Here again, a movement several paragraphs long explores the present meaning of the scriptural element in a very diverse and extensive survey of the human situation. Like the movement beginning with the ontological pride of the about-to-be-fallen angels and that pride's contrast to their unfallen status, this movement begins at a kind of cerebrally conceptualistic and absolute extreme: a definition of Christ's command to follow, by comparison with the paradoxically similar command to "get thee behind me." Yet the addition of Incarnational setting helps make the first paragraph in this movement more existential than the first in the earlier movement, even though each is the most philosophical in its series. Here Christ speaks; we are given not just a recurring concept but a unique voice. He speaks the "get thee behind me" once to a fallen angel, yes, but once to the historical individual Peter. In an age and society like Donne's, ignorance or indifference to Christ's claims was scarcely relevant. So not following Christ would logically (if colloquially) be "a going behind Christ," either scheming self-preoccupation or casuistical scheming. But such a "going" is paradoxically and "fearfull[y]"—as in nightmare—a "station, a . . . retrogradation." Yet Peter's case is made to reassure the listener alive to the fearfulness: the averted face of Christ may turn back; the self-averted eye may melt with saving tears. (Donne seems among other things here to have baptized the convention of tragic-illumination-concurrent-with-physical-darkness.) The whole exposition also works to suggest antitheses of similar life-worlds but opposite bearings. The same path can lead the wayfaring Christian up or down, depending on which way he faces; it can in either case undergo a radical metamorphosis—self-induced or Christ-induced.

The glance downgrade surveys the crude grotesquerie of religious orders jockeying for position from sheer pride in their own humility (para. 17). What remained when "the eighteenth of Queene *Elizabeths* Injunctions" cleared the ground of that *particular* unseemliness will presumably in somewhat different ways for each auditor give point to the preacher's following earnest appraisal of how better to follow Christ.

The question of doctrinal following, Donne characteristically and quickly resolves in historical terms, the advice to walk where "his Church hath walked from the beginning" (para. 17). However, such terms, meaningful to the individual but relatively general and static, quickly yield to five vigorous paragraphs (para. 18–22) on the grounds of individual moral choice, where the sweaty struggle sweeps continually.

The proposal of "foure stages, foure resting . . . places in this progresse" inaugurates four paragraphs whose formal purpose is more or less ostensibly that of definition, needful because it can clarify options often masked or muddled in practical life. The first (para. 19) fits that pattern, distinguishing real crosses to be taken up from ordinary afflictions. Yet the sick and much-tried Donne invests the distinction with stunning intensity.

Here we are in a world of sober attitude distant from the limbo of vanity where Nullanos jostled Ignorantes. The first burst of imagery develops the by now familiar idea of withdrawal and self-regard, develops it in language like our everyday locutions *frozen* and *confirmed,* but even more like the imagery frequent in schizophrenics' dreams and self-descriptions:[8] "The afflictions of the wicked exasperate them, enrage them, stone and pave them, obdurate and petrifie them . . . ." The exact converse comes as the typological fulfillment of "Elisha . . . raising the *Shunamits* dead child," the intimate but outgoing and self-dedicating approach to the crucified Christ and adoption by touch of his words, to witness: "my afflictions are truly a crosse . . . doe truly crucifie me, and souple me, and mellow me, and knead me, and roll me out, to a conformity with Christ."

From this crucial center of intimacy and immediacy, false crosses can be recognized and appraised by their *distance,* "remote . . . out of my way" (para. 20, 21).

Typologically the crucified Christ fulfills the figure of Elisha breathing new life into the dead child. Typology is a way in which calendar history is superseded by kinships in meaning. In exploring the present meaning of Christ's commission to be fishers of men (para. 23–32), he begins with painstaking and anxious attention to the literal truth and particular uniqueness of history. In effect he accused latter-day bishops of Rome of a casually symbolic, insufficiently historical apprehension of biblical narrative. He argues that apostolic "jurisdiction over all the world," like prophetic authority to castigate society, like a marshal's authority "in time of rebellion and other necessities"—all are "Extraordinary" offices. But the argument moves in a direction which mutes the force of its logical point. Instead of his frequent tactic of beginning with the familiar thing and placing the unfamiliar thing just beyond it (hence, not so *very* unfamiliar), here he reverses the order. His argument and initial topic is the uniqueness of the twelve apostles' office; his first analogy in support of this point is the prophetic office, arguably unique but historically more diffuse, and the second analogy—martial law—although admittedly special is scarcely uncommon. Although it is difficult to appraise the final effect of such a curiously downhill argument, there can be no doubt of Donne's preoccupaion with the comic. For him, comedy inheres in ordinary offices of ministers, justices, and judges, and men in general surviving, no doubt with some laughter; it contrasts not so much with tragedy as with Puritan (or any other) apocalypticism.

After defining apostleship by contrast with later claims, he defines in tones of earnest care the metaphoric title "fishers of men" and its present relevance by analogy. He places it on a specturum of iconicity, between God's title for Himself, which has a unique validity and reliability, and all the evanescent "Titles and Honours" of fallen men. There is, the argument goes, a graceful validity and reliability in these men's title of fishers. They are constantly fishers, past and future, but not so rigidly so as to deny "a Renovation, though not an Innovation." Nor are they so uniquely and literally fishers that their instruments and catch cannot change, nor so restrictively fishers of men that they cannot afford legitimate analogy: "Christ puts no man out of his way . . . to goe to heaven."

The witty and impressive exposition of the world as a sea, and the gathering of those "respects and assimilations" into a critical implication for action (para. 29–31), almost epitomize early seventeenth-century employment of metaphor. With classical and Renaissance copiousness and baroque wit he introduces some nine similarities between properties or transitions or boundaries or inhabitants or traverse of sea and world. To *varying* degees each world-sea metaphoric kinship does double work, thanks to the conventional equation "every man is a world." "The world is like a sea because of x. I am a little world in myself. Therefore I partake of the x-ness of the sea." Not incidentally he insists on elements of mystery in social and individual life and on faith in any means of accommodating to those mysteries. Not incidentally the list's climax (para. 30–31) is application, the mode for continuing response to the reality of what has gone before. And as all priests are fishers of men and any believer's good action may preach as good a sermon as the priest's and any man's work may offer roadway to heaven, we are left with the implication that any man's course of working life may afford good fishing.

In diction, syntax, and tone the remarks on the world as a sea have moved as a composite discovery, tabulation, and exhortation to the preacher's self and to all the "we" in the congregation. The smaller-scale exposition of Gospel as net, on the other hand, displays preacher as anxious teacher, addressing himself to "thou . . . thou . . . thou," because he can without vanity or presumptuous judgment claim that better than they do he already knows the net (para. 32). That address to "thy soule" and "thy consolation" emphasizes by contrast the fellow feeling of the following paragraph, which begins with the conglomerate "we" of fallen man, modulates to the "I" of any lonely believer—"My first end in serving God, must not be my selfe, but he and his glory"—and comes to resolution in the "we" of the company of faithful people: "If we doe it, (though not because we doe it) we shall have eternall life." Other sermons by Donne, at such a point with regard to their texts and with such a conclusive phrase, might have ended there with a formula of praise for the Trinity.

Remarkably this does not. He begins the final paragraph forcefully with an assured appraisal of Andrew and Peter's action: "Therefore did [they] . . . faithfully beleeve." But the crisp retrospect quickly shifts and gains resonance with a sense of "us" who may be all priests, perhaps all believers as workers and priests, but emphatically includes himself. Donne was aging and ill when he revised this sermon, a vocation-buoyed man long given to quoting as he does here *"St Pauls Vae si non* . . . (Woe be unto us if we doe not preach)." We might almost expect the closing vision he gives of fish and fisher and Master of the Sea and of the Marriage Feast; he has prepared us for that. But would we expect his penultimate note? "That is truly the comfort that refreshes us in all our Lucubrations, and night-studies, through the corse of our lives, that that God that sets us to Sea, will prosper our voyage . . . will open the hearts of those Congregations to us, and blesse our labours to them." Is that ring of a valediction any less engaging than those in his "Sermon of Valediction" or in his celebrated valedictory poems?

ii. General Conclusion

It invites us at any rate to a summary review of his lucubrations and imaginative labors, as a valedictory to this study. How restricted are this study's claims for itself? How large are its claims for the Sermons?

Some of the effort in Chapter Two sought to identify a certain limited form of relativism as not only present in the sermons but usual there. Donne's form of conditional relativism seems to me altogether sensible. This conviction frames and affects the study's contention that the sermon is a greatly significant literary mode of articulating experience (a generic sector). Likewise, the conviction of relativism frames the study's attempt to deal with the sermons in a largely comprehensive way and to identify a bevy of their typical features. Insofar as that framing relativism is sensible, to that extent this study's view of the sermons may take its place with ones already articulated and others yet to appear, without dogmatic opposition.

That fact—multiple readings of the sermons, current and to come, many of them supplementary to one another—should not, however, obscure the organization this reading does imply in the Donne canon. The *Essays in Divinity* have long been recognized as prefatory studies and warming-up exercises for the sermons. The *Devotions upon Emergent Occasions* may readily be seen as nonliturgical (and frequently brilliant) analogues to the sermons. In their relatively private mode of man-to-self or man-to-God or man-to-individual reader (rather than listening congregation) the organizing structure of Prayer-Book worship yields to the recurring private devotional pattern of meditation, expostulation, and prayer. The recurrence of that pattern depends, in turn, not on the larger cycle of the Christian Year but instead on authorial will and natural history (the course of the illness, specifically). Since the Christian Year represents both history, and willed interpretation and response to history, as Donne's sermons within its context are biblical text and response, the *Devotions* are analogous to the sermons in these ways too.

A case could be made—if anyone cared to bother—that *Biathanatos* and *Pseudo-Martyr* and *Ignatius his Conclave* and the *Catalogus Librorum* are all tangent to particular elements of the sermons. Those earlier prose pieces give us argument in varieties that are expository, ironic, scornful, or mocking. They marshall dialectical adversaries and redoubts of names, as the sermons frequently do, but all this without the context of liturgical order and liturgical significance, nor of congregational-ministerial personal relationship.

Those unifying, organizing, and mellowing features of the sermons are also absent from the *Songs and Sonets,* of course; hence this reading of the sermons reveals particularly how the *Songs and Sonets* can usefully be seen as a brilliant inventory of existential options. Of course some of those options—those life-worlds, really—are mutually exclusive. Naturally some of them materialize around quite particular events like sunrises or leave-takings while others materialize amid general considerations of celestial mechanics or shadows or conflicting ideologies. We need not conclude as some annoyed undergraduates do that the *Songs and Sonets* are held together by a lowest human denominator of cynicism and nothing else. Nor need we worry much about which life-world was most present or attractive or real to Donne as he wrote each poem, which religion of love or of self or sense or flux or ratiocination.

Those poems as a group recognize not just two but many "divided and distinguished worlds" as simultaneously possible human habitations. Each such life-world is not just a superficial matter of differing attitude, but a kind of self-fulfilling prophecy. Such recognition would seem to be a necessary preliminary to the life-world exploration and options of the sermons. We can be thankful for their range and the stunning conclusiveness of their definitions. We may be less thankful for the adapter in the *Elegies,* even for the citizen or friend in the *Verse Letters,* but at least equally thankful for the whole man so busy-minded and busy-hearted in the *Divine Poems.*

But in the sermons he does a better thing than all the worthies did, those diverse self-definers who speak in the poems. In the sermons he does a very considerable job for himself, for his ecclesiastically defined auditory, and for his modern reading audience who are all in some measure noncommunicants (at least in that no one of us is a seventeenth-century Anglican).

For himself, he connects. By voice from deep within, to a perceived congregation, he connects his inner self to a social world "out there." His ranges of tones and of subject matter and of roles (now apart, now complimentary, now integrated) all enrich and reinforce that connection. Such multiple responses to the multiple challenges of a biblical text, eventuating in loving concord and trust, exercise and orient and in some always challengeable measure *move* the coherent self.

To his auditors he has by these activities at the same time issued an urgent invitation: to do likewise, or at least to go a course analogously faithful and integrated, while recognizing their radical freedom and its radical risks. To noncommunicants, as to himself and his initial auditors, he presents the figure of existential man moving anew in each sermon toward a total commitment to noble trust and ideals which reach beyond himself and cannot be fully grasped. As such, he is not the alarming "True Believer," still less any sinister Gnostic *duce*, but rather a person whose strength is as the strength of one plus One.

Part III
Sermon Texts

A SERMON OF VALEDICTION AT MY GOING INTO GERMANY, AT LINCOLNS-INNE, APRIL 18. 1619[1]

"Remember now thy Creator in the dayes of thy youth."
Ecclesiastes **12.1.**

1. Wee may consider two great virtues, one for the society of this life. Thankfulness, and the other for attaining the next life, Repentance; as the two pretious Mettles, Silver and Gold: Of Silver (of the virtue of thankfulness) there are whole Mines, books written by Philosophers, and a man may grow rich in that mettle, in that virtue, by digging in that Mine, in the Precepts of moral men; of this Gold (this virtue of Repentance) there is no Mine in the Earth; in the book of Philosophers, no doctrine of Repentance; this Gold is for the most part in the washes; this Repentance in matters of tribulation; but God directs thee to it in this Text, before thou come to those waters of Tribulation, remember now thy Creator before those evill dayes come, and then thou wilt repent the not remembring him till now. */Divisio/* Here then the holy-Ghost takes the neerest way to bring a man to God, by awakening his memory; for, for the understanding, that requires long and cleer instruction; and the will requires an instructed understanding before, and is in it self the blindest and boldest faculty; but if the memory doe but fasten upon any of those things which God hath done for us, it is the neerest way to him. Remember therefore, and remember now, though the Memory be placed in the hindermost part of the brain, defer not thou thy remembring to the hindermost part of thy life, but doe that now *in die,* in the day, whil'st thou hast light, now *in diebus,* in the days, whilst God presents thee many lights, many means; and in *diebus juventutis,* in the days of thy youth, of strength, whilst thou art able to doe that which thou purposest to thy self; And as the word imports, *Bechurotheica,*[2] *in diebus Elec-*

tionum tuarum, in the dayes of thy choice, whilst thou art able to make thy choyce, whilst the Grace of God shines so brightly upon thee, as that thou maist choose the way, and so powerfully upon thee, as that thou maist walke in that way. Now, *in this day,* and *in these dayes* Remember first the Creator, That all these things which thou laborest for, and delightest in, were created, made of nothing; and therefore thy memory looks not far enough back, if it stick only upon the Creature, and reach not to the Creator, Remember the Creator, and remember thy Creator; and in that, first that he made thee, and then what he made thee; He made thee of nothing, but of that nothing he hath made thee such a thing as cannot return to nothing, but must remain for ever; whether happy or miserable, that depends upon thy *Remembring thy Creator now in the dayes of thy youth.*

2. /*Memento*/ First *remember;* which word is often used in the Scripture for considering and taking care: for, God remembred *Noah*/Genesis 8.1/and every beast with him in the Ark; as the word which is contrary to that, forgetting, is also for the affection contrary to it, it is neglecting, *Can a woman forget her child, and not have compassion on the son of her womb?* /Esay 49.15/ But here we take not remembring so largly, but restrain it to the exercise of that one faculty, the memory; for it is *Stomachus animae.* The memory, sayes St. *Bernard,* is the stomach of the soul, it receives and digests, and turns into good blood, all the benefits formerly exhibited to us in particular, and exhibited to the whole Church of God: present that which belongs to the understanding, to that faculty, and the understanding is not presently setled in it; present any of the prophecies made in the captivity, and a Jews understanding takes them for deliverances from *Babylon,* and a Christians understanding takes them for deliverances from sin and death, by the Messias Christ Jesus; present any of the prophecies of the Revelation concerning Antichrist, and a Papist will understand it of a single, and momentane, and transitory man, that must last but three yeer and a half; and a Protestant may understand it of a succession of men, that have lasted so 1000. yeers already: present but the name of Bishop or of elder, out of the Acts of the Apostle[s], or their Epistles, and other men will take it for a name of equality, and parity, and we for a name and office of distinction in the Hierarchy of Gods Church. Thus it is in the understanding[,] that's often perplexed; consider the other faculty, the will of man, by those bitternesses which have passed between the Jesuits and the Domini-

cans, (amongst other things belonging to the will) whether the same proportion of grace, offered to men alike disposed, must necessarily work alike upon both their wills? And amongst persons neerer to us, whether that proportion of grace, which doth convert a man, might not have been resisted by perversness of his will? By all these difficulties we may see, how untractable, and untameable a faculty the wil of man is. But come not with matter of law, but matter of fact, *Let God make his wonderful works to be had in remembrance:*/Psalm 111.4/ present the history of Gods protection of his children, from the beginning, in the ark, in both captivities, in infinite dangers; present this to the memory, and howsoever the understanding be beclouded, or the will perverted, yet both Jew and Christian, Papist and Protestant, are affected with a thankfull acknowledgment of his former mercies and benefits, this issue of that faculty of their memory is alike in them all: And therefore God in giving the law, works upon no other faculty but this, *I am the Lord thy God which brought thee out of the land of Egypt;* /Exodus 20/ He only presents to their memory what he had done for them. And so in delivering the Gospel in one principal seal thereof, the sacrament of his body, he recommended it only to their memory, *Do this in remembrance of me.* This is the faculty that God desires to work upon; And therefore if thine understanding cannot reconcile differences in all Churches, if thy will cannot submit it self to the ordinances of thine own Church, go to thine own memory; for as St. *Bernard* calls that the stomach of the soul, we may be bold to call it the Gallery of the soul, hang'd with so many, and so lively pictures of the goodness and mercies of thy God to thee, as that every one of them shall be a catachism to thee, to instruct thee in all thy duties to him for those mercies: And as a well made, and well plac'd picture, looks alwayes upon him that looks upon it; so shall thy God look upon thee, whose memory is thus contemplating him, and shine upon thine understanding, and rectifie thy will too. If thy memory cannot comprehend his mercy at large shewed to his whole church, (as it is almost an incomprehensible thing, that in so few yeers he made us of the Reformation, equall even in number to our adversaries of the Roman Church,) If thy memory have not held that picture of our general deliverance from the Navy; (if that mercy be written in the water and in the sands, where it was perform'd, and not in thy heart) if thou remember not our deliverance from that artificiall Hell, the Vault, (in which, though his instruments failed of their plot, they did not blow us up; yet the Devil goes forward with his plot, if ever he can blow out; if he can get that deliverance to be forgotten.) If these be too large pictures for thy gallery, for thy memory, yet every man hath a pocket picture about him, a manuall, a bosome book, and if he will turn over but one leaf, and remember what God hath done for him even since yesterday, he shall find even by that little branch a navigable river, to sail into that great and endless Sea of Gods mercies towards him, from the beginning of his being.

3. /*Nunc*/ Do but remember, but remember now: Of his own wil begat he us with the word of truth, that we should be as the first fruits of his creatures: That as we consecrate all his creatures to him, in a sober, and religious use of them, so as the first fruits of all, we should principally consecrate our selves to his service betimes. Now there were three payments of first fruits appointed by God to the Jews: The first was, *Primitiae Spicarum,* of their Ears of Corn, and this was early about *Easter;* The second was *Primitiae panum,* of Loaves of Bread, after their corn was converted to that use; and this, though it were not so soon, yet it was early too, about *Whitsontide;* The third was *Primitiae frugum,* of all their Fruits and Revenues; but this was very late in Autumn, at the fall of the leaf, in the end of the yeer. The two first of these, which were offered early, were offered partly to God, and partly to Man, to the Priest; but in the last, which came late, God had no part: He had his part in the corn, and in the loaves, but none in the latter fruits. Offer thy self to God; first, as *Primitias spicarum,* (whether thou glean in the world, or bind up whole sheaves, whether thy increase be by little and little, or apace;) And offer thy self, as *primitias panum,* (when thou hast kneaded up riches, and honor, and favour in a setled and established fortune) offer at thy *Easter,* whensoever thou hast any resurrection, any sense of raising thy soul from the shadow of death; offer at thy Pentecost, when the holy Ghost visits thee, and descends upon thee in a fiery tongue, and melts thy bowels by the power of his word; for if thou defer thy offering til thy fal, til thy winter, til thy death, howsoever they may be thy first fruits, because they be the first that ever thou gavest, yet they are such, as are not acceptable to God; God hath no portion in them, if they be not offered til then; offer thy self now; for that's an easie request; yea offer to thy self now, that's more easie; *Viximus mundo; vivamus reliquum nobis ipsis;* /Basil/ Thus long we have served the world; let us serve our selves the rest of our time, that is, the best part of our selves, our souls. *Expectas ut febris*

te vocet ad poenitentiam? /Idem/ Hadst thou rather a sickness should bring thee to God, than a sermon? hadst thou rather be beholden to a Physitian for thy salvation, than to a Preacher? thy business is to remember; stay not for thy last sickness, which may be a Lethargy in which thou mayest forget thine own name, and his that gave thee the name of a Christian, Christ Jesus himself: thy business is to remember, and thy time is now; stay not till that Angel come which shall say and swear, that time shall be no more. /Apocalypse 10.6/

4. /*In Die*/ Remember then, and remember now; *In Die* in the day; The Lord will hear us *In die qua invocaverimus,* in the day that we shall call upon him/Psalm 19.10/; and *in quacunque die,* in what day soever we call, and *in quacunque die velociter exaudiet,* as soon as we call in any day. But all this is *Opus diei*/Psalm 138.3/, a work for the day; for in the night, in our last night, those thoughts that fall upon us, they are rather dreams/Psalm 102.2/, then true remembrings; we do rather dream that we repent, then repent indeed, upon our death-bed. To him that travails by night a bush seems a tree, and a tree seems a man, and a man a spirit; nothing hath the true shape to him; to him that repents by night, on his death-bed, neither his own sins, nor the mercies of God have their true proportion. Fool, saies Christ, this night they will fetch away thy soul; but he neither tels him, who they be that shall fetch it, nor whether they shall carry it; he hath no light but lightnings; a sodain flash of horror first, and then he goes into fire without light. *Numquid Deus nobis ignem paravit? non, sed Diabolo, et Angelis*/Chrysostom/: did God ordain hell fire for us? no, but for the Devil, and his Angels. And yet we that are vessels so broken, as that there is not a sheard left, to fetch water at the pit, /Esa.30/ that is, no means in our selves, to derive one drop of Christs blood upon us, nor to wring out one tear of true repentence from us, have plung'd our selves into this everlasting, and this dark fire, which was not prepared for us: A wretched covetousness, to be intruders upon the Devil; a wretched ambition to be usurpers upon damnation. God did not make the fire for us; but much less did he make us for that fire; that is, make us to damn us. But now the Judgment is given, *Ite maledicti,* go ye accursed/[Matthew 25.41]/; but yet this is the way of Gods justice, and his proceeding, that his Judgments are not alwaies executed, though they be given. The Judgments and Sentences of Medes and Persians are irrevocable, but the Judgments and Sentences of God, if they be given, if they

be published, they are not executed. The Ninevites had perished, if the sentence of their destruction had not been given; and the sentence preserv'd them; so even in this cloud of *Ite maledicti,* go ye accursed, we may see the day break, and discern beams of saving light, even in this Judgment of eternal darkness, if the contemplation of his Judgment brings us to remember him in that day, in the light and apprehension of his anger and correction.

5. /In Diebus/ For this circumstance is enlarged; it is not *in die,* but *in diebus,* not in one, but in many dayes; for God affords us many dayes, many lights to see and remember him by. This remembrance of God is our regeneration, by which we are new creatures; and therefore we may consider as many dayes in it, as in the first creation. The first day was the making of light; and our first day is the knowledg of him, who saies of himself, *ego sum lux mundi,* I am the light of the world, and of whom St. *John* testifies, *Erat lux vera,* he was the true light, that lighteth every man into the world/John 8.12, 9.5, 1.9/. This is then our first day the true profession of Christ Jesus. God made light first, that the other creatures might be seen; *Frustra essent si non viderentur,* It had been to no purpose to have made creatures, if there had been no light to manifest them/Ambrose/. Our first day is the light and love of the Gospel; for the noblest creatures of Princes, (that is, the noblest actions of Princes, war, and peace, and treaties) *frustra sunt,* they are good for nothing, they are nothing, if they be not shew'd and tried by this light, by the love and preservation of the Gospel of Christ Jesus: God made light first, that himself (for our example) might do all his other works in the light: that we also, as we had that light shed upon us in our baptism, so we might make all our future actions justifiable, by that light, and not *Erubescere Evangelium,* not be ashamed of being too jealous in this profession of his truth. Then God saw that the light was good: the seeing implies a consideration; that so a religion be not accepted blindly, not implicitly; and the seeing it to be good implies an election of that religion, which is simply good in itself, and not good by reason of advantage, or conveniency, or other collateral and by-respects. And when God had seen the light, and seen that it was good, then he severed light from darkness; and he severed them, *non tanquam duo positiva,* not as two essential, and positive, and equal things; not so as that a brighter and a darker religion, (a good and a bad) should both have a beeing together, but *tanquam positivum et primitivum,* light and darkness are primitive, and positive, and figure

this rather, that a true religion should be established, and continue, and darkness utterly removed; and then, and not till then, (till this was done, light severed from darkness) there was a day; And since God hath given us this day, the brightness of his Gospel, that this light is first presented, that is, all great actions begun with this consideration of his Gospel; since all other things are made by this light, that is, all have relation to the continuance of the Gospel, since God hath given us such a head, as is sharp-sighted in seeing the several lights, wise in discerning the true light, powerful in resisting forraign darkness; since God hath given us this day, *qui non humiliabit animam suam in die hac,* as *Moses*/Leviticus 23/speaks of the dayes of Gods institution, he that will not remember God now in this day, is impious to him, and unthankful to that great instrument of his, by whom this day spring from on high hath visited us. 6. To make shorter dayes of the rest, (for we must pass through all the six dayes in a few minuts) God in the second day made the firmament to divide between the waters above, and the waters below; and this firmament in us, is *terminus cognoscibilium,* the limits of those things which God hath given man means and faculties to conceive, and understand: he hath limited our eyes with a firmament beset with stars, our eyes can see no farther: he hath limited our understanding in matters of religion with a starry firmament too; that is, with the knowledg of those things, *quae ubique, quae semper,* which those stars which he hath kindled in his Church, the Fathers and Doctors, have ever from the beginning proposed as things necessary to be explicitely believ'd for the salvation of our souls; for the eternal decrees of God, and his unreveal'd mysteries, and the inextricable perplexities of the School, they are waters above the firmament: here *Paul* plants, and here *Apollo*[*s*] waters/[I Cor. 3.6]/; here God raises up men to convey to us the dew of his grace, by waters under the firmament; by visible sacraments, and by the word so preach'd and so interpreted, as it hath been constantly, and unanimously from the beginning of the Church. And therefore this second day is perfited in the third, in the *congregentur aquae,* let the waters be gathered together; God hath gathered all the waters, all the waters of life in one place; that is, all the doctrine necessary for the life to come, into his Church: And then *producet terra,* here in this world are produced to us all herbs and fruits, all that is necessary for the soul to feed upon. And in this third daies work God repeats here that testimony, *vidit quod bonum,* he saw that it was good; good, that here should be a gathering of waters in one place, that is, no doctrine receiv'd that had not been taught in the Church; and *vidit quod bonum,* he saw it was good that all herbs and trees should be produced that bore seed; all doctrines that were to be proseminated and propagated, and to be continued to the end, should be taught in the Church: but for doctrines which were but to vent the passion of vehement men, or to serve the turns of great men for a time, which were not seminal doctrines, doctrines that bore seed, and were to last from the beginning to the end; for these interlineary doctrines, and marginal, which were no part of the first text, here's no testimony that God sees that they are good. And, *In diebus istis,* if in these two daies, the day when God makes thee a firmament, shewes thee what thou art, to limit thine understanding and thy faith upon, and the day where God makes thee a sea, a collection of the waters, (showes thee where these necessary things must be taught in the Church) if in those daies thou will not remember thy Creator, it is an irrecoverable Lethargy.

7. In the fourth daies work, let the making of the Sun to rule the day be the testimony of Gods love to thee, in the sunshine of temporal prosperity, and the making of the Moon to shine by night, be the refreshing of his comfortable promises in the darkness of adversity; and then remember that he can make thy sun to set at noon/Amos/, he can blow out thy taper of prosperity when it burns brightest, and he can turn the Moon into blood, he can make all the promises of the Gospel/Act. 2.20/, which should comfort thee in adversity, turn into despair and obduration. Let the fift daies work, which was the creation *Omnium reptibilium,* and *omnium volatilium* of all creeping things, and of all flying things, produc'd out of water, signifie and denote to thee, either thy humble devotion, in which thou saist of thy self to God, *vermis ego et non homo*/[Psalm 22.6]/, I am a worm and no man; or let it be the raising of thy soul in that, *pennas columbae dedisti*/[Psalm 55.6]/, that God hath given thee the wings of a dove to fly to the wilderness, in a retiring from, or a resisting of tentations of this world; remember still that God can suffer even thy humility to stray, and degenerate into an uncomly dejection and stupidity, and senselessness of the true dignity and true liberty of a Christian: and he can suffer this retiring thy self from the world, to degenerate into a contempt and despising of others, and an overvaluing of thine own perfections. Let the last day in which both man and beasts were made out of the earth, but yet a living soul breath'd into man,

remember thee that this earth which treads upon thee, must return to that earth which thou treadst upon; thy body, that loads thee, and oppresses thee to the grave, and thy spirit to him that gave it. And when the Sabbath day hath also remembered thee, that God hath given thee a temporal Sabbath, plac'd thee in a land of peace, and an ecclesiastical Sabbath, plac'd in a Church of peace, perfect all in a spirituall Sabbath, a conscience of peace, by remembering now thy Creator, at least in one of these daies of the week of thy regeneration, either as thou has light created in thee, in the first day, that is, thy knowledg of Christ; or as thou hast a firmament created in thee the second day, that is, thy knowledg what to seek concerning Christ, things appertaining to faith and salvation; or as thou hast a sea created in thee the third day, that is, a Church where all the knowledg is reserv'd and presented to thee; or as thou hast a sun and moon in the fourth day, thankfulness in prosperity, comfort in adversity, or as thou hast *reptilem humilitatem, or volatilem fiduciam,* a humiliation in thy self, or an exaltation in Christ in thy fift day, or as thou hast a contemplation of thy morality and immorality the sixth day, or a desire of a spiritual Sabbath in the seaventh, In those daies remember thou thy Creator.

8. /*Juventutis*/Now all these daies are contracted into less room in this text, *In diebus Bechurotheica,* is either, *in the daies of thy youth,* or *electionum tuarum,* in the daies of thy hearts desire, when thou enjoyest all that thou couldest wish. First, therefore, if thou wouldst be heard in *Davids* prayer; *Delicta juventutis;* O Lord remember not the sins of my youth/Psalm 25.7/; remember to come to this prayer, *In diebus juventutis,* in the dayes of thy youth. *Job* /29.4/remembers with much sorrow, how he was in the dayes of his youth, when Gods providence was upon his Tabernacle: and it is a late, but a sad consideration, to remember with what tenderness of conscience, what scruples, what remorces we entred into sins in our youth, how much we were afraid of all degrees and circumstances of sin for a little while, and how indifferent things they are grown to us, and how obdurate we are grown in them now. This was *Jobs* sorrow, and this was *Tobias* comfort/[Tobit 1.41]/, when I was but young, all my Tribes fell away; but I alone went after to *Jerusalem*. Though he lacked the counsail, and the example of his Elders, yet he served God; for it is good for a man, that he bear his yoke in his youth /Threnody 3.27/: For even when God had delivered over his people purposely to be afflicted, yet himself complains in their behalf, *That the persecutor laid the very heaviest*

yoke upon the ancient/Esay 47.6/: It is a lamentable thing to fall under a necessity of suffering in our age. *Labore fracta instrumenta, ad Deum ducis, quorum nullus usus?*/Basil/wouldst thou consecrate a Chalice to God that is broken? no man would present a lame horse, a disordered clock, a torn book to the King. *Caro jumentum*/Augustine/, thy body is thy beast; and wilt thou present that to God, when it is lam'd and tir'd with excesse of wantonness? when thy clock (the whole course of thy time) is disordered with passions, and perturbations; when thy book (the history of thy life,) is torn, 1000. sins of thine own torn out of thy memory, wilt thou then present thy self thus defac'd and mangled to almighty God? *Temperantia non est temperantia in senectute, sed impotentia incontinentiae*/Basil/, chastity is not chastity in an old man, but a disability to be unchast; and therefore thou dost not give God that which thou pretendest to give, for thou hast no chastity to give him. *Senex bis puer,* but it is not *bis juvenis;* an old man comes to the infirmities of childhood again; but he comes not to the strength of youth again.

9. /*Electionum*/Do this then *In diebus juventutis,* in thy best strength, and when thy natural faculties are best able to concur with grace; but do it *In diebus electionum,* in the dayes when thou hast thy hearts desire; for if thou have worn out this word, in one sense, that it be too late now, *to remember him in the dayes of youth,* (that's spent forgetfully) yet as long as thou art able to make a new choise, to chuse a new sin, that when thy heats of youth are not overcome, but burnt out, then thy middle age chooses ambition, and thy old age chooses covetousness; as long as thou art able to make thy choice thou art able to make a better than this; God testifies that power, that he hath given thee; *I call heaven and earth to record this day, that I have set before you life and death; choose life*/Deuteronomy 30.19/: If this choice like you not, *If it seem evil unto you to serve the Lord,* saith *Joshuah* then, *choose ye this day whom ye will serve*/24.15/. Here's the election day; bring that which ye would have, into comparison with that which ye should have; that is, all that this world keeps from you, with that which God offers to you; and what will ye choose to prefer before him? for honor, and favor, and health, and riches, perchance you cannot have them though you choose them; but can you have more of them than they have had to whom those very things have been occasions of ruin? The Market is open till the bell ring; till thy last bell ring the Church is open, grace is to be had there: but

trust not upon that rule, that men buy cheapest at the end of the market, that heaven may be had for a breath at last, when they that hear it cannot tel whether it be a sigh or a gasp, a religious breathing and anhelation after the next life, or natural breathing out, and exhalation of this; but find a spiritual good husbandry in that other rule, that the prime of the market is to be had at first: for howsoever, in thine age, there may be by Gods strong working, *Dies juventutis,* A day of youth, in making thee then a new creature; (for as God is *antiquissimus dierum,*/[Daniel 7.9]/ so in his school no man is super-annated,) yet when age hath made a man impotent to sin, this is not *Dies electionum,* it is not a day of choice; but remember God now, when thou hast a choice, that is, a power to advance thy self, or to oppress others by evil means; now *in die electionum,* in those[3] thy happy and sun-shine dayes, *remember him.*

10. /*Creatorem*/This is then the faculty that is excited, the memory; and this is the time, now, now whilest ye have power of election: The object is, the Creator, *Remember the Creator:* First, because the memory can go no farther than the creation; and therefore we have no means to conceive, or apprehend any thing of God before that. When men therefore speak of decrees of reprobation, decrees of condemnation, before decrees of creation; this is beyond the counsail of the holy Ghost here, *Memento creatoris,* Remember the Creator, for this is to remember God a condemner before he was a creator: This is to put a preface to *Moses* his *Genesis,* not to be content with his *in principio,* to know that *in the beginning God created heaven and earth,* but we must remember what he did *ante principium,* before any such beginning was. Moses his *in principio,* that beginning, the creation we can remember; but St. *Johns in principio,* that beginning, eternity, we cannot; we can remember Gods *fiat* in *Moses,* but not Gods *erat* in St. *John:* what God hath done for us, is the object of our memory, not what he did before we were: and thou hast a good and perfect memory, if it remember all that the holy Ghost proposes in the Bible; and it determines in the *memento Creatoris:* There begins the Bible, and there begins the Creed, *I believe in God the Father, maker of Heaven and Earth;* for when it is said, *The holy Ghost was not given, because Jesus was not glorified.* /John 7.39/ it is not truly *Non erat datus,* but *non erat;* for, *non erat nobis antequam operaretur;* It is not said there, the holy Ghost was not given, but it is the holy Ghost was not: for he is not, that is, he hath no being to us-ward, till he

works in us, which was first in the creation: *Remember the Creator then,* because thou canst remember nothing backward beyond him, and remember him so too, that thou maist stick upon nothing on this side of him, That so neither *height, nor depth, nor any other creature may separate thee from God*[4] /Romans 8 ult./; not only not separate thee finally, but not separate so, as to stop upon the creature, but to make the best of them, thy way to the Creator; We see ships in the river; but all their use is gone, if they go not to sea; we see men fraighted with honor, and riches, but all their use is gone, if their respect be not upon the honor and glory of the Creator; and therefore sayes the Apostle, *Let them that suffer, commit their souls to God, as to a faithful Creator;* /I Peter 4 ult./ that is, He made them, and therefore will have care of them. This is the true contracting, and the true extending of the memory, to *Remember the Creator,* and stay there, because there is no prospect farther, and to *Remember the Creator,* and get thither, because there is no safe footing upon the creature, til we come so far.

11. /*Tuum*/Remember then the Creator, and *remember thy Creator,* for, *Quis magis fidelis Deo?* who is so faithful a Counsailor as God? *Quis prudentior Sapiente?* /Basil/ who can be wiser than wisdome? *Quis utilior bono?* or better than goodness? *Quis conjunctor Creatore?* or neerer then our Maker? and therefore remember him. What purposes soever thy parents or thy Prince have to make thee great, how had all those purposes been frustrated, and evacuated if God had not made thee before? this very being is thy greatest degree; as in Arithmetick how great a number soever a man expresse in many figures, yet when we come to number all, the very first figure is the greatest and most of all; so what degrees or titles soever a man have in this world, the greatest and the foundation of all, is, that he had a being by creation: For the distance from nothing to a little, is ten thousand times more, than from it to the highest degree in this life: and therefore *remember thy Creator,* as by being so, he hath done more for thee than all the world besides; and remember him also, with this consideration, that whatsoever thou art now, yet once thou wast nothing.

12. /*Ex nihilo*/ He created thee, *ex nihilo,* he gave thee a being, there's matter of exaltation, and yet all this from nothing; thou wast worse than a worm, there's matter of humiliation; but he did not create thee *ad nihilum,* to return to nothing again, and there's matter for thy consideration, and study, how to make thine immortality profitable unto thee, for it is a deadly immortality, if

thy immortality must serve thee for nothing but to hold thee in immortal torment. To end all, that being which we have from God shall not return to nothing, nor the being which we have from men neither. As St. *Bernard* sayes of the Image of God in mans soul, *uri potest in gehenna, non exuri* /Bernard/, That soul that descends to hell, carries the Image [of] God in the faculties of that soul thither, but there that Image can never be burnt out, so those Images and those impressions, which we have received from men, from nature, from the World, the image of a Lord, the image of a Counsailor, the image of a Bishop, shall all burn in Hell, and never burn out; not only these men, but these offices are not to return to nothing; but as their being from God, so their being from man, shal have an everlasting being, to the aggravating of their condemnation. And therefore *remember thy Creator,* who, as he is so, by making thee of nothing, so he will ever be so, by holding thee to his glory, though to thy confusion, from returning to nothing; for the Court of Heaven is not like other Courts, that after a surfet of pleasure or greatness, a man may retire; after a surfet of sin there's no such retiring, as a dissolving of the soul into nothing; but God is from the beginning the Creator, he gave all things their being, and he is still thy Creator, thou shalt evermore have that being, to be capable of his Judgments.

13. Now to make up a circle, by returning to our first word, remember: As we remember God, so for his sake, let us remember one another. In my long absence, and far distance from hence, remember me, as I shall do you in the ears of that God, to whom the farthest East, and the farthest West are but as the right and left ear in one of us; we hear with both at once, and he hears in both at once; remember me, not my abilities; for when I consider my Apostleship that I was sent to you, I am in St. *Pauls quorum, quorum ego sum minimus*/I Corinthians 15.9/, the least of them that have been sent; and when I consider my infirmities, I am in his *quorum,* in another commission, another way, *Quorum ego maximus*/I Timothy 1.15/; the greatest of them; but remember my labors, and endeavors, at least my desire, to make sure your salvation. And I shall remember your religious cheerfulness in hearing the word, and your christianly respect towards all them that bring that word unto you, and towards myself in particular far [a]bove my merit. And so as your eyes that stay here, and mine that must be far off, for all that distance shall meet every morning, in looking upon that same Sun, and meet every night, in looking upon that

same Moon; so our hearts may meet morning and evening in that God, which sees and hears every where; that you may come thither to him with your prayers, that I, (if I may be of use for his glory, and your edification in this place) may be restored to you again; and may come to him with my prayer that what *Paul* soever plant amongst you, or what *Apollos* soever water, God himself will give the increase: That if I never meet you again till we have all passed the gate of death, yet in the gates of heaven, I may meet you all, and there say to my Saviour and your Saviour, that which he said to his Father and our Father, *Of those whom thou hast given me, have I not lost one*. Remember me thus, you that stay in this Kingdome of peace, where no sword is drawn, but the sword of Justice, as I shal remember you in those Kingdomes, where ambition on one side, and a necessary defence from unjust persecution on the other side hath drawn many swords; and Christ Jesus remember us all in his Kingdome, to which, though we must sail through a sea, it is the sea of his blood, where no soul suffers shipwrack; though we must be blown with strange winds, with sighs and groans for our sins, yet it is the Spirit of God that blows all this wind, and shall blow away all contrary winds of diffidence or distrust in Gods mercy; where we shall be all Souldiers of one Army, the Lord of Hostes, and Children of one Quire, the God of Harmony and consent: where all Clients shall retain but one Counsellor, our Advocate Christ Jesus, nor present him any other fee but his own blood, and yet every Client have a Judgment on his side, not only in a not guilty, in the remission of his sins, but in a *Venite benedicti,* in being called to the participation of an immortal Crown of glory: where there shall be no difference in affection, nor in mind, but we shall agree as fully and perfectly in our *Allelujah,* and *gloria in excelsis,* as God the Father, Son, and Holy Ghost agreed in the *faciamus hominem* at first; where we shall end, and yet begin but then; where we shall have continuall rest, and yet never grow lazie; where we shall be stronger to resist, and yet have no enemy; where we shall live and never die, where we shall meet and never part.

THE THIRD SERMON ON JOHN 1.8

"He was not that light, but was sent to beare witnesse of that light."
Preached at Saint Pauls 13. October, 1622.

1. This is the third time that I have *entertained* you (in a businesse of this nature, intended for Gods service, and your edification, I must not say, *troubled* you) with this Text. I begun it at *Christmas,* and in that *darke* time of the yeer told you *who,* and *what* was this *light* which *John Baptist* is denied to be. I pursued it at *Midsommer,* and upon *his owne* day, insisted upon the *person* of *John Baptist, who,* though *he were not this light, was sent to beare witnesse of this light.* And the third consideration, which (as I told you then) was not tied nor affected to any particular *Festivall,* you shall (by Gods grace) have now, the *office* of *John Baptist,* his *testimony;* and in that, these two parts; /Divisio/ first, *a problematicall part, why* so evident a thing as light, and *such* a light, *that* light, required testimony of *man:* and then a *dogmaticall* part, *what testimony* this man gives of this light. And in the first of these we shall make these two steps, first, *why any* testimony *at all,* then *why,* after so many others, *this of John.*

2. /I Part/ First then God made *light* first, *ut innotescerent omnia /Cur testis.* Ambrose/, that man might glorifie God in seeing the creature, and *him* in it; for, *frustra fecisset,* (says the same Father) it had been to no purpose to have a world, and no light. But though light discover and manifest every thing else to us, and it selfe too, if all be well disposed, yet, in the *fifth* verse of this chapter, there is reason enough given, why this light in our text, requires testimony; that is, *the light shines in darknesse,* and *the darknesse comprehends it not;* and therefore, *Propter non intel-*

ligentes, propter incredulos, propter infirmos, Sol lucernas quaerit; /Augustine, *Propter non intelligentes*/ for their sakes that are weak in their *understanding,* and not enlightened in that faculty, the *Gentiles;* for their sakes who are weake in their *faith,* that come, and heare, and receive light, but *beleeve* not; for their sakes that are perverse in their *manners,* and course of life, that heare, and beleeve, but practise not, *sol lucernas quaerit,* this light requires testimony. There may be light then and we not know it, because we are *asleep;* and asleep so, as *Jairus daughter* was, of whom Christ says, *the maid is not dead but asleep.* /Matthew 9.24/ The maide was absolutely dead; but because he meant forthwith to raise her, he calls it a sleep. The *Gentiles,* in their ignorance, are *dead;* we, in our *corrupt nature,* dead, as dead as they, we cannot heare the voice, we cannot see the light; without Gods *subsequent grace,* the *Christian* can no more proceed, then the *Gentile* can beginne without his *preventing grace.* But, because, amongst us, he hath established the *Gospell,* and in the ministery and dispensation thereof, ordinary meanes for the conveyance of his farther grace, we now are but *asleep* and may wake. A sodain *light* brought into a room doth awaken some men; but yet a *noise* does it better, and a *shaking,* and a pinching. The exalting of *naturall faculties,* and good *morall life, inward inspirations,* and private *meditations, conferences, reading,* and the like, doe awaken some; but the testimony of the messenger of God, the *preacher,* crying according to Gods ordinance, shaking the soule, troubling the conscience, and pinching the bowells, by denouncing of Gods Judgements, these beare witnesse of the light, when otherwise men would sleep it out; and so *propter non intelligentes,* for those that lye in the suddes of *nature,* and *cannot,* or of *negligence,* and *will* not come to heare, *sol lucernas,* this light requires testimony.

3. /*Propter incredulos*/ These testimonies, Gods ordinances, may have wakened a man, yet he may *winke,* and *covet darknesse,* and grow weary of instruction, and angry at increpation; And, as the *eye of the adulterer waiteth for the twilight,* /Job 24.15/ so, the eare of this fastidious and impatient man, longeth for the end of the Sermon, or the end of that point in the Sermon, which is a thorne to his conscience; But as, if a man wink in a cleare day, he shall for all that discerne light thorough his eylids, but not light enough to keep him from stumbling: so the most perverse man that is, either in *faith* or *manners,* that winkes against the light of *nature,* or light of the *law,* or light of *grace* exhibited in the Christian Church, the

most determined *Atheist* that is, discernes through all his stubbornnesse, though not light enough to rectifie him, to save him, yet enough to condemne him, though not enough to enable him, to reade his owne name in the book of life, yet so much, as makes him afraid to read his own story by, and to make up his owne *Audit* and account with God. And doth not this light to this man need testimony, That as he does see, it is a light, so he might see, that there is warmth and nourishment in this light, and so, as well see the way to God by that light, as to see by it, that there is a God; and, this he may, if he doe not sleep nor winke; that is, not forbeare comming hither, nor resist the grace of God, always offred here, when he is here. *Propter incredulos,* for their sakes, who though they do heare, heare not to beleeve, *sol lucernas,* this light requires testimony; and it does so too, *propter infirmos,* for their sakes, who though they do *heare,* and *beleeve,* yet doe not *Practise.*

4. /*Propter infirmos*/ If he neither *sleep,* nor *wink,* neither forbeare, nor resist, yet how often may you surprise and deprehend a man, whom you thinke directly to look upon such an object, yet if you aske him the quality or colour of it, he will tell you, he saw it not? That man sees as little with *staring,* as the other with *winking.* His eye hath seen, but it hath returned nothing to the *common sense.* We may pore upon *books,* stare upon *preachers,* yet if we reflect nothing, nothing upon our *conversation,* we shall still remaine under the increpation and malediction of Saint *Paul,* out of *Esay, Seeing yee shall see, and shall not perceive;* /Act. 21.26/ seeing and hearing shall but aggravate our condemnation, and it shall be easier at the day of Judgement, for the *deaf* and the *blinde* that never saw *Sacrament,* never heard *Sermon,* then for *us,* who have frequented both; *propter informos,* for their sakes, whose strength though it serve to bring them hither, and to beleeve here, doth not serve them to proceed to practise, *sol lucernas,* this light requires testimony.

5. /*Propter Relapsos*/ Yet, if we be neither *dead,* nor *asleep,* nor *winke,* nor *looke negligently,* but doe come to some degrees of holinesse in *practise* for a time, yet if at any time, we put our selves in such a position and distance from this light, as that we suffer dark thick bodies to interpose, and eclipse it, that is, *sadnesse* and *dejection* of spirit, for worldly losses; nay, if we admit inordinate *sadnesse* for sinne it selfe, to eclipse this light of comfort from us, or if we suffer such other lights, as by the corrupt estimation of the world, have a greater splendour to come in; (As the light of *Knowl-*

edge and *Learning,* the light of *Honour* and *Glory,* of popular *Applause* and *Acclamation*) so that this light which we speake of, (the light of former *Grace*) be darkned by the accesse of other lights, worldly lights, then also you shall finde that you need more and more Testimony of this light. God is light in the Creature, in nature; yet the *natural Man* stumbles and falls, and lies in that ignorance;[1] Christ bears witnesse of this light, in establishing a *Christian Church;* yet many Christians fall into *Idolatry* and *Superstition,* and lie and die in it. The Holy Ghost hath born further witnesse of this light, and, (if we may take so low a Metaphore in so high a Mystery) hath *snuffed* this candle, mended this light, in the *Reformation* of Religion; and yet there is a damp, or a cloud of *uncharitablenesse,* of *neglecting,* of *defaming* one another; we deprave even the *fiery,* the *cloven tongues* /Act. 2.3/ of the Holy Ghost: Our tongues are *fiery* onely to the consuming of another, and they are *cloven,* onely in speaking things contrary to one another. So that still there need more witnesses, more testimonies of this light. God the Father is *Pater Luminum* the *Father* /Jas. 1.17/ of all Lights; God the *Sonne,* is *Lumen de lumine,* Light of light, of the Father; God the *Holy Ghost* is *Lumen de luminibus,* Light of lights, proceeding both from the Father, and the Sonne; and this light the *Holy Ghost* kindles more lights in the Church, and drops a coale from the Altar upon every lamp, he lets fall beams of his Spirit upon every man, that comes in the name of God, into this place; and he sends you one man to day, which beareth witnesse of this light *ad ignaros,* that bends his preaching to the convincing of the *naturall man,* the ignorant soul, and works upon him. And another another day, that bears witnesse *ad incredulos,* that fixeth the promises of the *Gospell,* and the *merits* of Christ Jesus, upon that startling and timorous soul, upon that jealous and suspicious soul, that cannot beleeve that those promises, or those merits appertain to him, and so bends all the power of his Sermon to the binding up of such broken hearts, and faint beleevers. He sendeth another to bear witnesse *ad infirmos,* to them who though they have shaked off their sicknesse, yet are too weake to walke, to them, who though they doe beleeve, are intercepted by tentations from preaching, and his Sermon reduces them from their ill manners, who thinke it enough to come, to hear, to beleeve. And then he sendeth another *ad Relapsos,* to bear witnesse of this light to them who have relapsed into former sinnes, that the merits of Christ are inexhaustible, and the mercies of God in him indefatigable: As God cannot be deceived with a false repentance, so he cannot resist a true, nor be weary of multiplying his mercies in that case. And therefore thinke not that thou hast heard witnesses enow of this light, *Sermons enow,* if thou have heard all the points preached upon, which concerne thy salvation. But because *new Clouds of Ignorance,* of *Incredulitie,* of *Infirmitie, of Relapsing,* rise every day and call this light in question, and may make thee doubt whether thou have it or no, every day, (that is, as often as thou canst) heare more and more witnesses of this light; and bless that God, who for thy sake, would submit himselfe to these *Testimonia ab homine,* /John 5.34/ these Testimonies from men, and being all light himselfe, and having so many other testimonies, would yet require the Testimony of *Man,* of *John;* which is our other branch of this first part.

6. */A seipso/* Christ, (who is still the light of our Text, *That light,* the *essentiall light* had testimony enough without *John.* First, he bore witness of *himselfe.* And though he say of himself, (*If I beare witnesse of my self, my witnesse is not true*) /John 5.31/ yet that he might say either out of *legall* and *proverbiall* opinion of theirs, that ordinarily they thought, That a witness testifying for himself, was not to be beleeved, whatsoever he said; Or, *as Man,* (which they then took him to be) he might speake it of *himselfe* out of his own opinion, that, in *Judicature* it is a good rule, that a man should not be beleeved in his own case. But, after this, and after he had done enough to make them see, that he was more then man, by multiplying of *miracles,* then he said, *though I beare witnesse of my selfe, my witnesse is true.* /8.14/ So the onely infallibility and unreproachable evidence of our *election,* is in the *inward word of God,* when *his Spirit beares witnesse with our Spirit, that we are the Sonnes of God;* for, if the Spirit, (the Spirit of *truth*) say he is in us, he is in us. But yet the Spirit of God is content to submit himselfe to an ordinary triall, to be tried by God and the Countrey; he allowes us to *doubt,* and to be *afraid* of our *regeneration,* except we have the testimony of *sanctification.* Christ bound them not to *his own* testimony, till it had the seale of *workes,* or *miracles;* nor must we build upon any testimony in our selves, till other men, that see our life, testifie for us to the world.

7. */A Patre/* He had also the testimony of *his Father,* (the *Father himselfe which hath sent me, beareth witnesse of me.*) /John 5.37/ But where should they see the Father, or heare the Father speak? That was all which *Philip* asked at his hands, (*Lord show us the Father, and it sufficeth us.*) /14.8/ He had the testimony of an

Angel, /Ab Angelo/ who came to the shepheards so, as no where in all the Scriptures, there is such an *Apparition* expressed, (*the Angel of the Lord came upon them, and the glory of the Lord shone round about them*) /Luke 2.8/ but where might a man *talke* with his Angel, and know more of him? As Saint *Augustine* says of *Moses, Scripsit et albiit,* he hath written a little of the Creation, and he is gone; *Si hic esset, tenerem et rogarem,* if *Moses* were here, says he, I would hold him fast, till I had got him to give me an exposition of that which he writ. For, beloved, we must have such witnesses, as we may consult farther with. I can see no more by an *Angel,* then by *lightning.* A *star /A stella/* testified of him, at his birth. But what was that star? was it any of those stars that remaine *yet? Gregory Nissen* thinkes it *was,* and that it onely then changed the naturall course, and motion for that service. But almost all the other Fathers thinke, that it was a light but *then created,* and that it had onely the *forme of a star,* and no more; and some few, that it was the *holy Ghost* in that forme. And, if it were one of the fixed *stars,* and remaine *yet,* yet it is not now in that office, it testifies nothing of Christ *now. /A magis/* The wise men of the East testified of him, too; But *what* were they, or *who,* or *how many,* or *from whence,* were they? for, all these circumstances have put Antiquity it selfe into more distractions, and more earnest disputations, then *circumstances* should doe. *Simeon /A Simeone/* testified of him, who had a revelation from the holy Ghost, that he should not *see death, till he had seen Christ. /Ab Anna/* And so did the *Prophetess Anna, who served God, with fasting and prayer, day and night. Omnis sexus et aetas,* /Luke 2.25 Ambrose/ both *sexes,* and all *ages* testified of him; and he gives examples of all, as it was easie for him to doe. Now after all these testimonies, from *himselfe,* from the *Father,* from the *Angel,* from the *star,* from the *wise men,* from *Simeon,* from *Anna,* from all, what needed the testimony of *John?* All those witnesses had been *thirty years before John* was cited for a witnesse, to come from the wildernesse and preach. And in *thirty years,* by reason of his obscure and retired life, in his father *Josephs* house, all those personall testimonies of Christ might be forgotten; and, for the most part, those witnesses onely testified that he was *borne;* that he was come into the world, but for all their testimony, he might have been gone out of the world long. Before this, he might have perished in the generall flood, in that flood of innocent blood, in which *Herod* drowned all the young children of that Countrey. When therefore Christ came forth to *preach,* when he came to call *Apostles,* when he came to settle a *Church,* to establish meanes for our ordinary salvation, (by which he is the light of our text, the *Essentiall light* shining out in his Church, by the supernaturall light of *faith* and *grace*) then he admitted, then he required *Testimonium ab homine,* testimony from man. And so, for our conformity to him, in using and applying those meanes, which convay this light to us, in the Church, we must doe so too; we must have the seale of *faith,* and of the *Spirit,* but this must be in the testimony of men; still there must be that done by us, which must make men testifie for us.

8. */Scripturas esse/* Every Christian is a state, a common-wealth to *himselfe,* and in him, the Scripture is his law, and the conscience is his *Judge.* And though the Scripture be inspired from God, and the conscience be illumined and rectified by the *holy Ghost* immediately, yet, both the *Scriptures* and the *Conscience* admit *humane arguments.* First, the Scriptures doe, in all these three respects; first that there are *certaine Scriptures,* that are the revealed will of God. Secondly, that these books which we call *Canonicall,* are those Scriptures. And lastly, that this and this is the true sense and meaning of such and such a place of Scripture. First, that there is a manifestation of the will of God in certain Scriptures, if we who have not power to infuse *Faith* into men, (for that is the work of the Holy Ghost onely) but must deal upon the *reason* of men, and satisfie that, if we might not proceed, *per testimonia ab homine,* by humane Arguments, and argue, and infer *thus,* That if God will save man for worshipping him, and damne him for not worshipping him, so as he will be worshipped, certainly God hath revealed to man, how he will be worshipped, and that in some visible, in some permanent manner in *writing,* and that that writing is *Scripture,* if we had not these testimonies, these necessary consequences derived even from the *naturall reason* of man to convince men, how should we convince them, since our way is not to create *Faith,* but to satisfie *reason?* And therefore let us rest in this testimony of men, that all *Christian* men, nay *Jewes* and *Turkes* too, have ever beleeved, that there are certain Scriptures, which are the revealed will of God, and that God hath manifested to us, in those Scriptures, all that he requires at our hands for *Faith* or *Manners.* Now, which are those Scriptures?

9. */Hos eos libros esse/* As for the whole body intirely together, so for the particular limbs and members of this body, the *severall books* of the Bible, we must accept *testimonium ab homine,* humane Ar-

guements, and the testimony of men. At first, the Jewes were the Depositaries of Gods Oracles; and therefore the first Christians were to aske the Jewes, *which* books where those Scriptures. Since the Church of God is the *Master* of those *Rolls,* no doubt but the *Church* hath *Testimonium a Deo,* The Spirit of God to direct her, in declaring *what Books* make up the Scripture; but yet even the *Church,* which is to deal upon men, proceedeth also *per testimonium ab homine,* by humane Arguments, such as may work upon the *reason* of man, in declaring the Scriptures of God. For the *New Testament,* there is no question made of any Book, but in *Conventicles* of *Anabaptists;* and for the *Old,* it is testimony enough that we receive all that the Jews received. This is but the testimony of man, but such as prevails upon every man. It is somewhat boldly said, (not to permit to our selves any severer, or more bitter animadversion upon him) by a great man in the *Roman Church,* /Melchior Canus/[2] that perchance the book of *Enoch,* which St. *Jude* cites in his Epistle, was not an *Apocryphal* book, but *Canonicall Scripture* in the time of the *Jews.* As though the *holy Ghost* were a time-server, and would sometimes issue some things, for present satisfaction, which he would not avow nor stand to after; as though the *holy Ghost* had but a Lease for certain years, a determinable estate in the Scriptures; which might expire, and he be put from his evidence; that that book might become none of *his,* which was his before. We therefore, in receiving these books for *Canonicall,* which we do, and in post-posing the *Apochryphall,* into an inferior place, have *testimonium ab homine,* testimony from the People of God, who were, and are the most competent, and unreproachable witnesses herein: and we have *Testimonium ab inimico,* testimony from our adversary himself, *Perniciosius est Ecclesiae librum recipere pro sacro, qui non est, quàm sacrum rejicere, /Idem ex Aquinus/* It is a more pernicious danger to the Church, to admit a book for *Canonicall,* which is *not so,* then to reject one that is so. And therefore, *ne turberis novitie,* (saith another great Author of theirs) /Cajetan/ Let no young student in Divinity be troubled, *si alicubi repererit, libros istos supputari inter Canonicos,* if he finde at any time, any of these books reckned amongst the Canonical, *nam ad Hieronymi*[3] *limam, verba Doctorum et Conciliorum reducenda,* for saith he, *Hieroms* file must passe over the Doctors, and over the Councels too, and they must be understood, and interpreted according to St. *Hierom.* Now this is but *testimonium ab homine,* St. *Hieroms* testimony, that prevailed upon *Cajetan,* and it was but *testimonium ab homine* the testimony of the *Jews,* that prevailed upon St. *Hierom* himself.

10. /*Sensus locorum*/ It is so for the whole body, *The bible;* it is so for all the limbs of this body, *every particular book of the Bible;* and it is so, for the soul of this body, the true *sense of every place,* of every book thereof; for, for that, (the sense of the place) we must have *testimonium ab homine,* the testimony, that is, the interpretation of other men. Thou must not rest upon thy self, nor upon any private man. *John* was a witnesse that had witnesses, the *Prophets* had prophesied of *John Baptist.* The men from whom we are to receive testimony of the sense of the Scriptures, must be men that have witnesses, that is, a visible and outward *calling in the Church of God.* That no sense be ever admitted, that derogateth from God, that makes him a false, or an impotent, or a cruell God, That every contradiction, and departing from the Analogy of *Faith,* doth derogate from God, and divers such grounds, and such inferences, as every man confesses, and acknowledges to be naturally and necessarily consequent, these are *Testimonia ab homine,* Testimonies that passe like currant money, from man to man, obvious to every man, suspicious to none. Thus it is in the generall; but then, when it is deduced to a more particular triall, (what is the sense of such or such a place) when Christ saith, *Scrutamini Scripturas,* /*John* 5.39/ search the Scriptures, *non mittit ad simplicem lectionem, sed ad scrutationem exquisitam,* It is not a bare *reading,* but a diligent *searching,* that is enjoyned us. Now they that will search, must have a warrant to search; they upon whom thou must rely for the sense of the Scriptures, must be sent of God by his Church. Thou art robbed of all, devested of all, if the Scriptures be taken from thee; Thou hast no where to search; blesse God therefore, that hath kept thee in possession of that sacred Treasure, the *Scriptures;* and then, if any part of that treasure ly out of thy reach, or ly in the dark, so as that thou understandest not the place, *search,* that is, apply thy self to them that have warrant to *search,* and thou shalt lack no light necessary for thee. Either thou shalt understand that place, or the not understanding of it shall not be imputed to thee, nor thy salvation hindred by that Ignorance.

11. It is but to a woman that Saint *Hierome* saith, *Ama Scripturas, et amabit te Sapientia*/Hierome/, Love the Scriptures, and Wisdome will love thee: The weaknesse of her *Sex* must not avert her from *reading* the Scriptures. It is instruction for a *Childe,* and for a *Girle,* that the same Father giveth, *Septem annorum discat*

memoriter Psalterium, As soone as she is *seaven yeares old,* let her learn all the *Psalmes* without book; the tendernesse of her age, must not avert her from the Scriptures. It is to the whole Congregation, consisting of all sorts and sexes, that Saint *Chrysostome* saith, *Hortor, et hortari non desinam,* I alwayes doe, and alwayes will exhort you, *ut cum domi fueritis, assiduae lectioni Scripturarum vacetis*/Chrysostome/, that at home, in your owne houses, you accustome your selves to a dayly reading of the Scriptures. And after, to such men as found, or forced excuses for reading them, he saith with compassion, and indignation too, *O homo, non est tuum Scripturas evolvere, quia innumeris curis distraheris?* Busie man, belongeth it not to thee to study the Scriptures, because thou art oppressed with worldly businesse? *Imo magis tuum est,* saith he, therefore thou hadst the more need to study the Scriptures; *Illi non tam egent, etc.* They that are not disquieted, nor disordered in their passions, with the cares of this world, doe not so much need that supply from the Scriptures, as you that are, doe. It is an Authour that lived in the obedience of the *Romane Church,* that saith, the Councell of *Nice* did decree, That every man should have the Bible in his house/Cornelius Agrippa/. But another Authour in that Church saith now, *Consilium Chrysostomi Ecclesiae nunc non arridet*/Escalante/; The church doth not now like *Chrysostomes* counsell, for this generall reading of the Scriptures, *Quia etsi ille locutus ad plebem, plebs tunc non erat haeretica,* Though Saint *Chrysostome* spoke that to the people, the people in his time were not an Hereticall people: And are the people in the Roman Church now an Hereticall people? If not, why may not they pursue Saint *Chrysostomes* counsel, and reade the Scriptures? Because they are dark? It is true, in some places they are dark; purposely left so by the Holy Ghost, *ne semel lectas fastidiremus,* /Augustine/ lest we should think we had done when we had read them once; so saith St. *Gregory* too, In plain places, *fami occurrit*/Gregory/, he presents meat for every stomach; In hard and dark places, *fastidia detergit,* he sharpens the appetite: *Margarita est, et undique perforari potest* /Hierom/; the Scripture is a Pearl, and might be bored through every where. Not every where by *thy self;* there may be many places, which thou of thy self canst not understand; not every where by *any other man;* no not by them, who have warrant to search, Commission from God, by their calling, to interpret the Scriptures, not every where by the *whole Church,* God hath reserved the *understanding of some places of Scripture, till the time come for the fulfilling of those Prophecies;* as many places of the *Old Testament* were not understood, till Christ came, in whom they were fulfilled. If therefore thou wilt needs know, whether, when Saint *Paul* took his information of the behaviour of the *Corinthians,* /I Corinthians 1.2/ from those of *Chloe,* whether this *Chloe,* were a *woman,* or a *place,* the Fathers cannot satisfie thee, the latter Writers cannot satisfie thee, there is not *Testimonium ab homine,* no such humane Arguments as can determine thee, or give thee an Acquittance; the greatest pillars whom God hath raised in his Church, cannot give a satisfaction to thy curiosity. But if the Doctrine of the place will satisfie thee, which Doctrine is, that St. *Paul* did not give credit to light rumors against the *Corinthians,* nor to clandestine whispers, but tells them who accused them, and yet, as well as he loved them, he did not stop his eares against competent witnesses, (for he tells them, they stood accused, and by whom) then thou maist *bore this pearle* thorough, and make it fit for thy use, and wearing, in knowing so much of Saint *Pauls* purpose therein, as concerns thy edification, though thou never know, whether *Chloe* were a *Woman,* or a *Place. Tantum veritati obstrepit adulterer sensus, quam corruptor stylus;* /Tertullian/ a false interpretation may doe thee as much harme, as a false translation, a false Commentary, as a false copy; And therefore, forbearing to make any interpertation at all, upon dark places of Scripture, (especially those, whose understanding depends upon the future fulfilling of prophecies) in places that are clear, and evident thou maist be thine own interpreter; In places that are more obscure, goe to those men, whom God hath set over thee, and either they shall give thee that sense of the place, which shall satisfie thee, by having the sense thereof, or that must satisfie you, that there is enough for your salvation, though that remaine uninterpreted. And let this *Testimonium ab homine,* this testimony of man establish thee for the Scripture, that there is a Scripture, a certain book, that is the word, and the revealed will of God; That these books which we receive for *Canonicall,* make up that book; And then, that this and this is the true sense of every place, which the holy Ghost hath opened to the present understanding of his Church.

12. /*Conscientia*/ We said before, that a Christian being a Commonwealth to himselfe, the *Scripture* was his *law,* (and for that law, that Scripture, he was to have *Testimonium ab homine,* the testimony of man) And then, his *Conscience* is his *Judge,* and for that he is to have the same testimony too. Thou must not rest upon the

testimony and suggestions of thine owne conscience; *Nec illud de trivio paratum habere,* /Hierom/ thou must not rest in that vulgar saying *sufficit mihi etc.* As long as mine owne Conscience stands right, I care not what all the world say. Thou must care what the world says, and study to have the approbation and testimony of good men. Every man is enough defamed in the generall depravation of our whole *nature: Adam* hath cast an infamy upon us all: And when a man is defamed, it is not enough that he purge himselfe by *oath,* he must have *compurgators* too: other men must sweare, that they beleeve he sweares a truth. Thine owne conscience is not enough, but thou must satisfie the world, and have *Testimonium ab homine,* good men must thinke thee good. A conscience that admits no search from others, is *cauterizata,* burnt *with a hot Iron;* not *cured,* but *seared;* not at peace, but stupefied. And when in the verse immediately before our test, it is said *That John came to beare witnesse of that light,* it is added, that through him, (that is, through that man, through *John,* not through it, through that light) that *through him all men beleeve.* For though it be efficiently the operation of the light it selfe, (that is Christ himselfe) that all men beleeve yet the holy Ghost directs us to that that is nearest us, to this testimony of man, that instrumentally, ministerially works this beliefe in men. If then for thy *faith,* thou must have *testimonium ab homine,* the testimony of men, and maist not beleeve as no man but thy selfe beleeves, much more for thy *manners,* and conversation. Thinke it not enough to satisfie thy self, but satisfie *good men;* nay *weake men;* nay *malicious men:* till it comes so far, as that for the desire of satisfying man, thou leave God unsatisfied, endeavor to satisfie all. God must waigh down all; thy selfe and others; but as long as thy selfe onely art in one balance, and other men in the other, let this preponderate; let the opinion of other men, waigh downe thine owne opinion of thy selfe. 'Tis true, (but many men flatter themselves too far, with this truth) that it is a sin, to do anything in *Conscientia dubia,* when a man doubts whether he may doe it, or no, and in *Conscientia scrupulosa,* when the conscience hath received any single scruple, or suspicion to the contrary, and so too *in conscientia opinante,* in a conscience that hath conceived, but an *opinion,* (which is far from a debated, and deliberate determination) yea *in conscientia errante,* though the conscience be in an error, yet it is sin to do aright against the conscience; but then, as it is a sin, to do against the conscience labouring under any of these infirmities, so it is a greater sin, not to labour to recover the conscience, and devest it of those scruples, by *their* advise, whom God hath indued with knowledg, and power, for that purpose. For, (as it is *in civill Judicature*) God refers causes to *them,* and according to their *reports,* Gods ordinary way is to decree the cause, to *loose* where they loose, to *binde* where they binde. Their imperfections, or their corruptions God knowes how to punish in them; but thou shalt have the recompense of thy humility and thy obedience to his ordinance, in harkening to *them,* whom he hath set over thee, for the rectifying of thy conscience. Neither is this to erect a *parochiall papacy,* to make every minister a *Pope* in his own parish, or to re-enthrall you to a necessity of communicating all your sinnes, or all your doubtfull actions to *him;* God forbid. God of his goodnesse hath delivered us, from that bondage, and butchery of the conscience, which our Fathers suffered from *Rome,* and *Anathema,* and *Anathema Maran-atha,* /I Corinthians 16.22/ cursed be he till the Lord comes, and cursed when the Lord comes, that should go about to bring us in a relapse, in an *eddy,* in a whirlpoole, into that disconsolate estate, or into any of the pestilent errors of that Church. But since you think it no diminution to you, to consult with a *Physician* for the state of your body, or with a *Lawyer* for your Lands, since you are not borne, nor grown good Physicians, and good Lawyers, why should you think your selves born, or grown so good *Divines,* that you need no counsell, in doubtful cases, from other men? And therefore, as for the *Law* that governs us, that is, the *Scripture,* we go the way that Christ did, to receive the testimony of man, both for the *body,* that Scriptures there are, and for the limbs of that body, that these books make up those Scriptures, and for the soule of this body, that this is the sense of the holy Ghost in that place; so, for our Judge, which is the *conscience,* let that be directed before hand, by their advise whome God hath set over us, and setled, and quieted in us, by their testimony, who are the witnesses of our conversation. And so we have done with our Problematicall part; we have asked and answered both these questions, Why this light requires *any* testimony, (and that is because exhalations, and damps, and vapours arise, first from our *ignorance,* then from our *incredulity,* after from our *negligence* in *practising,* and lastly, from our *slipperinesse in relapsing,* and therefore we need more and more attestations, and remembrances of this light) and the other question, Why after so many *other* testimonies, (from the *Magi,* from *Simeon,* from *Anna,* from many, many, very many more) he required this testimony of *John;* and that is, because all those other witnesses had testified *long before,* and because *God* in all matters belonging to *Religion* here, or to *salvation* hereafter, refers us to *man,* but to man sent, and ordained by God, for our direction, that we may do well; and to the testimony of *good men,* that we have done well. And so we passe to our *dogmaticall* part, *what* his testimony was; what *John Baptist* and his successors in preaching, and preparing the ways of Christ, are sent to do; he was sent *to beare witnesse of that light.*

13. /2 Part./ Princes which send Ambassadors, use to give them a *Commission,* containing the generall scope of the businesse committed to them, and then *Instructions,* for the fittest way to bring that businesse to effect. And upon due contemplation of both these, (his *Commission,* and his *Instructions*) arises the use of the Ambassadors judgement and discretion, in making his Commission, and his Instructions, (which do not always agree in all points, but are often various, and perplext) serve most advantagiously towards the ends of his negotiation. *John Baptist* had both; therefore they minister three considerations unto us; first, his *Commission,* what *that* was; and then his *Instructions,* what *they* were; and lastly, the *execution,* how he proceeded therein.

14. /*Commissio*/ His Commission was drawn up, and written in Esay, and recorded and entred into Gods Rolls by the Evangelists. It was, *To Prepare the way of the Lord, to make streight his paths,* /Esay 40.3/ that therefore *every valley should be exalted, every mountaine made low;* /Mark 1.3/ and all this he was to *cry* out, to make them inexcusable, who contemne the outward Ministery, and relie upon private inspirations. This Commision lasts during Gods pleasure; and Gods pleasure is, that is should last to the end of the world; Therefore are *we* also joyned in Commission with *John,* and we *cry out* still to you to all those purposes.

15. /*Preparate viam* [4]/ First, that you *prepare the way of the Lord.* But when we bid you do so, we do not meane, that this preparing or pre-disposing of your selves, is *in your selves,* that you can prevent Gods *preventing grace,* or mellow, or supple, or fit your selves for the entrance of that grace, by any *naturall faculty* in your selves. When we speak of a *co-operation,* a joint working with the grace of God, or of a *post-operation,* an after working upon the virtue of a former grace, this *co-operation,* and this *post-operation* must be mollified with a good concurrent cause with that grace. So there is a good sense of *co-operation* and *post-operation,* but *praeopera-*

tion, that we should work, *before* God work upon us, can admit no good interpretation. I could as soon beleeve that I had a being before *God* was, as that I had a *will* to good, before God moved it. But then, God having made his way into you, by his *preventing grace, prepare that way,* not *your* way, but *his* way, (sayes our Commission) that is that way that he hath made in you, prepare that by forbearing and avoiding to cast new hinderances in that way. In *sadnesse* and *dejections* of spirit, seek not your comfort in *drinke,* in *musique,* in *comedies,* in *conversation;* for, this is but a preparing a way of your owne. To prepare the *Lords way,* is to look, and consider, what way the Lord hath taken, in the like cases, in the like distresses with other servants of his, and to prepare that way in thy self, and to assure thy selfe, that God hath but practised upon *others,* that he might be perfect when he comes to *thee,* and that he intends to thee, in these thy tribulations, all that he hath promised to all, all that he hath already performed to any one. Prepare *his way;* apply that way, in which he hath gone *to others,* to thy self.

16. */Rectas facite semitas Dei/* And then, by our Commission we cry out to you, *to make streight his paths.* In which we do not require, that you should absolutely rectifie all the deformities and crookednesses, which that *Tortuositas Serpentis,* /Tertull./ the winding of the old Serpent hath brought you to; for, now the streame of oure corrupt nature, is accustomed to that crooked channell, and we cannot divert that, we cannot come to an absolute directness, and streightnesse, and profession in this life; and, in this place, the holy Ghost speakes but of *a way,* a path; not of *our rest* in the end, but of our labour in the way. Our Commission then is not to those *sinlesse* men, that think they have nothing for God to *forgive;* But, when we bid you make streight *his paths,* (as before we directed you, to take knowledge what *his* wayes towards *others* had been) so here we intend, that you should observe, which is the Lords path into you, by what way he comes oftnest into you, who are his *Temple,* and do not lock that doore, do not pervert, do not crosse, do not deface that path. The ordinary way, even of the *holy Ghost,* for the conveying of *faith,* and supernaturall graces, is (as the way of worldly knowledge is) by the *senses:* where his way is by the eare, by hearing his word *preached;* do not thou crosse that way of his, by an inordinate delight, in hearing the eloquence of the preacher; for, so thou hearest the man, and not *God,* and goest *thy way,* and not *his.* God hath divers wayes into

divers men; into some he comes at noone, in the sunshine of prosperity; to some in the *dark* and *heavy* clouds of adversity. Some he affects with the musick of the Church, some with some particular Collect or Prayer; some with some passage in a Sermon, which takes no hold of him, that stands next him. Watch the way of the Spirit of God, into thee; that way which he makes his path, in which he comes oftnest to thee, and by which thou findest thy self most affected, and best disposed towards him, and pervert not that path, foule not that way. *Make streight his paths,* that is, keepe them *streight;* and when thou observest, which is his path in thee, (by what means especially he workes upon thee) meet him in that path, embrace him in those meanes, and alwayes bring a facile, a fusil, a ductile, a tractable soule, to the offers *of his grace,* in his way.

17. /*Omnis Vallis exaltetur*/ Our Commission reaches to the exalting of your *valleys, Let every valley be exalted;* In which, we bid you not to raise your selves in this world, to such a *spirituall heighth,* as to have no regard to this world, to your *bodies,* to your *fortunes,* to your *families.* Man is not all soule, but a body too; and, as God hath married them together in thee, so hath he commanded them mutuall duties towards one another; and God allowes us large uses of *temporall blessings,* and of recreations too. To *exalt valleyes,* is not to draw up flesh, to the heighth of spirit; that cannot be, that should not be done. But it is to draw you so much towards it, as to consider (and consider with an application) that the very *Law,* which was but *the schoolmaster* to the Gospell, was given upon a *mountaine;* /Exodus 24.18, Deuteronomy 32.49/ That *Moses* could not so much as see the Land of promise, till he was brought up into a *mountaine;* That the inchoation of Christs glory, which was his *transfiguration,* was upon a *mountaine,* /Matthew 17.2, 14.23, Acts 1.10/ That his conversation with God in prayer; That his returne to his eternall Kingdom by his *ascension,* was so too, from a *mountaine;* even his exinanition, his evacuation, his lowest humiliation, his crucifying was upon a *mountaine;* and he calls, even that *humiliation,* an *exaltation, Si exaltatus, If I be exalted, lifted up,* sayes Christ, *signifying what death he should die.* /John 12.32/ Now, if our depressions, our afflictions be exaltations, (so they were to Christ, so they are to every good Christian) how far doth God allow us, an *exalting of our vallies,* in a considering with a spirituall boldnesse, the heighth and dignity of *mankind,* and to what glory God hath created us. Certainly man

may avoid as many sinnes, by this *exalting his vallies,* this considering the heighth and dignity of his nature, as by the humblest meditations in the world. For, upon those words of *Job, Manus tuae fecerunt me,* Saint *Gregory* says, *Misericordiae judicis, dignitatem suae conditionis opponit;* /10.8 Gregory/ *Job* presents the dignity of his creation, by the hand of God, as an inducement why God should regard him; It is not his valley, but his mountaines, that he brings into Gods sight; not that dust which God took into his hands, when he made him, but that person which the hands of God had made of that dust. Man is an abridgement of all the world; and as some *Abridgements* are greater, then some other authors, so is one man of more dignity, then all the earth. And therefore *exalt thy vallies,* raise thy selfe above the pleasures that this earth can promise. And above the sorrowes, it can threaten too. A painter can hardly diminish or contract an Elephant into so little a forme, but that that Elephant, when it is at the least, will still be greater then an Ant at the life, and the greatest. Sinne hath diminished man shrowdly, and brought him into a narrower compasse; but yet, his *naturall immortality,* (his soule cannot dye) and his *spirituall possibility,* even to the last gaspe, of spending that immortality in the kingdome of glory, and living for ever with God, (for otherwise, our immortality were the heaviest part of our curse) exalt this valley, this clod of earth, to a noble heighth. How ill husbands then of this dignity are we by *sinne,* to forfeit it by submitting our selves to inferior things? either to *gold,* then which every worme (because a worme hath life, and gold hath none) is in nature, more estimable, and more precious; Or, to that which is lesse then gold, to *Beauty;* for there went neither labour, nor study, nor cost to the making of that; (the Father cannot diet himselfe so, nor the mother so, as to be sure of a faire child) but it is a thing that hapned by chance, wheresoever it is; and, as there are Diamonds of divers waters, so men enthrall themselves in one clime to a black, in another to a white beauty. To that which is lesse then *gold,* or *Beauty, voice, opinion, fame, honour,* we sell our selves. And though the good opinion of good men, by good ways, be worth our study, yet popular applause, and the voice of inconsiderate men. is too cheape a price to set our selves at. And yet, it is hardly got too; for as a ship that lies in harbour within land, sometimes needs most of the points of the Compasse, to bring her forth; so if a man surrender himselfe wholly to the opinion of other men, and have not his *Criterium,* his touchstone within him, he will need both *North* and *South,* all the points of the Compasse, the breath of all men; because, as there are contrary Elements in every body, so there are contrary factions in every place and when one side cries him up, the other will depresse him, and he shall, (if not *shipwrack*) lie *still.* But yet we doe forfeit our dignity, for that which is lesse then all, then *Gold,* then *Beauty,* then *Honour;* for *sinne;* sinne which is but a privation, (as darknesse is but a privation) and privations are nothing. And therefore exalt every valley, consider the dignity of man in his *nature,* and then, in the *Sonne of God* his assuming that nature, which gave it a new dignity, and this will beget in thee a *Pride* that God loves, a valuing of thy selfe above all the tentations of this world.

18. /*Omnis mons humiliabitur*/ But yet exalt this valley temperately, consider and esteem this dignity modestly, for our Commission goes farther, not onely to the exalting of every valley, but, *Omnis mons humiliabitur, every mountain must be made low:* which is not to bring our mountainous, and swelling affections, and passions, to that flatnesse, as that we become stupid, and insensible. Mortification is not to kill nature, but to kill sinne. Bring therefore your *Ambition* to that bent, to covet a place in the kingdome of heaven, bring your *anger,* to flow into *zeale,* bring your *love* to enamour you of that face, which is *fairer then the children of men,* /Psalm 45.2/ that face, on which the Angels desire to look, Christ Jesus, and you have brought your mountains to that lownesse, which is intended, and required here.

19. /*In Deserto*/ Now, this Commission, *John Baptist* was, and we are, to publish *in deserto,* in the Desert, in the wildernesse; that is, as Saint *Hierome* notes, not in *Jerusalem,* in a tumultuary place, a place of distraction, but in the *Desert,* a place of solitude, and retirednesse. And yet this does not imply an abandoning of society, and mutuall offices, and callings in the world, but onely informes us, that every man is to have a *Desert in himself,* a retiring into himself, sometimes of emptying himself of worldly businesses, and that he spend some houres in such solititudes, and lay aside, (as one would lay aside a garment) the *Lawyer,* the *Physician,* the Merchant, or whatsoever his profession be, and say *Domine hîc sum,* Lord, I am here, I, he whom thou madest, and such as thou madest him, not such as the world hath made me, *Hîc sum,* I am here, not where the affairs of the world scatter me, but *here,* in this retiredness, Lord, *I am here, command what thou wilt;* in this retirednesse, in this solitude, (but is not a Court, is not an

Army, is not a Fair a solitude, in respect of this association, when God and a good soul are met?) but in this home solitude, in this home Desert, are we commanded to publish this Commission, as the fittest time to make impressions of all the parts thereof, *Prepare the way of the Lord, make streight his paths, exalt your vallies, and bring down your mountains.* And this was *John Baptists* Commission, *What* to do; And then he had *Instructions* with his *Commission, how to doe it;* which is another consideration.

20. /Instructions/ His Commission was long before in *Esay,* so he was *Legatus natus,* born an Ambassadour; his *Instructions* were delivered to him by God immediately, when *The Word of God came unto* John, *in the wildernese.* /Luke 3.2/ Princes oftentimes vary their Instructions from their Commissions, and do perplex their Ambassadours. God proceeded with *John Baptist,* and doth with us directly. Our Commission is to conform you to him, our Instructions are to doe that, that way, *By preaching the Baptisme of Repentance,* for the *remission of sinnes.* It is, in a word, by the *Word* and *Sacraments.* First, he sends us not as *Spies,* to lie, and learn, nor to learn and lie; but to deale apertly, manifestly, to publish, to preach; which as it forbids forcible and violent pressing the Conscience by secular or Ecclesiasticall authority, so it forbids clandestin and whispering *Conventicles;* It is a *Preaching,* a publique avowing of Gods Ordinance, in a right Calling. He gives us not our Instructions to offer Peace and reconciliation to all, and yet he not mean it to all; He bids us preach unto *all,* he bids all *hearers repent,* and he allowes us to set to his seales of reconciliation, to *all* that come as penitents. He knowes *who will,* and who *will not repent,* we doe not; but both he knowes, and so doe we, that *all may,* so far as that, if they doe not, they finde enough in themselves to *condemne* themselves, and to discharge God and us. Our Instructions are to preach, that is our way, and to preach *Repentance;* there begin you in your own bosoms: He that seeks upwards to a River, is sure to finde the head; but he that upon every bubling spring, will think to finde a River, by that may erre many wayes. If thou repent truely, thou art sure to come up to *Gods Decree* for thy salvation; but if thou begin above at the *Decree,* and say, *I am saved,* therefore *I shall repent,* thou mayest misse both. Repent, and you shall have the Seals; the Seals are the *Sacraments; Johns* was *Baptisme;* but to what? *He baptized to the amendment of life.* This then is the chain; we *preach,* you *repent;* then we give you the *Seals,* the *Sacraments,* and you *plead* them, that is, declare them a holy life; for, till that (*Sanc-*

tification) come, *Preaching,* and *Repentance,* and *Seals,* are ineffectual. A good life inanimates all. And so, having done with his Commission, *what* he was to do, and his Instructions, *how* he was to do it, we passe to our last branch, in this last part, The execution of his Commision, and Instructions, what, and how he did it, what Testimony he gave of this light.

21. /*Se non esse*/ First, he testified, *se non esse,* that *he was not this light,* this Christ, this Messias. And secondly, *Christum esse,* that this light, this Christ, this Messias was come into the world, there was no longer expectation: And lastly, *hunc esse,* that this particular person whom he designed and specified in the *Ecce Agnus, behold the Lambe of God,* was this Light, this Christ, this Messias. *He* was not, One was, Christ was; In these three consists his Testimony. First, he testified that himself was not the Messias, he confessed and denied not, and said plainly, *I am not the Christ.* /John 1.20/ Therefore, lest *John Baptist* might be overvalued, and their devotions fixed and determined in him, St. *Augustine* enlarges this consideration, *Erat Mons illustratus, non ipse Sol; John Baptist* was a hill, and a hill gloriously illustrated by the Sun, but he was not that Sun; *Mirare, mirare, sed tanquam montem; John Baptist* deserves a respect, and a regard; but regard him, and respect him but as an hill, which though high, is but the same earth; and *mons in tenebris est, nisi luce vestiatur,* A hill hath no more light in it self, then the valley, till the light invest it; *Si montem esse lucem putas; in monte naufragium facies,* If you take the hill, because it shines, to be the light it self, you shipwrack upon the top of a hill. If we rest in the person, or in the gifts of any man, to what heighth soever this hill be raised in opinion, or in the Church, still we mistake; *John Baptist,* men of the greatest endowments, and goodnesse too, are but instruments, they are not the workman himself. And therefore as they are most inexcusable, that put an infallibility in the breast of *one man,* (our adversaries of *Rome*) so do they transgresse too farre that way, that runne, and pant, and thrust after *strange preachers,* and leave their owne *Church* deserted, and their owne *Pastour* discouraged; for some one family, by the greatnesse thereof, or by the estimation thereof, may induce both those inconveniences. Truly, though it may seeme boldly said, it may be said safely, that we were better heare some *weaknesses* from our own Pastour, then some excellencies from another; go farther, some *mistakings,* from our own, then some truths from another; for, all the truths are not necessary; nor all mistakings pernicious; but obedi-

ence to order is necessary, and all disorder pernicious. Now what a way had *John Baptist* open to him, if he had been popularly disposed. Amongst a people, that at that time expected their *Messias,* (for, all the Prophecies preceding his coming were then fulfilled) and such a *Messias* as should be a *Temporall King,* and had invested an opinion, that he, *John Baptist,* was that Christ, what rebellions, what earthquakes, what inundations of people might he have drawne after him, if he would have countenanced and cherished their error to his advantage? They would have lacked no *Scriptures,* to authorize their actions. They would have found particular places of the *Prophets,* to have justified any act of theirs, in advancing their *Messias,* then expected. Therein he is our patterne; not to preach *our selves, but Christ Jesus;* /II Corinthians 4.5/ not to preach for admiration, but for edification; not to preach to advance *civill ends,* without *spirituall ends;* to promote all the way the peace of all *Christian Kingdomes,* but to refer all principally to the Kingdome of peace, and the King of peace, the God of heaven. He confessed, and denied not, and said plainly, *I am not the Christ;* That was his Testimony; we confesse, and deny not, and say plainly, That our *own parts,* our *owne passions,* the purpose of great persons, the purpose of any State, is not Christ; *we preach Christ Jesus, and him crucified;* /I Corinthians 1.23/ and whosoever preaches any other Gospell, or any other thing for Gospell, let him be accursed.

22. */Esse Natum/* I *am not* the man, sayes *John Baptist,* for, that *man* is *God* too; but yet that man, that God, that *Messias* consisting of both, is come, though I be not he. *There is one amongst you, whom you know not, whose shooe-latchet I am not worthy to loose.* /John 1.26/ In which, he sayes all this; *There is one among you;* you need seek no farther; all the promises, and Prophecies, (the *Semen mulieris,* That the *seed of the woman should bruise the Serpents head;* the *appropriation* to *Abraham, In semine tuo, In thy seed shall all Nations be blessed:* the fixation upon *David, Donec Shiloh,* till *Shiloh* come; *Esay's Virgo concipiet, Behold a Virgin shall conceive; Micah's Et tu Bethlem,* that *Bethlem should* be the place, *Daniels seventy Hebdomades,* That that should be the time,) /Genesis 3.15, Genesis 26.4, Genesis 49.10, Isaiah 7.14, Micah 5.2, Daniel 9.24/ all promises, all prophecies, all computations are at an end, the *Messias* is come.

23. */Hunc esse/* Is he come, and amongst you, and do you not know him? what will make you know him? You beleeve you need

a *Messias;* you cannot restore your selfe. You beleeve this *Messias* must come at a certain time, specified by certain marks; were all these marks upon *any other?* or lacks there any of these in *him?* Do you thus magnifie *me,* and neglect a person, *whose shooe-latchet I am not worthy to loose? John Baptist* was a Prophet, *more then a Prophet, The greatest of the sonnes of women:* Who could be so much greater then *he,* and not the *Messias?* we must necessarily enwrap all these three in one another, and into one another they do easily and naturally fall: He testifies that *he* was not the man, (he preaches not himself) he testifies that *that* man is *come;* (future expectations are frivolous) and he testifies, that the *characters* and *marks* of the expected *Messias,* can fall upon *none* but *this man,* and therefore he delivers him over to them with that confidence, *Ecce Agnus Dei, Behold the Lambe of God,* /John 1.29/ there you may see him; and this is his Testimony.

24. /*Conclusio*/ These three, *we,* we to whom *John Baptists* Commission is continued, testifie too. First, we tell you, what is *not Christ;* austerity of life, and outward sanctity is not *hee; John Baptist* had *them* abundantly, but yet permitted not, that they should have that opinion of him. But yet, much lesse is chambring and wantonnesse, and persevering in sinne, *that Christ,* or the way to him. We tell you, *stetit in medio,* /John 1.26/ he hath been amongst you, you have heard him *preached* in your ears; yea yee have heard him knock at your hearts, and for all that, we tell you that you *have not known him.* Which, though it be the discomfortablest thing in the world, (not to have known Christ in those approches) yet we tell it you somewhat to your comfort; and to your excuse, for *had you knowne it, you would not have crucified the Lord of glory* /I Corinthians 2.8/ as we doe *all,* by our daily sinnes. And though God have winked at these times of ignorance, pretermitted your former *inconsiderations*) /Acts 17.30/ now, he commandeth all men every where to *repent.* /Luke 19.42/ And therefore, that thou maist know, even thou, (as Christ iterates it) at least in this thy day, the things which belong to thy Peace, we tell you who he is, and where he is; *Ecce agnus Dei, Behold the lambe of God, Here, here* in this his ordinance he supplicates you, when the Minister, how meane soever, prays you, *in his stead, be yee reconciled to God.* /II Corinthians 5.20/ Here he proclaims, and cries to you, *Venite omnes, come all that are weary and heavy laden.* /Matthew 25.34/ Here he bleeds in the *Sacrament,* here he takes away the sinnes of the world in deriving a jurisdiction upon us, to binde and loose upon earth,

that which he will binde and loose in heaven. This we testifie to you; Doe you but receive this testimony. Till you hear that voice of consummation in heaven, *Venite benedicti, come yee blessed,* /Matthew 25.34/ you shall never heare a more comfortable Gospell then this, which was preached by Christ himselfe, *the Spirit of the Lord is upon me, to preach the Gospell to the poore, to heale the broken hearted, to preach deliverance to the captives, and the acceptable yeare of the Lord:* /Luke 4.18, Esay 61.1/ for, this was not a deliverance from their brick-making in *Egypt,* nor from their *scornes* and *contempts* in *Babylon,* but a deliverance from that unexpressible, that unconceivable bondage of *sinne,* and *death,* not by the hand of a *Moses,* but a *Messias. Optat dare qui praecipit petere,* /Augustine/ he that commands us to aske, would faine give: *Cupit largiri, qui desiderat postulari,* he that desires us to pray to him, hath that ready, and a readinesse to give that, that he bids us pray for. If the King give a *generall pardon,* will any man be so suspiciously trecherous in his own behalfe, as to say, for all this large extent of his mercy, he meant not *me,* and therefore I will sue out no pardon? If the King cast a *donative,* at his Coronation, will any man lie still and say, he meant none of that money to *me?* When the master of the feast sent his servants for guests, had it become those *poor,* and *maimed,* and *halt,* and *blind,* to have stood and disputed with the steward, and said, Surely Sir, you mistooke your Master, your Master did not meane *us?* Why should any man thinke that God meanes not *him?* When he offers grace, and salvation, to *all,* why not to him? Should God exclude him *as a man?* Why, God made him good, and, as a man and his creature, he is good still. But, *non Deus Esau hominem odit, sed odit Esau peccatorem?* /Augustine/ God did not hate *Esau,* as he was a *man,* but as he was a *sinner.* Should he exclude him as a *sinner?* Why then he should receive *none,* for we are all so; and he came for none but such, but sinners. *Perfectiorum est nihil in peccatore odiisse praeter peccata,* /Mark 2.17, Augustine/ To hate nothing in a sinner, but his sinne, is a great degree of perfection; God is that perfection; he hates nothing in thee but thy sinne; and that sinne he hath taken upon himself, and sees it not in thee. Should he exclude thee because thou art *impenitent,* because thou hast not repented? Doe it now. *Peccasti, poenitere,* Hast thou sinned? repent. *Millies peccasti? millies poenitere.* /Chrysostome/ Hast thou multiplied thy sinnes by thousands? multiply thy penitent teares so too. Should he exclude thee, because thou art *impenitible,* thou canst not repent; how knowest thou thou *canst* not repent? Doest thou try, doest thou endeavour, doest thou strive? why, this, this holy contention of thine is repentance. Discredit not Gods evidence; he offers thee *Testimonium ab homine,* the testimony of man, of the man of God, the Minister, that the promises of the Gospell belong to *thee*. Judge not against that evidence; confesse that there is *no other name given under heaven,* to be *saved, but the name of Jesus,* /Acts 4.12/ and that *that is*. And then, when thou hast thus admitted his witnesses to *thee,* that his *preaching* hath wrought upon thee, be thou his witnesse to *others,* by thy *exemplar life,* and holy conversation. In this chapter, in the calling of the Apostles some such thing is intimated, when of those two Disciples, which, upon Johns testimony /verse 40/, followed Christ, one is named, (Andrew) and the other is not named. No doubt, but the other is also written in the book of life, and long since enjoyes the blessed fruit of *that* his forwardnesse. But in the testimony of the Gospell, written for posterity, onely *Andrew* is named, who sought out his brother *Simon,* and drew *him* in, and so propagated the Church, and spread the Glory of God. They who testifie their faith by *works,* give us the better comfort, and posterity the better example. It will be but Christs first question at the last day, *What hast thou done for me?* If we can answer *that,* he will aske, *What hast thou suffered for me?* and if we can answer *that,* he will aske at last, *Whom hast thou won to me, what soul hast thou added to my Kingdome?* Our thoughts, our words, our doings, our sufferings, if they bring *but our selves* to Heaven, they are not *Witnesses;* our example brings *others;* and that is the purpose, and the end of all we have said, *John Baptist* was a witnesse to *us,* we are so to *you,* be you so to *one another*.

THE SERMON ON PSALM 63.7

The second of my Prebend Sermons upon my five Psalmes. Preached at St. Pauls, January 29.1625. (1625/6)

Psal. 63.7. BECAUSE THOU HAST BEEN MY HELPE, THEREFORE IN THE SHADOW OF THY WINGS WILL I REJOYCE.[1]

1. The Psalmes are the Manna of the Church. As Manna tasted to every man like that he liked best, so doe the Psalmes minister Instruction, and satisfaction, to every man, in every emergency and occasion. /Wisdom 16.20/ *David* was not onely a cleare Prophet of Christ himselfe, but a Prophet of every particular Christian; He fortels what I, what any shall doe, and suffer and say. And as the whole booke of Psalmes is *Oleum effusum,* (as the Spouse speaks of the name of Christ) /Canticle 1.3/ an Oyntment powred out upon all sorts of sores, A Searcloth that souples all bruises, A balme that searches all wounds; so are there some certaine Psalmes, that are Imperiall Psalmes, that command over all affections, and spread themselves over all occasions, Catholique, universall Psalmes, that apply themselves to all necessities. This is one of those; for, of those Constitutions which are called Apostolicall, one is, That the Church should meet every day, to sing this Psalme. And accordingly, *St. Chrysostome* testifies, That it was decreed, and ordained by the Primitive Fathers, that no day should passe without the publique singing of this Psalme. Under both these obligations, (those ancient Constitutions, called the Apostles, and those ancient Decrees made by the primitive Fathers) belongs to me, who have my part in the service of Gods Church, the especiall meditation, and recommendation of this Psalme. And under a third obligation too, That it is

one of those five psalmes, the daily rehearsing whereof, is injoyned to me, by the Constitutions of this Church, as five other are to every other person of our body. As the whole booke is Manna, so these five Psalmes are my Gomer, which I am to fill and empty every day of this Manna.

2. /*Divisio*/ Now as the spirit and soule of the whole booke of Psalmes is contracted into this psalme, so is the spirit and soule of this whole psalme contracted into this verse. The key of the psalme, (as St. *Hierome* calls the Titles of the psalmes) tells us, that *David* uttered this psalme, *when he was in the wildernesse of Judah;* There we see the present occasion that moved him; and we see what was passed between God and him before, in the first clause of our Text; (*Because thou hast been my helpe*) And then we will see what was to come, by the rest, (*Therefore in the shadow of thy wings will I rejoyce.*) So that we have here the whole compasse of Time, Past, Present, and Future; and these three parts of Time, shall be at this time, the three parts of this Exercise; first, what *Davids* distresse put him upon for the present; and that lyes in the Context; secondly, how *David* built his assurance upon that which was past; (*Because thou hast been my help*) And thirdly, what he established to himselfe for the future, (*Therefore in the shadow of thy wings will I rejoyce.*) First, His distresse in the Wildernesse, his present estate carried him upon the memory of that which God had done for him before, And the Remembrance of that carried him upon that, of which he assured himselfe after. Fixe upon God any where, and you shall finde him a Circle; He is with you now, when you fix upon him; He was with you before, for he brought you to this fixation; and he will be with you hereafter, for *He is yesterday, and to day, and the same for ever.* /Heb. 13.8/

3. For *Davids* present condition, who was now in a banishment, in a persecution in the Wildernesse of Judah, (which is our first part) we shall onely insist upon that, (which is indeed spread over all the psalme to the Text, and ratified in the Text) That in all those temporall calamities *David* was onely sensible of his spirituall losse; It grieved him not that he was kept from *Sauls* Court, but that he was kept from Gods Church. For when he sayes, by way of lamentation, *That he was in a dry and thirsty land, where no water was* /Ver. 1/, he expresses what penury, what barrennesse, what drought and what thirst he meant; *To see thy power, and thy glory, so as I have seene thee in the Sanctuary.* /Ver. 2/ *For there, my soule shall be satisfied as with marrow, and fatnesse,* /Ver. 5/ and there,

my mouth shall praise thee with joyfull lips. /Ver. 5/ And in some few considerations conducing to this, That spirituall losses are incomparably heavier then temporall, and that therefore, The Restitution to our spirituall happinesse, or the continuation of it, is rather to be made the subject of our prayers to God, in all pressures and distresses, then of temporall, we shall determine that first part. And for the particular branches of both the other parts, (The Remembring of Gods benefits past, And the building of an assurance for the future, upon that Remembrance) it may be fitter to open them to you, anon when we come to handle them, then now. Proceed we now to our first part, The comparing of temporall and spirituall afflictions.
4. /1 Part. *Afflictio Universalis*/ In the way of this Comparison, falls first the Consideration of the universality of afflictions in generall, and the inevitablenesse thereof. It is a blessed Metaphore, that the Holy Ghost hath put into the mouth of the Apostle, *Pondus Gloriae* /II Corinthians 4.17/, That our *afflictions* are but *light,* because there is an *exceeding,* and an *eternall waight of glory* attending them. If it were not for that exceeding waight of glory, no other waight in this world could turne the scale, or waigh downe those infinite waights of afflictions that oppresse us here. There is not onely *Pestis valde gravis,* (*the pestilence grows heavy upon the Land*) /Exodus 9.3/ but there is *Musca valde gravis* /8.24/, God calls in but the fly, to vexe Egypt, and even the fly is a heavy burden unto them. It is not onely *Job* that complains, *Aggravabit compedes, That he was a burden to himselfe,* but even *Absaloms* haire was a burden to him, till it was polled /II Samuel 14.26/. It is not onely *Jeremy* that complains, *Aggravavit compedes* /Lamentations 3.7/, That God had made a faire day heavy unto them, (*We have borne the heat, and the burden of the day.*) /Matthew 20.12/ *Sand is heavy,* /Proverbs 27.3. sayes *Solomon;* And how many suffer so? under a sand-hill of crosses, daily, hourely afflictions, that are heavy by their number, if not by their single waight? And *a stone is heavy;* (sayes he in the same place) And how many suffer so? How many, without any former preparatory crosse, or comminatory, or commonitory crosse, even in the midst of prosperity, and security, fall under some one stone, some grindstone, some mil-stone, some one insupportable crosse that ruines them? But then, (sayes *Solomon* there) *A fooles anger is heavier then both;* and how many children, and servants, and wives suffer under the anger, and morosity, and peevishnesse, and jealousie of foolish Masters, and Parents, and Husbands, though they must not say so? *David* and *Solomon* have cryed out, That

all this world is *vanity* and *levity;* and (God knowes) all is waight, and burden, and heavinesse, and oppression; And if there were not a waight of future glory to counterpoyse it, we should all sinke into nothing.

5. I aske not *Mary Magdalen,* whether lightnesse were not a burden; (for sin is certainly, sensibly a burden) But I aske *Susanna* whether even chast beauty were not a burden to her; And I aske *Joseph* whether personall comelinesse were not a burden to him. I aske not *Dives,* who perished in the next world, the question; but I aske them who are made examples of *Solomons* Rule, of that *sore evill,* (as he calls it) *Riches kept to the owners thereof for their hurt* /Eccles. 5.13/, whether Riches be not a burden.

6. All our life is a continuall burden, yet we must not groane; A continuall squeasing, yet we must not pant; And as in the tendernesse of our childhood, we suffer, and yet are whipt if we cry, so we are complained of, if we complaine, and made delinquents if we call the times ill. And that which addes waight to waight, and multiplies the sadnesse of this consideration is this, That still the best men had most laid upon them. As soone as I heare God say, that he hath found *an upright man, that feares God, and eschews evill* /[Job 1.1]/, in the next lines I finde a Commission to Satan, to bring in Sabeans and Chaldeans upon his cattell, and servants, and fire and tempest upon his children, and loathsome diseases upon himselfe. As soone as I heare God say, That he hath found *a man according to his own heart* /[I Samuel 13.14]/, I see his sonnes ravish his daughters, and then murder one another, and then rebell against the Father, and put him into straites for his life. As soone as I hear God testifie of Christ at his Baptisme, *This is my beloved Sonne in whom I am well pleased,* I finde that sonne of his *led up by the Spirit, to be tempted of the Devill* /Matthew 3.17, 4.1/. And after I heare God ratifie the same testimony againe, at his Transfiguration, (*This is my beloved Sonne in whom I am well pleased*) /Matthew 17.5/ I finde that beloved Sonne of his, deserted abandoned, and given over to Scribes, and Pharisees, and Publicans, and Herodians, and Priests, and Souldiers, and people, and Judges, and witnesses, and executioners, and he that was called the beloved Sonne of God, and made partaker of the glory of heaven, in this Transfiguration, is made now the Sewer of all the corruption, of all the sinnes of this world, as no Sonne of God, but a meere man, as no man, but a contemptible worme. As though the greatest weaknesse in this world, were man, and the greatest fault in man were to be good, man is more

miserable than other creatures, and good men more miserable then any other men.

7. /*Afflictio spiritualis*/ But then there is *Pondus Gloriae, An exceeding waight of eternall glory,* and that turnes the scale; for as it makes all worldly prosperity as dung, so it makes all worldly adversity as feathers. And so it had need; for in the scale against it, there are not onely put temporall afflictions, but spirituall too; And to these two kinds, we may accommodate those words, *He that fals upon this stone,* (upon temporall afflictions) may be bruised, broken, *But he upon whom that stone falls,* (spirituall afflictions) *is in danger to be ground to powder.* /Matthew 21.44/ And then, the great, and yet ordinary danger is, That these spirituall afflictions grow out of temporall; Murmuring, and diffidence in God, and obduration, out of worldly calamities; And so against nature, the fruit is greater and heavier then the Tree, spirituall heavier then temporall afflictions.

8. They who write of Naturall story, propose that Plant for the greatest wonder in nature, which being no firmer then a bull-rush, or a reed, produces and beares for the fruit thereof no other but an intire, and very hard stone. /Pliny 1.27.11, Litho-spermus/ That temporall affliction should produce spirituall stoninesse, and obduration, is unnaturall, yet ordinary. Therefore doth God propose it, as one of those greatest blessings, which he multiplies upon his people, *I will take away your stony hearts, and give you hearts of flesh* /Ezekiel 11.19 and 36.26/; And, Lord let mee have a fleshly heart in any sense, rather then a stony heart. Wee finde mention amonst the observers of rarities in Nature, of hairy hearts, hearts of men, that have beene overgrowne with haire; but of petrified hearts, hearts of men growne into stone, we read not; for this petrefaction of the heart, this stupefaction of a man, is the last blow of Gods hand upon the heart of man in this world. /Revelations 16/ Those great afflictions which are powred out of the Vials of the seven Angels upon the world, are still accompanied with that heavy effect, that the affliction hardened them. *They were scorched with heats and plagues.* /ver. 9/ by the fourth Angel, and it follows, *They blasphemed the name of God, and repented not, to give him glory.* Darknesse was induced upon them by the fift Angel, and it followes, *They blasphemed the God of heaven, and repented not of their deeds.* /ver. 11/ And from the seventh Angel there fell hailestones of the waight of talents /ver. 21/, (perchance foure pound waight) upon men; And yet these men had so much life left, as to

blaspheme God, out of that respect, which alone should have brought them to glorifie God, *Because the plague thereof was exceeding great.* And when a great plague brings them to blaspheme, how great shall that second plague be, that comes upon them for blaspheming?

9. Let me wither and weare out mine age in a discomfortable, in an unwholesome, in a penurious prison, and so pay my debts with my bones, and recompence the wastfulnesse of my youth, with the beggery of mine age; Let me wither in a spittle under sharpe, and foule, and infamous diseases, and so recompence the wantonnesse of my youth, with that loathsomnesse in mine age; yet, if God withdraw not his spirituall blessings, his Grace, his Patience, If I can call my suffering his Doing, my passion his Action, All this that is temporall, is but a caterpillar got into one corner of my garden, but a milldew fallen upon one acre of my Corne; The body of all, the substance of all is safe, as long as the soule is safe. But when I shall trust to that, which wee call a good spirit, and God shall deject, and empoverish, and evacuate that spirit, when I shall rely upon a morall constancy, and God shall shake, and enfeeble, and enervate, destroy and demolish that constancy; when I shall think to refresh my selfe in the serenity and sweet ayre of a good conscience, and God shall call up the damps and vapours of hell it selfe, and spread a cloud of diffidence, and an impenetrable crust of desperation upon my conscience; when health shall flie from me, and I shall lay hold upon riches to succour me, and comfort me in my sicknesse, and riches shall flie from me, and I shall snatch after favour, and good opinion, to comfort me in my poverty; when even this good opinion shall leave me, and calumnies and misinformations shall prevaile against me; when I shall need peace, because there is none but thou, O Lord, that should stand for me, and then shall finde, that all the wounds that I have, come from thy hand, all the arrowes that stick in me, from thy quiver; when I shall see, that because I have given my selfe to my corrupt nature, thou hast changed thine; and because I am all evill towards thee, therefore thou has given over being good towards me; When it comes to this height, that the fever is not in the humors, but in the spirits, that mine enemy is not an imaginary enemy, fortune, nor a transitory enemy, malice in great persons, but a reall, and irresistible, and an inexorable, and an everlasting enemy, The Lord of Hosts himselfe, the Almighty God himself, the Almighty God himselfe onely knowes the waight of this affliction, and except hee put in that *pondus gloriae,* that exceeding waight of

an eternall glory, with his owne hand, into the other scale, we are waighed down, we are swallowed up, irreparably, irrevocably, irrecoverably, irremediably.

10. This is the feareful depth, this is spirituall misery, to be thus fallen from God. But was this *Davids* case? was he fallen thus farre, into a diffidence in God? No. But the danger, the precipice, the slippery sliding into that bottomlesse depth is, to be excluded from the meanes of comming to God, or staying with God; And this is that that David laments here, That by being banished, and driven into the wildernesse of Judah, hee had not accesse to the Sanctuary of the Lord, to sacrifice his part in the praise, and to receive his part in the prayers of the Congregation; for Angels passe not to ends, but by wayes and meanes, nor men to the glory of the triumphant Church, but by participation of the Communion of the Militant. To this note *David* sets his Harpe, in many, many Psalms: Sometimes, that God had suffered his enemies to possesse his Tabernacle, (*Hee forsooke the Tabernacle of Shiloh, Hee delivered his strength into captivity, and his glory into the enemies hands*) /Psalm 78.60/ But most commonly he complaines, that God disabled him from comming to the Sanctuary. In which one thing he had summed up all his desires, all his prayers, (*One thing have I desired of the Lord, that will I looke after; That I may dwell in the house of the Lord, all the dayes of my life, to behold the beauty of the Lord, and to enquire in his Temple*) /Psalm 27.4/ His vehement desire of this, he expresses againe, (*My soule thirsteth for God, for the living God; when shall I come and appeare before God?*) /Psalm 42.2/ He expresses a holy jealousie, a religious envy, even to the sparrows and swallows, (*yea, the sparrow hath found a house, and the swallow a nest for her selfe, and where she may lay her yong, Even thine Altars, O Lord of Hosts, my King and my God.*) /Psalm 84.3/ Thou are my King, and my God, and yet excludest me from that, which thou affordest to sparrows, *And are we not of more value then many sparrows?* /Luke 12.7/

11. And as though *David* felt some false ease, some half-tentation, some whispering that way, *That God is in the wildernesse of Judah,* in every place as well as in his *Sanctuary,* /Psalm 84.3/ there is in the Originall in that place, a patheticall, a vehement, a broken expressing expressed, *O thine Altars;* It is true, (sayes *David*) thou are here in the wildernesse, and I may see thee here, and serve thee here, but *O thine Altars, O Lord of hosts, my King and my God.* When *David* could not come in person to that place, yet he bent

towards the Temple, (*In thy feare will I worship towards thy holy Temple.*) /Psalm 5.7/ Which was also *Daniels* devotion; when he prayed, *his Chamber windowes were open towards Jerusalem* /Daniel 6.10/; And so is *Hezekias* /Esay 38.2/ turning to the wall to weepe, and to pray in his sick bed, understood to be to that purpose, to conforme, and to compose himselfe towards the Temple. In the place consecrated for that use, God by *Moses* fixes the service, and fixes the Reward /Deuteronomy 31.11/; And towards that place (when they could not come to it) doth *Solomon* direct their devotion in the Consecration of the Temple, (*when they are in the warres, when they are in Captivity, and pray towards this house, doe thou heare them.*) /Kings 8.44/ For, as in private prayer, when (according to Christs command) we are shut in our chamber, there is exercised *Modestia fidei,* The modesty and bashfulnesse of our faith, not pressing upon God in his house: so in the publique prayers of the Congregation, there is exercised the fervor, and holy courage of our faith, for *Agmine facto obsidemus Deum,* /Tertullian/ It is a Mustering of our forces, and a besieging of God. Therefore does *David* so much magnifie their blessednesse, that are in this house of God; (*Blessed are they that dwell in thy house, for they will be still praising thee*) /Psalm 84.4/ Those that looke towards it, may praise thee sometimes, but those men who dwell in the Church, and whose whole service lyes in the Church, have certainly an advantage of all other men (who are necessarily withdrawne by worldly businesses, in making themselves acceptable to almighty God, if they doe their duties, and observe their Church-services aright.

12. /*Excommunicatio*/ Man being therefore thus subject naturally to manifold calamities, and spirituall calamities being incomparably heavier then temporall, and the greatest danger of falling into such spirituall calamities being in our absence from Gods Church, where onely the outward meanes of happinesse are ministred unto us, certainely there is much tendernesse and deliberation to be used, before the Church doores be shut against any man. If I would not direct a prayer to God, to excommunicate any man from the Triumphant Church, (which were to damne him) I would not oyle the key, I would not make the way too slippery for excommunications in the Militant Church; For, that is to endanger him. I know how distastfull a sin to God, contumacy, and contempt, and disobedience to Order and Authority is; And I know, (and all men, that choose not ignorance, may know) that our Excommunications (though

calumniators impute them to small things, because, many times, the first complaint is of some small matter) never issue but upon contumacies, contempts, disobediences to the Church. But they are reall contumacies, not interpretative, apparant contumacies, not presumptive, that excommunicate a man in Heaven; and much circumspection is required, and (I am far from doubting it) exercised in those cases upon earth; for, though every Excommunication upon earth be not sealed in Heaven, though it damne not the man, yet it dammes up that mans way, by shutting him out of that Church, through which he must goe to the other; which being so great a danger, let every man take heed of Excommunicating himselfe. The imperswasible Recusant does so; The negligent Libertin does so; The fantastique Separatist does so; The halfe-present man, he, whose body is but halfe here, his limbes are here upon a cushion, but his eyes, his eares are not here, does so: All these are selfe-Excommunicators, and keepe themselves from hence. Onely he enjoyes that blessing, the want whereof *David* deplores, that is here intirely, and is glad he is here, and glad to finde this kinde of service here, that he does, and wishes no other.

13. And so we have done with our first Part, *Davids* aspect, his present condition, and his danger of falling into spirituall miseries, because his persecution, and banishment amounted to an Excommunication, to an excluding of him from the service of God, in the Church. And we passe, in our Order proposed at first, to the second, his retrospect, the Consideration, what God had done for him before, *Because thou hast beene my helpe.*

14. /2 Part./ Through this second part, we shall passe by these three steps. First, That it behoves us, in all our purposes, and action, to propose to our selves a copy to write by, a patterne to worke by, a rule, or an example to proceed by, Because it hath beene thus heretofore, sayes *David,* I will resolve upon this course for the future. And secondly, That the copy, the patterne, the precedent which we are to propose to our selves, is, The observation of Gods former wayes and proceedings upon us, Because God hath already gone this way, this way I will awaite his going still. And then, thirdly and lastly, in this second part, The way that God had formerly gone with *David,* which was, That he had been his helpe, (*Because thou hast beene my helpe.*)

15. */Ideae/* First then, from the meanest artificer, through the wisest Philosopher, to God himselfe, all that is well done, or wisely undertaken, is undertaken and done according to pre-conceptions, fore-

imaginations, designes, and patterns proposed to our selves beforehand. A Carpenter builds not a house, but that he first sets up a frame in his owne minde, what kinde of house he will build. The little great Philosopher *Epictetus,* would undertake no action, but he would first propose to himselfe, what *Socrates,* or *Plato,* what a wise man would do in that case, and according to that, he would proceed. Of God himselfe, it is safely resolved in the Schoole, that he never did any thing in any part of time, of which he had not an eternall pre-conception, an eternall Idea, in himselfe before. Of which Ideaes, that is, pre-conceptions, predeterminations in God, St. *Augustine* pronounces, *Tanta vis in Ideis constituitur,*[2] There is so much truth, and so much power in these Ideaes, as that without acknowledging them, no man can acknowledge God, for he does not allow God Counsaile, and Wisdome, and deliberation in his Actions, but sets God on worke, before he have thought what he will doe. And therefore he, and others of the Fathers read that place, (which we read otherwise) *Quod factum est, in ipso vita erat;* /John 1.3, 4/ that is, in all their Expositions, whatsoever is made, in time, was alive in God, before it was made, that is, in that eternall Idea, and patterne which was in him. So also doe divers of those Fathers read those words to the Hebrews, (which we read, *The things that are seene, are not made of things that doe appeare*) *Ex invisibilibus visibilia facta sunt, Things formerly invisible, were made visible;* /Heb. 11.3/ that is, we see them not till now, till they are made, but they had an invisible being, in that Idea, in that pre-notion, in that purpose of God before, for ever before. Of all things in Heaven, and earth, but of himselfe, God had an Idea, a patterne in himselfe, before he made it.

16. And therefore let him be our patterne for that, to worke after patternes; To propose to our selves Rules and Examples for all our actions; and the more, the more immediately, the more directly our actions concerne the service of God. If I aske God, by what Idea he made me, God produces his *Faciamus hominem ad Imaginem nostram* /Genesis 1.26/, That there was a concurrence of the whole Trinity, to make me in *Adam,* according to that Image which they were, and according to that Idea, which they had predetermined. If I pretend to serve God, and he aske me for my Idea, How I meane to serve him, shall I bee able to produce none? If he aske me an Idea of my Religion, and my opinions, shall I not be able to say, It is that which thy word, and thy Catholique Church hath imprinted in me? If he aske me an Idea of my prayers, shall I not be able to say, It is

that which my particular necessities, that which the forme prescribed by thy Son, that which the care, and piety of the Church, in conceiving fit prayers, hath imprinted in me? If he aske me an Idea of my Sermons, shall I not be able to say, It is that which the Analogy of Faith, the edification of the Congregation, the zeale of thy worke, the meditations of my heart have imprinted in me? But if I come to pray or to preach without this kind of Idea, if I come to extemporall prayer, and extemporall preaching, I shall come to an extemporall faith, and extemporall religion; and then I must looke for an extemporall Heaven, a Heaven to be made for me; for to that Heaven which belongs to the Catholique Church, I shall never come, except I go by the way of the Catholique Church, by former Idea's, former examples, former patterns, To beleeve according to former meditations. God does nothing, man does nothing well, without these Idea's, these retrospects, this recourse to pre-conceptions, pre-deliberations.

17. */Via Domini/* Something then I must propose to my selfe, to be the rule, and the reason of my present and future actions; which was our first branch in this second Part; And then the second is, That I can propose nothing more availably, then the contemplation of the history of Gods former proceeding with me; which is *Davids* way here, Because this was Gods way before, I will looke for God in this way still. That language in which God spake to man, the Hebrew, hath no present tense; They forme not their verbs as our Westerne Languages do, in the present *I heare,* or *I see,* or *I reade,* But they begin at that which is past, *I have seene* and *heard,* and *read.* God carries us in his Language, in his speaking, upon that which he hath done already; I cannot have better security for present, nor future, then Gods former mercies exhibited to me. *Quis non gaudeat,* sayes St. Augustine, Who does not triumph with joy, when hee considers what God hath done? *Quis non et ea, quae nondum venerunt, ventura sperat, propter illa, quae jam tanta impleta sunt?* Who can doubt of the performance of all, that sees the greatest part of a Prophesie performed? If I have found that true that God hath said, of the person of Antichrist, why should I doubt of that which he sayes of the ruine of Antichrist? *Credamus modicum quod restat,* sayes the same Father, It is much that wee have seene done, and it is but little that God hath reserved to our faith, to beleeve that it shall be done.

18. There is no State, no Church, no Man, that hath not this tie upon God, that hath not God in these bands, That God by having done

much for them already, hath bound himselfe to doe more. Men proceed in their former wayes, sometimes, lest they should confesse an error, and acknowledge that they had beene in a wrong way. God is obnoxious to no error, and therefore he does still, as he did before. Every one of you can say now to God, Lord, Thou broughtest me hither, therefore enable me to heare; Lord Thou doest that, therefore make me understand; And that, therefore let me beleeve; And that too, therefore strengthen me to the practise; And all that, therefore continue me to a perseverance. Carry it up to the first sense and apprehension that ever thou hadst of Gods working upon thee, either in thy selfe, when thou camest first to the use of reason, or in others in thy behalfe, in thy baptisme, yet when thou thinkest thou art at the first, God had done something for thee before all that; before that, hee had elected thee, in that election which St. *Augustine* speaks of *Habet electos, quos creaturus est eligendos,* God hath elected certaine men, whom he intends to create, that he may elect them; that is, that he may declare his Election upon them. God had thee, before he made thee; He loved thee first, and then created thee, that thou loving him, he might continue his love to thee. The surest way, and the nearest way to lay hold upon God, is the consideration of that which he had done already. So *David* does; And that which he takes knowledge of, in particular, in Gods former proceedings towards him, is, Because God had been his helpe, which is our last branch in this part, *Because thou hast beene my helpe.*

19. /*Quia auxilium*/ From this one word, That God hath been my *Helpe,* I make account that we have both these notions; first, That God hath not left me to my selfe, He hath come to my succour, He hath helped me; And then, That God hath not left out my selfe; He hath been my Helpe, but he hath left some thing for me to doe with him, and by his helpe. My security for the future, in this consideration of that which is past, lyes not onely in this, That God hath delivered me, but in this also, that he hath delivered me by way of a Helpe, and Helpe alwayes presumes an endeavour and co-operation in him that is helped. God did not elect me as a helper, nor create me, nor redeeme me, nor convert me, by way of helping me; for he alone did all, and he had no use at all of me. God infuses his first grace, the first way, meerly as a Giver; intirely, all himselfe; but his subsequent graces; and we alwayes receive them, when we endevour to make use of his former grace. *Lord, I beleeve.* (sayes the Man in the Gospel to Christ) *Helpe mine unbeliefe* /Mark 9.24/. If there had not been unbeliefe, weaknesse, unperfectnesse in that faith, it

had not been capable of helpe and assistance, but it must have been an intire act, without any concurrence on the mans part.

20. So that if I have truly the testimony of a rectified Conscience, That God hath helped me, it is in both respects; first, That he hath never forsaken me, and then, That he hath never suffered me to forsake my selfe; He hath blessed me with that grace, that I trust in no helpe but his; and with this grace too, That I cannot looke for his helpe, except I helpe my selfe also. God did not helpe heaven and earth to proceed out of nothing in the Creation, for they had no possibility of any disposition towards it; for they had no beeing: But God did helpe the earth to produce grasse, and herbes; for, for that, God had infused a seminall disposition into the earth, which for all that, it could not have perfected without his farther helpe. As in the making of Woman, there is the very word of our Text, *Gnazar,* God made him a *Helper,* one that was to doe much for him, but not without him. So that then, if I will make Gods former working upon me, an argument of his future gracious purposes, as I must acknowledge that God hath done much for me, so I must finde, that I have done what I could, by the benefit of that grace with him; for God promises to be but a helper. *Lord open thou my lips,* sayes *David;* that is Gods worke intirely; and then, *My mouth, My mouth shall shew forth thy praise* /Psalm 51.15/; there enters *David* into the worke with God. And then, sayes God to him, *Dilata os tuum, Open thy mouth,* (It is now made *Thy mouth,* and therefore doe thou open it) *and I will fill it* /Psalm 81.10/; All inchoations and consummations, beginnings and perfectings are of God, of God alone; but in the way there is a concurrence on our part, (by a successive continuation of Gods grace) in which God proceeds as a Helper; and I put him to more then that, if I doe nothing. But if I pray for his helpe, and apprehend and husband his graces well, when they come, then he is truly, properly my helper; and upon that security, that testimony of a rectified Conscience, I can proceed to *Davids* confidence for the future, *Because thou hast been my Helpe, therefore in the shadow of thy wings will I rejoyce;* which is our third, and last generall part.

21. /*Divisio* 3 Part./ In this last part, which is, (after *Davids* aspect, and consideration of his present condition, which was, in the effect an Exclusion from Gods Temple, And his retrospect, his consideration of Gods former mercies to him, That he had been his Helpe) his prospect, his confidence for the future, we shall stay a little upon these two steps; first, That that which he promises himselfe, is not

an immunity from all powerfull enemies, nor a sword of revenge upon those enemies; It is not that he shall have no adversary, nor that that adversary shall be able to doe him no harme, but that he should have a refreshing, a respiration, *In velamento alarum,* under the shadow of Gods wings. And then, (in the second place) That this way which God shall be pleased to take, this manner, this measure of refreshing, which God shall vouchsafe to afford, (though it amount not to a full deliverance) must produce a joy, a rejoycing in us; we must not onely not decline to a murmuring, that we have no more, no nor rest upon a patience for that which remains, but we must ascend to a holy joy, as if all were done and accomplished, *In the shadow of thy wings will I rejoyce.*

22. /*Umbra Alarum*/. First then, lest any man in his dejection of spirit, or of fortune should stray into a jealousie or suspition of Gods power to deliver him, As God hath spangled the firmament with starres, so hath he his Scriptures with names, and Metaphors, and denotations of power. Sometimes he shines out in the name of a *Sword,* and of a *Target,* and of a *Wall,* and of a *Tower,* and of a *Rocke,* and of a *Hill;* And sometimes in that glorious and manifold constellation of all together, *Dominus exercituum, The Lord of Hosts.* God, as God, is never represented to us, with Defensive Armes; He needs them not. When the Poets present their great Heroes, and their Worthies, they always insist upon their Armes, they spend much of their invention upon the description of their Armes; both the greatest valour and strength needs Armes, (*Goliah* himselfe was armed) and because to expose ones selfe to danger unarmed, is not valour, but rashnesse. But God is invulnerable in himselfe, and is never represented armed; you finde no shirts of mayle, no Helmets, no Cuirasses in Gods Armory. In that one place of *Esay,* /59.17/ where it may seeme to be otherwise, where God is said *to have put on righteousnesse as a breastplate, and a Helmet of Salvation upon his head;* in that prophecy God is Christ, and is therefore in that place, called *the Redeemer.* Christ needed defensive armes, God does not. Gods word does; His Scriptures doe; And therefore St. *Hierome* hath armed them, and set before every booke his *Prologum galeatum,* that prologue that armes and defends every booke from calumny. But though God need not, nor receive not defensive armes for himselfe, yet God is to us a Helmet, a Breastplate, a strong tower, a rocke, every thing that may give us assurance and defence; and as often as he will, he can refresh that Proclama-

tion, *Nolite tangere Christos meos,* Our enemies shall not so much as touch us. /Psalm 105.15/

23. But here, by occasion of his Metaphore in this Text, (*Sub umbra alarum, In the shadow of thy wings*) we doe not so much consider an absolute immunity, That we shall not be touched, as a refreshing and consolation, when we are touched, though we be pinched and wounded. The Names of God, which are most frequent in the Scriptures, are these three, *Elohim,* and *Adonai,* and *Jehovah;* and to assure us of his Power to deliver us, two of these three are Names of Power. *Elohim* is *Deus fortis,* The mighty, The powerfull God: And (which deserves a particular consideration) *Elohim* is a plurall Name; It is not *Deus fortis, but Dii fortes,* powerfull Gods. God is all kinde of Gods; All kinds, which either Idolaters and Gentils can imagine, (as Riches, or Justice, or Wisdome, or Valour, or such) and all kinds which God himself hath called gods, (as Princes, and Magistrates, and Prelates, and all that assist and helpe one another) God is *Elohim,* All these Gods, and all these in their height and best of their power; for *Elohim,* is *Dii fortes,* Gods in the plurall, and those plurall gods in their exaltation.

24. The second Name of God, is a Name of power too, *Adonai.* For Adonai is *Dominus,* The Lord, such a Lord, as is Lord and Proprietary of all his creatures, and all creatures are his creatures; And then, *Dominium est potestas tum utendi, tum abutendi,* sayes the law; To be absolute Lord of anything, gives that Lord a power to doe what he will with the thing. God, as he is *Adonai, The Lord,* may give and take, quicken and kill, build and throw downe, where and whom he will. So then two of Gods three Names are Names of absolute power, to imprint, and re-imprint an assurance in us, that hee can absolutely deliver us, and fully revenge us, if he will. But then, his third Name, and that Name which hee chooses to himselfe, and in the signification of which Name, hee employes *Moses,* for the reliefe of his people under Pharaoh, that Name *Jehovah,* is not a Name of Power, but onely of Essence, of Being, of Subsistence, and yet in the vertue of that Name, God relieved his people. And if, in my affliction, God vouchsafe to visit mee in that Name, to preserve me in my being, in my subsistence in him, that I be not shaked out of him, disinherited in him, excommunicate from him, devested of him, annihilated towards him, let him, at his good pleasure, reserve his *Elohim,* and his *Adonai,* the exercises and declarations of his mighty Power, to those great publike causes, that more concerne his

Glory, then any thing that can befall me; But if he impart his *Jehovah,* enlarge himselfe so far towards me, as that I may live, and move, and have my beeing in him, though I be not instantly delivered, nor mine enemies absolutely destroyed, yet this is as much as I should promise my selfe, this is as much as the Holy Ghost intends in this Metaphor, *Sub umbra alarum, Under the shadow of thy wings,* that is a Refreshing, a Respiration, a Conservation, a Consolation in all afflictions that are inflicted upon me.

25. Yet, is not this Metaphor of *Wings* without a denotation of Power. As no Act of Gods, though it seeme to imply but spirituall comfort, is without a denotation of power, (for it is the power of God that comforts me; To overcome that sadnesse of soule, and that dejection of spirit, which the Adversary by temporall afflictions would induce upon me, is an act of his Power) So this Metaphor, *The shadow of his wings,* (which in this place expresses no more, then consolation and refreshing in misery, and not a powerful deliverance out of it) is so often in the Scriptures made a denotation of Power too, as that we can doubt of no act of power, if we have this shadow of his wings. For, in this Metaphor of *Wings,* doth the Holy Ghost expresse the *Maritime* power, the power of some Nations at Sea, in Navies, (*Woe to the land shadowing with wings;*) /Esay. 18.1/ that is, that hovers over the world, and intimidates it with her sailes and ships. In this Metaphor doth God remember his people, of his powerfull deliverance of them, (*You have seene what I did unto the Egyptians, and how I bare you on Eagles wings, and brought you to my selfe.*) /Exodus 19.4/ In this Metaphor doth God threaten his and their enemies, what hee can doe, (*The noise of the wings of his Cherubims, are as the noise of great waters, and of an Army.*) /Ezekiel 1.24/ So also, what hee will doe, (*He shall spread his wings over Bozrah, and at that day shall the hearts of the mighty men of Edom, be as the heart of a woman in her pangs.*) /Jeremiah 49.22/ So that, if I have the shadow of his wings, I have the earnest of the power of them too; If I have refreshing, and respiration from them, I am able to say, (as those three Confessors did to *Nebuchadnezzar*) *My God is able to deliver me,* I am sure he hath power; *And my God will deliver me,* when it conduces to his glory, I know he will; *But, if he doe not, bee it knowne unto thee, O King, we will not serve thy Gods;* /Daniel 3.17/ Be it knowne unto thee, O Satan, how long soever God deferre my deliverance, I will not seeke false comforts, the miserable comforts of this world. I will not, for I need

not; for I can subsist under this shadow of these Wings, though I have no more.

26. The Mercy-seat it selfe was covered with the Cherubims Wings /Exodus 25.20/; and who would have more then Mercy? and a Mercy-seat; that is, established, resident Mercy, permanent and perpetuall Mercy; present and familiar Mercy; a Mercy-seat. Our Saviour Christ intends as much as would have served their turne, if they had laid hold upon it, when hee sayes, *That hee would have gathered Jerusalem, as a henne gathers her chickens under her wings* /Matthew 23.37/. And though the other Prophets doe (as ye have heard) mingle the signification of Power, and actuall deliverance, in this Metaphor of Wings, yet our Prophet, whom wee have now in especiall consideration, *David,* never doth so; but in every place where hee uses this Metaphor of Wings (which are in five or sixe severall Psalmes) still hee rests and determines in that sense, which is his meaning here; That though God doe not actually deliver us, nor actually destroy our enemies, yet if hee refresh us in the shadow of his Wings, if he maintaine our subsistence (which is a religious Constancy) in him, this should not onely establish our patience, (for that is but halfe the work) but it should also produce a joy, and rise to an exultation, which is our last circumstance *Therefore in the shadow of thy wings, I will rejoice.*

27. *Gaudium.* I would always raise your hearts, and dilate your hearts, to a holy Joy, to a joy in the Holy Ghost. There may be just feare, that men doe not grieve enough for their sinnes; but there may bee a just jealousie, and suspition too, that they may fall into inordinate griefe, and diffidence of Gods mercy; And God hath reserved us to such times, as being the later times, give us even the dregs and lees of misery to drinke. For, God hath not onely let loose into the world a new spirituall disease; which is, an equality, and an indifferency, which religion our children, or our servants, or our companions professe; (I would not keepe company with a man that thought me a knave, or a traitor; with him that thought I loved not my Prince, or were a faithlesse man, not to be beleeved, I would not associate my selfe; And yet I will make him my bosome companion, that thinks I doe not love God, that thinks I cannot be saved) but God hath accompanied, and complicated almost all our bodily diseases of these times, with an extraordinary sadnesse, a predominant melancholy, a faintnesse of heart, a chearlesnesse, a joylesnesse of spirit, and therefore I returne often to this endeavor

of raising your hearts, dilating your hearts with a holy Joy, Joy in the holy Ghost, for *Under the shadow of his wings,* you may, you should, *rejoyce.*

28. If you looke upon this world in a Map, you find two Hemisphears, two half worlds. If you crush heaven into a Map, you may find two Hemisphears too, two half heavens; Halfe will be Joye, and halfe will be Glory, for in these two, the joy of heaven, and the glory of heaven, is all heaven often represented unto us. And as of those two Hemisphears of the world, the first hath been knowne long before, but the other, (that of America, which is the richer in treasure) God reserved for later Discoveries; So though he reserve that Hemisphear of heaven, which is the Glory thereof, to the Resurrection, yet the other Hemisphear, the Joy of Heaven, God opens to our Discovery, and delivers for our habitation even whilst we dwell in this world. As God hath cast upon the unrepentant sinner two deaths, a temporall, and a spirituall death, so hath he breathed into us two lives; for so, as the word for death is doubled, *Morte morieris, Thou shalt die the death* /Genesis 2.17/, so is the word for life expressed in the plurall, *Chaiim, vitarum, God breathed into his nostrils the breath of lives,* of divers lives. Though our naturall life were no life, but rather a continuall dying, yet we have two lives besides that, an eternall life reserved for heaven, but yet a heavenly life too, a spirituall life, even in this world; And as God doth thus inflict two deaths, and infuse two lives, so doth he also passe two Judgements upon man, or rather repeats the same Judgement twice. For, that which Christ shall say to thy soule then at the last Judgement, *Enter into thy Masters joy* /Matthew 25.23/, Hee sayes to thy conscience now, *Enter into thy Masters joy.* The everlastingnesse of the joy is the blessednesse of the next life, but the entring, the inchoation is afforded here. For that which Christ shall say then to us, *Venite benedicti, Come ye blessed* /Verse 34/, are words intended to persons that are comming, that are upon the way, though not at home; Here in this world he bids us *Come,* there in the next, he shall bid us *Welcome.* The Angels of heaven have joy in thy conversion, /Luke 15.10/ and canst thou bee without that joy in thy selfe? If thou desire revenge upon thine enemies, as they are Gods enemies, That God would be pleased to renew and root out all such as oppose him, that Affection appertaines to Glory; Let that alone till thou come to the Hemisphear of Glory; There joyne with those Martyrs under the Altar, *Usquequo Domine,* /Revelation 6.10/ How long O Lord, dost thou deferre Judgement? and thou shalt have

thine answere there for that. Whilst thou art here, here joyne with *David,* and the other Saints of God, in that holy increpation of a dangerous sadnesse, *Why art thou cast downe O my soule? why art thou disquieted in mee?* /Psalm 42.5/ That soule that is dissected and anatomized to God, in a sincere confession, washed in the teares of true contrition, embalmed in the blood of reconciliation, the blood of Christ Jesus, can assigne no reason, can give no just answer to that Interrogatory, *Why art thou cast downe O my soule? why art thou disquieted in me?* No man is so little, as that he can be lost under these wings, no man so great, as that they cannot reach to him; *Semper ille major est, quantumcumque creverimus* /Augustine/, To what temporall, to what spirituall greatnesse soever wee grow, still pray wee him to shadow us under his Wings; for the poore need those wings against oppression, and the rich against envy. The Holy Ghost, who is a Dove, shadowed the whole world under his wings; *Incubabat aquis* /Genesis 1.2[3]/, He hovered over the waters, he sate upon the waters, and he hatched all that was produced, and all that was produced so, was good. Be thou a Mother where the Holy Ghost would be a Father; Conceive by him; and be content that he produce joy in thy heart here. First thinke, that as a man must have some land, or els he cannot be in wardship, so man must have some of the love of God, or els he could not fall under Gods correction; God would not give him his physick, God would not study his cure, if he cared not for him. And then thinke also, that if God afford thee the shadow of his wings, that is, Consolation, respiration, refreshing, though not a present, and plenary deliverance, in thy afflictions, not to thanke God, is a murmuring, and not to rejoyce in Gods wayes, is an unthankfulnesse. Howling is the noyse of hell, singing the voyce of heaven; Sadnesse the damp of Hell. Rejoycing the serenity of Heaven. And he that hath not this joy here, lacks one of the best pieces of his evidence for the joyes of his heaven; and hath neglected or refused that Earnest, by which God uses to binde his bargaine, that true joy in this world shall flow into the joy of Heaven, as a River flowes into the Sea; This joy shall not be put out in death, and a new joy kindled in me in Heaven; But as my soule, as soone as it is out of my body, is in Heaven, and does not stay for the possession of Heaven, nor for the fruition of the sight of God, till it be ascended through ayre, and fire, and Moone, and Sun, and Planets, and Firmament, to that place which we conceive to be Heaven, but without the thousandth part of a minutes stop, as soone as it issues, is in a glorious light, which is Heaven, (for all the way to Heaven is Heaven; And as those Angels, which came from Heaven hither, bring Heaven with them, and are in Heaven here, So that soule that goes to Heaven, meets Heaven here; and as those Angels doe not devest Heaven by comming, so these soules invest Heaven, in their going). As my soule shall not goe towards Heaven, but goe by Heaven to Heaven, to the Heaven of Heavens, So the true joy of a good soule in this world is the very joy of Heaven; and we goe thither, not that being without joy, we might have joy infused into us, but that as Christ sayes, *Our joy might be full* /John 16.24/, perfected, sealed with an everlastingnesse; for, as he promises, *That no man shall take our joy from us,* /John 16.22/, so neither shall Death it selfe take it away, nor so much as interrupt it, or discontinue it, But as in the face of Death, when he layes hold upon me, and in the face of the Devill, when he attempts me, I shall see the face of God (for, every thing shall be a glasse, to reflect God upon me) so in the agonies of Death, in the anguish of that dissolution, in the sorrowes of that valediction, in the irreversiblenesse of that transmigration, I shall have a joy, which shall no more evaporate, then my soule shall evaporate, A joy, that thall passe up, and put on a more glorious garment above, and be joy super-invested in glory. *Amen.*

THE TWO-PART SERMON ON FISHERS OF MEN

At the Haghe Decemb. 19. 1619. I Preached upon this Text. Since in my sicknesse at Abrey-hatche in Essex, 1630, revising my short notes of that Sermon, I digested them into these two.

Mat. 4.18, 19, 20. AND JESUS WALKING BY THE SEA OF GALILE SAW TWO BRETHREN, SIMON CALLED PETER, AND ANDREW HIS BROTHER, CASTING A NET INTO THE SEA, (FOR THEY WERE FISHERS,) AND HE SAITH UNTO THEM, FOLLOW ME, AND I WILL MAKE YOU FISHERS OF MEN; AND THEY STRAIGHTWAY LEFT THEIR NETS, AND FOLLOWED HIM.

1. Solomon presenting our Saviour Christ, in the name and person of Wisdome, in the booke of Proverbs, puts, by instinct of the Holy Ghost, these words into his mouth, *Deliciae meae esse cum filiis hominum, Christs delight is to be with the children of men*/Prov. 8.30/; And in satisfaction of that delight, he sayes in the same verse, in the person of Christ, *That he rejoyced to be in the habitable parts of the Earth,* (that is, where he might converse with men) *Ludens in orbe terrarum,* (so the Vulgat reads it) and so our former Translation had it, *I tooke my solace in the compasse of the Earth.* But since Christs adversary Satan does so too, (Satan came *from compassing the Earth to and fro, and from walking in it;*/Job 1.7/) since the Scribes and Pharisees doe more then so, *They compasse Land and Sea, to make one of their own profession,* the mercy of Christ is not lesse active, not lesse industrious then the malice of his adversaries, He preaches in populous Cities, he preaches in the desart wildernesse, he preaches in the tempestuous Sea: and as his Power shall collect the severall dusts, and atoms, and Elements of our scattered bodies at the Resurrection, as materialls, members of his Triumphant Church; so he collects the materialls, the living

stone, and timber, for his Militant Church, from all places, from Cities, from Desarts, and here in this Text, from the Sea, (*Jesus walking by the Sea, &c.*)

2. */Divisio/* In these words we shall onely pursue a twofold consideration of the persons whom Christ called here to his Apostleship, *Peter* and *Andrew;* What their present, what their future function was, what they were, what they were to be; They were *fishermen,* they were to be *fishers of men.* But from these two considerations of these persons, arise many Circumstances, in and about their calling; and their preferment for their chearfull following. For first, in the first, we shall survay the place, *The Sea of Galile;* And their education and conversation upon that Sea, by which they were naturally less fit for this Church-service. At this Sea he found them *casting their Nets;* of which act of theirs, there is an emphaticall reason expressed in the text, *For they were fishers,* which intimates both these notes, That they did it because they were fishers; It became them, it behoved them, it concerned them to follow their trade; And then they did it as they were fishers, If they had not been fishers they would not have done it, they might not have usurped upon anothers Calling; (*They cast their Nets into the Sea, for they were fishers*) And then, in a nearer consideration of these persons, we finde that they were *two* that were called; Christ provided at first against singularity, He called not one alone; And then they were *two Brethren,* persons likely to agree; He provided at first against schisme; And then, they were two such as were nothing of kinne to him, (whereas the second payre of brethren, whom he called, *James* and *John,* were his kinsmen) He provided at first, against partiality, and that kinde of Simony, which prefers for affection. These men, thus conditioned naturally, thus disposed at this place, and at this time, our blessed Saviour calls; And then we note their readinesse, they obeyed the call, they did all they were bid, They were bid *follow,* and they *followed,* and *followed presently;* And they did somewhat more then seemes expresly to have been required, for, *They left their Nets, and followed him.* And all these substantiall circumstances invest our first part, these persons in their first estate. For those that belong to the second part, Their preferment upon this obedience, (*Follow me, and I will make you fishers of men*) it would be an inpertinent thing, to open them now, because I doe easily foresee, that this day we shall not come to that part.

3. /Andreas/ In our first part, The consideration of these persons

then, though in this Text *Peter* be first named, yet we are to note, that this was not in the first time of their meeting; when Christ and they met first, which was, when *John Baptist* made that declaration upon Christs walking by him, *Behold the Lamb of God*/John/, *Peter* was not the first that applied himselfe to Christ, nor that was invited by Christ's presenting himselfe to him, to doe it; *Peter* was not there; *Peter* was not the second; for, *Andrew,* and another, who were then *John Baptists* Disciples, and saw Christ declared by him, were presently affected with a desire to follow Christ, and to converse with him, and to that purpose presse him with that question, *Magister, ubi habitas?* They professe that they had chosen him for their Master, and they desire to know where he dwelt, that they might waite upon him, and receive their instructions from him. And in *Andrews* thus early applying himselfe to Christ, we are also to note, both the fecundity of true Religion; for, as soone as he had found Christ, he sought his brother *Peter, Et duxit ad Jesum,* he made his brother as happy as himselfe, he led him to Jesus; (And that other Disciple, which came to Christ as soone as *Andrew* did, yet because he is not noted to have brought any others but himselfe, is not named in the Gospel) And we are to observe also, the unsearchable wisdome of God in his proceedings, that he would have *Peter,* whom he had purposed to be his principall Apostle, to be led to him by another, of inferior dignity, in his determination. And there *Conversus converte,* Thinke not thy selfe well enough preached unto, except thou finde a desire, that thy life and conversation may preach to others, and *Edoctus disce,* thinke not that thou knowest any thing, except thou desire to learne more; neither grudge to learne of him, whom thou thinkest lesse learned then thy selfe; the blessing is in Gods Calling, and Ordinance, not in the good parts of the man; *Andrew* drew *Peter,* The lesser in Gods purpose for the building of the Church, brought in the greater. Therefore doth the Church celebrate the memory of St. *Andrew,* first of any Saint in the yeare; and after they have been altogether united in that one festivall of *All-Saints,* St. *Andrew* is the first that hath a particular day. He was *Primogenitus Testamenti novi*/Bernard/, The first Christian, the first begotten of the new Testament; for, *John Baptist,* who may seeme to have the birthright before him, had his conception in the old Testament, in the wombe of those prophecies of *Malachy*/3.1/, and of *Esay*/40.3/, of his comming, and of his office, and so cannot be so intirely referred to the new Testament, as St. *Andrew* is. Because therefore, our adversaries of the Romane heresie distill, and racke every passage of Scripture, that may drop any thing for the advantage of St. *Peter,* and the allmightines of his Successor, I refuse not the occasion offered from this text, compared with the other, *John* I. to say, That if that first comming to Christ were but (as they use to say) *Ad notitiam et familiaritatem,* and this is our Text, *Ad Apostolatum,* That they that came there, came but to an acquaintance, and conversation with Christ, but here, in this text, to the Apostleship, yet, to that conversation, (which was no small happinesse) *Andrew* came clearly before *Peter,* and to this Apostleship here *Peter* did not come before *Andrew;* they came together.

4. */Mare Galilaeum/* These two then our Saviour found, *as he walked by the Sea of Galile.* No solitude, no tempest, no bleaknesse, no inconvenience averts Christ, and his Spirit, from his sweet, and gracious, and comfortable visitations. But yet, this that is called here, *The Sea of Galile,* was not properly a Sea; but according to the phrase of the Hebrews, who call all great meetings of waters, by that one name, A Sea, this, which was indeed a lake of fresh water, is called a Sea. From the roote of Mount Libanus, spring two Rivers, Jor, and Dan; and those two meeting together, joyning their waters, joyne their names too, and make that famous river Jordan; a name so composed, as perchance our River is, Thamesis, of Thame, and Isis. And this River Jordan falling into this flat, makes this Lake, of sixteene miles long, and some sixe in breadth. Which Lake being famous for fish, though of ordinary kinds, yet of an extraordinary taste and relish, and then of extraordinary kinds too, not found in other waters, and famous, because divers famous Cities did engirt it, and become as a garland to it, *Capernaum,* and *Chorazim,* and *Bethsaida,* and *Tiberias,* and *Magdalo,* (all celebrated in the Scriptures) was yet much more famous for the often recourse, which our Saviour (who was of that Countrey) made to it; For this was the Sea, where he amazed *Peter,* with that great draught of fishes, that brought him to say, *Exi a me Domine, Depart from me, O Lord, for I am a sinfull man*/Matt. 14.25; Luke 5.8/This was the sea, where himselfe *walked upon the waters* And where he *rebuked the tempest*/Matt. 8.23/;[1] And where he manifested his Almighty power many times. And by this Lake, this Sea, dwelt *Andrew* and *Peter,* and using the commodity and the place, lived upon fishing in this Lake; and in that act our Saviour found them, and called them to his service. Why them? Why *fishers?*

5. */Cur Piscatores/* First, Christ having a greater, a fairer Jeru-

salem to build then *Davids* was, a greater Kingdome to establish then Juda's was, a greater Temple to build then *Solomons* was, having a greater work to raise, yet he begun upon a lesse ground; Hee is come from his twelve Tribes, that afforded armies in swarmes, to twelve persons, twelve Apostles; from his Juda and Levi, the foundations of State and Church, to an *Andrew* and a *Peter* fisher-men, sea-men; and these men accustomed to that various, and tempestuous Element, to the Sea, lesse capable of Offices of civility, and sociablenesse, then other men, yet must be employed in religious offices, to gather all Nations to one houshold of the faithfull, and to constitute a Communion of Saints; They were Sea-men, fisher-men, unlearned, and indocil; Why did Christ take them? Not that thereby there was any scandall given, or just occasion of that calumny of *Julian* the Apostat, That Christ found it easie to seduce, and draw to his Sect, such poore ignorant men as they were; for Christ did receive persons eminent in learning, (*Saul* was so) and of authority in the State, (*Nicodemus* was so) and of wealth, and ability, (*Zacheus* was so, and so was *Joseph* of Arimathea) But first he chose such men, that when the world had considered their beginning, their insufficiency then, and how unproper they were for such an employment, and yet seene that great work so farre, and so fast advanced, by so weake instruments, they might ascribe all power to him, and ever after, come to him cheerfully upon any invitation, how weake men soever he should send to them, because hee had done so much by so weak instruments before: To make his work in all ages after prosper the better, he proceeded thus at first. And then, hee chose such men for another reason too; To shew that how insufficient soever he received them, yet he received them into such a Schoole, such an University, as should deliver them back into his Church, made fit by him, for the service thereof. Christ needed not mans sufficiency, he took insufficient men; Christ excuses no mans insufficiency, he made them sufficient.

6. /*Nequid Instrumentis*/ His purpose then was, that the worke should be ascribed to the Workman, not to the Instrument; To himselfe, not to them; *Nec quaesivit per Oratorem piscatorem,* He sent not out Orators, Rhetoricians, strong or faire-spoken men to work upon these fisher-men, *Sed de piscatore lucratus est Imperatorem*/Augustine, [*Enarrationes in Psalmos* 36.2. sec. 14] [2] /, By these fisher-men, hee hath reduced all those Kings, and Emperours, and States which have embraced the Christian Religion, these

thousand and six hundred yeares. When *Samuel* was sent with that generall Commission, to anoint a sonne of *Ishai King*/I Samuel 16.6/, without any more particular instructions, when hee came, and *Eliab* was presented unto him, *Surely,* sayes *Samuel,* (noting the goodlinesse of his personage) *this is the Lords Anointed.* But the Lord said unto *Samuel, Looke not on his countenance, nor the height of his stature, for I have refused him; for,* (as it followeth there, from Gods mouth) *God seeth not as man seeth;*[3] *Man looketh on the outward appearance, but the Lord beholdeth the heart.* And so *David,* in appearance lesse[4] likely, was chosen. But, if the Lords arme be not shortned, let no man impute weaknesse to the Instrument. For so, when *David* himselfe was appointed by God, to pursue the Amalekites, the Amalekites that had burnt Ziklag, and done such spoile upon Gods people, as that the people began to speak of stoning *David,* from whom they looked for defence/1 Samuel 30.6/, when *David* had no kind of intelligence, no ground to settle a conjecture upon, which way he must pursue the Amalekites, and yet pursue them he must, in the way he findes a poore young fellow, a famished, sicke young man, derelicted of his Master, and left for dead in the march, and by the meanes and conduct of this wretch, *David* recovers the enemy, recovers the spoile, recovers his honour, and the love of his people.

7. If the Lords arme bee not shortned, let no man impute weaknesse to his Instrument. But yet God will alwayes have so much weaknesse appeare in the Instrument, as that their strength shall not be thought to be their owne. When *Peter* and *John* preached in the streets, *The people marvelled,* (sayes the Text) why? *for they had understood that they were unlearned*/Acts 4.13/. But *beholding also the man that was healed standing by, they had nothing to say,* sayes that story. The insufficiency of the Instrument makes a man wonder naturally; but the accomplishing of some great worke brings them to a necessary acknowledgement of a greater power, working in that weake Instrument. For, if those Apostles that preached, had beene as learned men, as *Simon Magus,* as they did in him, (*This man is the great power of God*/Acts 8.10/, not that he had, but that he was the power of God) the people would have rested in the admiration of those persons, and proceeded no farther. It was their working of supernaturall things, that convinced the world. For all *Pauls* learning, (though hee were very learned) never brought any of the Conjurers to burne his bookes, or to renounce his Art; But when God wrought extraordinary works by him, That

sicknesses were cured by his napkins, and his handkerchiefs/Acts 19.11/, (in which cures, *Pauls* learning had no more concurrence, no more cooperation, then the ignorance of any of the fisher-men Apostles) And when the world saw that those Exorcists, which went about to doe Miracles in the Name of Jesus, because *Paul* did so, could not doe it, because that Jesus had not promised to worke in them, as in *Paul,* Then the Conjurers came, and burnt their bookes, in the sight of all the world, to the value of fifty thousand pieces of silver/Acts 19.13–19/. It was not learning, (that may have been got, though they that heare them, know it not; and it were not hard to assigne many examples of men that have stolne a great measure of learning, and yet lived open and conversable lives, and never beene observed, (except by them, that knew their Lucubrations, and night-watching) to have spent many houres in study) but it was the calling of the world to an apprehension of a greater power, by seeing great things done by weake Instruments, that reduced them, that convinced them. *Peter* and *Johns* preaching did not halfe the good then, as the presenting of one man, which had been recovered by them, did. Twenty of our Sermons edifie not so much, as if the Congregation might see one man converted by us. Any one of you might out-preach us. That one man that would leave his beloved sinne, that one man that would restore ill-gotten goods, had made a better Sermon then ever I shall, and should gaine more soules by his act, then all our words (as they are ours) can doe.

8. */Non inidoneos/* Such men he took then, as might be no occasion to their hearers, to ascribe the work to their sufficiency; but yet such men too, as should be no examples to insufficient men to adventure upon that great service; but men, though ignorant before, yet docil, and glad to learne. In a rough stone, a cunning Lapidary will easily foresee, what his cutting, and his polishing, and his art will bring that stone to.[5] A cunning Statuary discerns in a Marble-stone under his feet, where there will arise an Eye, and an Eare, and a Hand, and other lineaments to make it a perfect Statue. Much more did our Saviour Christ, who was himselfe the Author of that disposition in them, (for no man hath any such disposition but from God) foresee in these fisher-men, an inclinablenesse to become usefull in that great service of his Church. Therefore hee took them from their owne ship, but he sent them from his Crosse; He tooke them weather-beaten with North and South winds, and rough-cast with foame, and mud; but he sent them back soupled, and smoothed, and levigated, quickned, and inanimated with that Spirit, which he had

breathed into them from his owne bowels, his owne eternall bowels, from which the Holy Ghost proceeded; Hee tooke fisher-men, and he sent fishers of men. He sent them not out to preach, as soone as he called them to him; He called them *ad Discipulatum,* before hee called them *ad Apostolatum;* He taught them, before they taught others. As St. *Paul* sayes of himselfe, and the rest, *God hath made us able Ministers of the New Testament*/2 Corinthians 3.6/; *Idoneos,* fit Ministers, that is, fit for that service. There is a fitnesse founded in Discretion; a Discretion to make our present service acceptable to our present Auditory; for it be not acceptable, agreeable to them, it is never profitable.

9. As God gave his children such Manna as was agreeable to every mans taste, and tasted to every man like that, that the man liked best/Wisdom 16.20/: so are wee to deliver the bread of life agreeable to every taste, to fit our Doctrine to the apprehension, and capacity, and digestion of the hearers. For as St. *Augustine* sayes, That no man profits by a Sermon that he heares with paine, if he doe not [under]stand easily; so if he doe not understand easily, or if he doe not assent easily to that that he heares, if he be put to study one sentence, till the Preacher have passed three or foure more, or if the doctrine be new and doubtfull, and suspitious to him, this fitnesse which is grounded in discretion is not shewed. But the generall fitnesse is grounded in learning, St. *Paul* hath joyned them safely together, *Rebuke and exhort with all long suffering, and learning*/2 Timothy 4.2/. Shew thy discretion in seasonable Rebuking; shew thy learning in Exhorting. Let the Congregation see that thou studiest the good of their soules, and they will digest any wholesome increpation, any medicinall reprehension at thy hands, *Dilige et dic quod voles*/Augustine, [?*De Doctrina Christiana*]/. We say so first to God, Lord let thy spirit beare witnesse with my spirit, that thou lovest me, and I can endure all thy Prophets, and all the *vae's,* and the woes that they thunder against me and my sin. So also the Congregation sayes to the Minister, *Dilige et dic quod voles,* shew thy love to me, in studying my case, and applying thy knowledge to my conscience, speake so, as God and I may know thou meanest me, but not the Congregation, lest that bring me to a confusion of face, and that a hardnesse of heart; deale thus with me, love me thus, and say what thou wilt; nothing shall offend me. And this is the Idoneity, the fitnesse which we consider in the Minister, fitnesse in learning, fitnesse in discretion, to use and apply that learning. So Christ fits his.

10. */Mittebant rete in Mare/* Such men then Christ takes for the service of his Church; such as bring no confidence in their owne fitnesse, such as embrace the meanes to make them fit in his Schoole, and learne before they teach. And to that purpose he tooke *Andrew* and *Peter;* and he tooke them, when he found them casting their net into the Sea. This was a Symbolicall, a Propheticall action of their future life; This fishing was a type, a figure, a prophesie of their other fishing. But here (in this first part) we are bound to the consideration of their reall and direct action, and exercise of their present calling; *They cast their Net, for they were Fishers,* sayes the Text. In which, *for,* (as wee told you at first) there is a double reason involved.

11. */1 Quia piscatores/* First, in this *For* is intimated, how acceptable to God that labour is, that is taken in a calling. They did not forbeare to cast their nets because it was a tempestuous Sea; we must make account to meet stormes in our profession, yea and tentations too. A man must not leave his calling, because it is hard for him to be an honest man in that calling; but he must labour to overcome those difficulties, and as much as he can, vindicate and redeeme that calling from those aspersions and calumnies, which ill men have cast upon a good calling. They did not forbeare because it was a tempestuous Sea, nor because they had cast their nets often and caught nothing, nor because it was uncertaine how the Market would goe when they had catched. A man must not be an ill Prophet upon his own labours, nor bewitch them with a suspition that they will not prosper. It is the slothfull man that sayes, *A Lion in the way, A Lion in the street*/Proverbs 26.13/. Cast thou thy net into the Sea, and God shall drive fish into thy net; undertake a lawfull Calling, and clogge not thy calling with murmuring, nor with an ill conscience, and God shall give thee increase, and worship in it, *They cast their nets into the Sea, for they were fishers;* it was their Calling, and they were bound to labour in that.

12. */2 Quia piscatores/* And then this *For* hath another aspect, lookes another way too, and implies another Instruction, *They cast their nets into the Sea, for they were fishers,* that is, if they had not beene fishers, they would not have done it; Intrusion into other mens callings in an unjust usurpation; and, if it take away their profit, it is a theft. If it be but a censuring of them in their calling, yet it is a calumny, because it is not in the right way, if it be extrajudiciall. To lay an aspersion upon any man (who is not under our charge) though that which we say of him be true, yet it is a

calumny, and a degree of libelling, if it be not done judiciarily, and where it may receive redresse and remedy. And yet how forward are men that are not fishers in that Sea, to censure State Councels, and Judiciary proceedings? Every man is an *Absolom,* to say to every man, *Your cause is good, but the King hath appointed none to heare it*/2 Samuel 15.3/; Money brings them in, favour brings them in, it is not the King; or, if it must be said to be the King, yet it is the affection of the King and not his judgement, the King misled, not rightly informed, say our seditious *Absoloms,* and, *Oh that I were made Judge in the land, that every man might come unto me, and I would doe him justice,* is the charme that *Absolom* hath taught every man. They cast their nets into a deeper Sea then this, and where they are much lesse fishers, into the secret Councels of God. It is well provided by your Lawes, that Divines and Ecclesiasticall persons may not take farmes, nor buy nor sell, for returne, in Markets. I would it were as well provided, that buyers and sellers, and farmers might not be Divines, nor censure them. I speake not of censuring our lives; please your selves with that, till God bee pleased to mend us by that, (though that way of whispering calumny be not the right way to that amendment) But I speak of censuring our Doctrines, and of appointing our doctrines; when men are weary of hearing any other thing, then Election and Reprobation, and whom, and when, and how, and why God hath chosen, or cast away. We have liberty enough by your Law, to hold enough for the maintenance of our bodies, and states; you have liberty enough by our Law, to know enough for the salvation of your soules; If you will search farther into Gods eternall Decrees, and unrevealed Councels, you should not cast your nets into that Sea, for you are not fishers there. *Andrew and Peter cast their nets, for they were fishers,* (therefore they were bound to do it) and againe, *for they were fishers,* (if they had not been so, they would not have done so.)

13. /*Duo simul*/ These persons then thus disposed, unfit of themselves, made fit by him, and found by him at their labour, labour in a lawfull Calling, and in their owne calling, our Saviour Christ cals to him; And he called them by couples, by paires; two together. So he called his Creatures into the world at the first Creation, by paires. So he called them into the Arke, for the reparation of the world, by paires, two and two. God loves not singularity; The very name of Church implies company; It is *Concio, Congregatio, Coetus;* It is a Congregation, a Meeting, an assembly; It is not any

one man; neither can the Church be preserved in one man. And therefore it hath beene dangerously said, (though they confesse it to have beene said by many of their greatest Divines in the Roman Church) that during the time that our blessed Saviour lay dead in the grave, there was no faith left upon the earth, but onely in the Virgin *Mary;* for then there was no Church. God hath manifested his will in two Testaments; and though he have abridged and contracted the doctrine of both in a narrow roome, yet he hath digested it into two Commandements, *Love God, love thy neighbour.* There is but one Church; that is true, but one; but that one Church cannot be in any one man; There is but one Baptisme; that is also true, but one; But no man can Baptize himselfe; there must be *Sacerdos et competens,* (as our old Canons speake) a person to receive, and a Priest to give Baptisme. There is but one faith in the remission of sins; that is true too, but one; But no man can absolve himselfe; There must be a Priest and a penitent. God cals no man so, but that he cals him to the knowledge, that he hath called more then him to that Church, or else it is an illusory, and imaginary calling, and a dreame.

14. Take heed therefore of being seduced to that Church that is in one man; *In scrinio pectoris,* where all infallibility, and assured resolution is in the breast of one man; who (as their owne Authors say) is not bound to aske the counsell of others before, nor to follow their counsell after. And since the Church cannot be in one, in an unity, take heed of bringing it too neare that unity, to a paucity, to a few, to a separation, to a Conventicle. The Church loves the name of Catholique; and it is a glorious, and an harmonious name; Love thou those things wherein she is Catholique, and wherein she is harmonious, that is, *Quod ubique, quod semper* /Lyrinensis/, Those universall, and fundamental doctrines, which in all Christian ages, and in all Christian Churches, have beene agreed by all to be necessary to salvation; and then thou are a true Catholique. Otherwise, that is, without relation to this Catholique and universall doctrine, to call a particular Church Catholique, (that she should be Catholique, that is, universall in dominion, but not in doctrine) is such a solecisme, as to speak of a white blacknesse, or a great littlenesse; A particular Church to be universall, implies such a contradiction.

15. */Duo fratres/* Christ loves not singularity; he called not one alone; He loves not schism neither between them whom he cals; and therefore he cals persons likely to agree, two brethren, (*He saw*

two brethren, Peter and Andrew, etc.) So he began to build the Synagogues, to establish that first government, in *Moses* and *Aaron,* brethren; So he begins to build the Church, in *Peter* and *Andrew,* brethren. The principall fraternity and brotherhood that God respects, is spirituall; Brethren in the profession of the same true Religion. But *Peter* and *Andrew* whome he called here to the true Religion, and so gave them that second fraternity and brotherhood, which is spirituall, were naturall brethren before; And that God loves; that a naturall, a secular, a civill fraternity, and a spirituall fraternity should be joyned together; when those that professe the same Religion, should desire to contract their alliances, in marrying their Children, and to have their other dealings in the world (as much as they can) with men that professe the same true Religion that they do. That so (not medling nor disputing the proceedings of States, who, in some cases, go by other rules then private men do) we doe not make it an equall, an indifferent thing, whether we marry our selves, or our children, or make our bargaines, or our conversation, with persons of a different Religion, when as our Adversaries amongst us will not goe to a Lawyer, nor call a Physitian, no, nor scarce a Taylor, or other Tradesman of another Religion then their owne, if they can possibly avoid it. God saw a better likelihood of avoyding Schisme and dissention, when those whom hee called to a new spirituall brotherhood in one Religion, were naturall brothers too, and tied in civill bands, as well as spirituall.
16. /*Non cognati*/ And as Christ began, so he proceeded; for the persons whom he called were Catechisticall, instructive persons; persons, from whose very persons we receive instruction. The next whom he called, (which is in the next verse) were two too; and brethren too; *John* and *James;* but yet his owne kinsmen in the flesh. But, as he chose two together to avoid singularity, and two brethren to avoid Schisme, so he preferred two strangers before his own kindred, to avoid partiality, and respect of persons. Certainly every man is bound to do good to those that are neare him by nature; The obligation of doing good to others lies (for the most part) thus; *Let us do good to all men, but especially unto them which are of the household of the faithful*/Galatians 6.10/; (They of our owne Religion are of the *Quorum*) Now, when all are so, (of the household of the faithfull, of our owne Religion) the obligation looks home, and lies thus, *He that provideth not for his own, denieth the faith, and is worse then an Infidel*/1 Timothy 5.8/. Christ would therefore leave no example, nor justification

of that perverse distemper, to leave his kindred out, nor of their disposition, who had rather buy new friends at any rate, then relieve or cherish the old. But yet when Christ knew how far his stock would reach, that no liberality, howsoever placed, could exhaust that, but that he was able to provide for all, he would leave no example nor justification of that perverse distemper, to heape up preferments upon our owne kindred, without any consideration how Gods glory might be more advanced by doing good to others too; But finding in these men a fit disposition to be good labourers in his harvest, and to agree in the service of the Church, as they did in the band of nature, he calls *Peter* and *Andrew,* otherwise strangers, before he called his Cosins, *James* and *John.*

17. /*Continuo sequuti*/. These Circumstances we proposed to be considered in these persons before, and at their being called, The first, after their calling, is their chearfull readinesse in obeying, *Continuo sequuti,* They were bid *follow* and *forthwith they followed.* Which present obedience of theirs is exalted in this, that this was freshly upon the imprisonment of *John Baptist,* whose Disciple *Andrew* had been; and it might easily have deterred, and averted a man in his case, to consider, that it was well for him that he was got out of *John Baptists* schoole, and company, before that storme, the displeasure of the state fell upon him; and that it behoved him to be wary to apply himselfe to any such new Master, as might draw him into as much trouble; which Christs service was very like to doe. But the contemplation of future persecutions, that may fall, the example of persecutions past, that have falne, the apprehension of imminent persecutions, that are now falling, the sense of present persecutions, that are now upon us, retard not those, upon whom the love of Christ Jesus works effectually; They followed for all that. And they followed, when there was no more perswasion used to them, no more words said to them, but *Sequere me, Follow me.*

18. And therefore how easie soever *Julian* the Apostate might make it, for Christ to work upon so weake men, as these were, yet to worke upon any men by so weake means, onely by one *Sequere me, Follow me,* and no more, cannot be thought easie. The way of Rhetorique in working upon weake men, is first to trouble the understanding, to displace, and to discompose, and disorder the judgement, to smother and bury in it, or to empty it of former apprehensions and opinions, and to shake that beliefe, with which it had possessed it self before, and then when it is thus melted,

to powre it into new molds, when it is thus mollified, to stamp and imprint new formes, new images, new opinions in it. But here in our case, there was none of this fire, none of this practise, none of this battery of eloquence, none of this verball violence, onely a bare *Sequere me, Follow me,* and *they followed.* No eloquence enclined them, no terrors declined them: No dangers withdrew them, no preferment drew them; they knew Christ, and his kindred, and his means; they loved him, himselfe, and not any thing they expected from him. *Minùs te amat, qui aliquid tuum amat, quod non propter te amat*/Augustine/, That man loves thee but a little, that begins his love at that which thou hast, and not at thy selfe. It is a weake love that is divided between Christ and the world; especially, if God come after the world, as many times he does, even in them, who thinke they love him well; that first they love the riches of this world, and then they love God that gave them. But that is a false Method in this art of love; The true is, radically to love God for himselfe, and other things for his sake, so far, as he may receive glory in our having, and using them.

19. /*Relictis retibus*/ This *Peter* and *Andrew* declared abundantly; they did as much as they were bid; they were bid *follow, and they followed;* but it seemes they did more, they were not bid *leave their nets,* and yet *they left their nets, and followed him;* But, for this, they did not; no man can doe more in the service of God, then is enjoyned him, commanded him. There is no supererogation, no making of God beholden to us, no bringing of God into our debt. Every man is commanded *to love God with all his heart, and all his power,* and a heart above a whole heart, and a power above a whole power, is a strange extension. That therefore which was declared explicitly, plainly, directly by Christ to the young man in the Gospel, *Vade, et vende, et sequere, Goe and sell all, and follow me*/Matthew 19.21/, was implicitely implied to these men in our text, Leave your nets, and follow me. And though to doe so, (to leave all) be not alwayes a precept, a commandment to all men, yet it was a precept, a commandment to both these, at the time; to the young man in the Gospell, (for he was as expressly bid to sell away all, as he was to follow Christ) and to these men in the text, because they could not performe that that was directly commanded, except they performed that which was implied too; except they left their nets, they could not follow Christ. When God commands us to follow him, he gives us light, how, and in which way he will be followed; And then when we understand which is his way, that

way is as a commandment, as the very end it selfe, and not to follow him that way, is as much a transgression, as not to follow him at all. If that young man in the Gospel, who was bid sell all, and give to the poore, and then follow, had followed, but kept his interest in his land; If he had devested himselfe of the land, but let it fall, or conveyed it to the next heire, or other kinsmen; If he had employed it to pious uses, but not so, as Christ commanded, to the poore, still he had been in a transgression: The way when it is declared, is as much a command, as the end.

20. But then, in this command, which was implicitely, and by necessary consequence laid upon *Peter* and *Andrew,* to leave their nets, (because without doing so, they could not forthwith follow Christ) there is no example of forsaking a calling, upon pretence of following Christ; no example here, of devesting ones selfe of all means of defending us from those manifold necessities, which this life lays upon us, upon pretence of following Christ; It is not an absolute leaving of all wordly cares, but a leaving them out of the first consideration; *Primum quaerite regnum Dei,* so, as our first businesse be to seeke the kingdome of God. For, after this leaving of his nets, for this time, *Peter* continued owner of his house/Matthew 8.14/, and Christ came to that house of his, and found his mother in law sicke in that house, and recovered her there. Upon a like commandment, upon such a *Sequere, Follow me, Matthew* followed Christ too; but after that following, Christ went with *Matthew* to his house, and sate at meat with him at home/Matthew 9.10/. And for this very exercise of fishing, though at that time when Christ said, Follow me, they left their nets, yet they returned to that trade, sometimes, upon occasions, in all likelihood, in Christs life; and after Christs death, clearly they did returne to it/John 21.1/; for Christ, after his Resurrection, found them fishing.

21. They did not therefore abandon and leave all care, and all government of their own estate, and dispose themselves to live after upon the sweat of others; but transported with a holy alacrity, in this present and chearfull following of Christ, in respect of that then, they neglected their nets, and all things else. *Perfecta obedientia est sua imperfecta relinquere*/Augustine/, Not to be too diligent towards the world, is the diligence that God requires. St. *Augustine* does not say, *sua relinquere,* but *sua imperfecta relinquere,* That God requires we should leave the world, but that we should leave it to second considerations; That thou do not forbeare, nor defer thy conversion to God, and thy restitution to man, till

thou have purchased such a state, bought such an office, married, and provided such and such children, but *imperfecta relinquere,* to leave these worldly things unperfected, till thy repentance have restored thee to God, and established thy reconciliation in him, and then the world lyes open to thy honest endeavours. Others take up all with their net, and *they sacrifice to their nets, because by them their portion is fat, and their meat plenteous*/Habakkuk 1.16/. They are confident in their own learning, their own wisedome, their own practise, and (which is a strange Idolatry) they sacrifice to themselves, they attribute all to their own industry. These men in our text were far from that; they left their nets.

22. But still consider, that they did but leave their nets, they did not burne them. And consider too, that they left but nets; those things, which might entangle them, and retard them in their following of Christ. And such nets, (some such things as might hinder them in the service of God) even these men, so well disposed to follow Christ, had about them. And therefore let no man say, *Imitari vellem, sed quod relinquam, non habeo*/Gregory/, I would gladly doe as the Apostles did, leave all to follow Christ, but I have nothing to leave; alas, all things have left me, and I have nothing to leave. Even that murmuring at poverty, is a net; leave that. Leave thy superfluous desire of having the riches of this world; though thou mayest flatter thy selfe, that thou desirest to have onely that thou mightest leave it, that thou mightest employ it charitably, yet it might prove a net, and stick too close about thee to part with it. *Multa relinquitis, si desideriis renunciatis*/Idem/, You leave your nets, if you leave your over-earnest greedinesse of catching; for, when you doe [not] so.[6] You doe not onely fish with a net, (that is, lay hold upon all you can compasse) but, (which is strange) you fish for a net, even that which you get proves a net to you, and hinders you in the following of Christ, and you are lesse disposed to follow him, when you have got your ends, then before. He that hath least, hath enough to waigh him down from heaven, by an inordinate love of that little which he that, or in an inordinate and murmuring desire of more. And he that hath most, hath not too much to give for heaven; *Tantum valet regnum Dei, quantum tu vales*/Idem/, Heaven is alwayes so much worth, as thou art worth. A poore man may have heaven for a penny, that hath no greater store; and, God lookes, that he to whom he hath given thousands, should lay out thousands upon the purchase of heaven. The market changes, as the plenty of money changes; Heaven costs a rich man

more then a poore, because he hath more to give. But in this, rich and poore are both equall, that both must leave themselves without nets, that is, without those things, which, in their own Consciences they know, retard the following of Christ. Whatsoever hinders my present following, that I cannot follow to day, whatsoever may hinder my constant following, that I cannot follow to morrow, and all my life, is a net, and I am bound to leave that.

23. And these are the pieces that constitute our first part, the circumstances that invest these persons, *Peter* and *Andrew,* in their former condition, before, and when Christ called them.

MAT. 4.18, 19, 20. AND JESUS WALKING BY THE SEA OF GALILE SAW TWO BRETHREN, SIMON CALLED PETER, AND ANDREW HIS BROTHER, CASTING A NET INTO THE SEA, (FOR THEY WERE FISHERS.) AND HE SAITH UNTO THEM, FOLLOW ME, AND I WILL MAKE YOU FISHERS OF MEN; AND THEY STRAIGHTWAY LEFT THEIR NETS, AND FOLLOWED HIM.

1. [*Divisio*] We are now in our Order proposed at first, come to our second part, from the consideration of these persons, *Peter* and *Andrew,* in their former state and condition, before, and at their calling, to their future estate in promise, but an infallible promise, Christs promise, if they followed him, (*Follow me, and I will make you fishers of men.*) In which part we shall best come to our end, (which is your edification) by these steps. First, that there is an Humility enjoyned them, in the *Sequere, follow,* come after. That though they bee brought to a high Calling, that doe not make them proud, nor tyrannous over mens consciences; And then, even this Humility is limited, *Sequere me, follow me;* for there may be a pride even in Humility, and a man may follow a dangerous guide; Our guide here is Christ, *Sequere me, follow me.* And then we shall see the promise it selfe, the employment, the function, the preferment; In which there is no new state promised them, no Innovation, (They were *fishers,* and they shall be *fishers* still) but there is an emprovement, a bettering, a reformation, (They were *fisher-men* before, and now they shall be *fishers of men;*) To which purpose, wee shall finde the world to be the Sea, and Gospel their Net. And lastly, all this is presented to them, not as it was expressed in the former part, with a *For,* (it is not, Follow me, for I will prefer you) he will not have that the reason of their following; But yet it is, Follow me, and I will prefer you; It is a subsequent addition of his owne goodnesse, but so infallible a one,

as we may rely upon; Whosoever doth follow Christ, speeds well. And into these considerations will fall all that belongs to this last part, *Follow me, and I will make you fishers of men.*

2. */Sequere Humilitas/* First then, here is an impression of Humility, in following, in coming after, *Sequere, follow,* presse not to come before; And it had need be first, if we consider how early, how primarie a sinne Pride is, and how soone it possesses us. Scarce any man, but if he looke back seriously into himselfe, and into his former life, and revolve his owne history, but that the first act which he can remember in himselfe, or can be remembred of by others, will bee some act of Pride. Before Ambition, or Covetousnesse, or Licentiousnesse is awake in us, Pride is working; Though but a childish pride, yet pride; and this Parents rejoyce at in their children, and call it spirit, and so it is, but not the best. Wee enlarge not therefore the consideration of this word *sequere, follow,* come after, so farre, as to put our meditations upon the whole body, and the severall members of this sinne of pride; Nor upon the extent and diffusivenesse of this sinne, as it spreads it selfe over every other sinne; (for every sinne is complicated with pride, so as every sinne is a rebellious opposing of the law and will of God) Nor to consider the waighty hainousnes of pride, how it aggravates every other sin, how it makes a musket a Canon bullet, and a peble a Milstone; but after we have stopped a little upon that usefull consideration, That there is not so direct, and Diametrall a contrariety between the nature of any sinne and God, as between him and pride, wee shall passe to that which is our principall observation in this branch, How early and primary a sin pride is, occasioned by this, that the commandment of Humility is first given, first enjoyned in our first word, *Sequere, follow.*

3. */Nihil tam contrarium Deo/* But first, wee exalt that consideration, That nothing is so contrary to God, as Pride, with this observation, That God in the Scriptures is often by the Holy Ghost invested, and represented in the qualities and affections of man; and to constitute a commerce and familiarity between God and man, God is not onely said to have bodily lineaments, eyes and eares, and hands, and feet, and to have some of the naturall affections of man, as Joy, in particular, (*The Lord will rejoyce over thee for good, as he rejoyced over thy Fathers*/Deuteronomy 30.9/) And so, pity too, (*The Lord was with Joseph, and extended kindnesse unto him*/ Genesis 39.21/) But some of those inordinate and irregular passions and perturbations, excesses and defects of man, are imputed to

God, by the holy Ghost in the Scriptures. For so, lazinesse, drowsinesse is imputed to God; (*Awake Lord, why sleepest thou?*/Psalm 44.23/) So corruptiblenesse, and deterioration, and growing worse by ill company, is imputed to God; (*Cum perverso perverteris*/ Psalm 18.26/, God is said to grow froward with the froward, and that hee learnes to go crookedly with them that go crookedly) And prodigality and wastefulnesse is imputed to God; (*Thou sellest thy people for naught, and doest not increase thy wealth by their price*/ Psalm 44.12/) So sudden and hasty choler; (*Kisse the Son lest he be angry, and ye perish In ira brevi, though his wrath be kindled but a little*/Psalm 2.12/) And then, illimited and boundlesse anger, a vindicative irreconciliablenesse is imputed to God; (*I was but a little displeased,* (but it is otherwise now) *I am very sore displeased*/Zecharia 1.15/) So there is *Ira devorans* (*Wrath that consumes like stubble*/Exodus 15.4; 15.7 c/) So there is *Ira multiplicata,* (*Plagues renewed, and indignation increased*/Job 10.17/) So God himselfe expresses it, (*I will fight against you in anger and in fury* /Jeremiah 21.5/) And so for his inexorablenesse, his irreconciliablenesse, (*O Lord God of Hosts, Quousque, how long wilt thou be angry against the prayer of thy people?*/Psalm 80.4/) Gods owne people, Gods own people praying to their owne God, and yet their God irreconciliable to them. Scorne and contempt is imputed to God; which is one of the most enormious, and disproportioned weakenesses in man; that a worme that crawles in the dust, that a graine of dust, that is hurried with every blast of winde, should find any thing so much inferiour to it selfe as to scorn it, to deride it, to contemne it; yet scorne, and derision, and contempt is imputed to God, (*He that sitteth in the Heavens shall laugh, the Lord shall have them in derision*/Psalm 2.4/) and againe, (*I will laugh at your calamity, I will mock you when your feare commeth.* /Proverbs 1.26/) Nay beloved, even inebriation, excesse in that kinde, Drunkennesse, is a Metaphor which the Holy Ghost hath mingled in the expressing of God's proceedings with man; for God does not onely threaten to make his enemies drunke, (and to make others drunke is a circumstance of drunkennesse) (so Jerusalem being in his displeasure complaines, *Inebriavit absynthio,* (*He hath made me drunke with wormewood*/Lamentations 3.15/) and againe, (*They shall be drunke with their owne blood, as with new Wine*/Esay 49.26/) Nor onely to expresse his plentifull mercies to his friends and servants, does God take that Metaphore, (*Inebriabo animam Sacerdotis, I will make the soule of the Priest drunke*

/Jeremiah 31.14/; fill it, satiate it) and againe, (*I will make the weary soule, and the sorrowfull soule drunke*/31.25/) But not onely all this, (though in all this God have a hand) not onely towards others, but God in his owne behalfe complaines of the scant and penurious Sacrificer, *Non inebriasti me, Thou hast not made me drunke with thy Sacrifices*/Esay 43.25/. And yet, though for the better applying of God to the understanding of man, the Holy Ghost impute to God these excesses, and defects of man (lazinesse and drowsiness, deterioration, corruptibleness, by ill conversation, prodigality and wastefulnesse, sudden choler, long irreconciliablenesse,[7] scorne, inebriation, and many others) in the Scriptures, yet in no place of the Scripture is God, for any respect said to be proud; God in the Scriptures is never made so like man, as to be made capable of Pride; for this had not beene to have God like man, but like the devill.

4. God is said in the Scriptures to apparell himself gloriously; (*God covers him with light as with a garment*/Psalm 104.2/) And so of his Spouse the Church it is said, (*Her cloathing is of wrought gold, and her raiment of needle worke*/Psalm 45.13/) and, as though nothing in this world were good enough for her wearing, she is said *to be cloathed with the Sun*/Revelation 12.1/. But glorious apparell is not pride in them, whose conditions require it, and whose revenews will beare it. God is said in the Scriptures to appeare with greatnesse and majesty, (*A streame of fire came forth before him; thousand thousands ministered unto him, and ten thousand times ten thousand stood before him*/Daniel 7.10/.) And so Christ shall come at Judgement, with his Hosts of Angels, in majesty, and in glory. But these outward appearances and acts of greatnesse are not pride in those persons, to whom there is a reverence due, which reverence is preserved by this outward splendor, and not otherwise. God is said in the Scriptures to triumph over his enemies, and to be jealous of his glory; (*The Lord, whose name is Jealous, is a jealous God*/Exodus 34.14/) But, for Princes to be jealous of their glory, studious of their honour, for any private man to be jealous of his good name, carefull to preserve an honest reputation, is not pride. For, Pride is *Appetitus celsitudinis perversus,* It is an inordinate desire of being better then we are.

5. Now there is a lawfull, nay a necessary desire of being better and better; And that, not onely in spirituall things, (for so every man is bound to be better and better, better today then yesterday, and to morrow then to day, and he that growes not in Religion, withers,

There is no standing at a stay, He that goes not forward in godlinesse, goes backward, and he that is not better, is worse) but even in temporall things too there is a liberty given us, nay there is a law, an obligation laid upon us, to endeavour by industry in a lawfull calling, to mend and improve, to enlarge our selves, and spread, even in worldly things. The first Commandment that God gave man, was not prohibitive; God, in that, forbad man nothing, but enlarged him with that *Crescite, et multiplicamini, Increase and multiply*/Genesis 1.28/, which is not onely in the multiplication of children, but in the enlargement of possessions too; for so it followes in the same place, not onely *Replete,* but *Dominamini,* not onely replenish the world, but subdue it, and take dominion over it, that is, make it your owne. For, *Terram dedit filiis hominum,* As God hath given sons to men, so God gives the possession of this world to the sons of men. For so when God delivers that commandment, the second time, to *Noah,* for the reparation of the world, *Crescite et multiplicamini, Increase and multiply,* he accompanies it with that reason, *The feare of you, and the dread of you shall be upon all, and all are delivered into your hands*/Genesis 9.1/; which reason can have no relation to the multiplying of Children, but to the enlarging of possessions. God planted trees in Paradise in a good state at first; at first with ripe fruits upon them; but Gods purpose was, that even those trees, though well then, should grow greater. God gives many men good estates from their parents at first; yet Gods purpose is that they should increase those estates. He that leaves no more, then his father left him, (if the fault be in himselfe) shall hardly make a good account of his stewardship to God; for, he hath but kept his talent in a handkerchief/Matthew 18.25/.[8] And *the slothfull man is even brother to the waster*/Prov. 18.9/. The holy Ghost in *Solomon,* scarce prefers him that does not get more, before him that wasts all. He makes them brethren; almost all one. *Cursed be he that does the worke of God negligently;* /Jer. 48.10/ that does any Commandment of God by halves; And this negligent and lazy man, this in-industrious and illaborious man that takes no paines, he does one part of Gods Commandment, He does multiply, but he does not the other, he does not increase; He leaves Children enow, but he leaves them nothing; not in possessions and maintenance, nor in vocation and calling.

6. And truly, howsoever *the love of money be the roote of all evill* /1 Timothy 6.10/, (He cannot mistake that told us so) Howsoever *they that will be rich* (that resolve to be rich by any meanes) *shall*

fall into many tentations, Howsoever a hasty desire of being suddenly and prematurely rich, be a dangerous and an obnoxious thing, a pestilent and contagious disease, (for what a perverse and inordinate anticipation and prevention of God and nature is it, to looke for our harvest in May, or to looke for all grains at once? and such a perversnesse is the hasty desire of being suddenly and prematurely rich) yet, to go on industriously in an honest calling, and giving God his leasure, and giving God his portion of the way, in Tithes, and in Almes, and then, still to lay up something for posterity, is that, which God does not onely permit and accept from us, but command to us, and reward in us. And certainly, that man shall not stand so right in Gods eye at the last day, that leaves his Children to the Parish, as he that leaves the Parish to his Children, if he have made his purchases out of honest gaine, in a lawful Calling, and not out of oppression.

7. In all which, I would be rightly understood; that is, that I speake of such poverty as is contracted by our owne lazinesse, or wastefulnesse. For otherwise, poverty that comes from the hand of God, is as rich a blessing as comes from his hand. He that is poore with a good conscience, that hath laboured and yet not prospered, knows to whom to go, and what to say, *Lord, thou hast put gladnesse into my heart, more then in the time when corne and wine increased* /Psalm 4.7/; (more now, then when I had more) *I will lay me downe and sleepe, for thou Lord onely makest me to dwell in safety.* Does every rich man dwell in safety? Can every rich man lye downe in peace and sleepe? no, nor every poore man neither; but he that is poore with a good conscience, can. And, though he that is rich with a good conscience may, in a good measure, do so too, (sleepe in peace) yet not so out of the sphere and latitude of envy, and free from the machinations, and supplantations, and underminings of malicious men, that feed upon the confiscations, and build upon the ruines of others, as the poore man is.

8. Though then St. *Chrysostome* call riches *Absurditatis parentes,* the parents of absurdities, That they make us doe, not onely ungodly, but inhumane things, not onely irreligious, but unreasonable things, uncomely and absurd things, things which we our selves did not suspect that we could be drawne to, yet there is a growing rich, which is not covetousnesse, and there is a desire of honor and preferment, which is not Pride. For, Pride is, (as we said before) *Appetitus perversus,* A perverse and inordinate desire, but there is a desire of honor and preferment, regulated by rectified Reason; and

rectified Reason is Religion. And therefore (as we said) how ever other affections of man, may, and are, by the Holy Ghost, in Scriptures in some respects ascribed to God, yet never Pride. Nay, the Holy Ghost himselfe seemes to be straitned, and in a difficulty, when he comes to expresse Gods proceedings with a proud man, and his detestation of him, and aversion from him. There is a considerable, a remarkable, indeed a singular manner of expressing it, (perchance you finde not the like in all the Bible) where God sayes, *Him that hath a high looke, and a proud heart, I will not*/Psalm 101.5/.[9] (in our last) *I cannot,* (in our former translation) Not what? Not as it is in those translations, *I cannot suffer him, I will not suffer him;* for that word of *Suffering,* is but a voluntary word, supplied by the Translators; In the Originall, it is as it were an abrupt breaking off on Gods part, from the proud man, and, (if we may so speake) a kinde of froward departing from him. God does not say of the proud man, I cannot worke upon him. I cannot mend him, I cannot pardon him, I cannot suffer him, I cannot stay with him, but meerly I *cannot,* and no more, I cannot tell what to say of him, what to doe for him; (*Him that hath a proud heart, I cannot*) Pride is so contrary to God, as that the proud man, and he can meet in nothing. And this consideration hath kept us thus long, from that which we made our first and principall collection, That this commandment of Humility, was imprinted in our very first word, *Sequere, follow,* be content to come after, to denote how early and primary a sin Pride is, and how soone it entred into the world, and how soone into us; and that consideration we shall pursue now.

9. /*Superbia in Angelis*/ We know that light is Gods eldest childe, his first borne of all Creatures; and it is ordinarily received, that the Angels are twins with the light, made then when light was made. And then the first act, that these Angels that fell, did, was an act of Pride. They [did] [10] not thanke nor praise God, for their Creation; (which should have been their first act) They did not solicite, nor pray to God for their Sustentation, their Melioration, their Confirmation; (so they should have proceeded) But the first act that those first Creatures did, was an act of pride, a proud reflecting upon themselves, a proud overvaluing of their own condition, and an acquiescence in that, in an imaginary possibility of standing by themselves, without any farther relation, or beholdingnesse to God. So early, so primary a sin is Pride, as that it was the first act of the first of Creatures.

10. /*Superbia positiva*/ So early, so primary a sin, as that whereas

all Pride now is but a comparative pride, this first pride in the Angels was a positive, a radicall pride. The Pharisee is but proud, *that he is not as other men are*/Luke 18.11/; that is but a comparative pride. No King thinks himselfe great enough, yet he is proud that he is independant, soveraigne, subject to none. No subject thinks himselfe rich enough, yet he is proud that he is able to oppresse others that are poorer, *Et gloriatur in malo, quia potens est*/Psalm 52.1/, He boasteth himselfe in mischiefe, because he is a mighty man. But all these are but comparative prides; and there must be some subjects to compare with, before a King can be proud, and some inferiors, before the Magistrate, and some poore, before the rich man can be proud. But this pride in those Angels in heaven, was a positive pride; There were no other Creatures yet made, with whom these Angels could compare themselves, and before whom these Angels could prefer themselves, and yet before there was any other creature but themselves, any other creature, to undervalue, or insult over, these Angels were proud of themselves. So early, so primary a sin is Pride.

11. /*Superbia in Paradiso*/ So early, so primary, as that in that ground, which was for goodnesse next to heaven, that is, Paradise, Pride grew very early too. *Adams* first act was not an act of Pride, but an act of lawfull power and jurisdiction, in naming the Creatures; *Adam* was above them all, and he might have called them what he would; There had lyen no action, no appeale, if *Adam* had called a Lyon a Dog, or an Eagle an Owle. And yet we dispute with God, why he should not make all us vessels of honor, and we complaine of God, that he hath not given us all, all the abundances of this world. Comparatively *Adam* was better then all the world beside, and yet we finde no act of pride in *Adam,* when he was alone. Solitude is not the scene of Pride; The danger of pride is in company, when we meet to looke upon another. But in *Adams* wife, *Eve,* her first act (that is noted) was an act of Pride, a hearkning to that voyce of the Serpent, *Ye shall be as Gods*/Genesis 3.5/. As soone as there were two, there was pride. How many may we have knowne, (if we have had any conversation in the world) that have been content all the weeke, at home alone, with their worky day faces, as well as with their worky day clothes, and yet on Sundayes, when they come to Church, and appeare in company, will mend both, their faces as well as their clothes. Not solitude, but company is the scene of pride; And therefore I know not what to call that practise of the Nunnes in Spaine, who thought they never see man,

yet will paint. So early, so primary a sin is Pride, as that it grew instantly from her, whom God intended for a *Helper,* because he saw *that it was not good for man to be alone*/Genesis 2.18/. God sees that it is not good for man to be without health, without wealth, without power, and jurisdiction and magistracy, and we grow proud of our helpers, proud of our health and strength, proud of our wealth and riches, proud of our office and authority over others.

12. So early, so primary a sin is pride, as that, out of every mercy, and blessing, which God affords us, (and, *His mercies are new every morning*) we gather Pride; wee are not the more thankfull for them, and yet we are the prouder of them. Nay, we gather Pride, not onely out of those things, which mend and improve us, (Gods blessings and mercies) but out of those actions of our own, that destroy and ruine us, we gather pride; sins overthrow us, demolish us, destroy and ruine us, and yet we are proud of our sinnes. How many men have we heard boast of their sinnes; and, (as St. *Augustine* confesses of himselfe) belie themselves, and boast of more sinnes then they committed? Out of every thing, out of nothing sin grows. Therefore was this commandment in our text, *Sequere, Follow* come after, well placed first, for we are come to see even children strive for place and precedency, and mothers are ready to goe to the Heralds to know how Cradles shall be ranked, which Cradle shall have the highest place; Nay, even in the wombe, there was contention for precedency; *Jacob* tooke hold of his brother *Esaus* heele, and would have been borne before him/Genesis 25.26/.

13. */Superbia in monumentis/* And as our pride begins in our Cradle, it continues in our graves and Monuments. It was a good while in the primitive Church, before any were buried in the Church; The best contented themselves with the Churchyards. After, a holy ambition, (may we call it so) a holy Pride brought them *ad Limina,* to the Church-threshold, to the Church-doore, because some great Martyrs were buried in the Porches, and devout men desired to lie neare them, as one Prophet did to lie neare another, (*Lay my bones besides his bones*/1 Kings 13.31/.) But now, persons whom the Devill kept from Church all their lives, Separatists, Libertines, that never came to any Church, And persons, whom the Devill brought to Church all their lives, (for, such as come meerly out of the obligation of the Law, and to redeem that vexation, or out of custome, or company, or curiosity, or a perverse and sinister affection to the particular Preacher, though

they come to Gods house, come upon the Devils invitation) Such as one Devill, that is, worldly repect, brought to Church in their lives, another Devill, that is, Pride and vain-glory, brings to Church after their deaths, in an affectation of high places, and sumptuous Monuments in the Church. And such as have given nothing at all to any pious uses, or have determined their almes and their dole which they have given, in that one day of their funerall, and no farther, have given large annuities, perpetuities, for new painting their tombes, and for new flags, and scutcheons, every certaine number of yeares.

14. O the earlinesse! O the latenesse! how early a Spring, and no Autumne! how fast a growth, and no declination, of this branch of this sin Pride, against which, this first word of ours, *Sequere, Follow,* come after, is opposed! this love of place, and precedency, it rocks us in our Cradles, it lies down with us in our graves. There are diseases proper to certaine things, Rots to sheepe, Murrain to cattell. There are diseases proper to certaine places, as the Sweat was to us. There are diseases proper to certaine times, as the plague is in divers parts of the Eastern Countryes, where they know assuredly, when it will begin and end. But for this infectious disease of precedency, and love of place, it is run over all places, as well Cloysters as Courts, And over all men, as well spirituall as temporall, And over all times, as well the Apostles as ours. The Apostles disputed often, *who should be greatest,* and it was not enough to them, that Christ assured them, *that they should sit upon the twelve thrones, and judge the twelve Tribes*/Matthew 19. 28/; it was not enough for the sonnes of *Zebedee,* to be put into that Commission, but their friends must solicite the office, to place them high in that Commission; their Mother must move, that one may sit at Christs right hand, and the other at his left, in the execution of that Commission. Because this sin of pride is so early and primary a sin, is this Commandment of Humility first enjoyned, and because this sin appeares most generally in this love of place, and precedency, the Commandment is expressed in that word, *Sequere, Follow,* Come after. But then, even this Humility is limited, for it is *Sequere me,* follow me, which was proposed for our second Consideration, *Sequere me.*

15. */Sequere me/* There may be a pride in Humility, and an overweaning of our selves, in attributing too much to our owne judgement, in following some leaders; for so, we may be so humble as to goe after some man, and yet so proud, as to goe before the

Church, because that man may be a Schismatike. Therefore Christ proposes a safe guide, himself, *Sequere me, follow me.* It is a dangerous thing, when Christ sayes, *Vade post me, Get thee behind me;* for that is accompanied with a shrewd name of increpation, Satan, *Get thee behind me Satan;* Christ speaks it but twice in the Gospell; once to *Peter,* who because he then did the part of an Adversary, Christ calls Satan, and once to Satan himselfe, because he pursued his tentations upon him/Matthew 16.23, 4.10/; for there is a going behind Christ, which is a casting out of his presence, without any future following, and that is a fearfull station, a fearefull retrogradation; But when Christ sayes, not *Vade retro, Get thee behind me,* see my face no more, but *Sequere me, follow me,* he meanes to look back upon us; so *the Lord turned and looked upon Peter, and Peter wept bitterly* /Luke 22.63/, and all was well, when hee bids us follow him, he directs us in a good way, and by a good guide.

16. The Carthusian Friers thought they descended into as low pastures as they could goe, when they renounced all flesh, and bound themselves to feed on fish onely; and yet another Order followes them in their superstitious singularity, and goes beyond them, *Foliantes,* the Fueillans, they eat neither flesh, nor fish, nothing but leafes, and rootes; and as the Carthusians in a proud humility, despise all other Orders that eat flesh, so doe the Fueillans the Carthusians that eat fish. There is a pride in such humility. That Order of Friers that called themselves *Ignorantes,* Ignorant men, that pretended to know nothing, sunk as low as they thought it possible, into an humble name and appellation; And yet the Minorits, (Minorits that are lesse then any) think they are gone lower, and then the Minimes, (Minimes that are lesse then all) lower than they. And when one would have thought, that there had not been a lower step then that, another Sect went beyond all, beyond the Ignorants, and the Minorits, and the Minimes, and all, and called themselves, *Nullanos,* Nothings. But yet, even these Diminutives, the Minorits, and Minimes, and Nullans, as little, as lesse, as least, as very nothing as they professe themselves, lie under this disease, which is opposed in the *Sequere me,* follow, come after, in our Text; For no sort nor condition of men in the world are more contentious, more quarrelsome, more vehement for place, and precedency, then these Orders of Friers are, there, where it may appeare, that is, in their publique Processions, as we finde by those often troubles, which the Superiours of the severall Orders,

and Bishops in their severall Dioces,[11] and some of those Councels, which they call Generall, have been put to, for the ranking, and marshalling of these contentious, and wrangling men. Which makes me remember the words, in which the eighteenth of Queene *Elizabeth* Injunctions is conceived, That to take away fond Curtesie, (that is, needlesse Complement) and to take away challenging of places, (which it seemes were frequent and troublesome then) To take away fond curtesie, and challenging of places, Processions themselves were taken away, because in those Processions, these Orders of Friers, that pretended to follow, and come after all the world, did thus passionately, and with so much scandalous animosity pursue the love of place, and precedence. Therefore is our humility here limited, *Sequere me, follow me,* follow Christ. How is that done?

17. */Sequendus in Doctrina/* Consider it in Doctrinall things first, and then in Morall; First how we are to follow Christ in beleeving, and then how in doing, in practising. First in Doctrinall things, There must have gone some body before, else it is no following; Take heed therefore of going on with thine owne inventions, thine owne imaginations, for this is no following; Take heed of accompanying the beginners of Heresies and Schismes; for these are no followings where none have gone before: Nay, there have not gone enow before, to make it a path to follow in, except it have had a long continuance, and beene much trodden in. And therefore to follow Christ doctrinally, is to embrace those Doctrins, in which his Church hath walked from the beginning, and not to vexe thy selfe with new points, not necessary to salvation. That is the right way, and then thou art well entred; but that is not all; thou must walke in the right way to the end, that is, to the end of thy life. So that to professe the whole Gospel, and nothing but Gospel for Gospel, and professe this to thy death, for no respect, no dependance upon any great person, to slacken in any fundamentall point of thy Religion, nor to bee shaken with hopes or fears in thine age, when thou wouldst faine live at ease, and therefore thinkest it necessary to do, as thy supporters doe; To persevere to the end in the whole Gospel, this is to follow Christ in Doctrinall things.

18. */Sequendus in vitae/* In practicall things, things that belong to action, wee must also follow Christ, in the right way, and to the end. They are both (way and end) laid together, *Sufferentiam Job audiistis, et finem Domini vidistis; You have heard of the patience of Job, and you have seen the end of the Lord*/James 5.11/; and you

must goe *Jobs* way to Christs end. *Job* hath beaten a path for us, to shew us all the way; A path that affliction walked in, and seemed to delight in it, in bringing the Sabaean upon his Oxen, the Chaldean upon his Camels, the fire upon his Sheep, destruction upon his Servants, and at last, ruine upon his Children. One affliction makes not a path; iterated, continued calamities doe; and such a path Job hath shewed us, not onely patience, but cheerfulnesse; more, thankfulnesse for our afflictions, because they were multiplied. And then, wee must set before our eyes, as the way of Job, so the end of the Lord; Now the end of the Lord was the crosse: So that to follow him to the end, is not onely to beare afflictions, though to death, but it is to bring our crosses to the Crosse of Christ. How is that progresse made? (for it is a royal progresse not a pilgrimage to follow Christ to his Crosse) Our Saviour saith, *Hee that will follow me, let him take up his crosse, and follow me*/Matthew 16.24/. You see foure stages, foure resting, baiting places in this progresse. It must bee a *crosse,* And it must be *my crosse,* and then it must be *taken up by me,* And with this crosse of mine, thus taken up by me, I must *follow Christ,* that is, carry my crosse to his.

19. /*Crux*/ First it must bee a *Crosse, Tollat crucem;* for every man hath afflictions, but every man hath not crosses. Onely those afflictions are crosses, *whereby the world is crucified to us, and we to the world*/Galations 6.14/. The afflictions of the wicked exasperate them, enrage them, stone and pave them, obdurate and petrifie them, but they doe not crucifie them. The afflictions of the godly crucifie them. And when I am come to that conformity with my Saviour as to *fulfill his sufferings in my flesh*/Colossians 1.24/, (as I am, when I glorifie him in a Christian constancy and cheerfulnesse in my afflictions) then I am crucified with him, carried up to his Crosse: And as *Elisha* in raysing the *Shunamits* dead child, put his mouth upon the childs mouth, his eyes, and his hands, upon the hands, and eyes of the child/2 Kings 4.34/; so when my crosses have carried mee up to my Saviours Crosse, I put my hands into his hands, and hang upon his nailes, I put mine eyes upon his, and wash off all my former unchast looks, and receive a soveraigne tincture, and a lively verdure, and a new life into my dead teares, from his teares. I put my mouth upon his mouth, and it is I that say, *My God, my God, why hast thou forsaken me?* and it is I that recover againe, and say, *Into thy hands, O Lord, I commend my spirit.* Thus my afflictions are truly a crosse, when those afflictions doe truely crucifie me, and souple me, and mellow me, and knead

me, and roll me out, to a conformity with Christ. It must be this *Crosse,* and then it must be *my crosse* that I must take up, *Tollat suam.*

20. /*Crux mea*/ Other mens crosses are not my crosses; no man hath suffered more than himselfe needed. That is a poore treasure which they boast of in the Romane Church, that they have in their Exchequer, all the works of superorogation, of the Martyrs in the Primitive Church, that suffered so much more then was necessary for their owne salvation, and those superabundant crosses and merits they can apply to me. If the treasure of the blood of Christ Jesus be not sufficient, Lord what addition can I find, to match them, to piece out them! And if it be sufficient of it selfe, what addition need I seek? Other mens crosses are not mine, other mens merits cannot save me. Nor is any crosse mine owne, which is not mine by a good title; It I be not Possessor *bonae fidei,* If I came not well by that crosse. And *Quid habeo quod non accepi?* is a question that reaches even to my crosses; what have I that I have not received?/1 Corinthians 4.7/ not a crosse; And from whose hands can I receive any good thing, but from the hands of God? So that that onely is my crosse, which the hand of God hath laid upon me. Alas, that crosse of present bodily weaknesse, which the former wantonnesses of my youth have brought upon me, is not my crosse; That crosse of poverty which the wastfulnesse of youth hath brought upon me, is not my crosse; for these, weaknesse upon wantonnesse, want upon wastfulnesse, are Natures crosses, not Gods, and they would fall naturally, though there were (which is an impossible supposition) no God. Except God therefore take these crosses in the way, as they fall into his hands, and sanctifie them so, and then lay them upon me, they are not my crosses; but if God doe this, they are. And then this crosse thus prepared, I must *take up; Tollat.*

21. /*Tollat*/ Forraine crosses, other mens merits are not mine; spontaneous and voluntary crosses, contracted by mine owne sins, are not mine; neither are devious, and remote, and unnecessary crosses, my crosses. Since I am bound to take up my crosse, there must be a crosse that is mine to take up; that is, a crosse prepared for me by God, and laid in my way, which is tentations or tribulations in my calling; and I must not go out of my way to seeke a crosse; for, so it is not mine, nor laid for my taking up. I am not bound to hunt after a persecution, nor to stand it, and not flye, nor to affront a plague, and not remove, nor to open my selfe to an injury, and not defend. I am not bound to starve my selfe by in-

ordinate fasting, nor to teare my flesh by inhumane whippings, and flagellations. I am bound to take up my Crosse; and that is onely mine which the hand of God hath laid for me, that is, in the way of my Calling tentations and tribulations incident to that.

22. /*Sequatur me*/ If it be mine, that is laid for me by the hand of God, and taken up by me, that is voluntarily embraced, then *Sequatur,* sayes Christ, I am bound to *follow him,* with that crosse, that is, to carry my crosse to his crosse. And if at any time I faint under this crosse in the way, let this comfort me, that even Christ himselfe was eased by *Simon* of Cyrene, in the carrying of his Crosse/Matthew 27.32/; and in all such cases, I must flye to the assistance of the prayers of the Church, and of good men, that God, since it is his burden, will make it lighter, since it is his yoake, easier, and since it is his Crosse, more supportable, and give me the issue with the tentation. When all is done, with this crosse thus laid for me, and taken up by me, I must follow Christ; Christ to his end; his end is his Crosse; that is, I must bring my crosse to his; lay downe my crosse at the foote of his; Confesse that there is no dignity, no merit in mine, but as it receives an impression, a sanctification from his. For, if I could dye a thousand times for Christ, this were nothing, if Christ had not dyed for me before. And this is truly to follow Christ, both in the way, and to the end, as well in doctrinall things as in practicall. And this is all that lay upon these two. *Peter* and *Andrew, Follow me.* Remaines yet to be considered, what they shall get by this; which is our last Consideration.

23. /*Piscatores hominum*/ They shall be *fishers;* and what shall they catch? *men.* They shall be fishers of men. And then, for that the world must be their Sea, and their net must be the Gospel. And here in so vast a sea, and with so small a net, there was no great appearance of much gaine. And in this function, whatsoever they should catch, they should catch little for themselves. The Apostleship, as it was the fruitfullest, so it was the barrennest vocation; They were to catch all the world; there is their fecundity; but the Apostles were to have no Successors, as Apostles; there is their barrennesse. The Apostleship was not intended for a function to raise houses and families; The function ended in their persons; after the first, there were no more Apostles.

24. And therefore it is an usurpation, an imposture, an illusion, it is a forgery, when the Bishop of Rome will proceed by Apostolicall authority, and with Apostolicall dignity, and Apostolicall jurisdiction; If he be St. *Peters* Successor in the Bishopricke of Rome, he

may proceed with Episcopall authority in his Dioces. If he be; for, though we doe not deny that St. *Peter* was at Rome, and Bishop of Rome; though we receive it with an historicall faith, induced by the consent of Ancient writers, yet when they will constitute matter of faith out of matter of fact, and, because St. *Peter* was (*de facto*) Bishop of Rome, therefore we must beleeve, as an Article of faith, such an infallibility in that Church, as that no Successor of St. *Peters* can ever erre, when they stretch it to matter of faith, then for matter of faith, we require Scriptures; and then we are confident, and justly confident, that though historically we do beleeve it, yet out of Scriptures (which is a necessary proofe in Articles of faith) they can never prove that St. *Peter* was bishop of Rome, or ever at Rome. So then, if the present Bishop of Rome be St. *Peters* Successor, as Bishop of Rome, he hath Episcopall jurisdiction there; but he is not St. *Peters* Successor in his Apostleship; and onely that Apostleship was a jurisdiction over all the world. But the Apostleship was an extraordinary office instituted by Christ, for a certaine time, and to certaine purposes, and not to continue in ordinary use. As also the office of the Prophet was in the Old Testament an extraordinary Office, and was not transferred then, nor does not remaine now in the ordinary office of the Minister.

25. And therefore they argue impertinently, and collect and infer sometimes seditiously that say, The Prophet proceeded thus and thus, therefore the Minister may and must proceed so too; The Prophets would chide the Kings openly, and threaten the Kings publiquely, and proclaime the fault of the Kings in the eares of the people confidently, authoritatively, therefore the Minister may and must do so. God sent that particular Prophet *Jeremy* with that extraordinary Commission, *Behold I have this day set thee over the Nations, and over the Kingdomes, to roote out, and to pull downe, to destroy and throw downe, and then to build, and to plant againe* /Jeremiah 1.10/; But God hath given none of us his Ministers, in our ordinary function, any such Commission over nations, and over Kingdomes. Even in *Jeremies* Commission there seemes to be a limitation of time; *Behold this day I have set thee over them,* where that addition (*this day*) is not onely the date of the Commission, that it passed Gods hand that day, but (*this day*) is the terme, the duration of the Commission, that it was to last but that day, that is, (as the phrase of that language is) that time for which it was limited. And therefore, as they argue perversely, frowardly, dangerously that say, The Minister does not his duty that speakes

not as boldly, and as publiquely too, and of Kings, and great persons, as the Prophets did, because theirs was an Extraordinary, ours an Ordinary office, (and no man will thinke that the Justices in their Sessions, or the Judges in their Circuits may proceed to executions, without due tryall by a course of Law, because Marshals, in time of rebellion and other necessities, may doe so, because the one hath but an ordinary, the other an extraordinary Commission) So doe they deceive themselves and others, that pretend in the Bishop of Rome an Apostolicall jurisdiction, a jurisdiction over all the world; whereas howsoever he may be St. *Peters* Successor, as Bishop of Rome, yet he is no Successor to St. *Peter* as an Apostle; upon which onely the universall power can be grounded, and without which that universall power fals to the ground: The Apostolicall faith remaines spread over all the world, but Apostolicall jurisdiction is expired with their persons.

26. */Piscatores, quia nomen humile/* These twelve Christ cals *Fishers;* why fishers? because it is a name of labour, of service, and of humiliation; and names that tast of humiliation, and labour, and service, are most properly ours; (fishers we may be) names of dignity, and authority, and command are not so properly ours; (Apostles wee are not in any such sense as they were) Nothing inflames, nor swels, nor puffes us up, more than that leaven of the soule, that empty, aery, frothy love of Names and Titles. We have knowne men part with ancient lands for new Titles, and with old Mannors for new honours; and as a man that should bestow all his money upon a faire purse, and then have nothing to put into it; so whole Estates have melted away for Titles and Honours, and nothing left to support them. And how long last they? How many winds blast them? That name of God, in which, *Moses* was sent to *Pharaoh,* is by our Translators and Expositors ordinarily said to be *I Am that I Am,* (*Go and say, I Am hath sent me,* sayes God there) /Exodus 3.14/ But in truth, in the Originall, the name is conceived in the future, it is, *I shall be.* Every man is that he is; but onely God is sure that he shall be so still. Therefore Christ cals them by a name of labour and humiliation. But why by that name of labour and humiliation, *Fishers?*

27. */Piscatores, quia nomen primativum/* Because it was *Nomen primitivum,* their owne, their former name. The Holy Ghost pursues his owne way, and does here in Christ, as hee does often in other places, he speakes in such formes, and such phrases, as may most worke upon them to whom he speaks. Of *David,* that was a

shepheard before, God sayes, he tooke him to feed his people/ Psalm 78.70/. To those *Magi* of the East, who were given to the study of the Stars, God gave a Star to be their guide to Christ at Bethlem/Matthew 2.2/. To those which followed him to Capernaum for meat, Christ tooke occasion by that, to preach to them of the spirituall food of their souls/John 6.24/. To the Samaritan woman, whom he found at the Well, he preached of the water of Life/John 4.11/. To these men in our Text accustomed to a joy and gladnesse, when they tooke great, or great store of fish, he presents his comforts agreeably to their tast, They should be fishers still. Beloved, Christ puts no man out of his way, (for sinfull courses are no wayes, but continuall deviations) to goe to heaven. Christ makes heaven all things to all men, that he might gaine all: To the mirthfull man he presents heaven, as all joy, and to the ambitious man, as all glory; To the Merchant it is a Pearle, and to the husbandman it is a rich field. Christ hath made heaven all things to all men, that he might gaine all, and he puts no man out of his way to come thither. These men he calls Fishers.

28. */Non Innovatio, sed Renovatio/* He does not call them from their calling, but he mends them in it. It is not an Innovation; God loves not innovations; Old doctrines, old disciplines, old words and formes of speech in his service, God loves best. But it is a Renovation, though not an Innovation, and Renovations are alwayes acceptable to God; that is, the renewing of a mans selfe, in a consideration of his first estate, what he was made for, and wherein he might be most serviceable to God. Such a renewing it is, as could not be done without God; no man can renew himselfe, regenerate himselfe; no man can prepare that worke, no man can begin it, no man can proceed in it of himselfe. The desire and the actuall beginning is from the preventing grace of God, and the constant proceeding is from the concomitant, and subsequent, and continuall succeeding grace of God; for there is no conclusive, no consummative grave in this life; no such measure of grace given to any man, as that that man needs no more, or can lose or frustrate none of that. The renewing of these men in our text, Christ takes to himselfe; *Faciam vos, I will make yee fishers of men;* no worldly respects must make us such fishers; it must be a calling from God; And yet, (as the other Evangelist in the same history expresses it) it is *Faciam fieri vos, I will cause yee to be made fishers of men* /Mark 1.16/, that is, I will provide an outward calling for you too. Our calling to this Manfishing is not good, *Nisi Dominus*

faciat, et fieri faciat, except God make us fishers by an internall, and make his Church to make us so too, by an externall calling. Then we are fishers of men, and then we are successors to the Apostles, though not in their Apostleship, yet in this fishing. And then, for this fishing, the world is the Sea, and our net is the Gospel.

29. */Mundus mare/* The world is a Sea in many respects and assimilations. It is a Sea, as it is subject to stormes, and tempests; Every man (and every man is a world) feels that. And then, it is never the shallower for the calmnesse, The Sea is as deepe, there is as much water in the Sea, in a calme, as in a storme; we may be drowned in a calme and flattering fortune, in prosperity, as irrecoverably, as in a wrought Sea, in adversity; So the world is a Sea. It is a Sea, as it is bottomlesse to any line, which we can sound it with, and endlesse to any discovery that we can make of it. The purposes of the world, the wayes of the world, exceed our consideration; But yet we are sure the Sea hath a bottome, and sure that it hath limits, that it cannot overpasse; The power of the greatest in the world, the life of the happiest in the world, cannot exceed those bounds, which God hath placed for them; So the world is a Sea. It is a Sea, as it hath ebbs and floods, and no man knowes the true reason of those floods and those ebbs. All men have changes and vicissitudes in their bodies, (they fall sick) And in their estates, (they grow poore) And in their minds, (they become sad) at which changes, (sicknesse, poverty, sadnesse) themselves wonder, and the cause is wrapped up in the purpose and judgement of God onely, and hid even from them that have them; and so the world is a Sea. It is a Sea, as the Sea affords water enough for all the world to drinke, but such water as will not quench the thirst. The world affords conveniences enow to satisfie Nature, but these encrease our thirst with drinking, and our desire growes and enlarges it selfe with our abundance, and though we sayle in a full Sea, yet we lacke water; So the world is a Sea. It is a Sea, if we consider the Inhabitants. In the Sea, the greater fish devoure the lesse; and so doe the men of this world too. And as fish, when they mud themselves, have no hands to make themselves cleane, but the current of the waters must worke that; So have the men of this world no means to cleanse themselves from those sinnes which they have contracted in the world, of themselves, till a new flood, waters of repentance, drawne up, and sanctified by the Holy Ghost, worke that blessed effect in them.

30. All these wayes the world is a Sea, but especially it is a Sea in

this respect, that the Sea is no place of habitation, but a passage to our habitations. So the Apostle expresses the world, *Here we have no continuing City, but we seeke one to come*/Hebrews 13.14/; we seeke it not here, but we seeke it whilest we are here, els we shall never finde it. Those are the two great works which we are to doe in this world; first to know, that this world is not our home, and then to provide us another home, whilest we are in this world. Therefore the Prophet sayes, *Arise, and depart, for this is not your rest*/Micah 2.10/. Worldly men, that have no farther prospect, promise themselves some rest in this world, (*Soule, thou hast much goods laid up for many yeares, take thine ease, eate, drinke, and be merry*/Luke 12.19/, sayes the rich man) but this is not your rest; indeed no rest; at least not yours. You must depart, depart by death, before yee come to that rest; but then you must arise, before you depart; for except yee have a resurrection to grace here, before you depart, you shall have no resurrection to glory in the life to come, when you are departed.

31. /*Status navigantium*/ Now, in this Sea, every ship that sayles must necessarily have some part of the ship under water; Every man that lives in this world, must necessarily have some of his life, some of his thoughts, some of his labours spent upon this world; but that part of the ship, by which he sayls, is above water; Those meditations, and those endevours which must bring us to heaven, are removed from this world, and fixed entirely upon God. And in this Sea, are we made fishers of men; Of men in generall; not of rich men, to profit by them, nor of poore men, to pierce them the more sharply, because affliction hath opened a way into them; Not of learned men, to be over-glad of their approbation of our labours, Nor of ignorant men, to affect them with an astonishment, or admiration of our gifts: But we are fishers of men, of all men, of that which makes them men, their soules. And for this fishing in this Sea, this Gospel is our net.

32. /*Rete Evangelium*/ Eloquence is not our net; Traditions of men are not our nets; onely the Gospel is. The Devill angles with hooks and bayts; he deceives, and he wounds in the catching; for every sin hath his sting. The Gospell of Christ Jesus is a net; It hath leads and corks; It hath leads, that is, the denouncing of Gods judgements, and a power to sink down, and lay flat any stubborne and rebellious heart, And it hath corks, that is, the power of absolution, and application of the mercies of God, that swimme above all his workes, means to erect an humble and contrite spirit, above

all the waters of tribulation, and affliction/*Rete nodosum*/. A net is *Res nodosa,* a knotty thing; and so is the Scripture, full of knots, of scruple, and perplexity, and anxiety, and vexation if thou wilt goe about to entangle thy selfe in those things which appertaine not to thy salvation; but knots of a fast union, and inseperable alliance of thy soule to God, and to the fellowship of his Saints, if thou take the Scriptures, as they were intended for thee, that is, if thou beest content to rest in those places, which are cleare, and evident in things necessary/*Rete diffusivum*/. A net is a large thing, past thy fadoming, if thou cast it from thee, but if thou draw it to thee, it will lie upon thine arme. The Scriptures will be out of thy reach, and out of thy use, if thou cast and scatter them upon Reason, upon Philosophy, upon Morality, to try how the Scriptures will fit all them, and beleeve them but so far as they agree with thy reason; But draw the Scripture to thine own heart, and to thine own actions, and thou shalt finde it made for that; all the promises of the old Testament made, and all accomplished in the new Testament, for the salvation of thy soule hereafter, and for thy consolation in the present application of them.

33. *Non quia tanquam causa.* Now this that Christ promises here is not here promised in the nature of wages due to our labour, and our fishing. There is no merit in all that we can doe. *The wages of sin is Death;* Death is due to sin, the proper reward of sin; but the Apostle does not say there, That eternall life is the wages of any good worke of ours. (*The wages of sinne is death, but eternall life is the gift of God, through Jesus Christ our Lord*)/Romans 6.23/. Through Jesus Christ, that is, as we are considered in him; and in him, who is a Saviour, a Redeemer, we are not considered but as sinners. So that Gods purpose works no otherwise upon us, but as we are sinners; neither did God meane ill to any man, till that man was, in his sight, a sinner. God shuts no man out of heaven, by a lock on the inside, except that man have clapped the doore after him, and never knocked to have it opened againe, that is, except he have sinned, and never repented. Christ does not say in our text, Follow me, for I will prefer you; he will not have that the reason, the cause. If I would not serve God, except I might be saved for serving him, I shall not be saved though I serve him; My first end in serving God, must not be my selfe, but he and his glory. It is but an addition from his own goodnesse, *Et faciam,* Follow me, and I will doe this; but yet it is a certaine, and infallible as a debt, or as an effect upon a naturall cause; Those propositions in nature are

not so certaine; The Earth is at such a time just between the Sunne, and the Moone, therefore the Moone must be Eclipsed, The Moone is at such time just between the Earth and the Sunne, therefore the Sunne must be Eclipsed; for upon the Sunne, and those other bodies, God can, and hath sometimes wrought miraculously and changed the naturall courses of them; (The Sunne stood still in *Joshua* And there was an unnaturall Eclipse at the death of Christ) But God cannot by any Miracle so worke upon himselfe as to make himselfe not himselfe, unmercifull, or unjust; And out of his mercy he makes this promise, (Doe this, and thus it shall be with you) and then, of his justice he performes that promise, which was made meerely, and onely out of mercy, If we doe it, (though not because we doe it) we shall have eternall life.

34. Therefore did *Andrew,* and *Peter* faithfully beleeve, such a net should be put into their hands. Christ had vouchsafed to fish for them, and caught them with that net, and they beleeved that he that made them fishers of men, would also enable them to catch others with that net. And that is truly the comfort that refreshes us in all our Lucubrations, and night-studies, through the course of our lives, that that God that sets us to Sea, will prosper our voyage, that whether he fix us upon our owne, or send us to other Congregations, he will open the hearts of those Congregations to us, and blesse our labours to them. For as St. *Pauls Vae si non,* lies upon us wheresoever we are, (We be unto us if wee doe not preach) so, (as St. *Paul* sayes too) we were of all men the most miserable, if wee preached without hope of doing good. With this net St. *Peter* caught three thousand soules in one day, at one Sermon, and five thousand in another/Acts 2.41, 4.4/. With this net St. *Paul* fished all the Mediterranean Sea, and caused the Gospel of Christ Jesus to abound from Jerusalem round about to Illyricum/Romans 15.19/. This is the net, with which if yee be willing to bee caught, that is, to lay downe all your hopes and affiances in the gracious promises of his Gospel, then you are fishes reserved for that great Mariage-feast, which is the Kingdome of heaven; where, whosoever is a dish, is a ghest too; whosoever is served in at the table, sits at the table; whosoever is caught by this net, is called to this feast; and there your soules shall be satisfied as with marrow, and with fatnesse, in an infallible assurance, of an everlasting and undeterminable terme, in inexpressible joy and glory. Amen.

NOTES

Chapter 1

1. Joan Webber, "Celebration of Word and World in Andrewes' Style," *Journal of English and Germanic Philology* 64 (1965): 257–269. There has of course been defense and praise of Donne's sermons. Specialized articles, and book-length studies will be acknowledged later, but three fine articles of a general nature claim notice here: Austin Warren, "The Very Reverend Doctor Donne," *Kenyon Review* 16 (1954): 268–277; Charles Coffin, rev. art. "Donne's Divinity," *Kenyon Review* 16 (1954): 292–298; and Thomas F. Merrill, "John Donne and the Word of God," *Neuphilologische Mitteilungen* 69 (1968): 597–616. Merrill argues for aligning Donne's views of preaching with those of the Puritan Cartwright who opposed the high-church Whitgift and Hooker (and Andrewes and Eliot). T. S. Eliot's remarks are preserved in the title essay of *For Lancelot Andrewes: Essays on Style and Order* (London: Faber and Gwyer, 1928), pp. 3–24.

2. This paradigm is discussed in more detail in my "Demythologizing Genre," *College English* 28 (1967): 495–501.

3. Further reflections on this formula and implications appear in "How Literary Things Go: Contra Hirsch," *Genre* 1 (1968): 195–208.

4. After writing this I was delighted to find agreement and support in Albert Cook's *The Classic Line* (Bloomington: Indiana University Press, 1966), Chapter One.

5. John Addleshaw and Frederick Etchells, *The Architectural Setting of Anglican Worship* (London: Faber and Faber Ltd., 1948), p. 35. That "tables of the Decalogue and other texts" were often in view should be kept in mind. Addleshaw and Etchells go on to explain that "the Royal arms . . . represented the royal supremacy; but the royal supremacy did not mean an authority external to the Church. Church

and State were two parts of one society finding its centre in the sovereign, who made provision for this society's welfare both as a Church and a State" (p. 101).

6. Addleshaw and Etchells, pp. 22–23, 245–247. For pictures of Blunham Church exterior and pulpit, see the Potter and Simpson edition, vol. 5, frontispiece and p. 21 (hereafter cited P and S); St. Dunstans-in-the-West, 8. p. 36; Old St. Paul's nave and choir, 7. p. 10, and 6. p. 24.

7. Donne was Reader in Divinity to Fellows and students at Lincoln's Inn (where he himself had studied law) from 24 October 1616 until 11 February 1621–22. See the chapter on the chapel in Sir Gerald Hurst's affectionate *Short History of Lincoln's Inn,* and picture of undercroft of the "new" chapel of 1623 (London, Constable, 1946). Potter and Simpson picture that chapel (2. p. 4) and its eighteenth-century pulpit (2. frontispiece), mistakenly identified as contemporary with Donne. Sadly, no drawing seems to survive of the old chapel where he preached a score of the surviving sermons.

8. J. Charles Cox, *English Church Fittings, Furniture, and Accessories* (London: B. T. Batsford, Ltd., 1933; first published 1923), pp. 121–122.

9. Ephraim Udall, rector of St. Augustine's, Old Change, London, complained in 1641 that if the celebrant brought the elements out to the communicants in the nave, and they awaited him in high pews, "this Communion seems to be rent and divided into so many single societies of twos and threes, as there be pewfulls in the church, more like so many private Masses and Houselings, than one Communion." [*To Trepon Eucharistikon*] i.e. *Communion Comelinesse* (London: 1641), pp. 8–13, as quoted by Addleshaw and Etchells, p. 120. They comment drily: "one remembers that many high square pews developed out of the medieval chantry chapels; the Puritans who owned them still retained the spiritual individualism of their medieval ancestors."

10. *Phenomenological Psychology:* Selected Papers, by Erwin W. Straus, trans. in part by Erling Eng (New York: Basic Books, 1966), pp. 20, 23, 56. See also Walter J. Ong, *The Presence of the Word* (New Haven: Yale, 1967).

11. *Phenomenological Psychology,* pp. 163–164, 173. See also Gaston Bachelard, *The Poetics of Space* (Boston: Beacon Press, 1969; original French edition 1958).

12. Berkeley and Los Angeles: Univ. of California Press; London: Cambridge Univ. Press, 1953–62; 10 vols.)

13. Christopher Morris, ed., *Of the Laws of Ecclesiastical Polity*

(London: J. M. Dent & Sons Ltd., 1954), 2: 94 ("Preface," chap. 2, para. 10).

14. *Phenomenological Psychology,* pp. 112–113.

15. "Beseech him to grant us true repentance, and his Holy Spirit, that those things may please him which we do at this present."

16. See Edward R. Hardy, "Priestly Ministries in the Modern Church," in *The Ministry in Historical Perspectives,* ed. H. Richard Niebuhr and Daniel D. Williams (New York: Harper & Brothers, 1956), pp. 149–179.

17. Wilson, *Arte of Rhetoric,* ed. G. H. Mair (Oxford: Clarendon Press, 1909). pp. 220–221. Fraunce, *The Arcadian Rhetoric,* ed. Ethel Seaton (Oxford: Basil Blackwell, 1950), p. 120. See also John Bulwer, *Chironomia,* pp. 133–134, published as a double illustrated volume with *Chirologia* (1644). And see the Anglican priest Henry Peacham's *The Garden of Eloquence,* facsimile of 1593 edition, with intro. William G. Crane (Gainesville, Florida: Scholars Facsimiles and Reprints, 1954), p. 54 (1st ed., 1577). Thomas Wright, in *The Passions of the Mind* (1604) wrote "to use no gestures argueth slownesse, too much . . . lightnesse: mediocritie proceedeth from wisedome and gravitie" (p. 213).

18. Thomas Crosfield, entry for 1 June 1630 in *The Diary,* ed. F. S. Boas (London: Oxford University Press, 1935); Jaspar Mayne, lines 57–64 of commendatory poem published with Donne's *Poems* (1633).

19. *De Doctrina Christiana, Patrologia Latina* 34, col. 60.

20. See also, for example, 1. S8. 144–165; 2. S1. 135–144.

21. Valuable analysis in this vein, with several pages on Donne's *Devotions* is to be found in Joan Webber's *The Eloquent "I": Style and Self in Seventeenth Century Prose* (Madison: Univ. of Wisconsin Press, 1968).

22. This at Lincoln's Inn, where he had served as Master of the Revels in 1593 (but declined the office of Steward of Christmas in 1594). The Inns of Court were known for theatrical entertainments; see A. Wigfall Green, *The Inns of Court and Early English Drama* (New Haven: Yale Univ. Press, 1931; reissued New York: Benjamin Blom, 1965). In any case, the young Donne was later described as "not dissolute but very neat; a great visitor of Ladies, a great frequenter of Playes, a great writer of conceited Verses." Sir Richard Baker, *A Chronicle of The Kings of England* (London: 1643), p. 156.

23. I have for clarity altered to a colon the comma of the Potter and Simpson text.

24. See, for example, Albert S. Cook, *The Dark Voyage and the Golden Mean* (Cambridge: Harvard Univ. Press, 1950).

25. *Creative Fidelity,* trans. Robert Rosthal (New York: Farrar, Straus & Co., 1964). Noonday Press edition, pp. 121–129. Orig. *Du Refus à L'Invocation.*

26. *Letters To Several Persons of Honor* (1651), ed. Charles E. Merrill (New York: 1910), p. 138 and note, p. 297.

27. See "Voice as Summons to Belief," *Literature and Belief,* English Institute Essays, 1957, ed. M. H. Abrams (New York: Columbia Univ. Press, 1958), pp. 80–105.

28. See the remarks by Arnold Stein on the "inconstant heart" in his excellent note on the sermons in *John Donne's Lyrics: the Eloquence of Action* (Minneapolis: Univ. of Minnesota, 1962), pp. 217–222.

Chapter 2

1. See, for example, P and S 1. pp. 117–119, 127; 2. pp. 12, 19; 3. p. 1, 28, 40; 7. p. 1. Charles M. Coffin's demurrer in "Donne's Divinity," *Kenyon Review* 16 (1954): 292–298. R. C. Bald argues that Donne "must have given convincing evidence of more than average competence as a preacher before the appointment was made" to Lincoln's Inn, and finds "few signs that his strength was failing" before his final illness. Bald draws on Walton's *Life,* Donne's correspondence, and pioneering studies by John Sparrow and John Hayward in summarizing the accepted presumptions that Donne regularly preached to great effect (and on rhetorically and elocutionarily sensitive auditories) from carefully prepared notes (pp. 405–410, 480).

2. *Theology of Culture* (New York: Oxford Univ. Press, 1959), p. 189. For work which outlines with even better lucidity and concision the risks, pitfalls, and gains of applying a later system of thought to an earlier, and convincingly argues the real affinity of biblical theology and existence philosophy, see John MacQuarrie, *An Existentialist Theology: A Comparison of Heidegger and Bultmann* (New York: Harper and Row, Torchbook edition 1965; first published London: S.C.M. Press, 1955). Brief supporting argument for existentialism in the sermons appears in William Mueller, *John Donne: Preacher* (Princeton: Princeton Univ. Press, 1962), p. 246; Thomas F. Merrill, "John Donne and the Word of God; *Neuphilologische Mitteilungen* 69:614–615; Sr. Mary Caroline, "The Existentialist Attitude of John Donne," *Xavier University Studies* 7 (1968): 37–50.

3. Compare the earnest irony of his petition to Christ concluding "A Litanie."

> But Patient and Physitian being free,
> As sinne is nothing, let it no where be.
>
> (probably 1608)

Compare 6. S11. 562–636 (1625) where the ontological question of sin's nature is put aside for attention to human redemption.

Compare also the mixture of earnest existential analysis with scorn for "school-shifts," at Lincoln's Inn, 2. S3: 154–205, perhaps 1618.

4. He scorns "the Schoole-men" for presuming to *measure* Hell, Heaven, and God (7. S4. 717–732).

5. Cf. Straus, *Phenomenological Psychology,* p. 55: "We are never *entirely* in any particular time and place. . . . The fact of never being complete needs to be understood in relation to the idea of Totality." See also 6. S11. 125–126; Augustine's *Enchiridion,* para. 101.

6. Cf. Gabriel Marcel's notion of *disponibilité.* See esp. "Belonging and Disposability" in *Creative Fidelity.*

7. *Letters,* ed. Merrill, p. 88 (and see his note, p. 289).

8. See also, for example, 7. S4. 795–804.

9. *Donne's Poetical Works,* ed. Grierson (Oxford, 1912), vol. 1, p. 393, vol. 2, p. 260.

10. Cf. D. R. Roberts, "The Death Wish of John Donne," *Publications of the Modern Language Association* 62 (1947): 958–976.

11. In the prehomiletic *Essays in Divinity,* ed. Evelyn Simpson (London; Oxford Univ. Press, 1952), he exhibits caution about biblical typology even as he praises the richness of the Bible:

> And as *Lyra* notes, being perchance too Allegoricall and Typick in this, it hath this in common with all other books, that the *words* signifie *things;* but hath this particular, that all the *things* signifie *other things.*
>
> (*ED* 8. 25–28; 1615?)

If anything, his caution increased with the years. See for example, 3. S5. 375–384 (1620), and 4. S1. 566–600 (1622).

12. For provocative statistics, and other observations, a few slightly at odds with the tenor of this study, see Potter and Simpson 10, pp. 346–358.

13. See also Sermon 22, "of the life of a Christian" on the same passage from 2 Corinthians (1. 6–10) adverted to by Augustine, above.

14. P and S 5, pp. 15–16.

15. Similarly 4. S6. 127–164, which uses the words *contracted, remote,*

near, and *close* to the same devotional end. Compare the secular parallel in Jonson's superb "To Penshurst," which seems to me to deal partly with existential presence; some "great men's tables," by their distinctions in fare and treatment, leave the guest dining "away," in contrast to Penshurst, where "high huswifery" made all the warmth of hospitality "nigh" for an unexpected visit by the king, despite the hostess's physical absence. Compare also Traherne's *Centuries,* for example at I, no. 21.

16. Likely to have been preached either in 1621 or 1623; see P and S 5, pp. 14–15.

17. And of course, by the nature of sound, hearing *again:* "since thou never thoughtest of it since that former hearing, till thou heardest it again now, thou didst not know that thou hadst heard it before" (5. S1. 738–740; on Acts 10.44 for a Whitsunday, probably at Lincoln's Inn, perhaps as early as 1617).

18. Cf. Ben Jonson's well-known remark: "Language most shewes a man: speake that I may see thee. It springs out of the most retired and inmost parts of us, and is the Image of the Parent of it, the mind." "Timber or Discoveries" in *Works,* ed. C. W. Herford, Percy and Evelyn Simpson (Oxford: Clarendon Press, 1947), Vol. 8, p. 625.

19. "R. B.," in *Poetical Works,* ed. Sir Herbert Grierson (Oxford: 1912), Vol. 1, p. 387. Perhaps R. Busby, headmaster of Winchester (see Bald, p. 409).

20. "Evolution and Cyclicism in Our Time," *In the Human Grain* (New York: Macmillan, 1967), p. 76.

21. Puttenham speaks of something like our four categories (pp. 116–117), and of levels of diction (pp. 82, 144–147, 251–253). Gladys Willcock and Alice Walker, speak of "the mill of oral tradition" (p. lxxxix) in their edition, *The Arte of English Poesie* (Cambridge: Cambridge Univ. Press, 1936).

22. These distinctions were first suggested to me by Prof. Marie Borroff.

23. For Donne, 2. S6. 673–692 (Lincoln's Inn, 1618), 6. S6. 597–620 (St. Dunstan's 1624), 9. S8. 790–828 (St. Paul's, 1630)—the next-to-last paragraph in each of the three sermons. For Andrewes, one representative paragraph each from a Whitehall sermon of 1610, of 1616, and of 1623; see *Sermons,* ed. G. M. Story (Oxford: Clarendon Press, 1967), p. 23, ll. 20–26; p. 54, ll. 8–21, p. 236, ll. 6–23.

24. Louis Martz points out the strategically and unusually wide range of diction from learned to colloquial in the poems of Taylor, the strategically narrower range in those of Herbert and Jonson; "Forward,"

The Poems of Edward Taylor, ed. Donald E. Stanford (New Haven: Yale Univ. Press 1960), p. xvi. For the best recent work on Andrewes, see Joan Webber, "Celebration," *JEGP* 64 (1965), and the selection of *Sermons* ed. G. M. Story (Oxford Univ. Press, 1967).

25. Cf. Harry Levin, "The War of Words . . ." in *Contexts of Criticism* (Cambridge: Harvard Univ. Press, 1957), esp. pp. 209–214. He quotes R. F. Jones on Shakespeare's and the Authorized Version's word derivations (90 percent and 94 percent Germanic, respectively), but draws simpler distinctions and conclusions than the "uniquely varied texture" of Renaissance prose asks.

26. *De Doctrina Christiana* 4:10. PL 34:100: Qui ergo docet, vitabit omnia verba quae non docent; et si pro eis alia integra, quae intelligantur, potest dicere, id magis eliget; si autem non occurrent, utetur etiam, verbis minus integris, dum tamen res ipsa doceatur atque discatur integre.

27. In 2. S2. 186, for example, where he accepts a reading of that edition, he calls it the "Vulgat."

28. See 3. S16. 6–11; seemingly none survive. One wonders if he chose not to preserve any.

29. See 1. S2. 166–186; 1. S8. 334–374, 444–456; 2. S1. 494–499; 3. S4. 560–566; *et passim*.

30. See also, for example, 1: S2: 536–538.

31. All this was (and is) further complicated by the language being in a state of unusually active flux, with infusions of loan words and many coinages, some frivolous. For a standard account, with report of attacks on "ink-horn" terms, see Richard Foster Jones, *The Triumph of the English Language* (Palo Alto: Stanford Univ. Press, 1953).

32. C. K. Ogden and I. A. Richards, *The Meaning of Meaning. A Study of the Influence of Language Upon Thought and of the Science of Symbolism* 8th ed. (London: Kegan Paul, Trench, Trübner and Co. Ltd., 1946), pp. 9–10.

33. Ernst R. Curtius, *European Literature and the Latin Middle Ages*. (New York: Harper Torchbook, 1963; first English edition 1953; first German edition 1948) See esp. pp. 495–500 for an entry to some linguistic norms in medieval Latinity.

34. Trans. D. W. Robertson, Jr. (Indianapolis and New York: Bobbs-Merrill Library of Liberal Arts, 1958), pp. 122, 164. "Our preaching is our speech, our good life is our eloquence" (9. S6. 10–13).

35. Cf. the sketchy but similar formulation of Augustine: *De Doctrina Christiana* 1: 6. PL 34: 21. "dicitur Deus. Non enim revera in strepitu istarum duarum syllabarum ipse cognoscitur; sed tamen omnes

latinae linguae scios, cum aures eorum sonus iste tetigerit, movet ad cogitandam excellentissimam quamdam immortalemque naturam."

36. See Curtius, *European Literature,* p. 123, and his citations from St. Jerome for "sails of interpretation" and "breeze of the Holy Ghost," another of numberless instances wherein Donne's Christian existentialism has roots in "the primitive church."

37. Austin Warren argued in a helpful but neglected article that "the phonetic consonance but stresses a parallelism or antithesis of conception." "The Very Reverend Dr. Donne," *Kenyon Review* 16 (1954): 268–277, p. 275.

38. My perception of this has been sharpened by the first chapter of Stanley Fish's fine study *Self-Consuming Artifacts,* which he kindly showed me in manuscript.

39. Donne's descriptions of heaven seem to me to suggest an atmosphere of dedicated, unwearying, devout play. In any case, I am taking play and game as profoundly significant, worthwhile activity, or at least potentially so. For the theoretical context of such a position, see Jacques Ehrmann's elegant demurrer to Huizinga and Caillois, "Homo ludens revisited," *Yale French Studies* 41 (1968): 31–57. Although I know of no one who has claimed significant and praiseworthy status for play and game in the seventeenth-century sermon, poetry has had such attention; see, for example, Frank Warnke, "Play and Metamorphosis in Marvell's Poetry," *Studies in English Literature* 5 (1965): 23–30, and "Sacred Play: Baroque Poetic Style," *Journal of Aesthetics and Art Criticism* 22 (1964): 455–464.

40. Thus, a trail of minute particulars has brought us to a conclusion somewhat like James Smith's, in his more general and rationalistic essay on "the Many and the One" as the central concern animating "Metaphysical Poetry," in *Determinations,* ed. F. R. Leavis (London: Chatto and Windus, 1934), pp. 10–45.

41. Joan Webber has explicated such reconciliation as characteristic shift from analogy and emblem to symbol and sacrament; William Mueller has commented on various secular experience, body imagery, and light and water imagery as media; so did Miss Webber, with particular reference to the fallen understanding and its difficulty in seeing clearly. Webber, *Contrary Music, The Prose Style of John Donne* (Madison: Univ. of Wisconsin, 1963), chaps. 5 and 3; Mueller, *John Donne: Preacher* (Princeton: Princeton Univ. Press, 1962), pp. 114–144.

42. Sir Herbert Grierson observed in a late article that Donne saw his church not only in the conventional terms as a middle way between

Roman Catholicism and Calvinism, but also between corrupted pre-Reformation Church and perfect church of Christ. "John Donne and the 'via media'," *Modern Language Review* 43 (1948): 305–314, p. 313. Reprinted in his *Criticism and Creation.* Dame Helen Gardner's essay on the "Sonnet on the Church" rightly argues that "Show me dear Christ" shows a characteristic wish to proceed between complementary errors, yet without unchurching other Christians, toward the perfect and unified church. See Appendix C in her edition, *The Divine Poems* (Oxford: Clarendon Press, 1952), pp. 121–127. Molly M. Mahood spoke of him shepherding his flock "along the via media," warning "of the sloughs on either hand" in the Cockayne funeral sermon (7. S10). *Poetry and Humanism* (London: Jonathan Cape, 1950), p. 165.

43. Rosemond Tuve's last book has a chapter on the *Pèlerinage,* Chap. Three in *Allegorical Imagery* (Princeton: Princeton Univ. Press, 1966). Another handsome volume exploring these matters with similar emphasis on kinships in literary and pictorial treatments is Samuel Chew's last book, *The Pilgrimage of Life* (New Haven: Yale Univ. Press, 1964).

44. (London: 1616), pp. 44–50. On the first blank leaf of the Yale copy appears the note, in ink, "ABp. Sandys Sermons, superior to any of his contemporaries" and the information "G. Ellis, 1783."

45. For a recent and able summary and critique of this notion, see Wolfhart Pannenberg, "The Question of God," *Interpretation* 21 (1967): 289–314. Man's "life is a process of inquiry that continually drives him into the open" (p. 301). " 'God' is not anthropomorphic if the very idea of personality has origin in religious experience" (p. 312).

46. The earliest and still definitive treatment of this is an article by Louis Martz recently revised for his *The Poem of the Mind* (New Haven: Yale Univ. Press, 1966), Chap. 6.

47. Like Augustine before him (*On Christian Doctrine* 2.42) and Milton after him (*Paradise Regained* 4. 331–350), Donne ranks the Scriptures above classical literature in rhetorical art as well as thematic validity, e.g., "whatsoever hath justly delighted any man in any mans writings, is exceeded in the Scriptures" (2. S7. 246–247).

48. The editors' annotated lexicon of Donne's Hebrew and their comments on his use of various editions and translations document fully the matter of scholarly exactitude. Their general conclusion on that seems similar to mine; see 10. pp. 306–344. Their view on Donne's biblical interpretation, however, might be taken to narrow his "literalism;" see 10. pp. 361–364. Cf. Don Cameron Allen, "Dean Donne Sets

his Text," *English Literary History* 10 (1943): 212–229, and Charles M. Coffin, *John Donne and the New Philosophy* (New York: Humanities Press, 1958; 1st ed. 1937), chap. 12.

49. And so even with color, not a very conspicuous element of Donne's imagery. Whiteness without God is the pallor of "diffidence," with Him is purity *"all faire my Love.* Rednesse alone is anger," but in the presence of God, an "Erubescence . . . that God loves too . . . an aptnesse in the soule to blush" lest "any of these spots doe fall upon it" (6. S1. 665–682).

50. For argument as to the influence of the legal congregation on the sermons, see J. B. Leishman, rev. Vols. 1 and 6, *Review of English Studies* ns6 (1955): 423, rejoinder by E. M. Simpson, ns9 (1958): 292–293, and reply by Leishman, 293–294. For an account of Donne's continuing and surprisingly intensive legal activities, see Bald, pp. 414–423. For a negative view of the significance of legal imagery, see Milton A. Rugoff, *Donne's Imagery: A Study in Creative Sources* (New York: Corporate Press, Inc., 1939), esp. p. 222. The *Concordance* lists sixty appearances of just the word *law* and its derivatives (to seventy-five for *light, lights,* etc.). John Sparrow's notes to *Devotions* list eight places where legal metaphor is important (Cambridge: Cambridge Univ. Press, 1923), p. 151. For careful appraisal of the presence of immediate times and circumstances in one Whitehall sermon and one "Spittle" sermon (3. S10 and 4. S3. 53), see William Gifford, "Time and Place in Donne's Sermons," *Publications of the Modern Language Association* 82 (1967): 388–398.

51. *The English People on the Eve of Colonization, 1603–1630* (New York: Harper, 1954, p. 157. But cf. Gifford: "bribery was almost an inevitable subject for assize sermons" ("Time and Place" p. 393, n. 27). See also *The Decline of* [preaching about] *Hell,* D. P. Walker (Chicago: Univ. of Chicago Press, 1964).

52. Shawcross, number 113; he suggests retirement at Pyrford in 1602–4 as the "retirednesse" in ln. 28 (not quoted here). Milgate suggests mainly on manuscript evidence 1597 (p. 223). For our purposes we need not choose either date over the other, nor need we argue with Martz's contention that "primary" among the *early* "seeds of better Arts" was formal meditation. See *The Poem of the Mind,* p. 7.

53. Cf. Gaston Bachelard's whole fine monograph *The Psychoanalysis of Fire,* trans. Alan C. M. Ross (Boston: Beacon Press, 1964; original French edition, Gallimard, 1938).

54. King James in 1622 forbade "those neoterics, both Jesuits and Puritans, who are known to be meddlars in matters of State and mon-

archy." See D. Harris Willson, *King James VI and I* (New York: Holt, 1956), p. 293, and Donne, 4. S7. 797–802.

55. For a summary history of the late medieval revival of preaching, see Charles Smyth, *The Art of Preaching: A Practical Survey of Preaching in the Church of England, 747–1934* (London: SPCK, 1940), esp. pp. 13, 17, 19. For an earlier, more extensive treatment of manuals and sermon-making, see G. R. Owst, *Preaching in Medieval England. An Intro. to Sermon Manuscripts of the Period c. 1350–1450* (Cambridge; Univ. Press, 1926), chaps. 7, 8. For *exempla,* see Owst, *Literature and Pulpit in Medieval England. A Neglected Chapter in the History of English Letters and of the English People* (Cambridge: Univ. Press 1933; 2nd ed. Oxford: Basil Blackwell, 1966), chap. 4. On the background of *artes praedicandi,* and early and late abuses in preaching technique, see William Fraser Mitchell's long-standard *English Pulpit Oratory from Andrewes to Tillotson* (London: SPCK; New York: Macmillan, 1932), on Keckermann, pp. 94–99; other remarks on abuses, pp. 192–193; but note should be taken of Mitchell's almost antirhetorical bias in favor of plain style. On Ramism in general (antipathetic, of course, to Donne) and that of Keckermann in particular (his *Rhetoricae Ecclesiasticae* was in its 3rd ed. by 1606; 1st ed. Hanover, 1600), see Walter J. Ong's superb *Ramus, Method, and the Decay of Dialogue; from the Art of Discourse to the Art of Reason* (Cambridge: Harvard Univ. Press, 1958), esp. pp. 298–300. On Puritan and Anglican rationales of worship see Dom Gregory Dix's still valuable *The Shape of the Liturgy,* 2nd ed. (Westminster: Dacre Press, 1945), esp. pp. 1, 312, 647–677; for modifying arguments (not critical here), see C. W. Dugmore, *The Mass and the English Reformers* (New York: St. Martin's Press, 1958).

56. *The Secular City: Secularization and Urbanization in Theological Perspectives* (New York: Macmillan, 1965), p. 66.

57. Albert William Levi, *Literature, Philosophy and the Imagination* (Bloomington: Indiana Univ. Press, 1962), p. 139.

58. *Eras and Modes in English Poetry* (Berkeley and Los Angeles: University of California Press, 1957), pp. 21, 29. And see her list of "the fifty-odd words most used," with eighteen verbs, all prominent in the sermons, p. 231. For helpful discussion of the somewhat different Renaissance articulations of arguments about process or data, sense or status, rhetoric or philosophy, see Quirinus Breen, "Some Aspects of Humanistic Rhetoric and the Reformation," *Nederlands Archief voor Kerkegeschiedenis* 43 (1959): 1–14, "Giovanni Pico della Mirandola on the Conflict of Philosophy and Rhetoric," and "Melanchthon's Reply

to . . . Mirandola," *Journal of the History of Ideas* 13 (1952): 384–426; and Paul O. Kristeller, *The Classics and Renaissance Thought* (Cambridge: Harvard Univ. Press, 1955), esp. pp. 3–23.

59. 2. S1. 136; 2. S2. 30; 2. S7. 262; 2. S14. 824; 3. S13. 118; 4. S7. 483; 4. S7. 596; 4. S8. 780–790; 5. S6. 660; 6. S3. 447; 6. S4. 1015; 6. S5. 545–550; 6. S7. 201-220; 6. S9. 41; 6. S16. 95–96; 7. S4. 595; 7. S12. 1010; 7. S16. 173; 9. S12. 423; 10. S2. 129; 10. S5. 263.

60. Gabriel Marcel argues powerfully that *any* relationship of "belonging to" is assailed by counter pressures. *Creative Fidelity,* p. 96.

61. *Creative Fidelity,* p. 8.

62. Without reference exclusively to Donne, Charles and Katherine George see "pursuit of the unity of the church . . . above all the mark of the *via media*" in their valuable *The Protestant Mind of the English Reformation 1570–1640* (Princeton: Princeton Univ., 1961), p. 417. Irving Lowe's admirably clear "John Donne: The Middle Way" emphasizes Donne's *inclusive* way of maintaining "a balance between reason and faith from first to last" (*Journal of the History of Ideas* 22 (1951): 389–397. P. 392, n. 18).

63. *The Works* (Dublin: 1676), p. 953.

64. Theodore Roethke, "The Marrow," *Collected Poems* (Garden City, New York: Doubleday, 1966), p. 246.

Chapter 3

1. See the invaluable commentary and notes of Frank Manley in his edition of *John Donne: The Anniversaries* (Baltimore: Johns Hopkins Univ. Press, 1963).

2. Seemingly the nearest thing to an exception is 6. S15, on "Surely men of low degree are vanity, and men of high degree are a lie . . ." a text from one of his *assigned* prebend psalms. It concludes with a paragraph insisting on the reliability of God, which turns the earlier explication of worldly vanity into a definition-by-contrast far from vain.

3. See Bald, pp. 340–345. "A Hymne to Christ" speaks of "an everlasting Night."

4. See 4. S11. 688–692 for a similar paradigm of discord, including the disputes of the Jesuit and Dominican orders as a type of doctrinal wrangle. For historical annotation, see *Essays in Divinity,* ed. E. M. Simpson (Oxford: 1951), p. 127.

5. He was on casual footing with some of them years earlier. See

Essays in Divinity 32: 11–14. It is hardly to our purpose to speculate where he first met them—perhaps in Augustine (see *Patrologia Latina* 41. 472), perhaps in Ambrose (see *PL* 14. 387–388; I was led to both these by Manley). See also Jean Daniélou, *Primitive Christian Symbols,* trans. Donald Attwater (Baltimore: Helicon Press, 1964), "Ship of the Church." Evelyn Simpson in an article published posthumously rightly insists that Donne discounts the battle imagery employed so unhesitatingly by many another. But she dwells somewhat one-sidedly, it seems to me, on his nautical voyage-figures. "Two Notes on Donne," *Review of English Studies* 16 (1965): 140–150.

6. See also, for example, 4. S3. 225–243, 4. S7. 456–459; 8. S13. 482.

7. See also 8. S11. 297–328 (1628, on John 14. 26, at St. Dunstan's).

8. I cannot agree with Potter and Simpson, who stigmatize the passages on the Creation as a digression (2. p. 35).

9. Milton's speech for Raphael, a blank verse paragraph of 113 lines, makes an instructive comparison with Donne's paragraph on the second and third day, which would run nearly as long if printed one line per elocutionary phrase. "Raphael" is more ambivalent, more speculative, perhaps more worldly, Donne as high priest more psychological and social. But they harmonize significantly. The waters above and below the firmament are an interesting ancient notion which had become obscure to Augustine (in his *Retractations*) and in the Koran. Donne unwittingly (in para. 6) reconstitutes their significance along lines parallel to those in the Gilgamesh epic, where the waters above the firmament are alien to man, the abyssal salt sea, while the waters below are the fresh-water springs, friendly though from mysterious depths. See Geoffrey Bibby, *Looking for Dilmun* (New York: Knopf, 1969), pp. 255–261.

10. In the first version he translated *temperantia* "temperance" rather than "chastity," and he continued: *"senex bis puer,* an old man returnes to the ignorance and frowardness of a child againe, but it is not *Senex bis Juvenis* that he returns to the daies of youth againe, to present first fruits acceptable to God soe late in his yeare." He drops distracting references to time and the "first fruits" metaphor, and sharpens the contrast of *senex* and *puer* with *Juvenis* into the antithesis of "infirmities" and "strength." The terms he poses antithetically ring a final change on the issue of sexuality, which is conspicuous among the moral issues in the paragraph. A superb example of man talking and thinking his way into increasingly perspicuous thought.

11. Cf. the biblical injunction to forgive "seventy times seven." Or:

"To make a King of a Beggar is not so much, as to make a Worm of nothing" (4. S2. 822–823).

12. *The Sermons,* pp. 215–229.

Chapter 4

1. Donne evidently sometimes found it proper to endorse the king in terms normal to his generation (obsequious to ours). Yet instances like the present one in the sermons, and at least one outside, pose intriguingly the question of how independent he may privately have been. See John B. Gleason, "Dr. Donne in the Courts of Kings: A Glimpse from Marginalia," *Journal of English and Germanic Philology* 69 (1970): 599–612.

Chapter 5

1. Subtitled *An Existential Study in Sanity and Madness* (Baltimore: Penguin Books, 1965; orig. London: Tavistock, 1960; New York, 1964; © 1969 by R. D. Laing. Reprinted by permission of Pantheon Books, of Random House, Inc. See especially Chap. 3 on responses.

2. Psalm 38. 4; 2. S3, S4, S5; see also 2. S1 and S2 on Ps. 38. 2 and 3, and 2. S6 on Ps. 38. 9; the six form a stunning exploration of the existential world of sin, to which 2. S8 makes an interesting postscript (being on Matthew 21. 44, which is a text quoted in para. seven above).

3. Laing, pp. 47, 44, 50.

4. To call fortune an "imaginary enemy" (para. 9) is to deplore abstraction and to insist (against much Aristotelian and medieval tradition) on the unmediated closeness of God.

5. Laing, p. 52. Cf. (inevitably) "If a clod be washed away by the sea, Europe is the less. . . . any man's death diminishes me. . . . the bell tolls . . . for thee" (*Devotions,* Meditation XVII).

6. For penetrating discussion of anxious care and defensive indifference as concomitants of Renaissance overcrowding in the medieval urban setting, see Lewis Mumford's magnificent *The City in History* (New York: Harcourt, Brace and World, 1961), esp. Chap. 10.

Chapter 6

1. Potter and Simpson mention the medal Donne received for that preaching, but they feel little interest in what they notice in the surviving two-part sermon (2. pp. 36–39). Cf. Bald, p. 364.

2. See 1. S3, at Paul's Cross in 1617, 4. S3 at Spital Cross in 1622. On revision, and Spital Cross sermons, see Gifford, sections I and III; on civic sermonizing, see Millar MacLure's valuable *The Paul's Cross Sermons, 1534–1642* (Toronto: Univ. of Toronto Press, 1958). Izaak Walton said that on the same day he had preached one sermon, Donne would choose the biblical text for his next, "cast his Sermon into a form, and his Text into divisions," for study, meditation, and memorization during the week. Robert L. Hickey takes the preacher's "hour" very literally (whereas I do not) and finds "Few of the published sermons can be read aloud at a normal speaking rate in less than two hours and a quarter" (whereas I read most of them faster). So he believes Donne "amplified" his notes by "approximately one hundred percent' for publication ;"Donnes Delivery, *Tennessee Studies in Literature* 9 (1964): 39–47. But quartos published at royal behest and surviving manuscript copies similar in length to folio versions—all seem to me to suggest strongly that Donne's amplification ordinarily was only moderate, or even modest.

3. *Speculorum Romanorum Pontificum,* by Stephanus Kis, of Szegedin, Hungary (Basle, 1584).

4. Bernard of Clairvaux, "Ser. 1 in die [Festo] St. Andreae Apostolus.'

5. "The Baite," number 37 in *The Complete Poetry of John Donne,* ed. John Shawcross (Garden City: Doubleday Anchor, 1967).

6. If we use Laurence Michel's formula: "the dream of innocence is confronted by the fact of guilt, and acquiesces therein."' See "The Possibility of a Christian Tragedy," in *Tragedy: Modern Essays in Criticism,* ed. Laurence Michel and Richard Sewell (Englewood Cliffs: Prentice-Hall, 1963), p. 211.

7. Compare Hamlet labelling his hands "pickers and stealers" for the understanding of Rosencrantz and Guildenstern. Here the preacher is more at one with his audience and is on the way with them to a situation wherein the author of his terms ("the Holy Ghost") need not be seen in adversary terms either.

8. Laing, "Petrification and depersonalization," pp. 46–61, and "The Self and the false self in a schizophrenic," pp. 160–177.

Part Three: Sermon of Valediction

1. The texts for the sermons given complete here depend conservatively on the folios and aim to be bibliographically responsible but do not pretend to be bibliographically definitive. I have adopted modern usage as to i, j, u, and v, but have otherwise preserved the spelling of the folios. The Folio's spelling should give no modern reader difficulty, and the issue of Donne's modernity should not be obscured by doctoring the spelling. Greek words have been transliterated (as elsewhere in this study). Marginal hangers were ordinary in his day and handy, whereas now they are not ordinary. Footnotes are less handy. So I have moved the hangers into the text, between slants, because Donne uses frequently and differently the parentheses which many modern writers use for such material. And I have added paragraph numbering, because the paragraph is the true molecular unit of these sermons, as indeed it probably is of all prose but the most lapidary or statistic-laden (or formless). Abbreviations have been adjusted to modern usage (St. Paul rather than S. Paul). Obvious typographical errors, or inaccuracies, as in biblical references, have usually been corrected, often with a debt to Simpson and Potter, which is indicated in textual notes. This Sermon of Valediction was published separately in 1638 and 1639, in a modern edition by Mrs. Simpson (London: Nonesuch Press, 1932), and as one of two sermons included complete in *John Donne: Selected Prose.* Chosen by Evelyn Simpson, ed. Helen Gardner and Timothy Healy (Oxford: Clarendon Press, 1967).
2. *Bechurotheica* for Folio's *Bechurocheica* (Potter and Simpson note).
3. 2. S11. 390 and both Yale copies of the folio give *those,* perhaps an error for *these.*
4. This text appears in the Prayer Book burial service.

The Sermon on John 1.8

1. The Folio has only a comma (F50. S38. p. 344).
2. Simpson correction of the Folio's "Melchilanus."

3. Simpson, for "*Hiero*" in Folio.
4. Simpson corrects to *Praeparate.*

The Sermon on Psalm 63.7

1. This sermon has been reprinted by Eric Gill in a Meridian paperback now out of print, by Evelyn Simpson in a paperback collection of *Donne's Sermons on the Psalms and Gospels* taken from the Potter-Simpson complete edition (Berkeley and Los Angeles: 1963), by Edmund Fuller (in part) in *The Showing Forth of Christ* (New York: Harper & Row, 1964), and by Janel M. Mueller, *Donne's Prebend Sermons,* edited with an introduction and Commentary (Cambridge: Harvard Univ. Press, 1971).
2. *De Diversis Quaestionibus* LXXXIII, 46 (Simpson note).
3. Simpson.

The Two-part Sermon on Fishers of Men

1. Potter and Simpson correct marginal reference from Prov. 8.30 to Prov. 8.31, from John 1.35 to John 1.36, and this from Matthew 8.23 to 8.26. But the series as it stands may just possibly show Donne's fallibility rather than a compositor's. Was he relying on memory? or too infrequent glances at one of his Bibles?
2. Potter and Simpson 10.378.
3. Potter and Simpson for *setth.*
4. Folio has *appearance, lesse.*
5. Potter and Simpson for *too.*
6. *do so* perhaps should read *do not so;* otherwise the *so* refers awkwardly to *your . . . catching.*
7. Potter and Simpson for *irreconciablenesse.*
8. As Potter and Simpson point out, Donne actually refers here to the parable at Luke 19.20.
9. The Authorized Version reads *will not I suffer,* while the Prayer Book (which uses the Great Bible of 1539) reads *I will not know a wicked person.* "David" speaks in both, not God. Donne leans for his own purposes on the Bishops' Bible of 1568 and the Authorized Version

wording, and on the commonplace view that David was secretary to the Holy Spirit's dictation.

10. Alford's conjecture, followed by Potter and Simpson.

11. Simpson emends to *Dioceses,* but Donne might have said *dioceez* for euphony.

INDEX

DATE DUE

OCT 23 1986			
DEC 14 1989			
5-19-93			

30 505 JOSTEN'S